100 TOP PICKS

FOR
Homeschool Curriculum

Choosing the Right Curriculum and Approach
for Your Child's Learning Style

CATHY DUFFY

BROADMAN
& HOLMAN
PUBLISHERS

Nashville, Tennessee

Ten-digit ISBN: 0-8054-3138-1
Thirteen-digit ISBN: 978-0-8054-3138-4

Published by Broadman & Holman Publishers,
Nashville, Tennessee

Dewey Decimal Classification: 371.042
Subject Heading: HOME SCHOOLING—CURRICULA

Note: Contact information and prices listed for resources in the following chapters are the most current information available from publishers at the time this book is written. You will need to confirm current price information when you make your purchases.

6 7 8 09 08 07 06

Dedication

To the thousands of dedicated homeschoolers who have resisted the impulse to imitate "real schools" and have chosen instead to figure out what is best for each of their children, even if it meant writing their own curriculum. You have made the world of homeschool curriculum far richer than the most well-funded schools in the world.

—Cathy Duffy

Table of Contents

1

How on Earth Do I Figure Out What Curriculum to Use?

One of the saddest sights I've ever seen was opening day of a three-day homeschool convention. Day one had been designated only for new homeschoolers. Five hundred or more raw homeschooling recruits streamed into an exhibit hall featuring well over one hundred different vendors. Where to even start? Each vendor, naturally, claimed that his or her products were absolutely essential and the best thing on the market. If the newcomers had come with unlimited resources, they could easily have dropped a few thousand dollars at the first few displays they visited. I'm certain many felt overwhelming guilt when they did not buy what they were told they needed. That's probably why so many were in tears after the first few hours of the convention.

They knew they needed to buy curriculum, but how on earth could they figure out which one to buy when they didn't even know what they needed to teach? The escape route for many beginners is to simply go to the larger companies that have complete packages for each grade level. Whatever grade the child would have been enrolled in next year at the local school becomes the grade level of the curriculum purchased.

Sometimes, but not often enough, representatives of these major publishers will take time to explain to inquirers that even if they sell a "fourth grade" package, such a package might not be the best choice for this particular child. A nine-year-old might need fifth-grade-level math and third-grade-level reading material because math comes easily to him and reading does not.

That doesn't make him a poor student or a "problem." It does mean that he's a fairly normal child, whatever "normal" means. After all, our children are not standardized products. None of them look alike (at least not much) on the outside, so why should we expect them to be alike on the inside—the way they learn, their interests, their abilities, and their temperaments?

One of the beauties of homeschooling is that it allows us to recognize and nurture each one of our very special individual children. We have the glorious opportunity to help them figure out who they are, what they want to be, and how they might get there.

In homeschooling, we can take detours unimaginable in the traditional classroom. If a nine-year-old boy is interested in rocket science, homeschooling parents can nurture that interest by allowing him to move ahead of grade level science topics into this more specialized area. They can help him search the library for biographies and other books related to the subject. They can supervise and assist him while he builds his own rockets, fiddles with fuel cells, designs recovery parachutes, estimates trajectories, and learns safety precautions.

That fourteen-year-old girl who wants to be a veterinarian can arrange her "school" schedule so that she works two days a week with the local vet, getting hands-on experience in her potential career. She'll know for certain by the end of high school whether or not she really wants to spend all those years (and all that money) in college to achieve her goal. Her other schooling can also be designed to support her budding career. She can research and write about animals, physiology, and related topics. She might study uses of and attitudes toward different animals within different cultures. Math and economics studies might include cost comparisons for animal care in traditional zoos versus "natural" parks.

I think you get the idea. Asking a supplier for a standardized package of curriculum ignores the individuality and special needs and interests of your child.

You can see this more easily if you compare feeding your child's body to feeding his mind. You don't expect all children to eat exactly the same amounts and types of food. Some have particular food allergies. All have preferences and dislikes. And some burn up twice as many calories as others.

Likewise, mental nourishment should take into consideration the strengths and weaknesses of each child—teaching to their strengths and helping to overcome weak areas. It should have extra "nourishment" for those special areas of interest. It should be provided at a pace a child can handle—not too slow, not too fast.

If you are a new homeschooling parent, and you expected to just purchase a packaged curriculum and be done with it, this sounds like bad news. Where on earth do you begin? There are far too many choices. How do you know what your child needs? How can you figure this out?

That's the purpose of this book. First, in chapter 2 we will cover some basic approaches you might wish to use: traditional textbooks, Charlotte Mason/real books education, classical education, unit study, unschooling, independent study, working under an umbrella program, or an eclectic mixture of approaches.

I'll walk you through some questions that will help you identify which approach (or mixture of approaches) is best for you. In chapter 3, I have created examples for you as if I were filling in the charts and answering the questions in chapter 2 myself. This should give you a clear idea of how to proceed.

Then, in chapter 4, I help you narrow things down even further by identifying your children's learning styles and figuring out what features you should be looking for in a curriculum to achieve the best fit for each child.

Many parents wonder what should be covered at each grade level, especially if they choose "ungraded" curriculum. Are you doing enough? Too much? Might your child's frustration be due to expectations that are beyond his maturity level? In chapter 5 I discuss academic goals and how to figure out what you should cover in each subject area.

My purpose with these first few chapters is to help you become goal-oriented rather than "curriculum driven." Too many new homeschoolers let that grade-level package of curriculum they purchased dictate the content, methods, and even the schedule they follow. In other words, the curriculum itself drives their homeschooling.

To be goal oriented means working in almost a reverse fashion. You determine what your children need to learn. You decide what methods to use. And you set up your own schedule. Then you find

curriculum that has the content and methodology that fits *your* agenda, and you use it on your own timetable.

After you use the first few chapters to figure out what content and methods are right for your children, you will be ready to explore my Top 100 curriculum choices in chapter 6 to see what is likely to fit your situation. To make this easy, I have included charts that help you readily identify which resources have the features that you will be looking for, features you will have already identified in the early chapters of this book.

Each product featured as a Top Pick also has a complete review in the following chapters. The page number of the review is in the last column of the Top Picks charts. Select likely candidates from the charts, read the full reviews, then make your decisions. I have also included ordering and contact information in each review so you will know how to actually get your hands on each resource.

Obviously, there are many more products than the Top 100 that I have chosen for this book. You might have a specialized need or a specialized topic that is not addressed by any of these resources. If so, you might want to consult the Web site at www.CathyDuffyReviews.com for more possibilities.

Please fight the temptation to jump right to the chart of Top Picks and the reviews! Take the time to work out your own philosophy of education and discover what you really should be doing with your children before exposing yourself to the temptation of what is still an overwhelming number of resources from which to choose. I think you'll enjoy the journey of personal discovery that happens along the way.

2

"Drill and Kill," "Real Books," "Delight-Directed Studies" . . . What's Best?

Jane Jones has just shown up at her first homeschool support group meeting. One of the moms is sharing about the fantastic unit study they've just completed on trains. Since they live in the Sacramento area of California, they visited the marvelous train museum in Old Sacramento. A trip on the modern Amtrak train provided a contrast to the old trains her children explored at the museum. Books they read about the building of the transcontinental railroad and development of the frontier provided the historical background. The children learned a few "railroad songs" and each painted a picture of his or her favorite old train. It was great fun and a terrific way to learn history.

Listening to this, Jane feels absolutely overwhelmed. How on earth can she do that sort of study? How would she know what to do? How could she tell if her children were learning anything? What about meeting requirements? What Jane really wants to know right now is what phonics program works best. If she has to make up a unit study for every topic, homeschooling just isn't going to work for her family!

It is so easy to be intimidated into thinking that your homeschool should mimic those of seasoned veterans. They seem to have a handle on things. Their kids are impressive. They're obviously doing something right. But, the question you really need to consider is whether or not what they are doing is right for you.

It doesn't take long to figure out that veteran homeschoolers are, overall, very independent and strong-minded parents. Chances are you could poll half a dozen such moms and discover they have half a dozen different ways they homeschool. There is no single *right* way to homeschool that everyone figures out after a few years.

In fact, the diversity of resources and methods is one of the beauties of homeschooling. Need a cassette tape to teach parts of the body to your child who just loves to sing all the time? Need a math program that uses colorful blocks to teach multiplication for that child who just has to *see* how math works and not just memorize rules? Need a science program that lets you teach all your children the same topic at the same time? You name it, and there's likely something in the homeschool marketplace to meet your requirements.

But how do you figure out what you need? You can try to find a professional curriculum counselor to work through this with you. That's great if there's one available in your area and you can afford it. However, if that's not practical for you, the material in chapters 4 and 5 will help you sort this out by addressing curriculum selection from the two most important perspectives: what fits with your family's philosophy of education, and what works for each of your children's learning styles.

Establishing Your Own "Philosophy of Education"

We'll start at the family level to sort out some "big picture" ideas about education. What we come up with is actually a philosophy of education. Don't let the word *philosophy* turn you off, because figuring out a philosophy of education is not as difficult as it sounds. Someone once remarked that philosophy is nothing more than common sense dressed up in fancy dress clothes.

We will start with some common sense questions. I want you to really think this through as you read, so there are lines on which you can write down your thoughts as you consider these questions.

Content

Let's begin with a question about the big picture—about what the overall content of "school" should be.

What do you think is most important for your children to learn?

You are not likely to come up with just one answer to this question. Instead, you will come up with a number of things you consider important. Before you start writing, here are a few more questions that might help you think about content:

1. If there were no laws requiring you to educate your child, what would you want them to learn anyway?

2. Would that list include strong academics, work skills, study habits, a love for reading, familiarity with Scripture, physical fitness, artistic expression, practical life skills, computer knowledge, ethical attitudes?

3. What else might you add?

At this point you should be writing down only broad categories rather than specifics such as "I want my child to learn to write poetry in fifth grade." Your list might include words, phrases, or sentences. For example, you might write out a list with such items as:

- college prep academics
- strong independent study habits
- extensive reading from many genres
- Scripture study and memorization
- art appreciation and expression
- familiarity with computer programs such as Microsoft Word and Excel

Or you might write your ideas more expansively:

- I want my children to grow up to be self-directed learners who know how to teach themselves.
- I want my children to love to learn, so I want learning to be as fun as we can make it.
- I want my children to have high aspirations for both college and career.
- I want my children to have a virtuous character and a strong ethical foundation.
- I want my children to develop habits of physical fitness that will stick with them all their lives.
- I want my children to take challenging academic courses for high school so they will have opportunities to win scholarships to prestigious colleges.

Now it's time to write down your own thoughts. But make an extra copy of the blank chart that follows before you begin!

Once you have made your list, go back through and prioritize the ideas. Go through first and mark each idea with a 1, 2, or 3, with 1 identifying a top level priority, 2 a mid-level priority, and 3 a lower level priority. You might find yourself only writing down items that you would give a level 1 or 2 priority, and that's OK. Once you've made your list, if it is helpful, use the second copy of the chart to rewrite the list with level 1 items at the top of the list. You might automatically write these down with top priorities first. In that case, there's no need to rewrite them.

If you need to see what this might look like, you can jump ahead to the next chapter for a sample, but make sure to come back here and create your own list.

Priorities

I want my children to:	Priority Level

Methods

Now let's consider ideas about methods.

How do you think learning should happen?

Keep in mind that answers to this question are heavily influenced by your own children and your own experiences. If you have very compliant children who love to play school just for fun, you might naturally think learning should always happen in traditional school fashion. But that's not your only choice. If you have a rowdy group of very active children, you might already be thinking they need lots of activity, movement, and freedom in their schooling. This question might be difficult to answer at this point because you simply haven't thought about or investigated possible options. If so, jot down any ideas you have now and then come back to this question after you've read the rest of this chapter about some possible approaches you might want to use.

_____

_____

_____

_____

_____

_____

How do you want to teach or "run your school"?

As you consider this question, you will probably start to see that what you believe about content and methods shapes your thinking about how you will actually do things. For example, if you consider it a high priority that your children learn structure and discipline, you are more likely to follow a predictable schedule and use tests on a regular basis. On the other hand, if you put a higher value on developing creativity and delight in learning, you might keep the schedule flexible so your child can concentrate on that project she started without stopping to complete her language workbook exercise.

The following questions will help you think through how you might operate. Make some notes as you consider each question. You might also need to come back to this section after you've read through the various approaches summarized in the remainder of this chapter and have considered which one(s) will work best for you.

1. Do you want to try to teach most or all of your children together, at least for some subjects?

_____

_____

2. How much of the time do you want (or are you able) to work directly with your children?

_____

_____

3. How much of the time do you expect your children to work independently? (Caution: Don't expect children below about age 8 to do a lot of independent work.)

_____

_____

4. Do you want to use real books (biographies, historical novels, books written about particular science topics, etc.) as part of your curriculum?

_____

_____

5. Do you want to include field trips? What type of field trips?

_____

_____

6. Do you like to "make up" curriculum as you go, adapting to the needs and interests of your children, or do you prefer things well planned out in advance?

_____

_____

7. Do you need a set schedule to get things done, or would you prefer more flexibility?

_____

_____

8. Do you prefer a curriculum that is thoroughly laid out with lesson plans that tell you what to do when or do you prefer just an outline to follow?

_____

_____

9. Any additional thoughts about how you want to operate?

_____

_____

Which Approach to Education Should I Use?

Writing down your thoughts about the above questions should have helped you clarify some of your goals and preferences. Now you can use the following "Approaches to Learning" chart to begin to identify which of the possible approaches to homeschooling are most likely to work for you.

The chart lists possible features and/or methods you might be looking for. When you read one that reflects your own ideas, move over to the boxes to the right of the statement and circle every number in that row. This means that this targeted feature or method is present to some extent in each approach for which there is a number. If the box is gray, that means that this feature or method is not characteristic of that approach. For example: "predictable structure" is not something you usually find in unit studies. Unit studies tend to use a variety of books and activities, often emphasizing different subject areas from day to day. So the box under unit studies across from "predictable structure" is grayed out. Some characteristics are found in resources for a particular approach some of the time, but not always. Those boxes have the number ".5". For example, Charlotte Mason methodology doesn't always translate into a predictable structure. Some Charlotte Mason resources have predictable structure and some don't. In such cases, the ".5" gives this feature "half credit" when you add up your boxes.

Approaches to Learning

I prefer:	Traditional	Charlotte Mason	Classical	Unit Study	Unschooling	Independent Study	Eclectic	Umbrella Program
predictable structure.	1	.5	1			1	1	1
that children have many real life experiences for learning—nature studies in the woods, building projects, etc.		1	.5	1	1	1	1	
children read historical novels and biographies rather than textbooks.		1	1	1	1		1	
a program that is thoroughly laid out for the teacher and provides a feeling of security.	1					1		1
a grammar program that emphasizes rules and memorization	1		1			1	.5	1
workbooks, teachers manuals, and answer keys for most or all subjects.	1					1	.5	1
children to work independently as much as possible.	.5				1	1	.5	.5
mental training and mental discipline have higher priority than stimulating curiosity and interest.	1		.5			1	.5	.5
curriculum that ensures my children cover the same things other school children might be learning.	1					1	.5	1
informal evaluation of my child by talking over what they've read and looking at their work rather than by testing.		1	1	1	1		.5	
that my young children do a significant amount of memorization, repetition, and recitation.	.5		.5			.5	.5	.5
my teen to get a strong background in the great books of western civilization.		.5	1	.5	.5	.5	.5	.5
to emphasize developing a love for learning *more than* the ability to work in a structured, methodical way.		1		1	1		.5	
that teens develop a "life of the mind" more than vocational skills.	.5	1	1	1	.5	.5	.5	.5
presenting my children with information to learn rather than having them choose their own topics to investigate.	1	.5	1	.5		1	.5	1
highly structured resources that "script" what teacher/parent and child are supposed to say and do.	.5		.5			.5	.5	.5
lots of discussion and interaction in the learning process.		1	1	1	.5		1	.5
covering subjects (e.g., history, science, religion) at the same time with the same material with as many of my children as possible.		1	1	1			1	
making connections between different subject areas, showing relationships, and viewing that as a high priority in learning.		1	1	1	1		.5	
project-based learning.		.5		1	1		.5	
to teach my children one-on-one as much as possible	1	.5	.5		.5		1	1
that my children learn grammar in a casual manner—e.g., some instruction, use of a grammar handbook, then working on mastery in their own writing.		.5		1	1		.5	
Totals for each column for this page:								

I prefer:	Traditional	Charlotte Mason	Classical	Unit Study	Unschooling	Independent Study	Eclectic	Umbrella Program
to keep structure to a minimum so that my children and I are able to pursue interesting learning ideas when they arise.		.5		.5	1		.5	
to make frequent field trips an essential part of schooling.	.5	1	.5	.5	1		.5	
to give my children freedom to determine what they will study and when and how they will do so.					.5	1	.5	
An "investigative" approach that stimulates my children to pursue information and research on their own.		.5		1	1	.5	.5	
flexible curriculum and schedules so I can capitalize on "teachable moments."		.5	.5	1	1		.5	
a mixture of structured learning and experiential/discovery learning.		1		1			1	
to set my own goals and schedule rather than adopting someone else's.		.5	.5	.5	1		.5	
to select curriculum/methods that suit my child's learning style rather than curriculum/methods widely recognized and accepted by authorities.		.5	.5	1	1		.5	
that computer-based learning be a significant part of the curriculum.	.5					.5		.5
A. Total for each column for this page								
B. Totals for columns from first page								
Total for each column: add line A and B and enter total as the numerator (top number) of the fraction	‾11	‾15.5	‾14.5	‾17	‾17	‾12	‾18	‾11
Optional: Percentage for each column (divide numerator by denominator)								

After you've gone through the entire chart, add up the total in each column. Keep in mind that the column with the highest number doesn't win. The number in the denominator of the fraction at the bottom of each column is the number of possible boxes you could have checked that reflect this particular approach to education. The actual number you checked will be the numerator (top number) of the fraction—what you write in. If you look only at your total in each box, the "eclectic" approach is likely to come out on top every time since there are so many boxes (possible total of eighteen) you might check. That could be very misleading. Instead, you need to look at the fraction. Any approach with almost all the possible numbers selected is likely to be in line with your philosophy of education, and there might be more than one!

(If you're mathematically minded, divide the numerator by the denominator for each column total. You will then have percentage numbers for each column that you can easily compare.)

The goal is to identify the approach or approaches that are most likely to appeal to you. If you see that you have circled many numbers under both traditional and classical education, and few under unschooling or unit studies, you've already narrowed your likely curriculum choices dramatically.

It is important to repeat that you need not select only one approach to use. Many experienced homeschoolers blend one or more approaches. Some blend approaches so much that we call them "eclectic" homeschoolers.

Next, read the descriptions for the different education approaches to verify your conclusions from the chart. As you read through these descriptions, you will be refining your own educational philosophy.

Traditional

A traditionalist might use either textbooks or worktexts (worktexts contain both instruction and workpages to be completed by students in a single book), but there are distinct books for each subject area: math, language arts (often broken down further into separate spelling, grammar, composition, literature, and vocabulary books), history, science, etc. These books are usually written for use in regular school classrooms, although the publisher might have taken homeschool use into consideration.

When used as the publisher intends, such curricula generally help a homeschool function much like a regular day school. Children will be studying what many other students at their grade level are studying.

In most cases teacher's manuals, answer keys, and other teaching aids are available. Sometimes these are so classroom oriented that they are of little use to the homeschooling parent, but other times they are essential to the program. For example, Bob Jones University Press's language courses are designed to be taught from the teacher's manuals. Student books are simply adjuncts containing practice exercises or activities that support the course instruction found only in the teacher's manuals.

Traditional programs generally give parents a sense of security while helping establish routines and teaching methods. They sometimes make homeschooling a less frightening venture because the curriculum seems somewhat like what parents themselves used in school.

Many parents begin with a traditional approach, gradually shifting to other approaches as they gain experience. Others find a traditional approach easier for record keeping, scheduling, and accountability.

Some parents choose traditional approaches that allow their children to work independently because of time constraints or learning styles. Some students (especially those beginning homeschool past the primary grades) actually prefer this type of approach because it feels familiar and comfortable for them.

However, traditional curricula can take more time to use since they often include activities, presentations, practice, and review that are needed when teaching an entire classroom of children. Even self-paced programs such as Alpha Omega *LIFEPACs*—not designed for an entire class to use together—target the amount of practice and review to the average classroom situation. For example, traditional grammar programs frequently reteach and review the same grammar concepts year after year.

Sometimes traditionalists are chided for recreating "school at home" because the experience varies little from that of regular day school settings. Parents who slavishly follow such a curriculum often miss out on those special moments when a child comes up with a question that begs for immediate exploration. Many parents, however, manage to find a good balance using traditional curricula while still retaining enough flexibility to respond to teachable moments when they arise.

Some parents are just "trying out" the idea of homeschooling. They figure that if it doesn't work for them, they'll put their children back in school next year. These parents often want to use a traditional curriculum, frequently coupled with a fairly consistent schedule similar to that of day schools, so their children can easily integrate into a regular day school classroom in the future if need be. The big caution here is that the traditional methods might make the homeschool experience boring and unappealing, creating a self-defeating experience from the beginning.

The choice is rarely all or nothing when it comes to traditional curriculum. While some umbrella programs use traditional curricula (see that category further on in this chapter), most homeschoolers are free to choose one or more traditional resources along with resources that might reflect other approaches, as I describe under the "Eclectic" approach later in this section.

Examples of traditional curriculum publishers: A Beka Book, Bob Jones University Press, Modern Curriculum Press, Scott Foresman, McDougal Littell, Houghton Mifflin, Alpha Omega *LIFEPAC* Curriculum, School of Tomorrow *PACE* curriculum, and Rod and Staff.

Charlotte Mason

Charlotte Mason was a turn-of-the-century educator who frequently used the term *twaddle* to describe much of what passed for curriculum content in traditional texts as a useless waste of a child's time and energy. For example, she warned against children's history textbooks saying, ". . . for this intelligent teaching of history, eschew, in the first place, nearly all history books written expressly for children . . . and as for what are called children's books, the children of educated parents are able to understand history written with literary power, and are not attracted by the twaddle of reading-made-easy little history books."[1]

Through her many years of teaching, she determined that there were better ways to teach children that stimulated a love for learning and helped children retain knowledge more effectively than traditional methods, all while respecting the nature of the child. She believed in a child's innate ability and desire to learn and the need for teachers to restrain themselves from controlling all learning. Mason says: "The children might echo Wordsworth's complaint of 'the world,' and say, the teacher is too much with us, late and soon. Everything is directed, expected, suggested. No other personality out of book, picture, or song, no, not even that of Nature herself, can get at the children without the mediation of the teacher. No room is left for spontaneity or personal initiation on their part."[2]

Mason wrote about the importance of nature walks and outdoor learning. Throughout her writings, she stresses how much children learn through their own senses, especially as they interact with nature. To make that happen, children must be given lots of time for exercise and outdoor exploration that should not be eliminated in favor of more hours in the "school room."

Even so, Mason was not an advocate of unschooling. She believed in directed learning as well as teaching a child self-discipline and good habits. She says, "Even the child who has gained the habit of attention to *things*, finds *words* a weariness. This is a turning-point in the child's life, and the moment for the mother's tact and vigilance. . . . Never let the child *dawdle* over copybook or sum, sit dreaming with his book before him. When a child grows stupid over a lesson, it is time to put it away. Let him do another lesson as unlike the last as possible, and then go back with freshened wits to his unfinished task."[3]

Mason is well known for her use of narration rather than workbooks. She outlines the idea:

When the child is six . . . let him narrate the fairytale which has been read to him episode by episode, upon one hearing of each; the Bible tale read to him in the words of the Bible; the well-written animal story; or all about other lands from some such volumes as *The World at Home*. The seven-year-old boy will have begun to read for himself, but must get most of his intellectual nutriment, by ear, certainly, but read to him out of books. Geography, sketches from ancient history, *Robinson Crusoe*, *The Pilgrim's Progress*, *Tanglewood Tales*, *Heroes of Asgard*, and much of the same calibre, will occupy him until he is eight. . . . He should have no book which is not a child's classic; and . . . it must not be diluted with talk or broken up with questions, but given to the boy in fit portions as wholesome meat for his mind, in the full trust that a child's mind is able to deal with its proper food. [The teacher should read] two or three pages, enough to include an episode; after that, let her call upon the children to narrate.[4]

The child then retells what has been read in his own words.

Mason also emphasized the importance of developing the imagination and the value of making connections between topics studied to enhance memory. She says, "If the business of teaching be to furnish the child with ideas, any teaching which does not leave him possessed of a new mental image has, by so far, missed its mark. Now, just think of the listless way in which the children too often drag through reading and tables, geography and sums, and you will see that it is a rare thing for any part of any lesson to flash upon them with the vividness which leaves a mental picture behind. It is not too much to say that a morning in which a child receives no new idea is a morning wasted, however closely the little student has been kept at his books."[5]

Charlotte Mason's ideas are generally implemented in the elementary grade levels. Hallmarks of a Charlotte Mason approach to education are the use of real books rather than textbooks for reading, history, geography, and science; the narration technique; nature learning; hands-on learning; making connections between various topics; inclusion of study of the fine arts; and a focus upon development of good habits and a love for learning in children.

Charlotte Mason's ideas about education are incorporated into many unit studies to varying degrees, and that would be the easiest way to get started in this methodology. However, if you don't want to use a unit study, you can still learn how to easily implement Mason's ideas by reading one or more of the following books on her methodology.

To read more about Charlotte Mason's ideas:

- *A Charlotte Mason Education* and *More Charlotte Mason Education* by Catherine Levison (Champion Press, Ltd., 4308 Blueberry Road, Fredonia, WI 53021; 262-692-3897; e-mail: info@championpress.com, Web site: www.championpress.com)—These are very practical, to-the-point books that will quickly help you understand Mason's methods.
- *A Charlotte Mason Companion* by Karen Andreola (Charlotte Mason Research and Supply, P.O. Box 758, Union, ME 04862; www.charlottemason.com)—Andreola presents an in-depth journey through Mason's philosophy of education.
- *Real Learning: Education in the Heart of the Home,* by Elizabeth Foss (By Way of the Family Press, 1090 Payne Avenue, St. Paul, MN 55101; 651-778-0287; www.bywayofthefamily.com)—This practical guide helps Catholic homeschoolers implement Mason's ideas.

Classical

Classical education is based on models of learning that go back to the Middle Ages, although its earliest roots lay in the Greek and Roman civilizations. Dorothy Sayers was one of a number of scholars who repopularized this method of learning in the twentieth century. Two current proponents of classical education, Gene Veith Jr. and Andrew Kern, tell us in the introduction to their book on the subject: "Classical education provides a conceptual framework for mastering the entire range of objective knowledge. It also offers a theory of human character development, and it contains a teaching methodology that is demonstrably effective and eminently practical."[6] They go on to tell us, "Classical education cultivates wisdom and virtue by nourishing the soul on truth, goodness and beauty."[7]

Personally, I think the greatest value of classical education is that it engages learners with the most important ideas—ideas about God, about life, about purpose. Classical education challenges the vocational orientation of most modern education by concentrating on learning that forms the inner person. At the same time, classical students learn how to think, how to learn independently, and how to present their own ideas—all of which ultimately prepares them for a wide range of vocations.

Veith and Kern also tell us, "The substance of classical education is the liberal arts curriculum."[8] Among those "arts" are three stages or categories grouped as the trivium. The trivium's three stages are labeled grammar, logic or dialectic, and rhetoric. They provide a sequential focus for education in the elementary through high school years. You start with the grammar stage and work up through the rhetoric stage.

The word *grammar* as used within classical education means much more than the nuts and bolts of a language. Rather, it is the basic structure, skills, and knowledge of any subject. Thus, in the elementary grades a child learns the grammar of math, language arts, social studies, science, and, possibly, religion and other electives.

In the logic or dialectic stage, students analyze information and make connections. Rhetoric describes the stage where the young person has assimilated knowledge, thought creatively about what he or she has learned, and now expresses his or her own ideas through speech and writing at what would likely be considered adult levels.

Some classical education proponents follow the progression of the trivium, making significant changes in methods and materials as they move through the stages. Others tend to mix the stages; for example, children in elementary grades might participate in Socratic discussions (dialectic type activity) alongside studies of basic English grammar.

A major component of classical education for dialectic purposes is the reading and discussion of real books. Consequently, "Good Books" and "Great Books" programs have been developed that use classic fiction and nonfiction titles both for knowledge and as springboards into the world of ideas and questions. Socratic dialogues are used to stimulate students to think about what they have read, to work through important questions, and to move to higher levels of thinking.

There are actual lists of the Good Books and the Great Books, with the former identifying books appropriate for younger children through adults and the latter listing books for teens and adults. Some classical programs, particularly at high school level, work with books from these lists, while others apply the methods to their own selection of books. The following Web sites have lists or links to Great and Good Books.

Great Books lists:
- www.classicalhomeschooling.org/celoop/100.html
- http://books.mirror.org/gb.home.html
- www.anova.org
- www.interleaves.org/~rteeter/greatbks.html
- www.geocities.com/Athens/Atlantis/4360

Good Books lists:
- www.classicalhomeschooling.org/celoop/1000.html
- www.angelicum.net/html/the_good_books_in_print_list.html (for K–8)
- www.ccel.org/index/classics.html (links to books in electronic format)

Other classical education programs, especially for the elementary grades, focus on other learning strategies more than on Good Books or Great Books. For example, some follow Dorothy Sayers' beliefs about children's ability to memorize in the grammar stage, so they build much of their curriculum around memorization as a means of obtaining knowledge.

Personally, I believe that the goal of acquiring knowledge and skills at the grammar level does not necessarily dictate any particular methodology, so all these variations might be appropriate for building a foundation to move on to dialectic and rhetoric stages.

An even larger question is the role of classical languages in classical education. Historically, study of Latin and Greek was always at the foundation of classical education. More recently, emphasis on the structure of the trivium and reading the Great Books seems to have displaced the study of Greek almost entirely and even Latin to some extent.

As you can see, there is quite a bit of discussion (and even disagreement) about the nature of classical education. It will be up to you to decide which elements of a classical education are most important to you. One thing to keep in mind is that classical education generally requires more direct instruction and interaction than do some other approaches. It is often more parent controlled and directed than other approaches.

See the following to read more about classical education:

The Well-Trained Mind, 2004 revised edition, by Jessie Wise and Susan Wise Bauer, (W.W. Norton & Co.; order through bookstores or distributors) $39.95

This is a nonsectarian book that lays out comprehensive, detailed classical education programs for all grade levels with a strong college-prep emphasis. Even if you don't do everything the way they suggest, this is a treasure trove for anyone considering classical education.

Teaching the Trivium: Christian Homeschooling in a Classical Style by Harvey and Laurie Bluedorn (Trivium Pursuit, PMB 168, 429 Lake Park Boulevard, Muscatine, IA 52761; 309-537-3641; www.triviumpursuit.com) $27.00

The Bluedorns, pioneers in classical Christian education, temper their enthusiasm with cautions about pagan content. Rather than buying into the "Great Books" model of classical education, the Bluedorns apply the methodology while carefully selecting resources that support a biblical Christian worldview. They suggest numerous ideas for content, presentation, and timing but leave it to parents to decide what makes sense for their own children. They approach their subject from a Reformed Protestant perspective. Even those Christians who might not share the Bluedorn's theological perspective should find this book helpful if their goal is to use the classical model of education by drawing from it that which is worthy, while staying true to biblical principles.

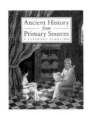

Ancient History from Primary Sources: A Literary Timeline by Harvey and Laurie Bluedorn (Trivium Pursuit; see contact information above) $59.00

This is a book and set of two CDs. The CDs contain primary source documents, while the book is a guide to their use. The Bluedorns direct us to excerpts from the various writings on the CD, so the prospect of using primary sources becomes much more manageable.

Natural Structure: A Montessori Approach to Classical Education at Home by Edward and Nancy Walsh (Catholic Heritage Curricula, P.O. Box 125, Twain Harte, CA 95383-0125; www.chcweb.com)

Natural structure is the name given to this form of education, which combines Montessori and classical education. Edward and Nancy Walsh have brought them together by adopting the framework of the trivium and quadrivium as outlined by Dorothy Sayers, then using Montessori's detailed teaching methodology to present the content. The program as presented in this book is Montessori-style education, but with resources selected to ensure content coverage reflective of the various stages of classical education. As children move past the prepara-tory and grammar stages of the trivium, Montessori materials are used less frequently and methodology becomes more similar to other forms of classical education. The Walshes rely on Montessori's original ideas, including her foundational Catholic perspective. While *Natural Structure* can be adapted by those with other religious beliefs, it does not readily fit nonreligious situations.

✓ ***Introduction to Classical Studies*** by Cheryl Lowe (Memoria Press, 4105 Bishop Lane, Louisville, KY 40218; 877-862-1097; e-mail: magister@memoriapress.com; www.memoiapress.com) $14.95

I suspect many parents like the idea of classical education but have no idea where or how to start. This guide solves that problem. Author Cheryl Lowe lays a foundation for classical education in the elementary grades (as early as third grade) by outlining a study of three key books: *The Golden Children's Bible, Famous Men of Rome,* and D'Aulaires's *Book of Greek Myths.* These three are key to a *Christian* classical education since classical studies center around Greek and Roman thought and history, and the Bible provides the foundational guidepost of truth.

The guide has daily lesson plans for a year and also shows how to recycle through the lessons at higher levels for a three-year plan. Children should begin Latin study along with these studies for the fullest benefit.

Classical Education: The Movement Sweeping America by Gene Edward Veith Jr. and Andrew Kern (Capital Research Center, 1513 Sixteenth Street, Northwest, Washington, D.C. 20036; 202-483-6900; www.capitalresearch.org)

This book covers the broad range of classical education, the different approaches and different settings as well as key organizations and resources. This is one of the most objec-tive resources if you are trying to sort out what approach within the classical education models you might use.

Unit Study

Unit study appears under many different names and formats but can be recognized by the presence of a unifying theme. Rather than approaching each subject and topic as isolated things to be learned, infor-mation is integrated across subject areas, thereby helping children better understand what they are study-ing. According to the theory behind the unit study approach, when children really understand what they are learning, they remember it better.

A unit study might focus on one primary subject area or on many subject areas. The major published unit studies generally encompass social studies, science, and the fine arts, with varying amounts of cover-age of language arts and religion, and very limited math.

Here's an example of a typical unit study that comes from the first chapter in *KONOS* Volume 1 on the character trait "attentiveness." First, we choose an aspect of attentiveness we wish to study, such as listening and sound. We study related Scriptures, then study about the human ear (science), listen to music (music), make musical instruments (crafts), study about musical composers (music history), practice listening games (character development), study about and apply the speeds of sound and light to thunder and lightning (math and science), and write a headache commercial describing irritating noises (language). These ideas are only a fraction of the choices offered within a typical *KONOS* unit!

There are also limited unit studies available that focus more narrowly on a single topic. For example, a study of horses might include the history of horses and the different breeds around the world, a study of their anatomy and physiology, and a written research paper on a horse-related topic. Thus history, science, and language arts are taught around a single theme selected primarily as a science topic.

You might also create your own limited unit study from resources on hand. For instance, if you are studying about the California Gold Rush, you could study those sections in a California history textbook along with sections about mining and minerals from a science textbook. You might also integrate a language arts activity by assigning a creative writing task related to the Gold Rush.

Unit studies typically use real books as sources for learning material rather than textbooks. Many unit studies incorporate Charlotte Mason's ideas on the use of real books, nature study, and narration.

Unit study is often, but not always, multisensory, using hands-on experiences or activities for more effective learning. Most unit studies are constructed so they can be used across a wide age span, with adaptations suggested for various levels.

Unit studies work best for families with more flexible schedules since activities might take more or less time on any given day. Most also require preparation and presentation time. You will need to gather materials and resources for the study and decide how to use them; the different published unit studies vary in how much of this work is already done for you.

The parent/teacher generally spends more time working directly with students in most unit studies—reading aloud, discussing, or leading an activity. The trade-off for extra time invested is that children retain the information that has been presented in such interesting ways, thereby relieving parents from reviewing and reteaching the same material again. An added bonus of this type of learning is that it tends to get children excited about the process—a real motivational boost.

Some parents are overwhelmed by the idea of unit studies, but there are programs available (e.g., *KONOS in a Box*) that are so thoroughly developed that they not only provide all the resources you need, they also tell you exactly what to do when.

Unit studies for high school level tend to be more book-based than activity-oriented. While unit studies at elementary levels require heavy parental involvement, those for older students frequently require a good deal of independent work.

Examples of comprehensive unit studies among my Top Picks are *Tapestry of Grace*, *KONOS*, and *Five in a Row*. Examples of limited unit studies are *Further Up and Further In* and *Media Angels Science* units.

Unschooling or Relaxed Homeschooling

The idea of letting children follow their own inclinations in their education has been called "unschooling." The philosophic ideas behind this approach are most often associated with John Holt, author of numerous books, such as *How Children Learn, How Children Fail, Instead of Education,* and *Teach Your Own.* Holt's books are available from libraries and bookstores, especially from John Holt's Book and Music Store.

A true unschooler would allow a child to determine what, when, how, and even "if" the child learns anything. But few people go to that extreme. What seems closer to reality in most unschooling situations is a much greater consideration for each child's interests and the timing of when they tackle various topics and skills. Also, unschooling parents often ask for their children's opinions about resources and learning methods. This approach is also sometimes called "relaxed" homeschooling.

Hallmarks of an unschooling approach are likely to be a very loose schedule, emphasis on developing a love for learning, rare use of traditional textbooks unless selected by the child, and more hands-on projects and/or field trips.

To learn more about unschooling, read one of John Holt's books listed above or one of the following:

- *The Unschooling Handbook* by Mary Griffiths (Prima Publishing, www.primapublishing.com; order through bookstores or distributors) $15.95—Mary helps explain what unschooling might look like, with anecdotes and examples from many different families. She also includes specific ideas about how to help your children become educated without the normal structure and curriculum.
- *The Relaxed Home School* by Mary Hood, Ph.D. (Ambleside Educational Press, P.O. Box 2524, Cartersville, GA 30120; 770-917-9141) $10.95—This is a practical book that seems to reflect what many families are actually doing. Mary stresses the need for goals coupled with an openness to many ways of attaining them. She suggests letting children have significant input into goal and strategy decisions, taking into consideration their talents and interests.

Independent Study

I include independent study as a distinct approach even though it often uses resources listed under other approaches. The key idea here is that parents use resources that allow a student to operate with little direct teaching or interaction regarding lessons. This means there must be a preset curriculum that is self-instructional.

School of Tomorrow, Alpha Omega (*LIFEPAC* curriculum), and Christian Light all have courses very similar in appearance that work this way, although these are not the only choices for independent study.

In the three aforementioned programs, a number of booklets (typically ten to twelve for a year-long course) comprise a course. Each booklet contains information students read (much like that found in textbooks). However, short sections of text are followed by questions. Students answer the questions referring back to what they have read. If they get most answers correct, they move on to the next section. If not, they review the material and answer questions again. Periodic tests operate the same way. So a student, theoretically, masters the material before moving on from each section. No direct teaching or parental interaction is required other than checking answers.

Alpha Omega took their *LIFEPACs* a step further by creating a computer-based version called *Switched-On Schoolhouse (SOS)*. (See the review of *SOS* in chapter 14.)

While the above-mentioned resources are designed for independent study, many textbooks may also be used this way. Some of *A Beka's* textbooks work well this way. *Saxon Math* from *Math 54* and up are primarily used for independent study.

Independent study works best for self-directed learners who are responsible about their use of time. Most young learners do not do well with independent study, but many high schoolers thrive on it.

Parents faced with difficult time constraints often see independent study resources as the only way they can manage to homeschool. However, it is important to keep in mind that when you choose independent study resources, you forsake the ability to adapt to meet the learning style needs of your child.

In addition, the format of independent study means that most learning is at the lower levels of thinking—knowledge and comprehension—rather than higher levels of synthesis and analysis. Answers for lower-level questions can be simple, factual answers, while those for higher-level questions tend to be complex and subjective—the type of answers that require sentences, paragraphs, or discussion rather than multiple choice or fill-in-the-blanks.

While the last paragraph describes resources designed particularly for independent study, there are many others that homeschoolers use for independent study that actually involve higher levels of thinking. Examples are the *Wordly Wise* vocabulary series, almost any of the *Critical Thinking Books*, *Apologia Science* courses, *Worldviews of the Western World*, and *KONOS History of the World*.

Eclectic

For want of a better name, we identify those who pick and choose from among a variety of philosophies and resources as "eclectic" homeschoolers. In reality, I suspect the large majority of homeschoolers are eclectic to some extent. Few use everything in a given curriculum. Homeschoolers tend to supplement even the best resources or programs with other interesting things they find.

The goal for eclectic homeschoolers is generally to combine the best ideas that work for their family. This might even mean using philosophic opposites, such as a very structured grammar program and a discovery approach to science.

Eclectic homeschooling requires more parental decision-making and responsibility, so it works best for those with some experience and/or confidence. Many homeschoolers start their first year with a traditional program or even a unit study. The next year, they branch out, keeping what they liked from the prior year and adding new ideas and different resources each year to the mix.

While using an eclectic program generally means putting it together yourself, *Sonlight Curriculum* actually has put together eclectic programs for you. Each level includes a mixture of workbooks and real books that you might say represents a mixture of traditional, Charlotte Mason, and classical approaches.

Sonlight is a great place to start if you really don't know which direction you would like to go. (See the complete review in chapter 14.)

Umbrella Program

I use the designation "umbrella program" to mean correspondence schools that have a preset curriculum with only a few possible options (e.g., Calvert with optional advisory teaching service or Christian Liberty Academy's full enrollment option). Enrollment in such programs provides parents with not only curriculum but guidance and evaluation assistance.

Umbrella programs can be a boon to parents who want assistance in choosing curriculum, planning schedules, and maintaining records. Generally, these programs don't require a great deal of preparation or teaching time. Some umbrella programs might even use resources for independent study, such as Alpha Omega *LIFEPACs* or *Switched-On Schoolhouse,* although most use a mix of resources from various publishers (unless the umbrella program is offered through a publishing company such as A Beka or Bob Jones University Press).

The negative trade off when using such programs is that you loose flexibility in curriculum choices and scheduling and in your ability to adapt to each child's needs. Nevertheless, such programs help parents who lack confidence, are disorganized, or do not have time and energy to go it alone.

Note: While I've restricted the meaning of umbrella programs in this manual, there are actually some that allow families to choose from among a broad range of curricula, and there are some—like the aforementioned Calvert and Christian Liberty Academy—that offer options where you can use their curriculum without reporting and accountability requirements.

Yes, this is confusing, so check out such programs carefully before enrolling. In addition to the obvious questions—How much does it cost? What grade levels do they offer? Is it Christian, nonsectarian, etc.?—ask what curriculum they use, what options are available, what sort of record keeping is required, if there are time limits, if there is any possibility of a refund once students have begun the program, and how much help is available and how quickly you can get it.

Finding Umbrella Programs

I've mentioned Calvert (see the review in chapter 14) and Christian Liberty Academy because they are the largest such programs, but there are many other such programs available that meet the needs of families with different educational and religious philosophies. Following are links to four very helpful Web sites that have lists of such programs with brief annotations:

- www.geocities.com/Athens/8259/umbrella.html
- www.gomilpitas.com/homeschooling/methods/DLPsCorrespondence.htm
- www.christianhomeschoolers.com/hs/satmisc.shtml
- www.homeschoolteenscollege.net/diplomaisp.htm

Figuring Out What Works For You

OK. You have added up the numbers on the chart and have read through the descriptions of different approaches, but perhaps you still have not developed a clear preference. Take heart! You can narrow this down even more as you consider some very practical issues. Your thoughts about the questions I pose next are so important that I've left space for you to jot down your responses on each one.

1. How much confidence and/or experience do you have homeschooling?

If you have a great deal of both, then you will probably do fine with unit studies, unschooling, and other more creative and loosely structured approaches. If not, you might easily be overwhelmed by resources that require you to make many choices, find resources, plan projects, and create your own assessment. It is sometimes better to start out with more structure, gradually adding more and more adventurous ideas as you gain confidence.

_____

_____

_____

2. How much time do you have available for working directly with your children and for planning and preparation?

Be realistic about this! If you've got two little ones in diapers (one of them still nursing), a beginning reader, and more work than hours in the day, choosing curriculum that requires lots of preparation, direct instruction, and your constant attention only proves that you have a death wish. It doesn't matter how much you love real books, project learning, and field trips if you don't have time to do them.

Figure out where your children _really_ need you and which subjects _must_ be taught this year, then find the most efficient resources you can for those. If there is time left over, add more interactive learning and more subjects. This doesn't mean your budding reader needs to learn how to read from a computer program. While that's possible, it will be much better if you squeeze in _some_ time for one-to-one work together.

Keep in mind that you can easily provide some reading instruction as you go about your daily routine. You can have magnetic letters on the refrigerator that your child identifies by sound while you're preparing a meal. You can have him or her find letters on signs as you drive to the grocery store. The same thing goes for math; counting silverware while setting the table, adding the total number of spoons and forks, and counting pennies that made it all the way through the laundry into the clothes dryer are examples.

If you are one of the fortunate few with plenty of time, you have much more freedom to choose time-consuming resources. However, most of us are somewhere in between the two extremes. We can usually function well if we balance some one-to-one time with some group time and some independent study time.

I strongly recommend trying to group your children together whenever you can for efficiency's sake. It's easiest to do this with religious devotions and instruction, history, science, and the arts. Math and language arts generally require more individualized work. Of course, methods like unit study and Charlotte Mason work better for grouping children than do traditional curriculum or correspondence courses, which have different books for each student for each subject.

So how much time do you really have to devote to homeschooling, both for direct teaching and for planning and preparation?

_____

_____

_____

_____

_____

3. How much money can you spend?

If the world were your oyster and cost were no problem, then choices would be simpler. Unfortunately, most of us have sacrificed a second income and operate on a limited budget, so we cannot buy everything we would like to own.

First, let me reassure you that the most expensive resources are not necessarily the best. Expensive resources sometimes provide more parental assistance, saving you time and energy. However, sometimes they only provide you with many more things that you will feel obligated to do but are really not essential to your goals. If your child does not need lots of hands-on work to grasp math concepts, money spent on a program with pricey math manipulatives would have been better budgeted for a family vacation.

Second, you might not need to purchase a lot of resources designed primarily for educational purposes. You already have a wealth of "unintentional" learning resources if you simply look for learning opportunities that surround your children in real life. Your kitchen is loaded with possibilities for learning and applying math. Building projects, board games, budgets, checkbooks, allowances, family businesses, and shopping add even more opportunities available to most of us. Children can practice language arts if you simply capitalize on opportunities all around you—writing thank-you notes for gifts, creating shopping lists, writing directions to their friend's home, and copying and posting a "quote for the week" or memorization verse on the refrigerator are just a few examples.

You *do* need information beyond your own limited knowledge, but your local library stocks more books than you can hope to own. Make friends with your librarian and get the most out of this marvelous resource.

The easiest way to tune into learning opportunities in your environment is to ask yourself what it is specifically that your child needs to learn and then think about how he or she might learn it with whatever is available. For example, your son needs to learn both standard and metric linear measurement. Grab a ruler and/or yardstick marked with both inches and centimeters and start measuring and comparing.

Need to teach about adjectives? Use them in abundance as you talk to your child—get flowery, silly, alliterative, and imaginative: "Just look at this fuzzy, filthy, fungus-covered floor covering! It must need vacuuming." Then challenge your child to come up with his or her own descriptive sentence. (Be careful not to include adverbs like "very" and prepositional phrases like "under piles of junk." Explaining the difference is another lesson.)

I could digress with many more examples, but I think you get the point: learning need not happen the way it happens in schools. This means you can save some of the money you might have spent to recreate a traditional school at home. Keep this in mind as you come up with a budget amount for your homeschooling. So, how much can you budget for homeschooling?

_____

_____

4. How do your religious beliefs impact your homeschooling?

Families have different feelings in this regard. For some families, spiritual knowledge and development is the highest priority. Other parents make academic excellence or raising independent, self-motivated learners their highest priority. Religion might be a lower priority, or it might have no place at all in their homeschooling. Many families haven't thought about their priorities enough to know how to answer this question. Thinking through this question is very important. Religious beliefs will play a role in your home education whether you plan for that to happen or not.

Many parents think that non-Christian textbooks present a "neutral" education, one that doesn't include any kind of spiritual viewpoint. In reality, all resources reflect a spiritual outlook. Now I can just picture some of you shaking your heads and saying, "Come on. There's no religion in my child's spelling book." Or, "Math doesn't have anything to do with religion!"

A humorous piece that has been wending its way around the Internet for a number of years illustrates my point. I have no idea who originated the first version, and it has been updated with additions to reflect ideological changes on a number of Web sites where it is posted. Here's a version I pulled from one Web site:

The Logger's New Math

Teaching Math in 1950: A logger sells a truckload of lumber for $100. His cost of production is 4/5 of the price. What is his profit?

Teaching Math in 1960: A logger sells a truckload of lumber for $100. His cost of production is 4/5 of the price, or $80. What is his profit?

Teaching Math in 1970: A logger exchanges a set "L" of lumber for a set "M" of money. The cardinality of set "M" is 100. Each element is worth one dollar. Make 100 dots representing the elements of the set "M." The set "C," the cost of production, contains 20 fewer points than set "M." Represent the set "C" as a subset of set "M" and answer the following question: What is the cardinality of the set "P" for profits?

Teaching Math in 1980: A logger sells a truckload of lumber for $100. Her cost of production is $80 and her profit is $20. Your assignment: Underline the number 20.

Teaching Math in 1990: By cutting down beautiful forest trees, the logger makes $20. What do you think of this way of making a living? Topic for class participation after answering the question: How did the forest birds and squirrels feel as the logger cut down the trees? There are no wrong answers.

Teaching Math in 1996: By laying off 40% of its loggers, a company improves its stock price from $80 to $100. How much capital gain per share does the CEO make by exercising his stock options at $80? Assume capital gains are no longer taxed, because this encourages investment.

Teaching Math in 1997: A company outsources all of its loggers. The firm saves on benefits, and when demand for its product is down, the logging workforce can easily be cut back. The average logger employed by the company earned $50,000, had three weeks vacation, a nice retirement plan, and medical insurance. The contracted logger charges $50 an hour. Was outsourcing a good move?

Teaching Math in 1998: A laid-off logger with four kids at home and a ridiculous alimony from his first failed marriage comes into the logging company corporate offices and goes postal, mowing down 16 executives and a couple of secretaries, and gets lucky when he nails a politician on the premises collecting his kickback. Was outsourcing the loggers a good move for the company?

Teaching Math in 1999: A laid-off logger serving time in Federal Prison for blowing away several people is being trained as a COBOL programmer in order to work on Y2K projects. What is the probability that the automatic cell doors will open on their own as of 00:00:01, 01/01/00?

(Taken from www.geocities.com/geminilaz1/newmath.html on March 22, 2003.)

These are mostly exaggerated examples of what folks have found in math textbooks over the years. You might have noticed that there's no mention of religion in any of them. But what does it imply when feelings take precedence over the facts of math as in the 1990 example? Or what about the other agendas (like ecology) that work their way into supposedly neutral subjects? And what do you think of presenting business ethic questions as mere mathematical calculations rather than moral challenges?

Do you doubt that some very different beliefs about God and man, man's purpose in life, and man's responsibilities in relationship to others shape many texts used in schools?

Even more subtle are the choices of what to include and what to leave out of textbooks. For example, history books that start with an evolutionary explanation of the origins of life proceed as if the theory has been proven. They ignore the possibility of man being a special creation of God. They also ignore all historical evidence of God being a real part of history. Less subtle are science texts that teach that accident and random chance are what brought us out of a primordial stew to our present evolving state.

In literature texts and readers we often find folk tales of various pagan gods that show us how each of the gods "blessed" those who followed their instructions. The implication is that all "gods" are created equal. Those same texts probably include no stories about the one true God, and certainly none that imply that He is the only one we should obey.

Even those that try to leave *all* spirituality out of learning are inadvertently teaching their children a materialistic philosophy. If spirituality and transcendence never enter the discussion, we are teaching children that the world consists only of what they experience with their senses and know with their minds. Some will admit that God might exist, but if He does, He is so irrelevant that He has nothing to do with important things like history and science. While parents might believe in God, if they don't show their children that that belief makes a difference in the way they look at all areas of life, they are teaching their children to be materialists—a religious belief.

If, on the other hand, you believe in God, it should be important enough to impart to your children— or else what's the point of believing in Him at all? If faith and knowledge of God are important, then they need to be incorporated into the learning process, both into the content and method of presentation. You teach what you believe and you demonstrate your belief by the way you act, how you speak, and how you treat people.

So, you must keep spiritual goals and influences in mind as you select your curriculum. A resource might be very popular with homeschoolers in general, but it might not reflect your family's spiritual beliefs. Sometimes you can work around these issues with minimal effort, but sometimes it's more trouble than it's worth. Be especially careful when selecting resources that your children will be using independently. You might seldom look at the curriculum once they start working, and you won't have opportunity to spot content that undermines your family's beliefs.

Back to the question: How will your spiritual beliefs affect your homeschooling—your goals and your choices of resources and methods? Do you want to use religiously oriented materials? Will there be some resources you will avoid for spiritual reasons?

_____

_____

_____

_____

Before you pull all this together, look at the samples in the next chapter to see how to combine the information you've gleaned thus far to put together your own philosophy of education.

3

Putting Together Your Philosophy of Education

There was a lot to work through in chapter 2, and you might be confused at this point. That's why I have created a sample of how this might look as you work through each section. I've written responses and completed charts as I would have when my sons were about ages seven, ten, and twelve.

After you read through these completed questions and charts, I'll show you how it all comes together. Let's begin with the first three questions.

Content and Methods

What do you think is most important for your children to learn?

Sample (remember that 1 indicates highest priority, 2 the next highest, and 3 the lowest):

Priorities

I want my children to	Priority Level
have a strong sense of God's reality in all aspects of their education	1
love to learn so they will become self-educators	1
have a broad education so they can consider lots of possibilities for their future	2
develop excellent reading skills	1
develop excellent thinking skills	1
develop excellent communication skills	2
learn how to work with other children/adults in groups	2
develop good work habits	2
develop excellent knowledge of Scripture and religious beliefs	1
prepare for college so that they have more life choices	1
develop a heart for service to others	1
cover all the normal subjects so they can pass tests when necessary	2
figure out their special talents and gifts	2
be computer literate	2
have exposure to the arts and develop some "artistic" skills	2
be physically fit	2
develop a strong Christian worldview	1
read widely from both classic and good books	1

Note: Notice there are still some blank lines. You don't have to fill them all in just because they're there. However, if you need even more space, feel free to grab another piece of paper and make your list longer. Also notice that there are no level 3 entries. I realized that I had so many level 1 and 2 entries that things that might be level 3 were too low on my priority list to even bother writing them down. However, you might write out your own list, then find on reflection that some of your entries actually rate a level 3.

How do you think learning should happen?

I have three very active boys who need to be able to move around and do lots of hands-on learning. I want lots of interaction and experiential learning. I also want them to learn how to operate independently and learn to teach themselves through their independent reading, especially as they get older. So a balance that combines these two ideas is best for us.

How do you want to teach or "run your school"?

1. Do you want to try to teach most or all of your children together, at least for some subjects? *Absolutely.*

2. How much of the time do you want (or are you able) to work directly with your children?

I want to start together in the mornings for about 1½ to 2 hours, do some group classes or park days a few afternoons a week, and have them work independently or one-to-one with me the rest of the time.

3. How much of the time do you expect your children to work independently?

My middle son works independently better than the other two—at least a few hours a day. My youngest will do a few scattered fifteen minute to half hour periods of independent work. My eldest will do at least two hours of independent work as long as I check on him frequently.

4. Do you want to use real books (biographies, historical novels, books written about particular science topics, etc.) as part of your curriculum?

Definitely.

5. Do you want to include field trips? If so, what type of field trips?

Yes! Field trips related to unit study topics plus any good opportunities that come up!

6. Do you like to "make up" curriculum as you go, adapting to the needs and interests of your children, or do you prefer things well planned out in advance?

I like to have a general plan completed during the summer, then adapt as I go.

7. Do you need a set schedule to get things done, or would you prefer more flexibility?

Flexibility, although we need to start with together time first thing in the morning.

8. Do you prefer a curriculum that is thoroughly laid out in advance and that tells you what to do when?

No.

9. Any additional thoughts about how you want to operate?

I want my lesson plans to become my record-keeping books, so I work from my spiral notebook that I use during each summer to make general plans for the year. I periodically fill in my lesson plan/record book for the next few weeks with specific books and page numbers, activities, field trips, etc., so it is easy to make changes to my original plan.

I'm not concerned about grading in the elementary grade levels, but I will give grades once in a while so they have concrete feedback about how I think they are doing. Grading becomes more important to me in junior high.

Approaches

Which approach to education should I use?

Approaches to Learning

I prefer:	Traditional	Charlotte Mason	Classical	Unit Study	Unschooling	Independent Study	Eclectic	Umbrella Program
predictable structure.	1	.5	1			1	1	1
that children have many real life experiences for learning—nature studies in the woods, building projects, etc.		(1)	(.5)	(1)	(1)	(1)	(1)	
children read historical novels and biographies rather than textbooks.		(1)	(1)	(1)	(1)		(1)	
a program that is thoroughly laid out for the teacher and provides a feeling of security.	1					1		1
a grammar program that emphasizes rules and memorization	1		1			1	.5	1
workbooks, teachers manuals, and answer keys for most or all subjects.	1					1	.5	1
children to work independently as much as possible.	.5				1	1	.5	.5
mental training and mental discipline have higher priority than stimulating curiosity and interest.	1		.5			1	.5	.5
curriculum that ensures my children cover the same things other school children might be learning.	1					1	.5	1
informal evaluation of my child by talking over what they've read and looking at their work rather than by testing.		(1)	(1)	(1)	(1)		(.5)	
that my young children do a significant amount of memorization, repetition, and recitation.	.5		.5			.5	.5	.5
my teen to get a strong background in the great books of western civilization.		(.5)	(1)	(.5)	(.5)	(.5)	(.5)	(.5)
to emphasize developing a love for learning *more than* the ability to work in a structured, methodical way.		(1)		(1)	(1)		(.5)	
that teens develop a "life of the mind" more than vocational skills.	(.5)	(1)	(1)	(1)	(.5)	(.5)	(.5)	(.5)
presenting my children with information to learn rather than having them choose their own topics to investigate.	1	.5	1	.5		1	.5	1
highly structured resources that "script" what teacher/parent and child are supposed to say and do.	.5		.5			.5	.5	.5
lots of discussion and interaction in the learning process.		(1)	(1)	(1)	(.5)		(1)	(.5)
covering subjects (e.g., history, science, religion) at the same time with the same material with as many of my children as possible.		(1)	(1)	(1)			(1)	
making connections between different subject areas, showing relationships, and viewing that as a high priority in learning.		(1)	(1)	(1)	(1)		(.5)	
project-based learning.		(.5)		(1)	(1)		(.5)	
to teach my children one-on-one as much as possible	1	.5	.5		.5		1	1
that my children learn grammar in a casual manner—e.g., some instruction, use of a grammar handbook, then working on mastery in their own writing.		(.5)		(1)	(1)		(.5)	
Totals for each column for this page:	.5	9.5	7.5	10.5	8.5	2	7.5	1.5

I prefer:	Traditional	Charlotte Mason	Classical	Unit Study	Unschooling	Independent Study	Eclectic	Umbrella Program
to keep structure to a minimum so that I and my children are able to pursue interesting learning ideas when they arise.		(.5)		(.5)	(1)		(.5)	
to make frequent field trips an essential part of schooling.	(.5)	(1)	(.5)	(.5)	(1)		(.5)	
to give my children freedom to determine what they will study and when and how they will do so.				.5	1		.5	
an "investigative" approach that stimulates my children to pursue information and research on their own.		(.5)		(1)	(1)	(.5)	(.5)	
flexible curriculum and schedules so I can capitalize on "teachable moments."		(.5)	(.5)	(1)	(1)		(.5)	
a mixture of structured learning and experiential/discovery learning.		(1)		(1)			(1)	
to set my own goals and schedule rather than adopting someone else's.		(.5)	(.5)	(.5)	(1)		(.5)	
to select curriculum/methods that suit my child's learning style rather than curriculum/methods widely recognized and accepted by authorities.		(.5)	(.5)	(1)	(1)		(.5)	
that computer-based learning be a significant part of the curriculum.	.5					.5		.5
A. Total for each column for this page	.5	4.5	2	5.5	6	.5	4	0
B. Totals for columns from first page	.5	9.5	7.5	10.5	8.5	2	7.5	1.5
Total for each column: add line A and B and enter total as the numerator (top number) of the fraction	$\frac{1}{11}$	$\frac{14}{15.5}$	$\frac{9.5}{14.5}$	$\frac{16}{17}$	$\frac{14.5}{17}$	$\frac{2.5}{12}$	$\frac{11.5}{18}$	$\frac{1.5}{11}$
Optional: Percentage for each column (divide numerator by denominator)	9%	90%	66%	94%	85%	21%	64%	14%

Note: When I complete this chart, I come up with high numbers (and large fractions) for unit study, Charlotte Mason, unschooling, classical education, and eclectic approaches. Traditional education, independent study, and umbrella programs are clearly not my preferences.

Check Your Results

As I read through the actual descriptions in chapter 2, I find that there are elements of unschooling that appeal to me, but not enough of the philosophy that I would really consider unschooling as my own approach, even though it scored 85 percent.

I really like certain aspects of classical education—Great Books, discussions, higher level thinking—but I'm not enamored with some of the memorization-based programs that are also called classical education. This dilutes my strong preference for the aspects I like and makes my preference for classical education appear weaker than it actually is. (This should be a caution to others who, like me, prefer some aspects of what is labeled classical education. You need to investigate resources described as classical to ensure that they really are what you want.)

Yes!

With my highest numbers appearing for unit study and Charlotte Mason approaches, it would make sense for me to see if there isn't a way to incorporate the classical education and Charlotte Mason ideas I like within a unit study format. (Yes, such curriculum actually exists!)

The Next Four Questions—the Reality Check

Next, I wrote down some notes on the next four questions, thinking back a few years to when I had children in elementary grades through junior high:

1. How much confidence and/or experience do you have homeschooling?

I have lots of confidence and enough experience that I don't mind trying unusual approaches.

2. How much time do you have available for working directly with your children and for planning and preparation?

My time is very limited because of other demands. My husband doesn't have much time to help. But I can work with other families to do some group classes, so that will help on the time question. So I have about three hours a day available for direct teaching/interaction. I need to do a lot of planning over the summer when I have more time, then I should have about three or four hours each weekend to plan for each week.

3. How much money can you spend?

We're on a limited budget, so I should spend about $300 to $400 total this year.

4. How do your religious beliefs impact your homeschooling?

My religious beliefs are a critical part of homeschooling. They will underlie everything we do. I would like to use resources that reflect my beliefs, but I can work with others as long as they are not in direct conflict.

When I consider my answers to these four questions, I can see that my time constraints will make time-consuming planning and projects difficult to impossible. I need to compromise on my desire to do unit studies and lot of project learning. I also might not have the time to do classical education.

Money will be a limitation, but I'm not set on only one way of doing this, so I can look at many different options.

Incorporating religious beliefs is easy within Charlotte Mason and unit study approaches since they use real books and require discussion and interaction. If I do classical education's Great Books/Good Books approach, I can also incorporate religion easily.

Putting It All Together

Now, I am ready to gather what I have learned so that I can verbalize my own personal philosophy of education and what that might look like for our family. You can do this in any order you wish, but I will describe my own process.

First, I summarized my educational philosophy primarily from the first section, actually copying from some of what I wrote there. I did not need to include everything from that section.

My philosophy of education:

I believe that my children's education should help them develop a strong sense of God's reality in all aspects of their lives. I want my children to love to learn so they will become self-educators who choose to learn on their own. I also want them to have strong academic skills so they have the tools for independent learning. I want them to have a broad education since I do not know what direction God has for each of them.

Next, I looked at the chart where I'd checked boxes reflecting different educational approaches. I'd already come to some conclusions (noted above) about which approaches I like. In my notes following the last four questions, I already noted that one of my highest priorities—incorporating religious goals into education—is easier to do within one of the "real books" approaches.

Another priority I set in the first section—and one of my strongest—is that my children love to learn. That means I will want to be particularly attentive to methods and resources that are appealing to them and that encourage that love of learning. I know enough about learning styles to recognize that this might mean choosing different resources for each of them, if necessary.

However, as I noted in the last section, we have a limited budget. Therefore I might not be able to purchase everything I would like to use.

Time is also a precious commodity. I know I don't want to plunk my boys down with workbooks all the time if I really want them to love learning. On the other hand, they will have to do some independent work both for their sakes and mine. I do not have time to do everything with them, and I want them to eventually become independent learners, so they *do* need to learn how to work independently.

I will need to come up with a balance of interesting, interactive learning activities and independent work. I realize that I can primarily use the educational approaches I prefer, but I will probably have to include some traditional workbooks just to make things manageable.

I want to incorporate worldview education, even more so at junior high and high school level, so that will narrow down my choices in some ways. I would like to use classical methods from the dialectic and rhetoric stages for a good part of worldview education.

Realistically, I can see that my time demands are going to be heavy. One of the smartest things I can do is work with all three children together whenever possible. Unit studies might help me do that. Group classes with other families will be another way to help with the time issue.

All of this tells me that I should probably look to unit study ideas, looking for those that have a strong worldview orientation plus those based on either Charlotte Mason's ideas or classical education (the latter especially for my older sons). I can likely use traditional books for subjects not covered by the unit study.

• • •

Now, it's your turn. When you've completed this section, go on to chapter 4 to see how understanding both your own and your children's learning styles will help you fine-tune your curriculum choices.

4

Learning Styles: How Does *My* Child Learn Best?

If you are like me and most other parents I've asked, teaching your child to read is probably the scariest part of homeschooling. We have this sense that if we blow it with reading, then how can we possibly accomplish anything else?

Given that so many of us share this common insecurity, you might well be one of the thousands of parents who shelled out two hundred to three hundred dollars for one of those reading programs advertised on the radio. The glowing testimonials really convinced you that this would be money well spent.

Also like thousands of parents who invested in such programs, you might have had a very discouraging experience with the program. Let's say you bought the one that teaches the alphabet and phonetic sounds to rap tunes. When you plugged in the first cassette for your child to listen to, you discovered a couple of disconcerting things: your child doesn't like rap music, and your child couldn't make any connection between what he was hearing and the letters he was seeing on the paper. If you figured this out quickly enough, you were able to return the program within the allowable time and get your money back. If not, the program got added to your collection of white elephants.

So how do we save ourselves this sort of expensive grief? One of the best ways is tuning in to our children's learning styles.

Unfortunately, this was something I learned after making some big mistakes in my initial curriculum choices. When we first began homeschooling in 1982, my strongest conviction was that I wanted to use a Christian curriculum. The only Christian curriculum publisher I knew of was A Beka Book. This was the "dark ages" of homeschooling—a time when most publishers were not interested in selling to homeschoolers, even if they knew such a thing as homeschooling existed. Nevertheless, I went to a great deal of trouble to obtain *A Beka* worktexts to use with my two older sons, first and third graders at the time.

It took no more than two weeks to figure out that this sort of curriculum was about the worst choice for my eldest son, Chris. You'll understand why shortly when you read the description of the Wiggly Willy learning style. I had to get busy adapting and doing other things to enable Chris to learn. If it depended upon him working through *A Beka* lessons, reading the text and completing the activity pages, we were doomed.

Learning Modalities and Learning Styles

I first started using methods relating to learning modalities. You might already be familiar with learning modalities—the idea that people tend to prefer one of three types (or modes) of sensory input:

1. auditory (hearing)
2. visual (seeing)
3. kinesthetic (feeling or experiencing with one's body)

Understanding learning modalities might have helped the parent who bought the phonics program that uses cassette tapes for most of the teaching if she had known that her child was *not* an auditory learner. Learning by listening would not be the method of choice for such a child.

Learning modalities helped me with Chris since I knew he was a kinesthetic learner. I pulled out math manipulatives and other concrete objects to teach lessons even though A Beka made no provision for that sort of learning. But it was a lot of work to come up with such adaptations for the different subjects while also sorting out what parts of the A Beka worktexts I could still use.

Understanding learning modalities helps to a certain extent, but it's a bit too simplistic. For example, what do you do with a child who is a strong auditory learner but who can't sit still long enough to listen to a lesson being read to him?

That's where learning styles come in. The term *learning style* refers to the way (or style) a person most easily learns and processes new information or skills. Learning styles are just a bit more complex than learning modalities. They not only include awareness of the child's preferred learning modality, they go further to look at other personality/learning traits, such as a desire to work with other people or to work independently, an orientation toward either the big picture or the details, and preferences for a more or less structured environment.

Learning modalities play a partial role in understanding learning styles. For example, the kinesthetic learning modality is an obvious match with Wiggly Willy learners. However, visual and auditory modalities cross learning style boundaries and should be taken into account no matter what style learner our child seems to be.

Which System Is Best?

Experts have come up with many different systems and labels for identifying a person's learning style. All of them are useful. The most significant differences are in their complexity. Some systems are so complex that an expert needs to administer an assessment and analyze the results.

When I first read about learning styles, hardly anyone was using them to address the needs of children. The first book I found that did so was titled *Learning Patterns and Temperament Styles*[1] by Dr. Keith Golay. Dr. Golay discussed learning styles in relation to traditional, public school classroom settings. Although it was very useful, the fact that it lacked a Christian outlook and didn't address homeschooling motivated me to come up with my own approach, which I use in this book.

The learning styles I use fall into four categories. Yes, it could be much more complex, but our goal with learning styles is not a thorough analysis of each of our children so much as developing an awareness that each child will have ways of learning that are easier and ways that are tougher. By identifying learning styles, we are able to choose teaching methods and materials that are more likely to be successful for each child.

For example, one child's learning style might be very physical in a whole-body sense. This child learns math best when she puts two blocks plus two more blocks together, then counts to see that there are four. She needs to move her body as she counts each number. She learns prepositions best by putting her teddy bear *on* the chair, *under* the chair, *over* the chair, and *beside* the chair. You can imagine how challenging children with this learning style might be to teach in a typical classroom setting!

Another child with a different learning style responds well to traditional classroom textbooks. He learns just fine by reading textbooks and doing workbook exercises. He doesn't need to feel or experience things to learn. But he also depends upon the predictability and security of those workbooks. He really struggles when it comes to creative writing and art projects.

Yet another child learns best when it's a social experience. She thrives on "unit study day" when you get together with a few other families to do all those creative unit study activities together. She blossoms when she gets to role-play a character in a historical event. Her writing is impressive because she wants to do her very best in her correspondence with a pen pal.

Recognizing these differences within each of your children will help you make better choices in the methods and materials you use. But that's only part of the curriculum equation.

But of Course My Way of Learning Is Best!

The other part of the equation is the parent's own learning style. The reality is that we parents have our own learning style preferences, and we tend to teach our children in ways that *we* learn best rather than ways *they* learn best. Our preferred learning style, by default, becomes our teaching style. That's what we're most comfortable with. That's what comes naturally to us.

Structure, organization, and schedules will be important to some of us, while exploration, creativity, and flexibility will be higher priorities for another parent. Some parents love to do messy art projects, while others would rather their children watch an art appreciation video. There's no right and wrong to such choices. Rather, it is a matter of recognizing one's own preferences, then checking to see if those methods are really what work best with one's own children. I like to think that in God's graciousness and wisdom, He usually gives us children of contrasting learning styles so we have more opportunities to stretch and grow.

Adult Learning Styles

The following will help you identify your own learning/teaching style. Read through the description of each learning style. Don't get hung up on the names at the top (Wiggly Willy, Perfect Paula, etc.). These are the labels I use to help you remember each style, but that doesn't mean that only males can have a Wiggly Willy style or that Perfect Paulas are exclusively female.

It is unlikely that every item under any one learning style fits you while none on the other three do. More likely, you will find a number of items under one learning style that describe you and only a few under one or more of the other learning styles. As you read through the four learning style descriptions decide which one is most like you. Then consider which style has the next highest number of characteristics that fit you, continuing through all four figuring which learning style or styles are also least descriptive of you. If you should find that you are fairly evenly spread across one or more learning styles, that's fine too.

Adult Learning/Teaching Styles

Wiggly Willy

- Has trouble organizing and following through
- Would rather play and have fun than work
- Tends to do things impulsively
- Probably did poorly in school (often due to lack of interest or boredom)
- Looks for creative and efficient solutions to tasks
- Dislikes paperwork and record keeping
- Prefers activity over reading books
- Prefers to teach the fine arts, physical education, and activity-oriented classes

Perfect Paula

- Likes everything neatly planned ahead of time

- Likes to follow a schedule
- Is not very good at coming up with creative ideas
- Is comfortable with memorization and drill
- Gets upset easily when children don't cooperate
- Worries about meeting requirements
- Often prefers to work under an umbrella program for home educators
- Prefers to teach with preplanned curricula
- Is more comfortable with "cut and dried" subjects than with subjects that require exploration with no clear answers

Competent Carl

- Likes to be in control
- Thinks and acts logically
- Likes to understand reasoning and logic behind ideas
- Is selectively organized
- Likes to work alone and be independent
- Is impatient with those who are slow to grasp concepts and those who are disorganized
- Is often uncomfortable in social situations and has trouble understanding others' feelings and emotions
- Tends to avoid difficult social situations
- Likes to make long-term plans
- Prefers to teach math, science, and other logic-related subjects rather than language arts and social studies

Sociable Sue

- Enjoys social interaction
- Likes to belong to groups, especially for activities
- Worries about what other people think
- Tends to be insecure about how well he/she is doing with home education
- Is idealistic about expectations and goals
- May or may not be organized, depending upon accountability
- Is more interested in general concepts than details
- Prefers to teach subjects related to language arts, social studies, and possibly, the fine arts

The following analogy showing how different style learners might respond to a visit to a theme park might help you see the differences even better.

For Wiggly Willy it's all about the rides. He wants to experience all of them. Forget the shops and the shows you sit and watch. He wants to feel the action.

Perfect Paula is likely to have organized the event in the first place. She'll make sure there's a meeting place in case someone gets lost. She'll know what time various events take place and try to schedule out the day to make sure she gets to all the things that are on her list.

Competent Carl won't mind going off on his own if everyone else takes too long figuring out what they want to do. He'll choose rides over shops, but particular shows might also intrigue him. His choice activities will be ones with special effects because the fun for him is in figuring out "how they did it."

Sociable Sue will make sure all her friends have come along. Then she'll enjoy whatever happens as long as everyone sticks together. For her the fun is in the company. They could spend hours standing in lines waiting for rides and that would be as much or more fun than anything else.

The next time you go to a theme park, pay attention to your group and see if you can't identify some of these patterns!

If you found that most of your characteristics matched up with a single learning style and very few were described under the other three, you will have to pay more attention to learning styles than a parent who is more evenly spread across the learning styles. You might tend to be "lopsided" in the learning methods you use with your children, leaning heavily toward those that favor the especially strong learning style of yours.

On the other hand, if you recognized a number of your characteristics in two or more learning styles, you will probably have an easier time adapting to the needs of your children since you already have a tendency to work across one or more learning styles.

Now, keeping in mind what you've discovered about your own learning/teaching style, it's time to try to identify your children's learning styles. Remember that they, just like adults, will rarely fit neatly into only one category. They will perhaps have one stronger learning style, one or two that are weaker, and maybe one that doesn't fit them at all.

Children's Learning Styles

Wiggly Willy

Wiggly Willys are those children who learn best by doing—the hands-on learners. They like to be free to move around and act spontaneously. Do you have a little boy who just seems to fall off his chair if he has tried to stay put for more than ten minutes? That's typical for a Wiggly Willy.

They have short attention spans most of the time, although it's interesting to see how their attention spans lengthen when they get into something of their own choosing! These children are usually not interested in deep thinking or analysis if it means sitting still for very long.

On the other hand, they generally do very well with hands-on projects. They can be very creative and imaginative.

These are carefree children who live for the moment. However, they can be difficult to motivate. Wiggly Willys hate being bored. They'll create their own "interesting moments" to break the boredom.

They don't think ahead about consequences, positive or negative. Telling them "Study hard and get good grades so you can get into a good college ten years from now" will not motivate them. Ten years from now is a nonexistent concept for them, so why on earth would they sacrifice present pleasure for that? These children need short-term goals and immediate rewards.

Wiggly Willys can be disruptive in groups. Sometimes these children are labeled as having attention deficit disorder (a disorder that I *do* believe is real) when the actual problem is that, because of their age and temperament, they really need to be moving around more than is allowed in a typical classroom.

Perfect Paula

I call our second type of learner Perfect Paula. This is the responsible child who likes to see that everything is done correctly. She likes things to be clearly structured, planned, and organized.

Perfect Paulas have a narrow comfort zone. They feel more secure when things are orderly. Consequently, they seldom act spontaneously and are uncomfortable with creative activities that lack specific guidelines. For example, if you want them to do an art project, they will ask, "Show me what it's supposed to look like." They want to make sure they do it correctly rather than seize an opportunity to express their own creativity.

They follow rules and respect authority, and they often feel it their duty to make sure everyone else does likewise. They like to follow a typical school curriculum and feel that they are accomplishing the same things as other children their age. They prefer to be part of groups, and they need approval and affirmation to let them know that they are doing what is proper.

Perfect Paulas can be easier to homeschool than other learners, but you might have to work at helping them develop more flexibility and creativity.

Competent Carl

Competent Carls like to be in control of themselves and their surroundings. They tend to be analytical, constantly trying to figure out what makes things tick. Problem solving is typically something they enjoy.

Their analytical/logical bent typically makes math and science their strong subjects and the more subjective language arts their weaker subjects.

Social skills can also be a weak area. Often Competent Carls have difficulty understanding and relating to their peers. Because of this, and sometimes simply by choice, they enjoy solitary activity. They expect others to operate the same way they do, and they don't find it easy to adapt to other ways of doing things.

Competent Carls tend to be self-motivated and enjoy long-term, independent projects. They have their own ideas about what they want to learn, as well as when and how they want to learn it.

Some Competent Carls love to brainstorm—to think out loud. These more verbal Competent Carls often want a more interactive learning environment, or at least one that allows them to ask questions and talk through what they are learning. One-to-one teaching or small groups usually suit Competent Carls better than large groups.

Sociable Sue

Sociable Sues are, of course, sociable. They often have warm, responsive personalities. They are interested in people, and as they get older, that interest expands into ideas, principles, and values.

They tend to be big picture people; concepts are more interesting to them than details and technicalities. They don't like memorizing names and dates for history, but they want to understand how different cultures and events affect one another.

They love change and new things. They can be very excited about a new project or assignment but easily "lose steam" once the novelty has worn off. Sometimes you have to switch what you are doing or add something new with Sociable Sues to reignite their interest—a different curriculum, a new supplemental workbook, an educational game, a field trip, etc.

They are motivated by relationships and care a great deal about what others think of them. They like to be recognized and acknowledged for their achievements. Because of this they will sometimes be overachievers, putting out extraordinary effort to impress people. For the same reason, they are vulnerable to conflict and criticism. They often dislike and avoid competitions, preferring cooperation so that no one's feelings are hurt.

Caution

I have to throw out a few cautions here as we talk about children's learning styles. First of all, think of a typical two-year-old child in terms of learning styles. Most two-year-olds fit into the Wiggly Willy category. They don't sit still very well. They are totally hands-on as they explore their new and expanding world. They aren't interested in deep thinking, long-range planning, or delayed gratification. But they grow beyond their two-year-old world, and eventually, their true learning style becomes evident. This might happen at age five, eight, or ten. They might seem one learning style as they begin kindergarten, then seem a very different style at age ten. So don't try to peg your preschooler's learning style. And don't think you've figured out your older child's learning style and expect it to remain the same forever.

Another caution: It's tempting to use learning styles as an excuse to ignore bad behavior or spiritual issues: "My son's a Wiggly Willy, and he just can't sit still." So you let him drive everyone crazy with his uncontrollable behavior.

Every learning style has both positive and negative character qualities. Wiggly Willys can be enthusiastic and fun-loving, but they struggle with self-discipline. Perfect Paulas can be very self-disciplined, but they might also be bossy or self-righteous. Competent Carls can be so self-sufficient that they lack charity or concern for others. Sociable Sues can be very concerned about people but absolutely hopeless when it comes to other areas of personal responsibility.

Recognizing these strengths and weaknesses in each of our children helps us identify our job as parents. We build on their strengths, but we also help them overcome their weaknesses.

Conflicting Learning Styles

Maybe you have already spotted the biggest problem with learning styles—the potential conflict between the learning styles of parents and children. For example, let's say you identify many of your own characteristics under "Competent Carl." You tend to be a very logical, analytical person. You like independent work, and you've little patience with drama queens. You might have a hard time with your Sociable Sue daughter who tries to use emotional manipulation to get out of doing what she doesn't want to do.

Or consider a very common situation in homeschooling: Perfect Paula mom and Wiggly Willy son. Mom has her lesson plans all organized, her curriculum well planned, and her daily schedule on the refrigerator for all to see. Wiggly Willy would much rather be outside doing practically anything other than school. He freaks out at the sight of the inch-thick math workbook, not to mention the pile of other books mom has purchased to make schooling easy for her to manage.

A far less common situation might be the reverse of our last scenario: Wiggly Willy mom and Perfect Paula daughter. Mom gets up in the morning and it's a beautiful day for a field trip. Besides, she has yet to get around to creating any lesson plans, so a field trip is a good excuse to put off planning for another day. Meanwhile, her daughter has compared notes with her age-mates and knows that she is way behind in math. And she worries that their "real book and field trip" approach to history might not help her know enough to get a high score on the standardized test she'll have to take at the end of the year. She would just love it if her mom would get some *real* school books and let her stay home and do school.

Most of us parents tend to think that the way we like to approach homeschooling will be equally appealing to our children. One of the most important lessons we can take from learning styles is that the opposite is more likely true. As parents, we need to stretch ourselves out of our own learning style comfort zones to try to meet our children's needs.

For parents without a single strongly dominant learning/teaching style, this will likely be easier. Such parents will more easily adapt to their children's needs than will the parent with a narrower range of personal learning styles.

Teaching to Their Strengths: Methods That Work Best For Different Learners

Meeting our children's needs in terms of learning styles does not mean we have to construct our entire curriculum around these learning styles. Generally, our children will have stronger subjects and weaker subjects.

Perhaps your child is good at math and weak in language arts. If you are using a math program that doesn't really use methods best for that child's learning style, but he is still learning just fine because math comes easily for him, then don't worry about it. Stick with what you are using. But if language arts are a challenge, then you will want to look for resources and methods for composition, grammar, spelling, etc., that work best with his learning style.

Use learning styles as a tool to help you tune into your child's needs and choose methods and materials that help in troublesome areas.

Let's look at methods that are most likely to work with different learning styles.

Wiggly Willy

Wiggly Willy is a kinesthetic learner. The more he can use his body and his senses to learn, the better. Hands-on learning works well. That might include math manipulatives, building projects, making 3-D maps, learning facts set to music, and anything else that involves both large and small muscle movement and as many senses as possible.

When you need to directly teach Willy, it's best to use audio-visual aids; the more he can hear, see, and touch what he's learning, the easier it will be for him to tune into and remember the lesson.

Willy has a short attention span, so if you have something important to say to him, say it quickly—don't use it as the final point in a five-minute lecture. He won't be listening past the first minute unless you've done something interesting to re-engage him.

These children really need freedom to move around. Often they learn best when their bodies are moving. Some therapists recommend that children with attention-deficit disorders do things like practice saying math facts while jumping on a trampoline. It also might be a good idea to let Willy play with something in his hands while you present a grammar or history lesson.

Project learning can work well with Wiggly Willys; however, these children do not think about consequences, so they need supervision. If they tackle a project, set up periodic checkpoints so you can ensure they are staying on task and making progress.

Likewise, unit studies often are a good choice for Wiggly Willys. Typically, unit studies include a healthy mix of book learning (including real books) and activities that stimulate and hold his interest. Unit studies that offer a number of activity options are especially good since Willy probably will need more hands-on activities than the average learner.

If you do not want to do a total unit study approach, you should still consider using real books rather than textbooks, especially for history and science, but also for other subjects. Essentially you will create your own mini unit studies that stay within a subject area. For example, for science in the elementary grades, choose only three or four topics to study during that school year. Find one or two good resource books on each topic to use as information sources—these will have far more information than a typical textbook and will invariably be more interesting. Find ideas for hands-on activities, experiments, and field trips related to each topic. Then study the selected topics in-depth instead of trying to cover ten to twenty topics superficially as do most textbooks. (Actually, this approach to science is good not just for Wiggly Willy but for all types of learners.)

Willys are easily overwhelmed by what seems to them to be too much reading or pencil-and-paper work. A math book with one hundred practice problems on a page might look impossible. However, half that number of problems broken down into twenty-five per worksheet and supplemented with practice using manipulatives or a computer game would be no problem at all, even if the total number of practice problems were higher.

Another example: an assignment for an older child to write a lengthy report should be broken down into manageable chunks that are due each day rather than simply assigning one big project due in two months.

If math is a problem area, use manipulatives like *Cuisenaire® Rods* or *Base Ten Blocks®* to teach new concepts. You can purchase these to use alongside a more traditional math text, or you can purchase a program that has manipulatives built in, such as *Math-U-See* or *Moving with Math*.

Consider supplementing manipulative-based programs even further with math games (card games, board games, computer games), applications through building projects, cooking activities, etc.

For beginning readers, use a movable alphabet—rubber or magnetic letters children can arrange into words, phonics games, and interesting reading material.

For Willys who are reluctant writers, first try making a shape book or some other interesting format for presentation of the writing project and *then* have Willy write what goes into the book. Dinah Zike's *Big Book of Books and Activities* (*Dinah-Might Activities,* available through teacher supply stores and home-school distributors) is packed with lots of great ideas for this sort of thing.

With Wiggly Willys you should probably reduce your use of traditional texts and workbooks and focus instead on resources that are stimulating and interesting.

Wiggly Willys pose special challenges, but the key is for parents to pay attention to what does and doesn't work for their child, no matter how unusual it might seem.

In summary, Wiggly Willy prefers:

- hands-on activity

- multisensory audio-visual aids
- short, dynamic presentations
- freedom to move around
- whole-body physical involvement
- project learning
- texts or workbooks that are not overwhelming
- learning games
- variety in learning methods

Perfect Paula

Many parents wish all their children were Perfect Paulas when it comes to homeschooling because these children actually care about doing what's expected and pleasing you. Perfect Paula tends to work well with typical school curriculum. She likes the security and predictability of knowing what's expected and how it is to be done each day. She can usually work well independently as long as instructions are clear.

However, recall that Paula has a narrow comfort zone. She's most comfortable with review, repetition, and drill because she's already familiar with most of the answers. New concepts can be challenging, so work closely with her when introducing new concepts. Give her lots of encouragement at this stage.

Paula would rather receive information than think creatively. She's not likely to do as well in a Socratic discussion (classical education method) as most other learners. If you are planning such a discussion or other activity that will take Paula out of her comfort zone, give her as much advance notice, reassurance, and encouragement as possible.

She's not likely to be enthusiastic about creative writing, dramatizations, or other self-expressive learning activities. You should not eliminate these from her experience, but introduce them gently, a little at a time. Unit studies might be a good tool for stretching Paula since most offer a variety of activities that can be used in this way.

One of the biggest problems for Paula is that she often does well memorizing and repeating information (typical for early elementary grades) but struggles when it comes time to start making connections, analyzing, and synthesizing information.

For example, *A Beka*'s math program might work fine up through third or fourth grade because Paula loves the continual practice, the clear presentation of the rules for each process, and the fact that she does well on timed drills. By fourth or fifth grade, however, she might struggle because *A Beka* has not explained concepts—why math processes work the way they do. She memorizes her math facts very well and knows how to do multidigit multiplication and division, but two-step word problems throw her for a loop. One solution would be to continue to use *A Beka* but add math manipulatives or supplemental books that present math "brain teasers," thereby helping to push her to deeper levels of thinking so she develops conceptual understanding. Or choose a different program altogether, one that includes understanding of math concepts such as *Modern Curriculum Press Mathematics* or *Horizons Math*.

Paulas probably will not need as much hands-on work as Wiggly Willy, so a manipulative-based program is generally not essential, although it might be helpful.

Since Perfect Paulas are generally weak in creative writing skills, look carefully at some of my Top Picks for developing writing skills.

Because the structure of most traditional curricula fits Perfect Paula's learning style fairly well, you will more often find yourself looking for supplements to help with difficult areas and to stretch her beyond her comfort zone.

In summary, Perfect Paula prefers:

- workbooks
- consistent structure in both schedule and curriculum
- rules and predictability
- lectures or lessons that follow an outline
- repetition and memorization
- drill and review
- time to prepare for any discussion
- gentle help to develop creativity and deeper thinking skills

Competent Carl

If you recall from looking at adult learning styles, control is a big issue for Competent Carl. He has lots of ideas of his own and has little patience for listening to others. Discussions are OK only if he gets to do a lot of talking. He'll tune out of an hour-long lecture. Unlike Perfect Paula, however, he might love Socratic discussions if questions are meaningful and such discussions are productive.

Carls like to think out loud or brainstorm. For example, you might find that he writes better when you first take plenty of time to talk through possible organizational strategies or ways to tackle writing assignments rather than leaving him on his own to figure it out.

Because of his logical mind, he prefers curriculum that is well-organized and purposeful rather than entertaining with lots of extra activity involved. He wants to know in advance what he is doing and why. Structured traditional curriculum can work well for Carl as long as it doesn't have too much busywork built into it.

Carl has plenty of his own ideas to explore, therefore long-term independent projects can work well for him. One approach is to present the learning objective and offer two or three possible ways for Carl to achieve it. Let him choose; then write up a learning contract that details what assignments will be completed and when they will be turned in.

Competent Carls are more likely than other learners to challenge you with "Why do I need to learn this?" Take time to explain to him since it will improve his motivation if he understands the purpose for each task.

He's also likely to challenge you about repetition, practice, and busywork. Sometimes Carl doesn't like to do review and practice once he's already covered something, even though he really needs the practice for proficiency. Choose curriculum that contains a minimal amount of busywork and review, or have him skip such material when it is unnecessary.

For instance, once Carl knows how to read fairly well, let him read books selected from your "approved" list rather than reading anthologies (textbooks). Use study guides for novels (see *Total Language Plus* and *Progeny Press* guides) or carefully selected supplemental activity/workbooks to work on comprehension, vocabulary, and other analytical skills. He will be more engaged in the process if he is able to select what he wants to read without being bogged down with what he considers redundant exercises in a reading text and workbook. You can focus on particular skills he needs to develop rather than that wide range of skills covered in a text.

While Competent Carls generally prefer independent work, group learning situations help them develop social skills. You might do a family unit study where everyone is together for foundational reading or discussion. Carl would then pursue the same topic as your other children by doing more independent research, reading, and writing while you continue with group activities with the rest of your children. You might also have Carl participate in a Friday afternoon art activity with the whole family.

Probably the most important thing to keep in mind with Carl is that he wants his learning to be efficient. Don't bog him down with manipulatives and hands-on activities if they aren't helpful. They can do more harm than good.

In summary, Competent Carl prefers:

- independent work
- logically organized lessons
- clear sense of purpose for lessons
- long-term projects
- talking rather than listening
- problem solving
- brainstorming

Sociable Sue

Sociable Sue is a perfect candidate for unit studies of the *KONOS*, *Tapestry of Grace*, and *Five in a Row* variety. She will thrive on group projects and interactive learning. Read-aloud sessions will also be appealing to her, so using real books rather than textbooks is a good choice.

Sue picks up on social dynamics better than other learners. She's sensitive to your attitude toward subjects, so choose curriculum about which you can be enthusiastic. If she senses that you don't like the curriculum, she won't like it either. You will also notice a dynamic that makes things even more complicated: if her friends like or use a particular resource, she's likely to have a positive attitude about it solely for that reason. This can make purchasing resources difficult since you're not likely to know ahead of time what her friends are going to be enthusiastic about.

Because approval from others matters so much to Sue, she generally likes "public presentations"—reading her writing assignment aloud, participating in a dramatic reenactment or dramatic reading of a poem or speech, performances (e.g., music, dance), or sharing her artwork.

Creative activities usually are more appealing than repetitive review and drill. Sue gets bored with the same learning format. She thrives on variety. Choosing a resource that alters the lesson format from time to time is wise. Otherwise, you will need to supplement or adapt what you're using to keep her motivated. Hands-on resources you might choose for Wiggly Willy often work well for Sue because they require social interaction.

One of the worst things you can do with Sociable Sue is purchase a workbook-based program that is designed for independent study and expect her to spend three hours a day in isolation as she works through her books. She can work alone for short periods, but not all day. If you must use independent workbooks, alternate them with sociable/interactive learning activities to keep her going.

Sue will also need help learning how to persevere even when learning isn't sociable and fun. She must develop the self-discipline to follow through on assignments even when it gets boring.

In summary, Sociable Sue prefers:

- real books
- unit studies
- discussions
- social interaction
- enthusiastic teaching
- variety in types of resources
- creative writing
- public presentations
- novelty and creativity in curriculum presentation
- situations where she is personally recognized and valued
- (needs but does not necessarily enjoy) repetition for detail

Keep Learning Modalities in Mind

As I mentioned earlier, our children might also have a strong learning modality—visual, auditory, or kinesthetic—where they learn best by either seeing, hearing, or touching/experiencing. Coupling what we discover about both learning styles and learning modalities gives us a lot of information we can use to make better curriculum choices for each of our children. A Sociable Sue who is kinesthetic will prefer more project-type learning, while an auditory Sociable Sue will prefer more sedentary read-aloud activity.

This does not mean, however, that we teach each type of learner only with methods that suit his personality and temperament. (For some children everything would be fun and games, and they would learn no self-discipline.) Instead, use methods that work best for each child when introducing new or difficult subject matter. Once they have grasped the concept, then using other more-challenging methods will be less likely to produce stress or failure.

We can help strengthen students' weak areas (such as short attention span or lack of creativity) by working on these problem areas within subjects that are especially interesting to them or in which they excel. For example, many Wiggly Willys do not like writing assignments. But reading an exciting historical adventure or biography aloud, then asking them to draw a picture about the story and write a few descriptive sentences will develop writing skills in a more enjoyable way than most workbook activities.

After initial instruction, review and reinforce learning through methods that will help each child stretch himself and strengthen his weak areas. For example, a very active Wiggly Willy can initially learn math by using objects, without paper and pencil. Once he has mastered a concept, he can then get out the paper and pencil to do review and practice.

To sum it up, with both younger and older children we should teach new concepts through a child's strongest sense (learning mode) or learning style and then review and practice through the other senses (modes) or learning styles.

It helps if we recognize those subjects that are easier and those that are more difficult for each child. While there are some typically strong subjects within each learning style, there are many exceptions. Wiggly Willys usually prefer physically active subjects such as music, the arts, and athletics. Perfect Paulas like more structured and predictable subjects like math, spelling, history, and geography. Competent Carls often excel in math and science, exhibiting less interest in the humanities. Sociable Sues often prefer whatever subjects are presented with the most enthusiasm and interaction, but their strong areas tend to be writing and literature, languages, social studies, and performing arts. Of course, these are very general observations that may or may not apply to your child.

You must observe which subjects consistently are handled with ease and which cause frustration. For those frustrating subjects, consider using teaching methods that better fit your child's learning style. Avoid using a child's "weak" methods until he understands the basic concept and has reached a review or application stage.

Matching Learning Styles to Curricula

When I put together the chart of the 100 Top Picks, I did not include columns headed "Only for Wiggly Willy," etc. This is because there are rarely direct matches between resources and learning styles. Instead, I included columns that rate how a curriculum tends to suit a primary aspect of each learning style. Thus, there are columns labeled multi-sensory/hands-on (WW), structure/rule-oriented (PP), appeals to logical/analytical learners (CC), and has social activity (SS).

You will also need to look at other columns that might be equally important, such as whether or not it works for independent study, how easy it is for the teacher to use, how much writing is required, or what methodology it reflects. Only you can decide which characteristics of a particular curriculum are most important.

Compromise Solutions

Sometimes your teaching style and your child's learning style are drastically different. Suppose your child really needs a unit study approach with lots of creative activity, but your Perfect Paula style makes you shudder at the thought of trying to gather all the stuff you need *plus* having to choose among activities. What if you choose the wrong ones? And then how will you know if your children did enough or too much?

There are what I call "compromise solutions" for such situations. For example, KONOS publishes *KONOS in a Box*, a unit study that includes step-by-step instructions plus all the books and materials (even craft materials) you need. Cornerstone Curriculum publishes *Making Math Meaningful*, a math program that includes manipulatives but has scripted lessons that tell parents exactly what to say and do. (This is not one of my Top Picks, but it works well in such situations. The address for Cornerstone Curriculum is under *Worldviews of the Western World.*)

So keep in mind that while you are looking for resources that suit your children's learning styles, you must also choose resources with which you can work.

Motivation

Motivation is often a two-part process. First, motivate your children to do well by providing a program that fits their learning style and makes it easier for them to grasp concepts. If you can make learning more enjoyable for children (not that it always will be!), you solve part of the motivation problem. By using creative approaches and relating learning to the interests of your children, you make learning more of a partnership than a struggle.

You also can try to improve motivation by using rewards or incentives. Just as different style learners are successful with different learning methods, they also respond to different types of rewards or incentives. Wiggly Willys often respond well to prizes, special trips, playtime, or food—the more immediate the reward, the more effective. Perfect Paula can be motivated with stickers, good grades, and other concrete affirmations as well as with personal praise. Competent Carl, who enjoys being independent, can be motivated by self-designed contracts or rewards of free time or money. Sociable Sue, more interested in people and relationships, tends to be motivated by personal affirmation (praise) and recognition or an opportunity to do something special with a friend.

Experiment with different types of motivation to figure out what works best with each child. Don't be afraid to use different incentives with each of your children.

Disguised Learning Disabilities

A word of caution is needed here. Sometimes we can mistake the characteristics or evidence of a learning disability for a learning style. If you have tried everything—paid attention to learning styles and methods and have retaught five different ways—and your child still "doesn't get it," he or she might have a learning disability. Sometimes a child will appear to be a Wiggly Willy because a learning disability interferes with reading, writing, or thinking processes. If the work is too difficult, your child might act bored, restless, or inattentive to avoid dealing with the "impossible" task. Active learning that requires less paper-and-pencil work or reading will appear successful, but it is only masking the real problem. This will be apparent when you've already taught a concept that they seem to understand—such as doing multiplication using blocks—but when you transition them to writing down what they have done, they are unable to make the shift.

If you suspect that your child has a learning disability, seek professional assistance. Generally, your local homeschool support group can recommend a professional in your area who can help you determine what is going on.

In Conclusion

The goal here is not labeling your child but becoming aware that each child will have strengths and weaknesses in the ways he or she learns. Likewise, you must recognize your own tendency to teach the way you like to learn rather than the way your children learn best. Then you need to look for resources and methods that best meet the needs of your children, while still being practical for you to use.

When you combine your philosophy of education and ideas about approaches you would like to use with what you have discovered about learning styles, you can fine-tune your curriculum choices. For example, I ended chapter 3 noting that unit study, Charlotte Mason, and classical education ideas should be part of the curriculum for my sons. When I add learning styles to the mix, I know that my Wiggly Willy eldest son still needs some projects and hands-on learning mixed in with the worldview/unit study type education I would like to pursue. I would still like to shift toward classical education, so when I look at the Top Picks charts in chapter 6, I find that *Tapestry of Grace* looks like it fits the situation quite well.

In addition, since math is my eldest son's most challenging subject, I need to be particularly careful about his math program and find one that still has manipulatives at junior high level. In chapter 6, I look for math programs with a 4 or 5 in the first column indicating that it is multisensory/hands-on, then go to the actual reviews in chapter 8 to find those that continue using manipulatives up into junior high and beyond. Either *Moving with Math* or *Math-U-See* might do, although *Math-U-See* looks to be a better bet since I suspect he will need to continue with some manipulative work on into high school.

• • •

Now there's one more thing to take into consideration before you choose your curriculum: what will you actually teach your children this year? The next chapter will help you figure that out.

5

Who Should Learn What and When?

Most home educators worry about whether or not their children are keeping up with what "other schools" are teaching. This concern can be a helpful prod to keep us focused and making progress. However, it can also be a distraction or even a diversion from what we really need to be teaching each of our children.

Curriculum Standards

On both state and national levels, there has been a push to develop common standards for each subject area that describe what all government school students should be learning. As those standards have been developed, textbooks have been rewritten to reflect them. While there are minor variations from state to state, standards are similar enough across the country to enable a handful of textbook publishers to produce books that can be used in just about every state.

The following examples of standards from California illustrate what I am talking about:

From kindergarten English language arts:

- Identify the front cover, back cover, and title page of a book.
- Follow words from left to right and from top to bottom on the printed page.

From fourth grade mathematics:

- Solve problems involving multiplication of multidigit numbers by two-digit numbers.
- Solve problems involving division of multidigit numbers by one-digit numbers.

From fifth grade science standards:

- Students know that each element is made of one kind of atom and that the elements are organized in the periodic table by their chemical properties.

From sixth grade English language arts:

- Identify the structural features of popular media (e.g., newspapers, magazines, online information) and use the features to obtain information.
- Clarify an understanding of texts by creating outlines, logical notes, summaries, or reports.
- Follow multiple-step instructions for preparing applications (e.g., for a public library card, bank savings account, sports club, league membership).

From Biology/Life Sciences for high school:

- Students know at each link in a food web some energy is stored in newly made structures but more much energy is dissipated into the environment as heat. This dissipation may be represented in an energy pyramid.

From eighth grade History/Social Science:

- Describe the significance of the Northwest Ordinance in education and in the banning of slavery in new states north of the Ohio River.
- Discuss the importance of the slavery issue as raised by the annexation of Texas and California's admission to the union as a free state under the Compromise of 1850.
- Analyze the significance of the States' Rights Doctrine, the Missouri Compromise (1820), the Wilmot Proviso (1846), the Compromise of 1850, Henry Clay's role in the Missouri Compromise and the Compromise of 1850, the Kansas-Nebraska Act (1854), the *Dred Scott* v. *Sandford* decision (1857), and the Lincoln-Douglas debates (1858).

Because these standards are so detailed, the compilation of standards for each state could fill an entire book per state! Consequently, I cannot include the standards themselves within this chapter. Instead, here are Web sites where you can access standards for most states.

➔ http://dir.yahoo.com/Education/K_12/Curriculum_Standards

This is the Yahoo! Directory for Curriculum Standards for various states and organizations. It's a great starting place since it has links to Web sites listing standards for most states and a number of organizations working on developing overarching national standards. Web site addresses might change from time to time, but this directory is likely to stay updated.

➔ http://www.cde.ca.gov/ci

This is the site for "Content Standards for California Public Schools, Kindergarten through Grade

Twelve." California, being one of the largest states, has some of the most well-developed and widely accepted standards.

→ www.pen.k12.va.us/VDOE/Superintendent/Sols/home.shtml

Like California, Virginia has also been a leader in developing standards. This is the site where you can view the "Standards of Learning Currently in Effect for Virginia Public Schools."

It is important that you notice how detailed and prescriptive these standards are. In years past, schools worked from "Scope and Sequence" documents that outlined goals in more general terms. For example, the previously quoted standards for eighth grade history might have been summarized as a more general directive: "Study the issue of slavery and its connection to the Civil War."

The more general language of "Scope and Sequences" left much to individual schools and teachers to determine as far as teaching each classroom of children. Now, to the contrary, these new standards leave little for schools or teachers to determine because coverage of so many topics is required.

Schools are held accountable to teach the standards by high-stakes standardized tests. These tests are still under development in most states, but this is the type of testing required under recent educational reforms. These tests ask questions based upon the content of the standards. Such tests have big consequences for students as well as for schools and teachers. Student advancement to the next grade level, summer school attendance, or even high school graduation might be based upon such tests. High-stakes tests might also determine whether schools (and teachers) gain or lose funding, whether principals and teachers lose their jobs, whether schools get taken over by the state, and even whether students might be given vouchers to attend private schools.

A side effect of the standards movement has been that private and homeschools have often adopted those same standards by default rather than on purpose. You might have noticed in advertisements for curricula and resources marketed to homeschoolers, that many mention that they "meet or exceed" national standards. Publishers of these resources have taken into consideration the large government school market and have made sure that they are creating resources that can be sold to those within government school systems. That means many homeschoolers end up teaching the same things as do government schools simply because that is what is in textbooks or other resources.

A Contrarian View

Most parents rarely question what their children are learning in school unless it has to do with sex or drug education. They assume that whatever the school has decided to teach must be what children need to learn. This may or may not be true.

There are two underlying assumptions that need to be challenged: the uniformity of children and the power of government to dictate education.

As to the uniformity of children, anyone who has spent any time at all around children knows that they are as different as pistachio ice cream and pepperoni pizza. The notion that they should be learning the same things as all other children who happen to be their age is silly when you think about it.

Children develop on their own personal timetables. Some are ready to read at age four, and others, at age six or seven. Some can easily learn their multiplication tables at age seven, and others, at age nine. As I discussed in the chapter on learning styles, some children can read something in a book and learn it while others need to touch, handle, or manipulate things to get information into their brains.

The notion that you can put thirty age-mates in a classroom and expect that all will learn at approximately the same rate and through the limited ways information is presented might work if children were machines to be programmed. But children are much more complex than this.

God created each one as an individual with particular gifts, abilities, and interests. He has a unique plan for every child. God's creativity gradually becomes visible within each child as he or she matures, an unfolding delight that we can either appreciate or deny. We appreciate it by recognizing and working with each child as an individual, or we deny it by trying to force children to adapt to others' ideas about how they should grow and learn.

In light of the individuality of each child, parents should view the state's educational standards with skepticism rather than accept them as a foundational directive for homeschooling.

The second problem with standards is that they challenge the right of government to dictate what a child should learn. In addition to the problem of children's individuality, there's a problem regarding the purpose of education and, consequently, its content.

Government management of schools springs from governmental concern to maintain peace and order—a sort of conformity—within society. It has nothing to do with religious beliefs and personal development except as it affects larger "societal" goals. At the present time, societal goals are primarily economic.

The mantra of much of the national education reform legislation over the past two decades has been "educating for the high-skill, high-wage jobs of the twenty-first century." Translation: children need to learn knowledge and skills that others have predetermined are necessary to prepare them for the workforce.

We see this very clearly in our present educational system at the high school level. Education is becoming primarily about vocational training rather than development of a human being with a body, mind, and soul. Part of that training might be learning enough to get into college, so they can get a degree, so they can get an even better job—simply a more complex form of vocational training.

While young people should be prepared to get a job when they get out of school, many parents believe that education is as much or more about personal development, learning to think, developing integrity, and spiritual development. After all, what profits a man if he has all the job skills in the world but he is a spiritual and cultural barbarian? And isn't this what we see with corporate executives who think nothing of using their "job skills" to siphon off money illegally and use their language arts skills to lie and convince others that they were just doing their jobs?

A Higher Goal for Education

Personally, I think one of the most important components of homeschooling is worldview education. This is where we address the most important life questions:

- Is there a God?
- Who is man in relation to God?
- What is the purpose of our life on earth?
- Is there life after death?

The way we answer these questions reveals our foundational philosophic and religious beliefs. Our worldview determines how we think about and shape our lives.

Everyone operates by one worldview or another. The default worldview of our modern society is a materialistic humanist worldview. (Some might call it secular humanism.) It teaches that man is an accidental product of evolution. There is nothing more to him than his physical existence. God doesn't exist, and there's nothing after death. Consequently, each person should try to get the most he can from this life because this is all there is.

A Christian worldview colors everything with the belief in God's existence. Because God is real, we believe He has revealed truth to us. Part of that revelation is the reality of life after death, the fact that we have a soul, the fact that Jesus Christ died for us so that we can have eternal life with God. This knowledge means there's much more to life than the present physical reality. There is a larger purpose and meaning to most everything. Our lives are not to be lived as if we are accidental entities. Instead, God calls us to live out our lives according to God's plan.

These conflicting worldviews produce some conflicting educational goals. While they share *some* common goals (such as acquiring reading, writing, and computation skills), they differ when it comes to making choices of other subjects to be taught, what is to be taught each year, the amount of time and attention we spend on each subject, and/or details within subject areas.

For example, religion or Bible study might be a major subject in your curriculum even though it is not on any standards list and none of the standardized tests asks any religion questions. It might be so important to you that it is the first subject covered every day of the week.

You might be a musically inclined family, and music education is a much higher priority for you than for most other families.

If you are following a classical education model, you might be teaching your children Greek and Latin in the elementary grades as a foundation for the study of primary sources in high school.

That same preference for a classical education might mean that your high school students study philosophy, logic, and rhetoric in place of, or in addition to, physics or calculus.

Even if you choose to teach the same subjects as do most schools, you might still have different ideas about what should be taught within each subject. One of the thorniest issues is evolution and creation.

Another one of the standards for high school Biology/Life Sciences reads: "Evolution is the result of genetic changes that occur in constantly changing environments. As a basis for understanding this concept: a. Students know how natural selection determines the differential survival of groups of organisms"[1] (emphasis in the original). This science standard requires students to parrot the evolutionary teaching that different species came about by natural selection. Since evidence for evolutionary theory is shaky at best, *requiring* children to learn and believe this is very much a part of a worldview that denies the existence of God. The implied logic is that if man came into existence as an accident through the process of evolution, then God did not make man, and the whole story of Genesis and the fall of man is nothing more than folklore. Logically, there is then no need of a Savior as a consequence of something that never happened.

Other worldview problems crop up in textbooks reflecting state goals. For example, multicultural goals translate into stories about pagan gods and goddesses who are presented as being every bit as credible as the Christian God. Students are taught they can make no value judgments regarding religion and morality because these are simply expressions of personal or cultural belief rather than reflections of any one reality or Truth that exists for everyone. Along the same line, literature is analyzed for whatever personal meaning a student might draw from it rather than to grasp an author's message or any transcendent meaning.

While purporting to be nonreligious, government schools actually have an agenda that turns out to be antireligious. Students learn what schools claim to be the essentials of education, and God is no part of any of it. This teaches them that God is irrelevant. They learn that all gods are created equal and that it is intolerant to expect others to accept your beliefs about God and His commands about how we should live. A parent who asks that her child not learn witchcraft spells in school is charged with narrow-mindedness. A parent who does not want her child to learn "safe" ways to fornicate is called "unrealistic."

I realize that much of this happens within government schools themselves and is not required by the standards, but the standards reflect the worldview that teaches and encourages the above (and even worse) classroom practices.

Beyond that, the time required to teach to government-selected standards steals time that could be devoted to other goals that are more important to you.

My point is, homeschooling parents should use state standards as well as the resources built around them with caution. Parents need to have goals for their children's education, but these should not simply be copied from government schools.

Choosing Your Own Goals

The *ideal* way to come up with your goals is to start from scratch and figure out what you think is important for your child to learn, then write it all out. The more *realistic* way to do this is to start by looking at one or more lists of standards, then work from those to come up with your own goals.

With standards readily available on the Internet, you can copy from these the standards you think are appropriate for your own child in each subject area. Look across a range of grade levels to find standards/goals that are appropriate for your child. Change ones that you think need rewriting and add any additional goals of your own.

For example, I agree with most of the California goals or standards for third grade mathematics, but I do not agree that children at this age need to be learning probability and graphing. However, if my children must take a standardized test, this is an item upon which they are likely to be tested. So I then have to decide whether a higher test score or sticking to my conviction is more important. Since I actually live in a state that does not require standardized testing, I would opt to drop probability and graphing from my goals for third grade. I also believe it important that children develop a Christian understanding of math from the earliest years, so I would add a goal that my child understand that mathematics reflects God's order and consistency. (I might illustrate this concept for my child by trying to get him to come up with a sum other than four when he adds two items plus two items. The impossibility helps him understand that the consistency of math reflects the nature of God.) So when it comes to third grade mathematics I copy the third grade standards and then make these deletions and additions.

The situation is a bit more complicated if my "third grader" already has mastered one quarter or more of the standards/goals listed for third grade. Then I look to the fourth grade list to see which goals might be better drawn from that level.

I do this for each subject as much as is practical. When it comes to history and science, I generally find my goals are so different from the state goals that I work from scratch. Later in this chapter I will share some ideas about studying those subjects.

Obviously, there are no goals or standards already written for religion or Bible, so you're on your own there. However, once you've worked through the other subjects, you should understand how you can establish goals for religion or Bible if you choose that as a subject for your curriculum. Likewise, you will not find goals for Latin or other foreign language class for the elementary grades, and you will have to come up with your own standards or goals.

Now some of you might be considering unit studies at this point and are wondering how on earth you can match up goals with a unit study. Actually, it works well as long as you understand that all of the goals/standards of a year-long unit study are unlikely to be found at only one grade level of a published list of goals/standards.

Unit studies assume that children in the study will be at many different grade levels. Some unit studies try to categorize learning activities by groups of grade levels (e.g., K–2, 3–6, 7–8, 9–12). Some are written for only grades 4–8 or some other limited audience. Still others leave it to you to sort through all the activity choices on your own to identify grade levels. You might find that the study you undertake this year and the activities you choose reflect goals from second, third, fourth, and fifth grade levels. You will not be covering all the "normal" goals for any one of those levels in a single year, but over the course of three or four years you will have done so. Consequently, unit studies require that you have a more long-range view of your goals.

In reality, if you stick with a comprehensive unit study program such as *KONOS*, *Tapestry of Grace*, or *A World of Adventure*, the authors have thought this through so that necessary material is covered over a span of years. Many unit studies will also tell you what subject areas they do and do not cover so you will know what other resources you might need to purchase.

What Do I Do with My Goals Now?

The next step is to use the reproducible form at the end of this chapter to write out your goals. (Be sure to make plenty of copies because you will need one for each subject for each child.) If you are trying to work from a preprinted list of goals or goals downloaded from the Internet, try to add three columns to the right as is done on the reproducible chart for writing out your own goals. In the sample below, I've adopted the California goals for second grade math,[2] and just added the columns to the right.

Sample Chart: Writing Out Your Own Goals

School Year 2004-2005   **Student Name: Brandon Smith**

Goals for Math	Introduction	Review/ Practice	Mastery
1.1 Count, read, and write whole numbers to 1,000 and identify the place value for each digit.			
1.2 Use words, models, and expanded forms (e.g., 45 = 4 tens + 5) to represent numbers (to 1,000).			
1.3 Order and compare whole numbers to 1,000 by using the symbols <, =, >.			
2.1 Understand and use the inverse relationship between addition and subtraction (e.g., an opposite number sentence for 8 + 6 = 14 is 14 - 6 = 8) to solve problems and check solutions.			
2.2 Find the sum or difference of two whole numbers up to three digits long.			
2.3 Use mental arithmetic to find the sum or difference of two two-digit numbers.			
3.1 Use repeated addition, arrays, and counting by multiples to do multiplication.			
3.2 Use repeated subtraction, equal sharing, and forming equal groups with remainders to do division.			
3.3 Know the multiplication tables of 2s, 5s, and 10s (to "times 10") and commit them to memory.			

The three additional columns are labeled "Introduction," "Review/Practice," and "Mastery." The reason for these columns is that teaching your child about a concept one time rarely means he or she has learned it. Generally, you'll need to review and/or practice the material, and at some point they will know it. By setting up the three columns, you will remind yourself to go back over these goals to make sure you work toward mastery.

These standards or goals can now help you in three ways:

1. figuring out what to teach,
2. checking progress through the school year, and
3. assessing year-end accomplishments.

Figuring Out What to Teach First

Sometimes when we start homeschooling, we have no idea where to begin. It really is helpful to have a list of standards or goals at least as a reference point to know what others might be doing. Assuming you are familiar with what your child already knows (through observation, your own experience, testing, or an evaluation by someone else), you can look at these lists and determine at what grade level your child seems to be functioning.

You want to choose goals that are challenging but not frustrating. If there are goals listed at a lower grade level that your child hasn't mastered, you need to consider whether it is important to make them a priority, put them off until later, or skip them altogether. Don't forget that you will be *adding* some of your own goals to whichever goals you choose to adopt.

Your lists of goals will also help you figure out what comes next. If your child has mastered the four punctuation marks for the ends of sentences, what punctuation comes next? Your goals will help you figure this out.

Checking Your Progress

Are you pushing your children too hard? Are you too lax in getting things accomplished?

Your list of goals can help answer this sort of question. At least once a quarter, you should refer back to these lists of goals for each subject. How many have been introduced, reviewed/practiced, and mastered? Are you making reasonable progress on checking them off? If you've checked them all off by the end of the first quarter, you might be pushing your children too hard. If by the end of that same first quarter you've checked off fewer than a third of the introduction boxes and nothing beyond that, you might need to get more focused on reinforcing your initial lessons. If you reach the end of the third quarter and half of your goals remain untouched, you need to do some serious evaluation of how you are operating. Too many field trips and park days? Lack of self-discipline on the part of parents, children, or both? Overly ambitious goals? Don't panic. You still have time to make midcourse corrections.

Assessing Year-End Accomplishments

At the end of the year, instead of judging your accomplishments by completed (or incomplete) text-books, judge by how many of your goals have reached mastery level. If you find that you have fallen far short, don't despair. If you've gone way beyond your goals, don't plan to take a year off.

Instead, spend some time evaluating. Did you set reasonable goals? Did you set too many goals? Did you include some that could have been skipped? Did you underestimate your child's ability? Did your child go through a period of emotional turmoil such that some of your goals had to be put on temporary hold? Did you move, have a baby, experience a death in the family or some other event that accounted for lost school time? Do you have too many books for your children to get through, some of which contain material that is purposeless busywork?

If you haven't a clue why you are having trouble, it might help to find a veteran homeschooler who will look over what you are doing and give you advice. Sometimes enrollment in a program that provides professional advice is the wisest investment.

After this, consider what you might do about what you've learned from your evaluation. Should you plan to do summer school? Should you consider following a different type school schedule—i.e., shifting from nine months on/three months off to year-round schooling with periodic week-long breaks? Do you need to get more organized or work out a different type schedule? Is your child having such difficulty accomplishing things that you ought to get him or her tested for learning disabilities? Are you all so unhappy with the way you are doing things that neither you nor your children are motivated to get things done, or do you need to rearrange things so that a particular child gets more one-to-one attention? Perhaps a different curriculum might help the situation.

I know you will be able to add more questions to these lists, but I think you get the idea. Your goals should be your touchstone to help you get focused, stay focused, and accomplish what needs to be done.

Of course, you never want to become a slave to those goals to the point where you ignore the needs of your children. Even the best of plans need to be modified from time to time. You might even find your-self adjusting your goals on a quarterly basis rather than waiting till the end of the year. That's great! It means you've taken control of what's going on and are really tuning in to your children's needs.

As you gain experience, generally you will feel freer to create your own goals and worry less about what everyone else is doing.

School Year _____   Student Name: _____

Goals for _____	Introduction	Review/ Practice	Mastery

6

Top 100 Picks

By this point you should have some insight into what philosophy of education appeals to you. You know what teaching style is most comfortable for you as well as which learning styles work best for each of your children. And you should have a fairly good idea of what subject matter and skills you actually need to teach this year.

That's a lot of information, but it doesn't do you much good unless you can match up what you've learned with the many curriculum options available to you. That's the purpose of this chapter.

I'll assume you've read through the first five chapters and have come to some conclusions about how you want to approach education. You've also figured out each of your children's learning styles. Now you're ready to use the chart at the end of this chapter.

The intent of the charts is to help you easily identify key features or characteristics of resources. The following descriptions of the meaning of each column will help you understand the information in the charts.

I have generally used a scale of 1 to 5 with 5 representing the highest correlation with the feature listed in that column. The number 1 usually means that it has none of this feature.

I'll explain the other "codes" below under their column headings.

1. Multisensory/hands-on (WW)

A 5 in this column means this is a particularly good choice for the kinesthetic learner, the one who needs movement and multisensory activity. This resource fits Wiggly Willys, but Sociable Sues often benefit from similar curriculum since it usually involves some sort of personal interaction.

2. Structure/rule-oriented (PP)

This is usually a more traditionally-structured resource that has a consistent format and/or a rules and memorization approach. Perfect Paulas generally prefer this sort of resource because it's predictable.

3. Appeals to logical/analytical learners (CC)

Resources with a 4 or 5 in this column require higher-level thinking and analysis and particularly appeal to Competent Carls.

4. Has social activity (SS)

Items with a 4 or 5 in this column require an interactive setting. Sociable Sues prefer learning in such social settings rather than independently. The interactive setting might be as minimal as a parent working directly with one child.

5. Needs parent/teacher instruction

A 4 or 5 means you will need to read, explain, or otherwise present information to your child. It might be only a short introduction, after which a child can work independently, in which case it will have a mid-range number of 2 or 3. If you are short on time, don't choose many resources with a high number in this column.

6. Independent study (ind), one-to-one (1 to 1), or group (g)

This very important column helps you plan your time as well as select the best resources for each child. Many resources can be used in a number of ways, so abbreviations for each possible setting are included. However, some are specifically designed for one type of setting. An *independent study* resource allows the student to do most or all of his work on his own. *One-to-one* means a parent works directly with a child as he or she progresses through the lesson. *Group* means the resource works well in a setting with two or more students. Most resources will still have independent assignments or other work to be done in addition to a required group or one-to-one presentation.

7. Amount of writing

If you have a child who is resistant to writing, you probably want to teach new concepts with resources that do not rely on a great deal of writing. On the other hand, if you have a child at a stage where he or she needs to practice writing skills, you might purposely choose a resource that requires more writing. Generally, you'll want no more than one or two resources that require a good deal of writing. A 5 indicates the resource requires a great deal of writing while a 1 means little to none. The letter *U* means it's "up to you"—that the parent has a great deal of discretion to decide how much writing to require.

8. Prep time

This one is fairly obvious. It will give you some idea about how much time you will need to spend preparing lessons or learning to teach the program. 5 means it will take a great deal of time.

9. Grade level specific (s) or multilevel (m)

If you want to teach children at more than one grade level using the same resource, ungraded resources obviously work better. These will generally address the needs of a span of grade levels, such as grades 1 to 5 or maybe even 1 to 12. An "m" indicates one of these multilevel resources. You might also want to use an ungraded resource for a third grade child who is working below grade level in reading and who will be discouraged by a textbook that advertises that fact with a "grade 2" designation. An "s" indicates resources designed to be used only for single grade levels.

10. Ease of use for teacher

A resource might be great once you can figure out how to use it, but getting past that hurdle might be impossible for one reason or another. Most resources are not that difficult to use, but some *do* require more time than others to sort out. The most challenging ones are marked 1 or 2. A 5 means it's easy to figure out. You should avoid "challenging" resources if you are short on time. Also, if you are easily discouraged or confused, stick with resources labeled 4 or 5.

11. Teacher's manual: e = essential, na = not available, nu = available but not useful, u = useful, a = answer key only

All teacher's manuals are not created equal. Some are essential (e)—the book or program cannot be used properly without them. Some are window dressing (nu)—save your money. Some are useful, but if you don't mind figuring out answers yourself and skipping the extra helps they offer, you can manage without them (u). Some serve only as an answer key (a)—usually you will want these if you are past second-grade-level material. And, of course, some resources do not have teacher's manuals (na).

12. Supports Charlotte Mason's philosophy

A 4 or 5 indicates that this resource is very much based upon or supportive of Charlotte Mason's ideas. Mason's ideas about secondary education are a bit different from those for the elementary grades, so it is difficult or impossible to rate upper level resources in this column. Those have been marked n/a (not applicable).

13. Supports classical education

Resources with a 4 or 5 are based on or supportive of classical education. However, keep in mind that folks have some different ideas about what classical education requires in the elementary grades, so read reviews of these items carefully.

14. Protestant (P), Catholic (C), Nonsectarian (N)

This column reflects the religious or nonreligious perspective presented. Check the full reviews for details or cautions. Some religion-based resources have minimal religious content or it is expressed in such a way that most everyone is able to use the resource. Similarly, many nonsectarian resources will be inoffensive to those wanting to provide their children with a religion-based education.

15. Page # for review

This is where you will go to find the complete review for each resource.

Working through the Chart

Let's consider one example. You've worked through the earlier chapters and you've discovered:
* You lean toward traditional curriculum, but you also like the idea of using real books to make learning more interesting.

- Your ten-year-old daughter, an only child, seems to be a Perfect Paula in regard to learning style.
- She is likely to thrive on traditional workbooks and independent study for just about every subject except composition.
- You want Christian curriculum.
- You like structured lessons that do most of the work for you.
- Teacher preparation and presentation time is not an issue since you have plenty of time.
- You don't really need hands-on or multi-sensory resources, but they might be more fun.
- She doesn't like to write, so that area needs special work this year.
- Your daughter will be working at fourth grade level.

You have read through the chart looking for resources that possess these characteristics. You really don't need items with a high rating in the first column. The second column will be more useful as a starting place since it lets you know which resources fit your daughter's Perfect Paula need for structure and order. Then the fifth column deals with direct teaching needed. She really likes to work independently, so you want to look for resources with a low number in this column.

The sixth column will help you spot items that will work for independent study, but you might also look for one or two that you can use one-to-one since you have time for some interaction with your daughter.

Also, you might specifically focus on a composition resource appropriate for a group so you can invite another child or two to join your daughter for a writing class to make that subject more interesting to her. "Amount of writing" is of concern in that she needs more writing practice than she's had, so you might look for at least one or two resources that require at least some writing and one that requires a great deal.

Prep time isn't an issue, and either multilevel or specific grade level resources will suffice since you don't need to worry about teaching another child. You want resources that are easy- to moderately-demanding for the teacher (5 to 3) because even though you have the time, you do not want to be bothered figuring out a complicated program. You are easily overwhelmed if you have to get very creative in putting together lessons.

You like to purchase teacher's manuals when they're available, so you'll order those that are marked as essential or useful.

You want Christian material, but you're willing to use nonsectarian resources as long as they're not offensive to you. (You will need to check the individual reviews on nonsectarian items for possible content problems.)

Resources that seem to fit the bill:

- *Horizons Math*—structured math program that has minimal hands-on work and works well for independent learners.
- *Switched-On Schoolhouse*—computerized course for social studies that allows independent study.
- *Progeny Press* study guides and the associated novels for literature/reading—allows student to read

real books while providing you, the parent, directions on how to ask appropriate questions and teach from the context of each book. It also includes some writing activity.

- *Wordsmith Apprentice*—for that group writing class you're going to organize. It is easy for you to use to lead an enjoyable, interactive small class.
- *Easy Grammar*—simple-to-use workbook approach for learning grammar independently.
- *BJUP* science or *Switched-On Schoolhouse*—since your daughter wants structure and accountability in her learning, and you like quizzes/tests to help ensure she is actually learning something, either of these programs could work. You might also plan to get together with another family to do science experiments, using those from the curriculum or experiments from a supplemental book.
- Your own Bible curriculum.

Let's take another example. We'll say you're a harried mom for whom time is the most critical element since you have five children. We'll focus on your eight-year-old son.

You've determined:

- You lean toward an eclectic approach to education.
- You put a high priority on making learning engaging so that your children will love to learn.
- You don't mind using Christian resources as long as they aren't too "preachy."
- You are not overly concerned about tests and grading in the early grade levels.
- Wiggly Willy describes your son, so you'll be looking for hands-on and multisensory resources.
- You have minimal preparation and presentation time.
- You want to teach all of your children together whenever possible to save time, energy, and the hassle of dealing with five different texts for every subject. You will look for resources that allow you to teach history, science, and fine arts to the whole group.
- Your Wiggly Willy can work independently in short bursts, so using some workbooks for independent study would be helpful.
- You want solid academic preparation for college.
- You son will be working at second/third grade level in math, a subject in which he struggles. Otherwise he will be working at approximately third grade level.

Given this challenging situation, you might choose the following:

- *Greenleaf Guide* for studying Greece and Rome along with the recommended supplementary books. You can read aloud and discuss these with all your children together. You will appreciate the minimal preparation time required. Susan Wise Bauer's *Story of the World, Volume I* might be another possibility for a read-aloud history resource, but you probably won't have time to use much from the companion Curriculum Guide this year.
- *Stratton House Home Science Adventures'* *Astronomy, Birds, and Magnetism*—All your children can participate together in these focused studies. The kit provides most everything you need for a full year of science learning and activity.

- *MCP's Comprehension Plus.* Your son reads fine on his own now, but you will use the third grade workbook from this series to develop better comprehension and vocabulary. No prep or presentation time is needed; he can use this on his own. You need only compare his responses to the answer key.

- *Easy Grammar*—Provides grammar basics in preparation for next year when you want to move into a more challenging grammar resource. Again, no prep or presentation required once you are past initial lessons on prepositions.

- Sandra Garant's *Creative Communications*—Great for whole-family writing activities. This one will require your preparation and interaction, but most of your children can participate.

- *MCP Spelling Workout*—Reinforces his phonics knowledge while teaching spelling. He can do this independently.

- *Math-U-See*—Since math is so difficult for him, the hands-on materials for this program make it easier for him to grasp math concepts. (Your six-year-old who grasps math easily can join him for these lessons.) You will need to watch the videos to understand how to present concepts, but once you've been through it, you'll be able to work much more efficiently with your other children. You can also let the children watch with you, stopping the tape and trying out what has been shown.

Why Aren't There Any Bible or Religion Top Picks?

Good question! I suspect that most who read this book will see Bible or religion as an essential part of their curriculum. In chapter 5, I also mentioned teaching worldviews as a possible goal very much related to Bible and religion. The problem here is the huge number of possible options.

Do you want to focus more on Scripture memorization, doctrinal teaching, developing a relationship with Jesus, studying church history, or some other area? Are you ready to get into heavy worldview study? Each of these might be appealing at one time or another to families, but you cannot do it all at once. And the content and methodology might differ based on each family's faith tradition. Consequently, I decided to leave those choices entirely up to you rather than state my own preferences. However, if you want to investigate some of the possibilities, check out the reviews online at www.CathyDuffyReviews.com.

One Last Note Regarding the Charts

Just because I have included an item within my Top Picks does not mean it is perfect. I have selected some items about which I have serious reservations, but I know they meet certain needs very well. After working through the chart, please take time to read through the reviews of items you think will meet your needs. Remember the saying, "One man's trash is another man's treasure"—things that bother me about a particular resource might be the very things that make that resource a good choice for you!

	Multisensory/ hands-on (Wiggly Willy)	Structure/rule-oriented (Perfect Paula)	Appeals to logical/analytical learners (Competent Carl)	Has social activity (Sociable Sue)	Needs parent/teacher instruction	Independent study (ind), one-on-one (1 to 1), or group (g)	Amount of writing: U = up to parent
Phonics, Reading, and Literature							
Alpha-Phonics	2	4	4	3	5	1 to 1	1
At Last! A Reading Method for Every Child	2	4	3	4	5	1 to 1/g	3
Explode the Code	1	5	3	2	2	ind	2
Happy Phonics	5	3	3	5	5	1 to 1/g	1
MCP Plaid Phonics	1	5	3	2	2	ind/1 to 1	2
Noah Webster's Reading Handbook	2	3	3	3	5	1 to 1	1
Phonics Pathways	3	4	4	4	5	1 to 1/g	2
Reading Made Easy	2	3	3	4	5	1 to 1	1
Sing, Spell, Read, and Write	4	3	1	5	3	1 to 1/g	1
Spell to Read and Write	2	5	5	2	5	1 to 1/g	5
Drawn into the Heart of Reading	3	3	4	5	3	ind/1 to 1/g	U
MCP Comprehension Plus	2	4	3	3	2	ind/1 to 1/g	4
Critical Thinking: Reading, Thinking, and Reasoning Skills	2	4	4	3	2	ind	2
Progeny Press Novel Study Guides	2	3	3	3	3	ind/1 to 1/g	U
Total Language Plus Novel Study Guides	2	3	4	4	3	ind/1 to 1/g	U
BJUP Literature Series	2	3	4	3	4	ind/1 to 1/g	U
Learning Language Arts through Literature, Gold Books	1	4	4	2	3	ind/1 to 1/g	4
Stobaugh's Literature Series	2	3	5	3	3	ind/1 to 1/g	5
Mathematics							
Horizons Math	3	5	4	3	4	ind/1 to 1	5
Math-U-See	5	4	5	5	4	1 to 1/g	3
MCP Math	2	4	4	3	2	ind/1 to 1	2
Moving with Math	4	3	4-if you skip most manipulative activities	4-if you use many manipulative activities	4	ind/1 to 1/g	3

Prep time	Grade level specific (s) or multilevel (m)	Ease of use for teacher	Teacher's manual: e = essential, na = not available, nu = available but not useful, u = useful, a = answer key only	Supports Charlotte Mason's philosophy, (n/a = not applicable)	Supports classical education	Suitablility/Content for Protestant (P), Catholic (C), Nonsectarian (N) audience	page # of review
1	m	4	e	3	3	N	81
2	m	3	e	3	2	N	82
1	m	5	a	4	4	N	84
5	m	3	e	4	3	N	85
1-more if you use Teacher Guide	s	5	u	4	4	N	86
1	m	5	e	3	3	P	87
2	m	5	e	3	3	N	88
3	m	3	e	4	3	P	90
0	m	3	e	2	3	N	91
3	m	3	e	4	4	P-but minute Christian content	93
4	m	3	e	5	4	P/C	98
1	s	4	u	2	3	N	100
1	s	5	u	3	3	N	101
1	m	4	e	5	4	P	102
3	m	5	e	5	4	P/C	104
depends on parent's familiarity with readings	s	3	e	3	3	P	106
3	m	4	e	5	4	P/C	113
2	m	3	e	4	4	P	109
2	s	4	e	3	4	P	133
3	m	3	e	4	3	N	137
1	s	5	u	3	2	N	142
3	s/m	2-unless you get the teacher guides	u	4	2	N	143

	Multisensory/ hands-on (Wiggly Willy)	Structure/rule-oriented (Perfect Paula)	Appeals to logical/analytical learners (Competent Carl)	Has social activity (Sociable Sue)	Needs parent/teacher instruction	Independent study (ind), one-on-one (1 to 1),	Amount of writing: U = up to parent or group (g)
Progress in Mathematics	4	4	3	5	5	1 to 1/g	K-2: 3 Gr. 3-8: 4
Singapore Math	2	4	5	3	4	ind/1 to 1/g	3
Algebra Classmate	4	4	4	2	1	ind	2
Chalk Dust	3	4	4	2	1	ind	3
Discovering Geometry	4	3	5	4	4	1 to 1/g	3
Elementary Algebra (Jacobs)	3	4	5	2	2	ind/1 to 1/g	3
Geometry (Jacobs)	2	4	5	2	2	ind/1 to 1/g	3
Keyboard Enterprises Algebra	3	5	4	2	1	ind	3
Saxon Math 54 and up	1	4	4	2	2	ind	3
Videotext Algebra	3	4	4	2	1	ind	3
Language Arts: Grammar and Composition							
A Beka Language Arts	1	4	4	1	2	ind/1 to 1/g	4
Building Christian English	1	5	2	2	3	ind/1 to 1	4
Create-A-Story Game	5	2	4	5	4	g	4
Creative Communications	4	2	3	5	4	1 to 1/g	3
Easy Grammar	2	5	3	1	2	ind	3
English for the Thoughtful Child	3	2	3	4	5	1 to 1/g	4
Fairview's Guide to Composition and Essay Writing	2	3	5	4	4	1 to 1/g	5
First Language Lessons	2	5	2	4	5	1 to 1	2
Format Writing	1	5	5	2	3	ind/1 to 1/g	5
Institute for Excellence in Writing	3	4	4	4	5	1 to 1/g	4
Learning Language Arts through Literature, Elementary Grades	2	3	3	4	3	ind/1 to 1	4
Winston Grammar	4	4	4	2	4	1 to 1/g	2
Wordsmith Series	3	3	4	depends on interaction provided	3	ind/1 to 1/g	4
WriteShop	2	4	3	4	5	1 to 1/g	4
Writing for 100 Days	2	3	3	3	5	1 to 1/g	5
Writing with a Point	2	3	5	4	4	ind/1 to 1/g	4

Prep time	Grade level specific (s) or multilevel (m)	Ease of use for teacher	Teacher's manual: e = essential, na = not available, nu = available but not useful, u = useful, a = answer key only	Supports Charlotte Mason's philosophy, (n/a = not applicable)	Supports classical education	Suitablility/Content for Protestant (P), Catholic (C), Nonsectarian (N) audience	page # of review
3	s	4	K-2: u Gr. 3-8: e	4	4	N	147
2	s	3	u	4	4	N	155
1	m	5	na	3	3	N	307
1	m	5	solutions guides instead	4	4	N	122
3	m	2	e	4	4	N	129
2	m	4	a	4	4	N	131
1	m	4	a	4	5	N	132
1	m	5	a	4	4	N	119
1	s	5	a-solutions guides	1	3	N	149
1	m	5	a-plus tests and quizzes in instructor's guide	4	4	N	158
1	s	5	a	2	5	P	161
1	s	4	u, e for upper grades	1	3	P	165
2	m	3	na	4	3	N	167
2	m	4	e	4	2	C	169
1	s/m	5	e	2	2	N	172
2	m	4	e	5	* see review	N	173
2	m	4	e	5	5	N	174
1	s	5	e	2	5	N	175
1	m	4	e	3	5	P	177
3-depends on how the course is used	m	4	e	5	5	N	179
2	s/m	4	e	5	2	P	181
2	m	4	e	3	3	N	184
2	m	4	e	4	3	N-subtle Christian influence	186
2	m	4	e	5	4	P	188
1	m	4	e	4	4	N	190
1	m	5	e	4	4	N	191

	Multisensory/ hands-on (Wiggly Willy)	Structure/rule-oriented (Perfect Paula)	Appeals to logical/analytical learners (Competent Carl)	Has social activity (Sociable Sue)	Needs parent/teacher instruction	Independent study (ind), one-on-one (1 to 1),	Amount of writing: U = up to parent or group (g)
Language Arts: Spelling and Vocabulary							
Building Spelling Skills	2	5	4	2	2	ind	3
English from the Roots Up	3	4	4	3	5	1 to 1/g	U
Spelling Power	3	4	4	3	4	ind/1 to 1/g	4
Spelling Workout	2	5	3	2	2	ind	3
Vocabulary from Classical Roots	2	5	5	2	3	ind/1 to 1/g	2
Wordly Wise	2	3	4	1	1	ind	2
History/Social Studies							
A Child's History of the World	2-higher with lesson activities	2	3	5	4	ind/1 to 1/g	1-more with student book
A Child's Story of America	2	3	3	4	5	1 to 1/g	U
Genevieve Foster series	2	2	4	3	2	ind/1 to 1/g	1
Greenleaf Guides	2	2	3	5	2	ind/1 to 1/g	U
Guerber History Series	2	3	3	4	2	ind/1 to 1/g	1
Mystery of History	4	3	3	5	5	ind/1 to 1/g	U
The Old World's Gifts to the New	2	3	3	3	3	ind/1 to 1/g	U
The Story of the World with study guide	4	3	4	5	5	1 to 1/g	U
TruthQuest History	3	3	4	4	4	1 to 1/g	U
Ultimate Geography and Timeline Guide	5	3	5	5	5	ind/1 to 1/g	3
Science							
AIMS Education Foundation	5	4	5	5	5	1 to 1/g	3
Backyard Scientist Series	5	3	5	5	5	1 to 1/g	1
Christian Kids Explore Biology	4	2	4	5	5	1 to 1/g	U
BJUP Science for Christian Schools, 1-6	3	4	3	3	4	1 to 1/g	U
Considering God's Creation	4	4	4	5	5	1 to 1/g	U
Exploring Creation Science Series (Apologia)	3	3	4	2	1	ind/g	3
Great Science Adventures	5	2	2	4	5	1 to 1/g	U
A History of Science	3	2	3	5	4	1 to 1/g	U
Janice VanCleave Science Books	5	4	4	5	5	1 to 1/g	U

Prep time	Grade level specific (s) or multilevel (m)	Ease of use for teacher	Teacher's manual: e = essential, na = not available, nu = available but not useful, u = useful, a = answer key only	Supports Charlotte Mason's philosophy, (n/a = not applicable)	Supports classical education	Suitablility/Content for Protestant (P), Catholic (C), Nonsectarian (N) audience	page # of review
1	s	5	a	2	5	P	192
5	m	2	e	4	5	N	194
2	m	3	e	3	4	N	195
1	s	5	u	3	5	N	197
1	m	5	e	3	5	N	198
1	m	5	a	2	5	N	199
1-higher with lesson manual	m	5 or 4 with lesson manual	u	5	5	N	214
1	m	5	a	4	5	P	215
1	m	5	na	4	3	N	216
1	m	5	e	4	4	P	217
1	m	5	na	3	4	P/C	219
4	m	4	e	5	2	P	221
1	m	4	na	3	4	C	223
3	m	3	e	5	5	P/C	224
3	m	2	e	4	4	P	226
4	m	2	e	5	4	N	228
4	m	3	e	5	5	N	235
5	m	4	e	5	3	N-Christian supplement available	236
5	m	2	e	5	3	P/C	241
4	s	4	e	3	3	P	239
4	m	2	e	5	4	P	242
2-except labs	m	4	a	4	4	P/C	252
5	m	1	e	3	2	N	243
2	m	4	e	5	5	N	245
5	m	2	na	5	3		237

	Multisensory/ hands-on (Wiggly Willy)	Structure/rule-oriented (Perfect Paula)	Appeals to logical/analytical learners (Competent Carl)	Has social activity (Sociable Sue)	Needs parent/teacher instruction	Independent study (ind), one-on-one (1 to 1),	Amount of writing: U = up to parent or group (g)
Living Learning Books	4	2	4	5	5	1 to 1/g	U
Media Angels Science	4	4	3	4	5	1 to 1/g	U
Rainbow Science	3	4	4	3	4	1 to 1/ind/g	3
Stratton House Home Science Adventures	5	4	4	5	5	1 to 1/g	2
TOPS Science	5	4	5	4	3	ind/1 to 1/g	2
Unit Studies							
Five in a Row	3	3	1	5	5-except oldest level	1 to 1/g	U
Further Up and Further In	2	3	3	3	4	1 to 1/g/ind	5
History Links	5	3	3	5	5	ind/1 to 1/g	U
KONOS	5	1-unless using Box or Bag	3	5-except high school level	5	g	U
Tapestry of Grace	4	2	3	5	5	g	U
A World of Adventure	3	3	3	3	4	1 to 1/g	U
World Views of the Western World	1	1	4	depends on interaction provided	2	ind/1 to 1/g	5
Foreign Language							
Henle Latin	1	5	4	2	3	ind/1 to 1/g	3
Latina Christiana	2	5	4	3	4	ind/1 to 1/g	3
Learnables	5	1	3	3	1	ind	1
Rosetta Stone	5	2	4	3	1	ind	1
Miscellaneous							
Total Health	1	3	3	2	2	ind/g	3
Critical Thinking Company	3	3	5	3	3	1 to 1/ind	2
The Fallacy Detective	1	3	5	2	2	ind	1
With Good Reason	1	2	5	3	5	1 to 1/g	3
Mark Kistler's Draw Squad	5	4	4	3	2	1 to 1/ind	5-art drawing
Feed My Sheep	5	2	4	4	4	ind/1 to 1/g	5-art drawing
Apex Learning	3	4	3	varies	2	ind/g	varies
The Potter's School	3	4	4	3	1	ind	4
Calvert School	3	4	3	3	3	ind/1 to 1	3
Sonlight	2	3	4	3	4-lots of reading together	1 to 1/g/ind	3
Switched-On Schoolhouse	2	5	2	1	1	ind	3-much on computer

Prep time (na = not applicable)	Grade level specific (s) or multilevel (m)	Ease of use for teacher	Teacher's manual: e = essential, na = not available, nu = available but not useful, u = useful, a = answer key only	Supports Charlotte Mason's philosophy, (n/a = not applicable)	Supports classical education	Suitablility/Content for Protestant (P), Catholic (C), Nonsectarian (N) audience	page # of review
4	m	2	e	5	4	P-supplement at end of Level 2	246
3	m	3	e	4	5	P	248
2	s	4	e	3	3	P/C	255
2	m	4	e	5	3	N	249
3	m	4	e	5	3	N	238
2	m	4	e	5	1	N/P with supplement	259
4	m	3	e	5	4	P	261
4	m	2	e	5	3	C	262
5-unless using Box or Bag	m	1-unless using Box or Bag	e	5	3-except high school level-5	P	265
5	m	1	e	5	5	P	269
3	m	4	e	4	3	P	272
2	m	3-depending upon student initiative	na	4	4	P	274
1	m	4	u	3	5	C	284
1	m	4	e	3	5	P/C	285
1	m	5	na	3	2	N	280
1	m	5	na	2	1	N	283
1	m	5	nu	2	2	P	289
1	m	4	e	3	5	N	291
1	m	5	na	5	5	P/C	293
2	m	4	na	5	5	N	294
1	m	5	na	5	4	N	295
3	m	4	e	5	4	P	296
n/a	m	5	na	1	1	N	300
n/a	m	5	na	varies	varies	P	301
1	s	5	e	1	2	N	303
2	m/s	4	e	5	3	P	304
1	s	5	na-except for specific courses	1	1	P	307

7

Phonics, Reading, and Literature

Phonics comes first. I need not belabor the necessity of a solid phonics foundation for reading since even the public schools are beginning to acknowledge its necessity.

You might choose to work with any one of the excellent phonics programs available. These programs are generally similar in their goals, but they vary greatly when it comes to methods and presentation. Some programs offer leeway for a less formal presentation, while others are more rigid and detailed. Some begin with the "consonant-vowel" approach (e.g., *ba, be, bi, bo, bu*) while others reverse this, beginning with "vowel-consonant" combinations (e.g., *at, am, ad*). Some programs include readers, while others don't. Some have games or hands-on activities, while others rely only on oral and written activity.

I have selected programs that are easily accessible, are appropriate for homeschool use, and ones that approach reading from a variety of educational philosophies. There is certainly something for everyone amidst all the choices.

I have to mention that there are many other excellent phonics programs that I could have included— this was the hardest section to make choices of the "best" programs. Please forgive me if I've left out your favorite!

I would be remiss if I didn't also mention one of the most valuable resources for teaching beginning reading, even though it isn't a program. Ruth Beechick's *A Home Start in Reading* is a small book, usually packaged in *The Three R's* set (Mott Media, 248-685-8773, www.homeschoolingbooks.com) that includes similar books on teaching arithmetic and language arts. *A Home Start in Reading* demystifies the process of teaching a child to read and gives you enough instructional material that you could actually teach your child to read from this twenty-eight-page book. I know that this approach is too "barebones" for most parents, but even if you choose to use a more complete program, this book will help you know what is and is not important so you're in control of your program rather than the reverse.

Following the reviews of phonics programs, I've listed some beginning readers that you might want to use alongside your program.

Once past the beginning reading/phonics stage, children need to shift their primary focus to comprehension and understanding, so I have included resources that address those needs. Then at the end of this chapter are reviews of resources that continue through junior and senior high school.

Phonics and Beginning Reading

Alpha-Phonics
by Samuel L. Blumenfeld
Paradigm Company
P.O. Box 45161
Boise, ID 83711
(208) 322-4440
www.alphaphonics.com
$29.95; CD—$39.95

Alpha-Phonics, Sam Blumenfeld's classic phonics manual, provides comprehensive phonics instruction in a simple, straightforward manner. Rules are presented along with lists of words, syllables, and eventually, sentences. A parent works through lessons with his or her child, working from the book. You can add extra activities, practice readers, or games if you wish.

Alpha-Phonics has heavy-duty plastic covers and a plastic comb binding so it will lie flat while you're working through lessons. Print is very large, making it suitable for young readers.

The methodology is solid phonics. Blending is taught via the vowel-consonant method, with initial consonants added next (e.g., *am* taught first, followed by *Sam* and *ham*). Words are taught in families (e.g., *an, ban, can, Dan, fan, Jan*). However, many nonsense syllables are included in the early stages to help students develop phonetic fluency. Some of the practice lists of such syllables get quite silly as students read through syllables and words like *gab, gac, gack, gad, gaf, gag, gal, gam, gan, gap, gas, gat, gav, gax*, and *gaz*. Students practice with quite a few such lists, but they also move quickly into reading actual sentences.

This program does not use pictures for key words as do many other programs. The print is very large and clear with no illustrations or other distractions. The intent is that students concentrate on the letters themselves so that they immediately recognize the sounds associated with a letter rather than taking an extra mental step to recall a key word associated with a picture.

Alpha-Phonics teaches forty-four different sounds for the letters of the alphabet. It teaches basic phonic rules, but not so many rules as we find in other programs such as *Writing Road to Reading* and *Saxon's Phonics*. You will want to use other reading material for additional practice once students have actually begun to read sentences. The publisher has a set of ten *Little Companion Readers* ($19.95 for the set) that work well alongside *Alpha Phonics*.

Parents must work with children through this book, but it requires no preparation time and is a very efficient, even if unexciting, way for children to learn phonics.

You can preview sample lessons at the Web site.

Computer fans might be interested in the CD version: *Alpha-Phonics the Book on CD-ROM*. This program mirrors the original book, but with both spoken and written instructions. Students respond with the mouse rather than keyboarding.

In addition, there is an *Alpha-Phonics/How To Tutor Workbook* ($14.95) that reinforces lessons in *Alpha-Phonics* with fill-in-the-blank and written exercises.

At Last! A Reading Method for EVERY Child!

by Mary Pecci

Pecci Educational Publishing

Order through Intrepid Group, Inc.

1331 Red Cedar Circle

Fort Collins, CO 80524

(970) 493-3793

www.OnlineReadingTeacher.com

$29.95

Mary Pecci has put together a phonetic reading program that she claims overcomes the problems of both intensive phonics and sight-reading programs. Sight programs fail to teach the "code" of reading, so children try to guess rather than decode. On the other hand, many phonics programs have too many rules and are sometimes complicated, making decoding a frustrating and laborious process for many children.

Mary has created a program with fewer rules than most and that uses a consistent decoding strategy that helps deal with exceptions. She teaches using a consonant-phonogram approach. The way this works is that children first practice reading lists with phonograms such as *ep*, *elt*, *ond*, and *unch*. The parent/teacher then introduces initial consonants that join with these phonograms to form words. For example, *l* combines with *unch* to form *lunch*.

Mary reduces the phonetic code to its simplest terms by dividing the entire English language into four clear-cut phonics groups: 1. Short Vowel Phonograms—such as *at, ent, ig, ock, ust*; 2. Long Vowel Phonograms with "e" on the End—such as *ake, ete, ide, ome, ute*; 3. Long Vowel Phonograms with Two Vowels Together—such as *ail, eat, een, ied, oap, ued*; and 4. Sight Phonograms—twenty-five phonograms that need to be memorized rather than sounded out, such as *alk, ight, ange, ought, tion*. By grouping phonograms this way, every word is decoded phonetically, syllable by syllable.

Part 1 of this book contrasts phonics and sight methods and the difficulties of both. You can skip this part if you want. Part 2 gets into Mary's actual method for teaching reading. The key to her system is the uniform approach in word decoding. Children learn phonics rules, but not with the fine-tuning you find in a *Writing-Road-to-Reading*-type program. For example, children are not explicitly taught different rules for figuring out the different sounds for *ea* as in *real, head, great, heart,* and *learn*. Mary claims that this only causes confusion, and children are capable of decoding words with the different sounds of *ea* on their own when they have a simplified rule as a focal point. For example, when only one sound for *ea* is taught with the "Two Vowels Together" rule, children automatically decode the word *head* as *heed*. When a word pronunciation comes close but is still not correct, children are told to identify these words as "twisters"— words we twist to fit into the context of the story to pronounce them correctly. For example, in the sentence "Put your hat on your head," children first sound out the last word as *heed*, but the context obviously requires twisting it to /hed/.

In the few cases when children cannot "twist" a word to get it right, they are taught to look up the phonetic pronunciation in the dictionary. These strategies simplify the number of rules children memorize.

Children work with word lists in the book as well as with flash cards and other visual aids that you, the teacher, will need to construct. Mary also shows you how to use beginning reading material other than phonetic readers that have only carefully contrived sentences such as "The rat sat on the mat." Using her decoding strategy, children decode and learn to read new words from basal readers. You also should be able to apply the method to other beginning reading storybooks like those by Dr. Seuss. This means children can soon read more natural sentences in meaningful contexts and enjoyable stories while simultaneously applying phonics skills that lead to independent reading.

Mary includes many ideas for seatwork, games, and other practice activities. However, much of this will not be practical outside a classroom situation since it is too much work for one or two children.

Many parents will appreciate the other extras in this book. For instance, there's a fifteen-minute reading skill diagnosis (for which you will need flash cards). She also addresses strategies for teaching spelling, vocabulary, reading comprehension, and handwriting.

In addition, Mary has written *Super Seatwork* books that many home educators will want to use. These have large, simple activities and exercises, including some cut-and-paste, writing, and drawing. The variety and simplicity are much more appealing to kids than the typical phonics workbooks. Titles include:

Color Words, Content Areas, Letter Recognition, Linguistic Exercises, Number Words, Phonic Grab Bag (these six are $12.95 each), and *Word Skills* ($18.95). *Letter Recognition* includes alphabet cards and strips, Bingo, follow-the-dots, letter-match games, puzzles, and more. *Linguistic Exercises* includes short-vowel families, long-vowel families, sight families, and 40 phonic review sheets. *Phonic Grab Bag* covers all basic phonic skills: consonants, blends, digraphs, long and short vowels, phonograms, and more. *Word Skills* covers skills related to reading such as contractions, possessives, prefixes and suffixes, alphabetizing, and dictionary skills. All *Super Seatwork* books are reproducible and are in 8½-inch by 11-inch format.

Mary Pecci maintains a message board on her Web site to answer any questions you might have.

Explode the Code
by Nancy M. Hall
Educators Publishing Service
P.O. Box 9031
Cambridge, MA 02139-9031
(800) 225-5750
www.epsbooks.com

Books 1–5—$6.75 each; books 6–8—$6.95 each; teacher's key for books 1–5 and 1½–4½—$2.15; teacher's key for books 6–8—$2.15

There are fourteen separate workbooks in this series, although you might not want to use them all. Most of the time you will use these for phonics reinforcement, but some families use them as their primary phonics teaching resource. Some families also use them with older children who have a weak phonics foundation.

Typically you would use these alongside something like *Alpha Phonics* or *Happy Phonics* programs that don't have a writing/workbook component.

The books review phonetic concepts individually rather than attempting to review all concepts repeatedly from book to book at increasing levels of difficulty. While phonic decoding skills are the primary focus, reading comprehension and vocabulary also get some attention.

Books are printed in black and white. They feature large print and less of it per page than some other phonics workbooks, making them a good choice for children who can do only limited amounts of writing or who have trouble focusing.

Students should be able to do most work independently once someone has read the instructions for that page to them. Eventually, most students become so familiar with the types of exercises that they seldom need even that assistance.

Books 1 through 8 are the most important. Content of each is as follows: Book 1—short vowels; Book 2—initial and final consonant blends; Book 3—open syllables, silent *e* rule, digraphs, and simple diphthongs; Book 4—syllable division rules; Book 5—word families, three-letter blends, *qu*, *-ey*, and the three sounds of *-ed*; Book 6—more difficult diphthongs and *r*-controlled vowels; Book 7—soft *c* and *g*, silent letters, sounds of *ear, ei, eigh,* and the digraph *ph*; Book 8—suffixes and irregular endings. Books 1½, 2½, 3½, 4½, 5½, and 6½ offer more practice on topics covered within books 1, 2, 3, etc., respectively. Post-tests are included within each book.

A single teacher's key covers Books 1 through 5 and 1½ through 5½, while another covers Books 6 through 8, including 6½. Keys include program description, answers, and dictations for the posttests.

Happy Phonics
by Diane Hopkins
Family Resources, Inc.
741 North State Road 198
Salem, UT 84653
(888) 771-1034 order
(801) 423-2009
e-mail: info@lovetolearn.net
www.lovetolearn.net
$39.95

I repeatedly say that you don't have to buy an expensive program to teach reading, but most parents want more direction and more activity than they get with a minimalist approach like *Alpha Phonics* or *Noah Webster's Reading Handbook.* Diane Hopkins has solved the problem by creating *Happy Phonics.*

A twenty-two-page, stapled teacher's guide directs you through a step-by-step process from learning letters and sounds into reading real books. The rest of *Happy Phonics* is heavy-duty, brightly colored paper stock printed with an alphabet desk strip, flash cards, words, letters, game pieces, and stories. These are cut apart and used for their various duties as explained in the instructions. If you dislike cutting things out and organizing, this might not be the program for you.

The games are manipulative learning materials rather than competitive devices, but young children love matching, flipping cards, and moving things around. The guide contains some of the same elements you find in reading workbooks or texts, but the format is more appealing, and the games are definitely more fun. You might even use these as a supplement to a phonics program like *Alpha Phonics* or *Noah Webster's Reading Handbook.*

While it does take some time to put this together, it's not overwhelming. A simple chart in the instructions shows which parts of *Happy Phonics* are used at which stages of learning. Diane also recommends using *Explode the Code* workbooks as part of your reading program and mentions other reading tools you might wish to use such as the *Bob Books.* She also encourages you to make your own beginning readers.

Spelling lists are included so children can learn to spell phonetically. *Happy Phonics* will suffice as a beginning spelling program.

The program includes instructions, games, little reading books, flashcards, and *My First Big Book*, which has an easy-to-read story for each phonic sound learned. If you prefer a clearly and thoroughly structured program, this *isn't* it. But if you are looking for a low cost, fun phonics program with games, this *is* it.

MCP *Plaid Phonics*

Modern Curriculum Press/Pearson Learning Group

P.O. Box 2500

Lebanon, IN 46052

(800) 393-3156

www.pearsonlearning.com

Levels K, A, B, and C (2003 editions)

Student editions: K—$9.95, A–C—$10.95 each; teacher's resource guide—$49.95 each

The *MCP Plaid Phonics* workbooks can be used for phonics instruction or reinforcement, although most homeschoolers use them as workbook supplements to other phonics programs.

The 2003 editions are colorfully illustrated with a combination of photographs and drawings. Some illustrations were commissioned from children's book illustrators. The variety of activities and colorful presentation make these workbooks appealing to children, and large print reduces the intimidation factor.

Their primary use is to help children develop both auditory and visual discrimination of sounds and letters. In the first three books, children do many exercises on recognition of beginning, ending, and middle sounds or phonograms.

Over the years, this series has changed, adding some features from the "whole language approach" to reading. Thus, the newest books (especially Levels B and C) include short stories and comprehension activities, make-it-yourself little storybooks, composition activities, and a "less-controlled" vocabulary. Unit openers are either a nonfiction reading passage related to science or social studies, or a poem. Other whole language activities (e.g., suggestions for related story books to read aloud) are in the teacher's resource guide.

Generally, these are positive improvements because the old editions repeated essentially the same information year after year. Level C reflects these changes the most. It reviews basic phonetic concepts within a variety of exercises, then goes on to extensive work with base words, prefixes, suffixes, plurals, syllables, synonyms, antonyms, homonyms, dictionary skills, and a few composition activities.

Level K introduces letters and sounds (both short and long vowels), working on identification and discrimination of individual letters. It includes a set of color flash cards in the back of the student book.

Level A reviews, then adds long vowels, blends, digraphs, contractions, and inflectional endings. Level B reviews more rapidly, then adds compound and two-syllable words, r-controlled vowels, vowel pairs and digraphs, diphthongs, and contractions. The final section introduces synonyms, antonyms, homonyms, and some prefixes.

In the newest editions, high-frequency words get more attention. There are word cards at the back of student books for levels K, A and B in addition to more work on such words throughout the entire series.

While *Plaid Phonics* could theoretically be used as your primary phonics instruction resource, it might not spend as much time as most children need on the critical blending stage. For example, most intensive phonics programs will have children spend a good deal of time working with word family groups like *at, sat, pat, hat, mat* to develop familiarity with the *at* phonogram. In *Plaid Phonics*, some work on blending is taught directly from the teacher resource guides, so if you want to use this as your primary tool, you will definitely need to purchase and use the guides, taking as much time as needed to work through the blending stage.

Teacher resource guides offer this sort of lesson-expanding help as well as lesson presentation instructions and workbook answers. However, if you only want to use *Plaid Phonics* as a supplement, you probably do not need the guides. Workbook activities have clear instructions, and answers are fairly obvious. Also, much of each guide's content is classroom oriented and unlikely to be used by many home educators. I suspect many homeschoolers purchase *Plaid Phonics* workbooks because they are so easy to use without the teacher guides and because their children enjoy them.

Noah Webster's Reading Handbook

Christian Liberty Press
502 W. Euclid Ave.
Arlington Heights, IL 60004
(847) 259-4444
e-mail: custserv@christianlibertypress.com
www.christianlibertypress.com
$7.00

This must be just about the cheapest resource for teaching phonics/beginning reading! It does a very adequate job, which should not be surprising since it's an updated version of Webster's original *Blue-Backed Speller* that was used to teach thousands (at least!) of children in past centuries.

It follows a fairly standard progression, introducing short vowels first, then using consonant-vowel practice to help beginning readers learn to blend. (This is the same method used by *A Beka* and *Sing, Spell, Read, and Write*.) Practice words and sentences are included on each page as soon as is appropriate. Lengthier reading selections (Bible-based) are at the back of the book. Rules are presented in boxes at the bottom of pages. A few pages of technical information are at the back of the book for parents who want to better understand the functions of the alphabet and sounds.

No frills, no confusion, straight-to-the-point phonics, and there seems to be little missing other than more work on sight words, complete treatment of the *ough* sounds, and the extra practice and review students need to really master reading skills.

Add this to your list of possibilities if you're looking for a simple, uncluttered approach. This book also suits remedial learners of all ages. If using it with beginning readers, consider using Christian Liberty Press's *Adventures in Phonics* workbooks, levels A, B, and C (and other levels as they become available) for written practice and reinforcement.

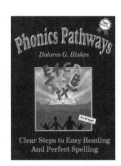

Phonics Pathways (eighth edition)
by Dolores G. Hiskes
Dorbooks, Inc.
1331 Red Cedar Circle
Fort Collins, CO 80524
(800) 852-4890 credit card orders
(970) 493-4793 check orders
(925) 449-6983 inquiries
e-mail: info@dorbooks.com
www.dorbooks.com
$32.95

Phonics Pathways is a complete phonics program, self-contained within one large book. There are extras from Dorbooks that you can use alongside *Phonics Pathways*, but they are not essential.

The program will work for all ages as well as for remedial readers. Sounds of the letters are taught, beginning with short vowels. As each consonant is taught, it is immediately used to begin making blends with the short vowels. Beginning blends are taught consonant-vowel (i.e., *ba, bi, bo,* etc.). Because of the quick movement into blending practice, children are reading three-letter words very soon.

Multisensory learning methods (hearing, saying, tracing, writing) are used with each letter. Dorbooks' supplemental card games add more hands-on activity for those who want it.

Uppercase and lowercase letters are shown from the beginning, although children work primarily with lowercase letters. You might need to take some extra time to work specifically on recognition and writing of uppercase letters, although this could be done late in the program.

Each new concept taught is followed by words, phrases, or sentences for practice, so no extra reading material is necessary. Reading practice is designed to improve tracking skills from left to right, which is especially important for preventing dyslexic problems. Some of the phrases and sentences are purposely nonsensical or humorous to keep it entertaining. The "Dewey the Bookworm" character and positive-thinking-type proverbs are also used throughout the book for the same reason.

The program covers all phonetic sounds, diacritical markings, suffixes and prefixes, plurals and possessives, contractions, and compound words. Teaching instruction is on each page. It is brief enough that no significant preparation time is needed.

One oddity pops up in the instructions. Sometimes they are written directly to students even though students of this program cannot yet read sentences as complex as those in the instructions. But this is no big deal. Parents/teachers just need to read through the instructions and present whatever is necessary to students.

An index to spelling rules, spelling and pronunciation charts, plural and suffix spelling charts, and two pages of "Vision and Motor Coordination Training Exercises" are found at the back of the book. Try some of these exercises if you have a child who seems to have minor learning disabilities.

Phonics Pathways introduces "pyramids" as another reading tool. Dorbooks also publishes an entirely separate book on the pyramid concept. The *Pyramid* book ($21.95) uses a gradually widening pyramid of words to help students "strengthen eye tracking, develop blending skills, increase eye span, and teach syllabication." This might also work well alongside other programs that use the same introductory approach (e.g., *Sing, Spell, Read, and Write*) to help students struggling with tracking and blending.

Dorbooks also publishes three other relatively simple supplements you might find useful, although none of these are essential. All three are printed on colorful card stock and must be laminated and cut apart before use.

The Train Game ($14.95) functions as a movable alphabet to be used as a learning activity rather than as a game. *Blendit!* ($34.95) has eleven bingo-type games for practice with various phonetic skills. *WordWorks* ($34.95) has ten sets of cards (thirty-six per set) that are used in games played like Memory, Old Maid, or Go Fish to reinforce phonics. If you have to choose only one of these, I would recommend *Blendit!* Like *Pyramid*, these supplements should also work well with other phonics programs that use the consonant-vowel approach.

One problem that crops up in this and other programs that begin with consonant-vowel combinations is that children are guessing at vowel sounds since actual vowel sounds are generally determined by what comes after the vowel—and in the early stages of the program, there's nothing "coming after" to give them a clue. When children start reading long-vowel words, they need to be taught to scan ahead for signals such as silent "e" that determine the vowel sound. *Phonics Pathways*, as well as the *Pyramid* book, have tried to address this problem in their newest editions by adding diacritical markings to vowels when children might run into problems determining the vowel sound.

Phonics Pathways is one of the top products because it does a great job teaching phonics, it is very reasonably priced for such a comprehensive program, it is easy for parents to use, and it has options that can make it more multisensory.

Reading Made Easy: A Guide to Teach Your Child to Read

by Valerie Bendt

Valerie Bendt

333 West Rio Vista Court

Tampa, FL 33604

(813) 758-6793

e-mail: ValerieBendt@earthlink.net

www.valeriebendt.com

$45.00

Veteran homeschooler and author Valerie Bendt has created a reading program that should be very appealing to even the most inexperienced parent. The program is contained in this single 500+ page book. It is scripted and illustrated so parent and child work together from the book. A little extra work is required: you will need a large quantity of blank index cards upon which each week's phonograms or words are written. Many times these are cut into two parts that are combined as you work through the lesson.

Valerie has created a unique coding system, similar in some ways to *Teach Your Child to Read in 100 Easy Lessons*. However, Valerie's system seems simpler and less confusing, especially since it doesn't use an artificial alphabet as does *100 Easy Lessons*. She uses a gray typeface for short vowels, dotted typeface for silent letters, bold typeface for long vowels, and circling for some digraphs. Children practice reading words, then sentences, then stories directly from this book. Valerie has tried to make the reading material meaningful and interesting. The occasional use of pictures invites the child to respond to both picture and words as they learn to understand context.

Valerie includes tracing, copying, and writing activities, continually cautioning against pushing children whose fine motor skills are too immature for such activities.

Parents will need to read through each lesson in advance to prepare index cards and the game activities used for learning sight words. Beginning with lesson 28, index cards are created while you present the lesson rather than in advance; children might actually help create the cards themselves at this point. Reproducible pages for the sight-word games are at the end of the book. Use of the index cards and games adds a multisensory dimension to lessons. So, although it might seem a bother, preparing the cards is an important part of the program.

The progression is a bit different from other reading programs—Valerie introduces both short and long "a" words before continuing with other short-vowel words, and she continues in this fashion throughout the program. She covers most other phonetic concepts, but there are some important ones that are not included, such as *eigh* as in *eight* and *sleigh*. However, on two pages at the end of the book, she lists those not covered along with example words and suggestions for covering them as a child encounters words containing them.

The last twelve lessons in the book incorporate a twelve-chapter story about a young boy named Gideon who wants to learn how to read. Each chapter is first presented as a read aloud by the parent. Then an abridged version is presented for the child to read aloud himself. The content of the book is essentially nonsectarian until the story of Gideon, which is loaded with spiritual content and lessons.

Throughout the book, Valerie has chosen to use the LucidaSansSchool font published by Portland State University. These are the folks who publish the *Italic Handwriting* series, which Valerie also recommends. However, you are not limited to that handwriting style by this book's presentation.

There are a few "rough" places. Only a few capital letters are specifically taught, but there are general instructions for the parent to teach them and keep track of which ones have been taught. I also found myself looking for fuller explanation when children were being introduced to some of the new phonograms/concepts. For example, two lists of *ow* words are presented—those with the long "o" sound then those with the /ou/ as in *ouch* sound. There's no mention that children will have to use familiarity and context to determine which sound is required, especially with words like *bow*.

Similarly, when some suffixes such as *er* and *ed* are introduced, there is no discussion about their grammatical purpose. They are simply presented as a way to make new words. Perhaps this is fine for young readers, but I know I would be adding additional comment as a teacher so that children saw the generalization and its broad application.

This program relies heavily upon parent/child interaction. Some early lessons conclude with the instruction to read a book aloud to your child. Valerie adds lists of suggested read-aloud and easy-reading books you might want to use.

Overall, this course looks to be both enjoyable and relatively easy-to-use, two features I consider very important when it comes to teaching reading. I understand from the publisher that it works well alongside *Five in A Row*. Also, *Learning Language Arts Through Literature Red Book* (second grade level) works well as a transition after *Reading Made Easy* since it reinforces and fills in the few gaps of the program.

Sing, Spell, Read, and Write, Kindergarten/Level 1 Home Kit (second edition)
Pearson Education
P.O. Box 2500
Lebanon, IN 46052
(800) 393-3156
www.pearsonlearning.com
Combo Kit—$272.50

This multisensory, phonics-based language arts program, appropriate for children ages five through eight, is especially good for active learners such as Wiggly Willys as well as for Sociable Sues. It covers phonics, reading, comprehension, spelling, beginning grammar, and manuscript printing. The *Kindergarten/Level 1 Home Kit* includes twenty-three full-color, phonetic, storybook readers; six cassette tapes with simple, catchy songs that teach the phonograms; a CD presentation of the songs (use either the tapes or the CD); five phonics games (bingo and card deck type games); phonogram "strips" for blending; a cardboard treasure chest with prizes (very inexpensive items); a phonics placemat; raceway chart and raceway car for tracking progress; a teacher's manual; four consumable student workbooks; an assessment book; and a teacher training video. Everything is very colorful and professionally put together. All of this comes packaged in an attractive, sturdy box. The back cover of each student book is a wipe-off writing "slate," as is the back of the placemat; a wipe-off marker and eraser for these are included.

Sing, Spell, Read, and Write uses the consonant-vowel approach (*ba, be, bi, bo, bu*) to teach reading. It's a fun program that is fairly easy to use. Instruction is provided by the parent with assistance from the cassettes or CD, a two-page folder for Kindergarten level, or the detailed instructor's manual that you use once you start Level 1. Lesson plans in the manual coordinate program elements plus lessons in grammar, reading, comprehension, and writing that are presented from the manual.

The program is truly multisensory as children listen to and sing the songs; practice saying and writing letters, phonograms, and words; manipulate letter cards; play the games; and complete workbook activities. There are thirty-six "steps" in the program, and progress is tracked on the Raceway Chart as children master each step.

The first workbook for Level 1, *Off We Go*, provides readiness activities plus an introduction to letters, their sounds, and their formation. The second workbook, the *Raceway Book*, is far more intensive, beginning with blends and continuing through all phonics instruction, while also working on manuscript handwriting, comprehension, and some grammar and spelling. If your child struggles with the written exercises, save them for later and focus on the oral work and games instead.

The songs are pleasant, child-oriented tunes to which children will sing along. If your children do not like singing, this is not the program for you! The games, raceway chart, and prizes add extra fun and incentive to both levels of the program. The *Assessment Book* is used after each reader to check on word recognition and comprehension. It also has three achievement tests to be used at different points in the program.

Seventeen of the phonetic readers used with Level 1 save us the trouble of looking elsewhere for practice material. There are more than one thousand pages in these readers. The last few readers in the set are often unnecessary since by that point many children have mastered phonics well enough to begin reading real books on their own. Still, the last few books cover the "oddities" of the English language, such as "ph" making the sound /f/, and these do need to be covered at some time.

Some parents found that the Level 1 kit moved too quickly for their kindergartners, particularly on short vowels, or that there was too much writing for younger children. So the publisher created a kindergarten level that covers the first fifteen of the program's thirty-six steps in a slower fashion with a separate set of two workbooks and six more readers. The two workbooks, *All Aboard* and *On Track*, spend more time on readiness activities and have larger print, more white space, and move at a slower pace than the presentation in Level 1. If you use the kindergarten materials, you can probably skip a good part of the lessons covering these same steps in the Level 1 program. The kindergarten books only cover a portion of what is in Level 1, so you will still need both levels if you start with the kindergarten materials.

Although kindergarten student books and readers are sold separately, you only get the rest of the components when you purchase either the Level 1 Kit or the Combo Kit. You would be missing the music, charts, games, and prizes without Level 1. So, for most families the Combo Kit makes the most sense.

There is also a separate *Pre-kindergarten Kit* with reading readiness activities for preschool level. The *Pre-kindergarten Kit* teaches colors, shapes, categorizing, sequencing, audio discrimination, and sound and letter recognition.

Additional materials for reading and grammar study are available for what are designated Levels 2 and 3. But since Level 1 is the heart of the phonics instruction, I do not include reviews of the higher levels here.

Spell to Write and Read
by Wanda Sanseri
Back Home Industries
P.O. Box 22495
Milwaukie, OR 97269
www.BHIbooks.org
Core Kit—$90.00; SWR—$35.00; WISE Guide for Spelling—$35.00

Wanda Sanseri wrote this guide for teaching the first four years of language arts—phonics, penmanship, spelling, reading, composition, logic, and introductory grammar—using methods originally presented by Romalda Spalding in *The Writing Road to Reading*. Because *The Writing Road to Reading* has a challenging organizational structure that makes it difficult for parents to use without assistance, Wanda came up with her own improved presentation.

The heart of *Spell to Write and Read* is the phonograms that children practice saying, writing, seeing, and reading. Phonetically taught spelling is the primary tool used for teaching writing and reading rather than a skill to be picked up later through reading.

The program uses its own system for marking the phonograms to identify sounds and spelling rules. This same system is applied to both spelling and reading.

This program has more rules and fewer sight words than most others. The result is that 99 percent of the one thousand most frequently used English words have rules that apply to them. So there's a trade off here; in most other programs, students memorize more sight words, but learn fewer rules.

Students build their own spelling textbook, so there is quite a bit more writing than in other programs. On first glance, this program seems designed more for Perfect Paula and Competent Carl learners who might like the detailed analysis of words than for Wiggly Willys and Sociable Sues who might be frustrated with the detail and notebook work. However, many teachers who have followed the program's suggestions have been able to keep the variety and pace moving and use it successfully with such children. (Wiggly Willy parents might still have trouble *teaching* the program.)

In addition, some learning disabled children who need a lot of repetition and very complete, specific instruction have benefited greatly from this method. Much depends upon the parent/teacher's ability to make the program enjoyable and to adapt lessons to meet the needs of each child.

Spell to Write and Read (SWR) is to be used with Wanda's *WISE Guide for Spelling*. *WISE Guide* covers two thousand basic words (plus hundreds of derivatives) to teach the foundational principles of English spelling. While *SWR* provides the methodology, *WISE Guide* provides much of the content.

Lesson plans each cover a set of twenty words in *SWR*. Recommended preliminary activities include warm-up drills and motivational comments for introducing the lesson. Sentences are provided to illustrate each word. Selections come from literature, quotes of famous people, or instructive comments. Each word is divided into syllables and highlighted to amplify phonograms and spelling rules. Information to explain the spelling is provided.

Creative ways to reinforce the spelling words are suggested. Rather than uninspiring activities like copying a word five times, students actively use spelling words in a variety of ways. The teacher is given simple instructions, and the student works from the words dictated for him to write into his spelling notebook. No worksheets are needed. Spelling lists actually cover up through twelfth grade level, so many parents have used this program as a spelling resource for older students.

WISE Guide is much more than a spelling resource. Enrichment activities involve a wide variety of topics: literature, grammar, antonyms, synonyms, derivatives, etymology, contractions, compound words, alphabetizing, keyboard instruction, punctuation, alliteration, homonyms, analogies, words of comparison, oxymorons, figures of speech, verb conjugation, poetry, plurals, subject and verb agreement, Greek and Latin roots, possession, and appositives. Assignments utilize art, pantomime, refrigerator magnets, deaf signing, and games. Numerous approaches used to improve composition skills include: creative writing, letter writing, diary work, vivid word selections, descriptive writing, feature writing, and dictation.

Other helps available from Back Home Industries include the *70 Basic Phonogram Cards*, *Phonogram Cassette Tape*, *Primary Learning Logs*, *SWR Charts*, *The Alpha List*, *The New England Primer*, *Play by the Sea* (a beginning reader), and *The McCall-Crabbs Test Lessons in Reading*. When purchased from the publisher, *SWR*, *WISE Guide*, the *Phonogram Cards*, *Spelling Rule Cards*, and the *Phonogram Tape* are sold as the Core Kit at a lower price than when purchasing individual items.

Wanda and fifteen other teachers she has trained and endorsed offer seminars for interested groups across the country and in Canada. I have received many positive reports from those who have attended Wanda's seminars and have used her materials. They tell me that Wanda gives them practical instruction that really works for homeschoolers while clearly explaining the basics so they have confidence in their knowledge and ability to teach their children.

Beginning Readers

When children are learning phonics, they need lots of practice with simple reading material. Beginning readers are sometimes included in phonics programs, but other times you need to find your own. Those listed below are not included in my 100 Top Picks since they are only representative of what is available.

Basic Phonics Readers

A Beka Book

P.O. Box 18000

Pensacola, FL 32532

(877) 223-5226

www.abeka.org

$11.50 for all twelve; teacher edition—$14.50

These are twelve small, colorful readers, divided into three sets of four books each. The sets progress in difficulty, reflected in the set titles: *I Learn to Read, I Do Read,* and *I Can Read Well.* They begin with short-vowel words, shift into long vowels by the fourth book, and continue up through words like *south, ground,* and *bright.* You can purchase the individual books, or you might purchase the teacher edition that includes all of the readers in one comb-bound book.

Bob Books

Scholastic, Inc.

(800) 325-6149

www.scholastic.com

$16.95 per set

Bob Books is actually five different sets of nonsectarian beginning readers. These are phonetically organized with controlled vocabulary, yet the stories are more interesting than many other such readers.

The first set of twelve little books, *Bob Books First* (#914544), concentrates on short-vowel words. The second set of twelve slightly longer books, *Bob Books Fun* (#912198), continues with short-vowel consistent words, while adding double consonants, blends, endings, some sight words and longer stories. The last three sets continue to add more complex phonics. The books get longer, so there are fewer per set. *Bob Books Kids* (#914546) has ten books with eight stories and two activity books. They continue work on short-vowel words. *Bob Books Pals* and *Bob Books Wow!* each have four books of sixteen pages each and four books of twenty-four pages each. *Pals* adds new blends, more sight words, and longer compound words. *Wow!* introduces long-vowel words.

Illustrations are simple black-and-white line drawings that children can imitate and color. Both the stories and drawings have an appealing childlike character. Teaching instructions are short and simple. These readers will work with any orderly phonics program.

Reading for Fun Enrichment Library
A Beka Book
(877) 223-5226
www.abeka.org
$36.00

Fifty-five small readers come in a boxed set. While they do not follow as strict a phonetic progression as the MCP readers, they do begin with short vowels and gradually increase the phonetic complexity. For most children you will still need additional practice with short-vowel words beyond these readers. While there are a few Bible stories and some character-building stories, most are about children, fairy tales, nature, and other common subjects. Books are illustrated in full color. The price is very reasonable for so much good quality reading material.

Phonics Practice Readers
Modern Curriculum Press/Pearson Learning
(800) 393-3156
www.pearsonlearning.com
$19.50 per set

For variety's sake, MCP offers three different series (A, B, and C) of these nonsectarian readers from which you can choose. You need not purchase them all. Within each series are four sets: short vowels, long vowels, blends, and digraphs. Each set consists of ten eight-page books. These are inexpensive and colorfully illustrated. You might need only short and long vowels before children are ready for many easy reading books.

Beyond Phonics

Once children have begun to read, the natural inclination is to get a reading program with readers and workbooks. However, here's another place where focusing on your goals can save you time, money, and effort and possibly produce better results with your children. Here are four things to think about before deciding what to do next:

1. If one of your goals is to improve decoding proficiency—which means being able to figure out how to say the words—just about any reading material that is not too difficult can be used as fodder for

practice. Those early reading books by Dr. Seuss and others can be much more fun than readers yet still provide essentially the same type decoding practice.

2. Other goals should focus on children understanding what they are reading. Beginning at lower levels of thinking, ask children to relate back simple data or events from what they have read. As they progress, you move on to more challenging levels of thinking. Children begin to interpret what they read, draw parallels to their own experience, or make connections to other things they know. Later they begin to compare and contrast, analyze, and otherwise focus more on the content than on the mechanics of reading. Reading programs can help with this, but simply applying Charlotte Mason's narration techniques with real books can accomplish the same thing.

3. Readers and workbooks were created to help teachers with classroom management not because they are the best way for children to develop reading skills. With groups of children, it's much easier to manage them if everyone is reading the same book and completing the same workbook pages. However, in our homeschools our children are generally all at different levels with reading, so we're not trying to keep all our children on the same page at the same time. In fact, I wish you luck if you even try to do such a thing!

4. A reading program might help you stay on track and focus on some of the necessary skills if you are working with a child individually. In other words, they might be more useful for the parent than for the child! The downside is that your child must read someone else's collected anthology of readings, many of which might have little appeal for your child. In addition, your child has to work through the exercises created to go with that particular anthology even if those exercises don't actually target skills your child needs at the time.

Although reading programs are not necessarily bad, I have found that selecting real books for my children to read and using supplemental resources to focus on particular skills has been far more fun and effective for all concerned. Consequently, the resources I've included for reading are ones that I believe work better than reading programs in most homeschool situations.

For those who might be leary of abandoning traditional reading programs, I suggest you pay particular attention to *Drawn into the Heart of Reading*. This "program" provides structure for this sort of "real books" approach, which might give you the confidence to give it a try.

I've included a few other reading skills resources that I think are particularly good. (*Note:* some resources for vocabulary are reviewed in chapter 9, and they might also be part of your reading skills development strategy.) The listed resources are just a sampling of the many other excellent resources you can easily find at teacher supply stores and in catalogs. Some will be broad in their skills coverage while others focus narrowly on comprehension, work with analogies, or other particular aspects.

I've also included some novel study guides for those who want to develop reading skills with real books their children are reading.

Those who still want traditional readers or reading programs might check out one of the following series. Phone numbers and/or Web sites follow each listing.

- A Beka Book has a number of readers with teacher's guides for each grade level. Many readers have a single theme such as nature, heroes, or fables; some are anthologies; and some are novels. (877) 223-5226, www.abeka.org

- *Christian Eclectic Readers* (Wm. B. Eerdmans Publishing Co.) is the latest reincarnation of the McGuffey series (and the best, in my opinion). (800) 253-7521, www.eerdmans.com

- Christian Liberty Press Readers (Christian Liberty Press) are an assortment of readers with different themes for different levels. (847) 259-4444, www.christianlibertypress.com

- *Little Angel Readers* (Stone Tablet Press) are a set of beginning readers for Catholic children. (636) 458-1515, www.stonetabletpress.com

- *Nature Readers* (Christian Liberty Press) feature science topics as the content. They are a bit more like "real books" than other readers. (847) 259-4444, www.christianlibertypress.com

- *Pathway Readers* (Pathway Books) are an excellent Amish series that reflect the rural, agricultural Amish community. Content is God-honoring and wholesome. These readers also have companion workbooks. http://www.anabaptists.org/places/pathway.html

- *Reading for Christian Schools* series (Bob Jones University Press) combines anthologies and novels in complete reading programs that include workbooks. (800) 845-5731, www.bjup.com

- Rod and Staff's *Bible Nurture and Reader* series has been very popular with homeschoolers looking for biblical content and no fantasy or modern sagas of cultural decadence. This series also includes workbooks. (606) 522-4348

Elementary and/or Upper Level

Drawn into the Heart of Reading
by Carrie Austin
Heart of Dakota Publishing, Inc.
1004 Westview Drive
Dell Rapids, SD 57022
(605) 428-4068
e-mail: carmikeaustin@msn.com
www.heartofdakota.com

Teacher's guide—$49.95; student books: Level 2/3—$18.00, Level 4/5—$23.00, Level 6/7/8—$28.00

Subtitled, "A Multi-Level Reading Program to Use with Any Books You Choose," this is a guide that can be used along with your choice of "real books" for children in grades 2 through 8. It consists of a teacher's guide plus student workbooks, available at three levels: grades 2–3, grades 4–5, and grades 6–8. Workbooks can be reproduced for use with all students within your family. You will also want to purchase the appropriate level of *Book Projects to Send Home*, small activity books published by McGraw-Hill and available through Heart of Dakota Publishing for $6.50 each.

You can use *Drawn into the Heart of Reading* as a core reading program (assuming young students are already able to read independently) or as a supplement. It is arranged into nine sections, each focused upon a different genre: biography, adventure, historical fiction, fantasy, mystery, folk tales, nonfiction, humor, and realistic fiction. You and/or your students select books representative of each genre. Because the program is structured for different levels of difficulty, you can reuse it for a number of years, even reusing the same level but having your student read different books from each genre.

The program is written for use with groups or with individual students; groups can be either your own children working at various levels or same-level groups. *Drawn into the Heart of Reading* is also a Christian character-building program that incorporates Scripture and biblical standards. For most families this means that your entire family will be reading books from the same genre, discussing and comparing similar story elements, and learning about the same character traits.

Some broader language arts skills are covered, and students do a good deal of writing, increasingly so as you move up each level. The writing assignments actually bring up one point of concern I have with the student workbooks. Workbook pages are formatted for students to fill in boxes, blanks, and circles in response to questions and instructions. However, occasionally the space allowed seems inadequate, especially in the Level 2/3 workbook. Also, young students may need to dictate some of their longer responses rather than write them themselves.

In addition to writing activities, the program incorporates a good deal of discussion, a little drawing, and lots of project ideas. This can be a strong multisensory program, depending upon which elements you choose to use.

The large, softbound teacher's guide (with lay-flat binding) features daily lesson plans with specific instructions for work to be done together with students as well as for independent work at each of the three levels. I really appreciate an extra feature found in each student book called "emergency options." On days when there is no time for the "together" activities, you can choose from these emergency options to fill in with independent assignments.

Overall, I like the flexibility of a reading program that allows parents and children to select their own reading material. The drawback to this approach is that children might be reading books with which parents are unfamiliar. Unless parents have time to also read the books, they might have trouble determining whether or not their children are identifying characters, actions, motives, plot, etc., correctly. Though children could narrate to a parent about what they are reading, the parent's ability to ask probing questions is limited. The teacher's guide *does* direct students in the first two levels to read some portions of their books aloud to parents, which helps somewhat to overcome this potential problem. Another possible strategy is for parents to provide a list of books as options—books with which they are already familiar.

Suggested questions range from simple comprehension through higher-level thinking skills. Thus, children learn to read more thoughtfully and analytically as they work through the "lessons."

I suspect that after working through a number of books using this program, parents will feel more comfortable allowing children to use unfamiliar books since children will have become accustomed to noticing key information and thinking beyond the surface of the story.

Comprehension Plus series, Levels A–F
by Dr. Diane Lapp and Dr. James Flood
Modern Curriculum Press
P.O. Box 2500
Lebanon, IN 46052
(800) 393-3156
www.pearsonlearning.com

Student workbooks: Level A—$7.95, B–D—$8.95 each, E and F—$9.50 each; teacher's guides—$11.95 each

If you choose to use real books rather than a reading program with your children, you can soothe your qualms about accountability by using a reading comprehension resource such as this series from Modern Curriculum Press. Books A through F are suggested for grade levels 1 through 6.

Student books are printed in full color. Each lesson begins with a short narrative followed by a variety of comprehension and vocabulary activities as well as some activities that stretch into areas such as grammar, map reading, and research. At the end of each lesson is a writing assignment to be done in a separate notebook. Since there are thirty lessons per book, you would likely use one per week.

Narrative selections in these books are wide ranging. While some fantasy is included, I found none of the narratives in the three books I looked through likely to be offensive to Christian parents.

Younger levels begin with concepts such as main idea and details, drawing conclusions, order of events, fantasy and reality, fact and opinion, and character. Each skill is continually developed each year at a more challenging level. At the top end of the series, students add skills in literary analysis (character, plot, theme, setting), comparing and contrasting, paraphrasing, recognizing the author's purpose and point of view, outlining, use of persuasion and propaganda, figurative language, and connotation and denotation. Most levels also work with analogies, synonyms, homonyms, and antonyms. They also cover reading of maps, tables, charts, and graphs plus using dictionaries, encyclopedias, the library, and the Internet.

While some answers are multiple choice, many are open-ended questions. That means they will take a bit longer for parents to check even though possible answers are in the teacher's guide.

Children can complete workbook lessons independently if need be, but lessons are designed to be taught. Teacher's guides have detailed lesson presentations that are very easy to use; however, you might find the presentation and discussion unnecessary. For example, there are new vocabulary words in each lesson. The teacher's guide instructs the teacher to discuss the meaning of these words with students before they tackle the vocabulary exercise, yet the student book has a glossary with definitions of these words that students can use on their own.

There are additional discussions and writing projects in the teacher's guide that are useful but not essential. The teacher's guide also has reproducible tests in a standardized test format and organizational forms for children to use for such activities as charting cause and effect, story sequence, or main ideas and details. I recommend getting a teacher's guide, then using as much as is practical in your situation.

There are other reading comprehension series that use only one-word or multiple-choice answers, but the extra writing and thinking required in this series will be more effective for developing reading skills.

Critical Thinking: Reading, Thinking, and Reasoning Skills
Harcourt Achieve, an imprint of Steck-Vaughn
P.O. Box 690789
Orlando, FL 32819
(800) 531-5015
www.HarcourtAchieve.com
$14.53 each; teacher's edition—$13.50 each

Yes, this is a critical thinking series, but it also happens to cover reading skills better than some books that are more narrowly focused. After all, analytical reading is little more than an application of critical thinking.

There are six books in the series, labeled A through F for grades 1 through 6. Books are based on Bloom's Taxonomy of Educational Objectives, which identifies six stages in developing thinking skills: comprehension, understanding, application, analysis, synthesis, and evaluation. The first two books address only the first four stages of Bloom's Taxonomy. Lessons cover five to seven different skills for each of the stages, so the comprehensiveness and variety of this series exceeds most others that typically address a narrower range of skills.

For example, under comprehension (or "knowing"), students work on classification, "real and fanciful," fact or opinion, definitions and examples, and outlining and summarizing. Under evaluation, they learn how to test generalizations, develop criteria, judge accuracy, make decisions, identify values, and identify the mood of a story. In the other stages they learn skills such as identifying main ideas, comparing and contrasting, inferring, recognizing fallacies, and drawing conclusions. You can see that some of these are typical reading skills, while others are generally relegated to specialized critical thinking classes.

Written for classroom situations, there are occasional lessons that assume a child's familiarity with the ways schools function. For example, children are asked to put four steps for getting ready for school in order. The steps are "leave home, eat and get dressed, board the school bus," and "get up." You might take such situations and have your children substitute their own steps in getting ready for school.

These are consumable workbooks, printed in two colors with some illustrations. Teacher's editions have student pages with answers overprinted. They also have a separate section with brief lesson plans. I suspect homeschool parents will not use these lesson plans very often, but some of the enrichment activity ideas found there are practical and worthwhile. In teacher's editions, there are also "School-Home Newsletters" that are intended to go home with students. These have some great activity ideas that are independent of the lessons. You should be able to use the first two levels without teacher's editions because answers are easy enough for you to figure out quickly. As you get into upper levels, however, you will probably need the teacher's editions as answer keys even if you use nothing else in them.

Children in the first two levels will probably need some direction on how to complete lessons, but older students should be able to work independently most of the time.

Progeny Press Study Guides for Literature

Progeny Press

P.O. Box 100

Fall Creek, WI 54742

(877) 776-4369

e-mail: progeny@progenypress.com

www.progenypress.com

Guides for lower elementary level—$10.99 each, guides for upper elementary and middle school levels—$14.99 each, guides for high school level—$16.99 each

Progeny Press study guides are tools for parents who want to use real books rather than reading anthologies with their children at all grade levels or for supplementing study of an anthology. These are less extensive than *Total Language Plus* in coverage of reading, composition, and spelling skills, but you can complete many more of them a year.

Although written by different authors, all come from a Christian perspective. Thus, we find questions that refer to Scripture, such as "Read Proverbs 17:17. 'A friend loves at all times, and a brother is born for adversity.' Tall John was Sarah's friend. At the end of Chapter 7, how did he comfort her?" (from *The Courage of Sarah Noble* study guide). Or another example from *The Hiding Place* study guide: "Read through 1 Corinthians 12:12–27. How does this passage reflect the importance of each individual within a church or family?"

The study guides deal with both literature as art and literature as a reflection or source of ideas, although, at the primary level, children study vocabulary and meaning with little attention to literary constructions or style. At older levels there are studies of vocabulary, literary terms, plot, etc., as well as studies about the characters, events, and ideas presented.

The format varies from one study guide to another but with many common characteristics. A synopsis and some background are first. Ideas for pre-reading (and sometimes mid- and post-reading) activities are next. Then studies are divided up to cover groups of chapters at a time. Questions go well beyond the recall level, asking students to infer meanings, identify symbolism, draw analogies, and apply principles to their own lives. Each study section has vocabulary activities along with comprehension, analysis, personal application, and thought questions. At older levels, a lengthier writing assignment completes each section. A variety of vocabulary activities are used within each guide, so the studies maintain a higher level of interest than those that use the same format for every lesson. Particularly at younger levels, guides include extra activity suggestions. For example, *The Courage of Sarah Noble* study guide includes some art, craft, game, and cooking suggestions.

Students might be able to work through the study guides independently if their reading skills are adequate, although discussion enhances any literature study. Answer keys are found at the back of each book, so each study guide is self-contained aside from the novel itself. All study guides are 8½-inch by 11-inch looseleaf and are reproducible for your family.

Within the Progeny Press series are a number of study guides geared for the primary grades. They are for books such as *Clipper Ship; The Courage of Sarah Noble; The Drinking Gourd; Frog and Toad Together; The Josefina Story Quilt; Keep the Lights Burning, Abbie; The Long Way to a New Land; Ox-Cart Man; Sam the Minuteman;* and *Wagon Wheels.* Another guide, *The Minstrel in the Tower,* straddles primary and middle grade levels.

Study guides geared for the upper elementary grades include such titles as *The Best Christmas Pageant Ever; The Bridge; The Cricket in Times Square; The Door in the Wall; Little House in the Big Woods; Sarah, Plain and Tall;* and *Charlotte's Web.*

Middle school titles stretch sometimes as low as fifth grade and up through eighth grade. Among them are *Amos Fortune, Free Man; Bridge to Terabithia; The Bronze Bow; Carry On, Mr. Bowditch; The Hiding Place; The Giver; Island of the Blue Dolphins; The Indian in the Cupboard; Johnny Tremain; The Magician's Nephew; Maniac Magee; Roll of Thunder, Hear My Cry; The Secret Garden;* and *The Lion, The Witch and the Wardrobe.*

For high school level, there are a number of study guides for both novels and plays, such as *The Red Badge of Courage; The Yearling; Heart of Darkness; Jane Eyre; The Merchant of Venice; Romeo and Juliet; Hamlet; Macbeth; Out of the Silent Planet; To Kill a Mockingbird; A Day No Pigs Would Die; The Great Gatsby; The Scarlet Letter; The Adventures of Huckleberry Finn; A Tale of Two Cities;* and *Perelandra.*

Guides for more than eighty books are available. The novels themselves are also available from Progeny Press if you need a source.

Total Language Plus

Total Language Plus, Inc.

P.O. Box 12622

Olympia, WA 98508

(360) 754-3660

e-mail: customer@totallanguageplus.com

www.totallanguageplus.com

$18.95 each, set of any four guides—$72.00

Total Language Plus "covers reading, comprehension, spelling, grammar, vocabulary, writing, listening, and analytical and critical thinking with a Christian perspective." Each volume is a student study guide/workbook that accompanies a novel. Study guides are written for various levels, from fifth grade up through twelfth. For example, the study of *Caddie Woodlawn* is suggested for grades 5 and 6 while *Anne of Green Gables* is suggested for grades 7 through 9.

Students read sections of the novel each week and answer comprehension questions. But that's only one aspect of *Total Language Plus*. The week's study also includes vocabulary work consisting of four lessons working with words drawn from the reading. There are also four activities for a list of spelling words drawn from the reading. Grammar worksheet activities include dictation exercises and grammatical work with the dictated material.

Lessons dealing with grammar, writing, and spelling rules are for application and review rather than instruction. A basic understanding is assumed. For example, since spelling words are selected from the chapter, there are no common patterns or spelling rules being covered.

Students create their own glossary toward the back of the book by entering definitions and parts of speech labels for their vocabulary words each week. At the beginning of each unit are Enrichment/Writing suggestions. These always include writing activities, but other activities depend upon the book being studied. For example, the guide for *Around the World in Eighty Days* includes map and geography work. Some activities are not tied directly to any one chapter, so you can use them when, if, and how you wish. You can select more activities to turn your study into an in-depth unit study or choose fewer and stick to the basics. You might use some of these for discussion and some for writing assignments. The activities are presented as suggestions rather than as fully developed plans, so they will require independent research and work beyond what is presented here. *Total Language Plus's* effectiveness in developing broader writing skills is dependent upon your selection of assignments from the Enrichment/Writing section as well as upon your work with your children on the writing process within those assignments.

Study guides get more challenging at high school level, especially with the addition of extensive writing activities and oral readings. I am particularly impressed with the quality of the writing activities. They teach and stress organization and planning, while offering students ideas about the main points they might wish to include. This is very helpful since this seems to be a challenging area for many students, and many parents are unsure about how to develop these writing skills. *Total Language Plus*'s writing assignments at upper levels should provide a significant part of your composition instruction.

In addition, the level of the vocabulary and spelling in advanced-level guides is quite challenging. The amount of both vocabulary and spelling practice is appropriate for high schoolers, although some students might need to work on additional vocabulary words that are at a less challenging level.

A "Note to Teachers and Students" in each book explains how to use each study guide. Answer keys are at the back of each book. Suggested responses are given for some questions, but parents really need to read the novels themselves in order to fairly evaluate all student responses as well as to be prepared for discussions. Other than that, preparation time is minimal. By the way, students will need access to a Bible, dictionary, and thesaurus for some of their work.

The number of lessons in the various volumes of *Total Language Plus* ranges from five to eight, so some books are likely to take longer to study than others. Generally, a volume should take from nine to ten weeks to complete, so plan to complete about one per quarter.

If impatient students want to read through the novel quickly rather than spread it out, they can do so covering the comprehension and critical thinking questions as they go and working through the remainder of each week's lessons on a slower schedule.

You need to obtain the novel for each study, so *Total Language Plus* sells inexpensive copies. Books have been selected to meet the needs of various age levels and interests. The catalog features brief descriptions of each novel. There are more than thirty-five guides for novels available at this time. Among the novels for which studies are available are *My Side of the Mountain*; *The Cricket in Times Square*; *The Light in the Forest*; *The Lion, the Witch and the Wardrobe*; *A Wrinkle in Time*; *Johnny Tremain*; *The Bronze Bow*; *Caddie Woodlawn*; *The Giver*; *Wheel on the School*; *The Trumpeter of Krakow*; *Where the Red Fern Grows*; *The Call of the Wild*; *The Hiding Place*; *The Swiss Family Robinson*; *Carry On, Mr. Bowditch*; *Rifles for Watie*; *Anne of Green Gables*; *The Scarlet Letter*; *Oliver Twist*; *To Kill a Mockingbird*; and *Jane Eyre*.

Three additional "anthology" guides are also available. *American Literature: Poetry* and *American Literature: Short Stories* are intended to be used along with the guides for *To Kill a Mockingbird* and *The Scarlet Letter* to comprise a high-school-level American Literature course. The *American Literature* guides include examples of poetry and short stories, but you will need to find most of the readings used along with the study guides within anthologies or on the Internet. These guides include planning schedules for completing the modules that might take from six to ten weeks each depending upon the academic needs of students and the time available.

The third anthology guide is *Christmas: Volume 1* ($15.95). It is a smaller guide covering three short stories: "A Pint of Judgment," "The Fir Tree," and "The Gift of the Magi." It is designed for multilevel use and should take about four weeks to complete. Unlike other guides, the three stories are included in the study guide.

In all guides, Scripture verses are often used for dictation, and exercises occasionally have very general Christian references, such as in the example sentence given for the word "approbation" which reads, "God bestows His approbation on all who seek to do His will" (TLP, *The Swiss Family Robinson,* p. 80).

Total Language Plus can serve as a supplement or as a primary learning tool depending upon the needs of each student. It should be your primary resource for reading skills; you do not need another reading program. It complements other instruction in grammar, composition, and spelling, except it might be your primary resource for composition at high school level.

Junior/Senior High Level

Literary analysis becomes more important with older students. There are some excellent series that use high quality literature and do a good job teaching literary analysis and appreciation. Some of my favorites use the literature as a springboard for teaching a Christian worldview.

Anthologies can be helpful for exposing students to a broad range of literary types without overwhelming them with ones they find less appealing. Some of the programs I review below use full-length books and fewer types of literature, so keep this in mind when making choices for your children. If they need broader exposure or if that better fits your educational goals, then you should use an anthology like the Bob Jones University Press books or extra resources such as the Norton Anthologies. If you would rather go in-depth on a few of the best books, then Stobaugh's or *Learning Language Arts through Literature* courses might better suit your situation.

No matter which way you go, junior and senior high school students should be reading more full-length books than are included within any program. After the reviews I've included lists of recommended reading for high school level (culled from a number of sources) that might help you make selections. Notice that some of these books are covered by study guides in the *Progeny Press* and *Total Language Plus* series reviewed above.

Bob Jones University Press literature series for grades 7–12
Bob Jones University Press
Greenville, SC 29614
(800) 845-5731
www.bjup.com

Literature courses are not all created equal. Some seem to have selected reading material to meet multicultural or social goals rather than as examples of good literature. Others seem to focus on simple comprehension questions (e.g., identify the protagonist and the antagonist) and never get into "meaty" discussion questions that really engage students.

The BJUP series for grades 7 through 12 does a great job on both ends—good literary selections and meaty questions—especially if you are interested in developing a strong Christian worldview in your students. Book in the series are *Explorations in Literature* (grade 7), *Excursions in Literature* (grade 8), *Fundamentals of Literature* (grade 9), *Elements of Literature* (grade 10), *American Literature* (grade 11), and *British Literature* (grade 12).

All feature an interesting mix of reading material. Many reading selections authored by non-Christians are included both for literary value and to help students learn how to identify different perspectives authors bring to their works. However, literary analysis and enjoyment is taught from a Protestant perspective, so much so in *American* and *British Literature* that those with other religious beliefs will have trouble with some of the selected readings, discussion questions, and the "application" part of the lessons presented in the teacher editions. Application sections at all levels almost always relate the reading selection to biblical ideas or principles.

One of the main purposes of this series is helping students progress beyond simply reading for pleasure to the point where they enjoy reading for inspiration and wisdom. Discussion questions are one of the primary tools used to make that happen.

The discussion questions are particularly good in this series, and they might be used for either oral discussion or writing assignments. At junior high level they focus more on recall and comprehension. *Fundamentals* and *Elements* shift toward more literary analysis. *American* and *British Literature* challenge students' thinking much more broadly. For example, *American Literature* includes the short story "The Minister's Black Veil" by Nathaniel Hawthorne. Among discussion questions are the following: "In your opinion, does Hooper's self-imposed isolation represent self-denial for the edification of others, or is it symbolic of misdirected religious zeal? Discuss Hawthorne's theme in light of 1 John 1:8–10" (p. 306).

Parents/teachers need to be familiar with the readings so they can lead discussions. While students can do a certain amount of work independently, parents will need to invest some time preparing for each lesson. Teacher's editions provide background, analysis, and suggested answers, so even teachers without a background in literature can teach these courses. As with all literature anthologies, parents/teachers are not expected to use every selection. Choose some from each section to fit your own goals and time schedule.

Each course has a hardbound student text and comb-bound teacher edition, with two volumes each for the teacher's editions for *American* and *British Literature*. Teacher's editions have reduced student pages printed in full color in the newest editions—*Fundamentals, American,* and *Elements of Literature*—and black-and-white in *Excursions, Explorations,* and *British Literature.* Below student pages and in side margins there is valuable teaching information. Tests and answer keys are in separate packets. Newest editions of *Elements* and *American Literature* have an extra feature in the teacher editions. Words, sentences, or paragraphs of the student text are highlighted in up to six different colors to match similarly colored notes to the teacher in the margins. They might indicate a point for discussion, a definition, an example of a literary element, or a cross-reference. I expect this helpful feature will be added to future revisions of other teacher editions. Reproducible supplemental activity pages and some teacher helps are at the back of each teacher's edition.

Reproducible tests and answer keys are available for *Fundamentals, Elements,* and *American Literature* (two separate items per course—$9.50 and $6.00 each respectively). An alternative, *TestBanks* ($19.50 per course), is a computer program from which you can select your own questions to create tests. Individual programs are available for *Explorations, Excursions,* and *British Literature,* with others in development. *TestBuilder* ($66.50) contains test questions for all courses for which *TestBanks* have been developed. Purchasers of *TestBuilder* will also have access to new banks of questions that can be downloaded from the BJUP Web site. If you plan to use at least three BJUP *TestBanks,* it makes sense to purchase *TestBuilder* instead. I personally love the flexibility of the *TestBanks/TestBuilder* since it allows me to make tests as long or as short as I desire, to focus on questions that we dwelled upon in lessons, and to easily create another test for retesting when necessary.

Explorations in Literature, second edition

Student text—$33.50, teacher's edition—$43.50, *or* set of both items—$73.50

This seventh-grade-level text covers a wide range of themes while emphasizing character. Content sections are titled Courage, Nature and Man, Generosity, Our Land, Humility, and Family. While some selections are by well-known authors (e.g., Carl Sandburg, O. Henry, Charles Finney, and James Thurber), most authors are not readily recognizable. Nevertheless, I would give a high rating to both literary quality and appeal for young teens. Selections are primarily prose, but there are some poems and one drama (a radio show script).

Excursions in Literature, second edition

Student text—$33.50, teacher's edition—$43.50, *or* set of both items—$73.50

The theme of this eighth grade text is a Christian's journey through life, including choices he must face. Illustrations from Scripture appear at the end of each unit. The text continues the character emphasis of the seventh grade book. Units are titled Choices, Friends, Viewpoints, Adventures, Discoveries, and Heroes and Villains. Some authors and writings (or excerpts) included are Lew Wallace (*Ben Hur*), Louisa May Alcott (*Little Women*), Charles Dickens (*A Christmas Carol*), Jack London (*The Banks of the Sacramento*), George MacDonald (*The Princess and Curdie*), and Amy Carmichael (*Make Me Thy Fuel*). A short novel, *In Search of Honor,* is studied in the final unit and included within the textbook. Lessons in the teacher's edition follow a format of overview, objectives, potential problems (e.g., objections to authors portraying animals as having human qualities), introductory discussion, the reading, analysis, application, and additional activities.

Fundamentals of Literature, updated version

Student text—$33.50, teacher's edition—$47.00, *or* kit with both books plus reproducible tests and key—$91.00

Suggested for grade 9, this textbook is the foundation for the study of literature. It studies conflict, character, theme, structure, point of view, and moral tone through both traditional and contemporary selections. Representative authors are Sir Arthur Conan Doyle, Lord Tennyson, Shakespeare, Carl Sandburg, Sir Walter Scott, John Donne, and Saki (H. H. Munro). The drama *Cyrano De Bergerac* is also included within the text, with a videocassette also available for $21.00.

Elements of Literature, updated version

Student text—$33.50, teacher's edition—$47.00, *or* kit with both books plus reproducible tests and key—$91.00, *Great Expectations*—$11.00, teacher's edition for *Great Expectations*—$28.50

Suggested for tenth grade, this text teaches students literary analysis at a more challenging level than *Fundamentals of Literature*. It delves into topics such as themes, allusions, symbolism, and irony, as well as teaching more about the forms of literature—fiction, poetry, biography, drama, etc. Shakespeare's *Romeo and Juliet* is included for study within the text. Study of *Great Expectations* by Charles Dickens is an optional part of the course. There is a separate teacher's edition for *Great Expectations* that includes reproductions of the student text pages as well as teaching information and helps. Time limitations will probably restrict most users to covering either *Romeo and Juliet* or *Great Expectations*, so plan accordingly.

American Literature, updated second edition

Student text—$33.50, teacher's edition—$47.00

Suggested for grade 11, this text covers American literature from the colonial period up through the twentieth century. Representative authors are William Bradford, Benjamin Franklin, Nathaniel Hawthorne, Henry David Thoreau, Herman Melville, Samuel Clemens, Thornton Wilder, and Bruce Catton. Selections are organized by historical literary periods, while addressing some of the philosophical movements that influenced literature. There is significant discussion of the worldviews reflected by authors and their works.

British Literature, second edition

Student text—$33.50, teacher's edition—$47.00

This twelfth grade course covers eight literary periods from Old English to Modern. Selections are often chosen to illustrate philosophical and cultural issues from various perspectives. Religious developments receive far more attention here than they do in other British literature texts. Representative authors include John Wycliffe, Geoffrey Chaucer, Thomas More, Shakespeare, Ben Jonson, William Wordsworth, and Robert Browning. The play *Macbeth* is also included for study.

Encouraging Thoughtful Christians to be World Changers series

by Dr. James P. Stobaugh
Broadman & Holman Publishers
127 Ninth Avenue North
Nashville, TN 37234
(800) 251-3225
www.broadmanholman.com

NOTE: Stobaugh's books have now been reedited and enhanced with DVDs that make these courses even better!

Dr. James Stobaugh has done a marvelous job of combining literature studies, composition, speech, vocabulary, and critical thinking, all within a Christian worldview context. Interestingly, Dr. Stobaugh manages to incorporate worldview concepts in the broad manner of C. S. Lewis so that no particular theological or denominational outlook dominates. Aside from only occasional and minor exceptions, lesson two of each book is devoted to the worldview exploration.

These courses should appeal to those trying to implement classical education not limited to the Great Books list, to those wanting to prepare their teens with challenging and rigorous coursework, and to those for whom worldview education is a high priority.

Stobaugh couples thorough development of writing and speaking skills with an analytical approach to literature. The first two books focus on basic skills in these areas that are then applied through all three literature courses. The first two books might be used in junior high or early high school, but each will take at least a year to complete.

Each book has thirty-four or thirty-five week-long lessons. Detailed lesson plans are provided for a year-long schedule for each course, but you might need to take longer to complete some of these lessons, especially if you are beginning in junior high and/or students do not already have fairly good reading and composition skills.

The series consists of the following books: *Skills for Literary Analysis*, *Skills for Rhetoric*, *American Literature*, *British Literature*, and *World Literature*.

All courses have both a teacher and student edition. The student editions of the *Skills* books allow students to work fairly independently through a good deal of their work since lesson plan schedules, background information, and examples are provided. However, these courses *do* require interaction, discussion, evaluation of papers and speeches. Two or more students working together would work best, but if that isn't possible, most of the lesson assignments can still be used with parents serving as audiences and reviewers.

The teacher editions add tests plus summaries or suggested responses for student questions and assignments, which are typically essays. All teacher's editions are essential.

All these courses require a great deal of writing and reading—daily journal writing, daily warm-up essays, analytical essays, biblical application essays, research papers, and tests. Each course can be adapted to the needs of the individual student. Parents can choose to include or omit any particular unit in the literature series.

The reading requirement seems to be a minimum of about two hundred pages per week—and it's often not light reading.

Some of the books suggest the use of a basic English grammar/writing style manual that can be used throughout these courses as well as in further academic pursuits. *Hodge's Harbrace College Handbook*, the *Bedford Handbook for Writers*, *Warriner's Handbook*, *MLA Style Manual*, and *The Gregg Reference Manual* are possibilities you might consider. While a writing style/grammar handbook is optional, I highly recommend that each student have a copy handy for reference.

Skills for Rhetoric, $24.99

Skills for Rhetoric focuses on developing skill in writing and speaking—the presentation of ideas through language. Stobaugh recommends it for students in grades eight through nine, but it assumes a higher level of learning than is typical of most students in those grades. I would also recommend it for older students.

Like Stobaugh's literature courses, *Rhetoric* stresses the importance of preparing young people for leadership by building a foundation of spiritual and academic strength. You will find worldview ideas throughout this text. Journal writing frequently requires reflection upon specified Scripture verses.

Each week-long lesson teaches a type of essay, beginning with an example of that essay. Warm-up essay topics are provided, and students are encouraged to tackle each of these daily. Students create vocabulary cards to work on learning the new words. A particular style issue, such as correct usage of "can" or "may" is reviewed. Students are required to read thirty-five to fifty pages a day from recommended reading lists. All of this is in addition to the major speeches—both extemporaneous and prepared—and essays assigned each week.

Students write every day. Between journal entries, daily essays, and other assignments, they do far more writing than in any other course that comes to my mind. Among the types of writing assignments: eyewitness account, summary report, character profile, analysis, historical profile, literary analysis, cause/effect, problem/solution, and evaluation. An extensive research paper with bibliography is an assignment through the last eleven lessons.

Stobaugh includes forms for some of the analytical assignments and for evaluation.

The biggest problem with *Rhetoric* is finding the appropriate time to use it if you also want to complete all of Stobaugh's literature courses since each requires a good deal of time and energy.

Skills for Literary Analysis, $24.99

While the five-year plan for this series suggests beginning with this book in eighth grade then using Skills for Rhetoric, you might reverse that order if you wish. Both courses can be used by students eighth grade or above. Some of the assigned reading excerpts are reprinted within the book, but you will have to obtain others. Among literary pieces for this study are *The Call of the Wild,* the Joseph narrative from Genesis, "Idylls of the King," *Alice in Wonderland, Screwtape Letters, Silas Marner, Anne of Green Gables, Ivanhoe,* and "The Midnight Ride of Paul Revere."

American Literature, $24.99

The second lesson in this book (and the second lesson in all other books in this series) helps students develop their own worldview, which is then applied to reading assignments throughout the lessons.

Like most high school literature courses, this one includes many short stories and other short readings, such as "Sinners in the Hands of An Angry God" and poems by Edwin Arlington Robinson and Ralph Waldo Emerson. Unlike other courses, however, it also requires students to read a number of complete books. Among them are *The Scarlet Letter, The Adventures of Huckleberry Finn, Billy Budd, Ethan Frome,*

The Red Badge of Courage, A Farewell to Arms, The Unvanquished, and *A Separate Peace.* A few of the short stories and poems are included within these volumes, but you will need to acquire most of the books yourself, including an anthology such as *The Norton Anthology of American Literature* for other short pieces. However, Stobaugh makes Web site addresses available for parents and students to use for acquiring poems, short stories, and even some books online.

Occasionally one book or reading is studied for two weeks, but generally each book or reading is to be read before each week's lesson. The lesson then focuses on critical thinking and "challenge" questions, with responses taking the form of essays and reports. Lessons vary in format including such things as background on the author or setting, recall questions, vocabulary words, literary analysis, and biblical/ worldview applications. Stobaugh's suggested answers help parents better understand how to discuss philosophical/worldview ideas as well as the literature.

British Literature, $24.99

Similar in format to Stobaugh's *American Literature,* this is a survey of British literature from the earliest Anglo-Saxon writings through the twentieth century. It also addresses worldview in the second lesson as a context for future lessons.

It begins with the narrative Anglo-Saxon poem "The Seafarer" and continues with ballads, poetry, sonnets, plays, short stories, essays, novels, and nonfiction books. Examples of the range of authors are Geoffrey Chaucer, Edmund Spenser, Shakespeare, Ben Jonson, Francis Bacon, George Herbert, John Milton, Daniel Defoe, Jonathan Swift, William Blake, John Henry Newman, Robert and Elizabeth Browning, C. S. Lewis, J. R. R. Tolkien, and T. S. Eliot.

Some of the shorter literary pieces are reprinted within the volume, but you should also purchase an anthology such as the two-volume *The Norton Anthology of English Literature.* Plan ahead to make sure you have the necessary literary pieces on hand before you begin the pertinent lessons.

Students are encouraged to read complete writings, although they are not always required to do so for each study. Stobaugh stresses composition skills, suggesting that students write for one hour per day. Stobaugh addresses literary elements through brief instruction and analytical questions. Worldview and faith issues come up frequently throughout the lessons, and most lessons also include one or more "Biblical Application" assignments.

World Literature, $24.99

Classical educators will find the Great Books well represented within this volume that includes study of *The Gilgamesh Epic, The Iliad* and *The Odyssey,* Plato's *Republic* and *The Death of Socrates, Oedipus Rex, The Aeneid,* Augustine's *Confessions,* the *Divine Comedy, Faust* by Goethe, *War and Peace,* and *Crime and Punishment.* In addition, students study writings of early church fathers, Scripture passages, and works by Chekhov, Camus, Ibsen, Remarque, and Paton. Some of the shorter writings are included in the book, but you will need to obtain copies of other literature. Many of these might be found on the Internet.

Learning Language Arts through Literature, Gold Books—American Literature and British Literature

Common Sense Press

Publisher sells only through distributors. Contact them for resellers in your area.

(352) 475-5757

e-mail: info@commonsensepress.com

www.commonsensepress.com

The *Gold Books,* written by Dr. Greg Strayer and Timothy Nichols (co-author only on *British Literature*) for high school level, are very different from other *Learning Language Arts through Literature* books reviewed in chapter 9. There are two *Gold Books*—one for British literature and one for American literature.

These books are written in units rather than as individual lessons, with students reading entire poems and pieces of literature rather than small excerpts.

In *American Literature,* students read from *Great American Short Stories, The Mentor Book of Major American Poets, The Red Badge of Courage, The Pearl,* and *The Old Man and the Sea.* A Bible and a concordance are required. *British Literature* requires *Frankenstein, Emma, A Tale of Two Cities, The Time Machine, Animal Farm,* and *The Mentor Book of Major British Poets.* You can use the books in whichever order you prefer.

Students study the elements of fiction and poetry as well as how to analyze the particular pieces. All of this is done within the context of a Christian worldview, but worldview study does not dominate as much as in Stobaugh's courses.

Writing assignments range from simple answers to essays, with significant attention given to essay writing. Discussion is an essential part of the learning process, so parents should also read the literature so they can lead the discussion. Suggested answers to questions are provided on pages following each set of questions.

These are excellent college preparatory courses. Other than the reading material, each course is self-contained within one nonconsumable book. Students do their writing in a separate notebook or on the computer.

I need to add a short note on *Norton Anthologies* since I mention them a number of times. There are a number of literary anthologies (priced from $35.00 to $40.00 each) published by Norton, including *Norton Anthology of English Literature, Norton Anthology of American Literature* (two volumes), *The Norton Anthology of World Masterpieces* (two volumes), *Norton Anthology of Literature by Women, Norton Anthology of Poetry,* and others.

These books emphasize classical selections unlike most anthologies written for high school students. Commentary is included, although it is written at college/adult level. Various editions of these books have been printed over many years, so it is fairly easy to find them in used bookstores at fantastic prices.

These are great for families who want to introduce their children to a wide variety of literary types, but who want to make their own selections. There are so many choices in these hefty books that you will certainly find plenty of selections to suit your purposes. Many selections are complete plays, complete books, or significant excerpts, which is made possible by use of small print and thin paper plus the fact that books range from about 1,500 to 2,500 pages each!

These are not high school level texts! I used them as resource books as does James Stobaugh. Parents need to select readings and guide discussion and assignments in some fashion rather than just handing these books to students to read on their own.

The books are nonsectarian, so commentary focuses on literary and historical background plus biographical information on authors.

Norton Anthologies

W. W. Norton and Co.

(800) 223-2584

www.wwnorton.com

Recommended Reading for High-School-Level Literature

The following are taken primarily from core literature recommendations for high school students, but I have added some titles I think important from a Christian perspective. Some of the listed titles are recommended by schools but are not necessarily titles I would recommend.

- *The Adventures of Huckleberry Finn* and other works by Mark Twain
- *The Aeneid* of Virgil
- *Alice's Adventures in Wonderland* by Lewis Carroll
- *All Quiet on the Western Front* by Erich Maria Remarque
- *All the King's Men* by Robert Penn Warren
- *Anna Karenina, War and Peace*, and other works by Leo Tolstoy
- *Anne Frank: Diary of a Young Girl* by Anne Frank
- *Anne of Green Gables* and other titles by Lucy Maud Montgomery
- *Billy Budd, Moby Dick*, and other works by Herman Melville
- *Black Like Me* by John Howard Griffin
- *Brave New World* by Aldous Huxley
- *Canterbury Tales* by Geoffrey Chaucer
- "The Charge of the Light Brigade" and other works by Alfred Lord Tennyson

- *The Chosen* by Chaim Potok
- *Christy* by Catherine Marshall
- *Crime and Punishment* by Fyodor Dostoyevsky
- *Cry the Beloved Country* by Alan Paton
- *David Copperfield, Great Expectations, A Tale of Two Cities*, and other works by Charles Dickens
- *The Death of Socrates* and other works by Plato
- "The Devil and Daniel Webster" and other works by Stephen Vincent Benet
- *The Divine Comedy* by Dante
- *Don Quixote* by Miguel de Cervantes
- *Exodus* by Leon Uris
- *A Farewell to Arms* by Ernest Hemingway
- *The Good Earth* by Pearl Buck
- *The Grapes of Wrath, The Pearl, The Red Pony, Of Mice and Men*, and other works by John Steinbeck
- *The Great Divorce, Screwtape Letters*, and *Mere Christianity* by C. S. Lewis
- *The Great Gatsby* by F. Scott Fitzgerald
- *Gulliver's Travels* and other works by Jonathan Swift
- *The Guns of August* by Barbara W. Tuchman
- *Hamlet, Henry V, Macbeth, A Midsummer Night's Dream, Othello, The Merchant of Venice*, and other works by William Shakespeare
- "The Hollow Men" and other works by T. S. Eliot
- *The Hound of the Baskervilles* and other works by Sir Arthur Conan Doyle
- *The Iliad* and *The Odyssey* by Homer
- *In His Steps* by Charles M. Sheldon
- *The Invisible Man* by Ralph Ellison
- *Jane Eyre* by Charlotte Brontë
- "The Legend of Sleepy Hollow" and other works by Washington Irving
- *Lés Miserables* by Victor Hugo
- *The Life and Times of Frederick Douglass* by Frederick Douglass
- *The Light in the Forest* by Conrad Richter
- *Little Women* by Louisa May Alcott
- *A Man for All Seasons* by Robert Bolt
- *The Marquis' Secret* and other works by George MacDonald (updated versions)
- *Martian Chronicles* and other works by Ray Bradbury
- *Men of Iron* by Howard Pyle
- *The Miracle Worker* by William Gibson

- *Moby Dick* by Herman Melville
- *1984* and *Animal Farm* by George Orwell
- *Oedipus Rex, Antigone,* and other plays by Sophocles
- *One Day in the Life of Ivan Denisovitch* by Aleksandr Solzhenitsyn
- "Ozymandias" and other works by Percy Bysshe Shelley
- *Paradise Lost* by John Milton
- *Perelandra, Out of the Silent Planet,* and other works by C. S. Lewis
- *Pilgrim's Progress* by John Bunyan
- "The Pit and the Pendulum" and other works by Edgar Allen Poe
- *Pride and Prejudice* by Jane Austen
- *The Prince* by Niccolo Machiavelli
- *The Princess Bride* by William Goldman
- *Pygmalion* by George Bernard Shaw
- *A Raisin in the Sun* by Lorraine Hansberry
- "The Road Not Taken" and other works by Robert Frost
- *Robinson Crusoe* by Daniel Defoe
- *The Scarlet Letter* by Nathaniel Hawthorne
- *Silas Marner* by George Elliott
- *The Spy* and other works by James Fenimore Cooper
- *Stranger in a Strange Land* by Robert A. Heinlein
- "Tiger, Tiger" and other poems by William Blake
- *The Time Machine* by H. G. Wells
- *To Kill a Mockingbird* by Harper Lee
- *Treasure Island, Kidnapped,* and other works by Robert Louis Stevenson
- *A Tree Grows in Brooklyn* by Betty Smith
- *The Lord of the Rings Trilogy* by J. R. R. Tolkein
- *Twenty Thousand Leagues under the Sea, Around the World in Eighty Days,* and other works by Jules Verne
- *Uncle Tom's Cabin* by Harriet Beecher Stowe
- *Wuthering Heights* by Emily Brontë
- *The Yearling, Cross Creek,* and other works by Marjorie K. Rawlings

Obviously, the above list is not comprehensive. You might also want to focus more on the Great Books, only a few of which are included in the above list. You might want to refer to the Great Books lists on the Internet at addresses listed on p. 17 or the Great Books lists for St. John's College's Great Books program, which can be found at http://home.comcast.net/~antaylor1/greatbooksstjohns.htm.

8

Mathematics

My top picks for math are a diverse assortment to suit different situations and learning styles. Since I've had to be selective, I have narrowed my choices to resources that fit the largest number of children.

You might notice that I have not included programs from A Beka or Bob Jones University Press (BJUP), and I should explain why. A Beka's math program is very traditional, does an excellent job developing computation skills, and has more than enough review and practice. Explanation of new concepts is included within student worktexts, so students can work independently most of the time. However, the series is weak in developing conceptual understanding, especially in comparison to programs like *Math-U-See* and *Singapore Math*. Curriculum guides offer some teaching assistance, but my experience is that homeschoolers rarely use them. Instead, they are more likely to purchase only the teacher editions that serve as answer keys. Some children are strong enough conceptual thinkers that A Beka still works very well for them.

In contrast, BJUP's math program is strong on conceptual development. The drawback with their program is that it needs to be taught from the teacher's edition—this is not a program for independent study. The teacher's editions include teaching strategies that explain concepts and address different learning styles. While this is very helpful, it also means that it takes longer to get through a lesson, either in planning and selecting what to use or in actually doing the lesson with your child. Consequently, I find that too many homeschoolers try to shortcut by just handing their children the workbook without adequate instruction. If you have time to use the program correctly, it is very good.

I have also left out the University of Chicago School Mathematics Project (UCSMP) math program from ScottForesman. This is one of the very best high-school-level math programs; however, it needs to be taught, and it assumes that the teacher has a good math background. Lack of time or expertise makes it very difficult for many homeschooling families to use. However, if you have a good supply of both, you should check it out at http://social-sciences.uchicago.edu/ucsmp/Secondary.html

Supplements

Narrowing down to the top hundred resources meant skipping all the wonderful supplemental items. This was especially frustrating when it came to math since there are so many great supplements that you really might need to use. You can check the Web site at www.CathyDuffyReviews.com for reviews of many math-related resources, but meanwhile, the following are a few ideas to consider. All of these type supplements can be found at teacher supply stores, homeschool stores and catalogs, and directly from their publishers.

• Focused topical books: When children struggle with a particular topic or skill, they often need to get a better understanding of the concept itself. Supplemental books are often the solution. The *Key to . . .* series workbooks from Key Curriculum Press are an example of this sort of thing. They have excellent series on *Fractions, Decimals, Measurement,* and *Geometry* (www.keypress.com). Other publishers offer single books on such topics.

• Computer-based computation drill programs: I hate to mention any single program since there are so many good ones. This is one area where computers are really useful. Drill can be so boring, but the computer can jazz things up, put it into a game format, add color, and make it fun.

• *Cuisenaire® Rods, Base Ten Blocks®,* and other manipulatives can be used as supplements alongside more traditional programs. If your children do not need *Math-U-See*'s immersion in manipulatives, it can be relatively inexpensive to purchase these other manipulatives and a few resource books on how to use them to teach particular concepts. *Cuisenaire* actually has some activity books for working with the rods that are just plain fun.

• Games: many traditional games like Monopoly and Life have quite a bit of math built in. Other games have been developed specifically to focus on math skills. Check homeschool distributors, educational product stores, and the catalogs below for ideas.

• Supplemental activity books: Some children love to do activity pages when the math practice is linked to a dot-to-dot picture, puzzle, or something that provides motivation for figuring out the correct answers. Drill and review in such formats is much more appealing than what is generally offered in math textbooks.

Some of the best catalogs that specialize in math supplements are:

Activities for Learning, (888) 272-3291, www.Alabacus.com

Creative Teaching Associates, (800) 767-4282, www.mastercta.com

Dale Seymour Publications, (800) 526-9907, www.pearson
learning.com/dalesey/dalesey_default.cfm

Learning Resources, (800) 333-8281, www.learningresources.com

Nasco Math, (800) 558-9595, www.eNasco.com

Programs

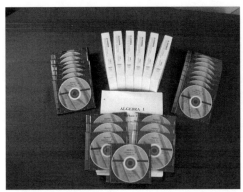

Algebra
by Leonard Firebaugh
Keyboard Enterprises
5200 Heil, #32
Huntington Beach, CA 92649
(800) 737-6284
(714) 840-8004
e-mail: info@mathrelief.com
www.mathrelief.com

Videotapes: $49.95 or $69.95 per phase; DVDs $69.95 per phase, $209.85 for full course

Reports I consistently hear from parents are that their children really understand algebra when they go through this course. It may not be exciting or colorful, but it really works.

This set of videos with accompanying worksheets and answer keys comprises a complete first-year algebra course and then some. Presentation is definitely not exciting, but it moves along at a steady pace without wasting time. Firebaugh uses a whiteboard to demonstrate problem solving, explaining concepts clearly as he goes.

Each video lesson presentation (145 in all) takes about fifteen minutes, then students practice on worksheets for about thirty to forty-five minutes. Answer keys showing full solutions are included as well as tests. About eight hundred pages of worksheets, solutions, and tests come with the course. No parent preparation or participation is necessary. Students can work independently through all course work.

The complete course consists of three groups of tapes, listed on the order form as Phase One, Phase Two, and Phase Three. One benefit of the "phase arrangement" is that you can purchase Phase One, try it out, then decide whether to invest in the complete program. A more important benefit is that you can use only Phases One and Two for a slower student who does not intend to pursue algebra any further. The material covered in the first two parts will still be sufficient for a first-year algebra course. Students who complete all three phases will have covered some coordinate geometry along with many Algebra 2 concepts.

The cost for videos varies according to different quality options for each phase—choices of good or better quality reproduction tapes. The better quality has improved clarity and is recorded on more tapes. (Compare these to taping on your VCR at varying speeds.) Of course, DVDs are the best quality reproduction, so they make the most sense as long as you have a DVD player or computer that can run them. When you think about the cost, keep in mind that the videos or DVDs are not consumable, and you can reuse or resell them.

Overall, this is a time- and cost-effective solution even though it lacks polish.

Firebaugh is also just completing *Geometry* and *Algebra II* courses. Contact Keyboard Enterprises for information about availability.

The Algebra 1 Classmate

Classmate, L.L.C.
3535 Westheimer, Suite 215
Houston, TX 77027
(800) 579-0470
e-mail: info@classmate.net
www.classmate.net/homeschool
$74.50 per course

Teacher Mike Maggart created the first in this series of CD-ROM based courses, *Algebra 1*, based upon his teaching experience at a rigorous private school in Houston, Texas. He then tested and developed it through actual use in a number of schools. Although developed through traditional school settings, it works especially well in independent tutorial situations such as homeschooling.

Algebra 1 and *Prealgebra* are available thus far, with *Geometry* and *Algebra 2* yet to come. Programs are delivered via CD-ROMs that run on either Windows (Win 95 or higher) or Mac (OS 7 or higher). These programs are very easy to use; there's no installation required. Just pop in the CD and it runs.

I'll begin with *Algebra 1* since it was the first Classmate course I reviewed. For *Algebra 1*, eleven CDs come in a compact, zip-up case. Three levels of tests for every unit as well as solutions for problems in the program are available either on an optional twelfth CD or in the "instructor's tools" section of the publisher's Web site.

In addition, the "E-book" feature in the software allows the student to print out summary notes for every chapter plus sets of extra practice problems. There are five thousand printable problems plus another one thousand printable problems designed for discussion. I suspect the notes feature will be especially useful for quick review if students print out these pages and store them in a binder.

The program incorporates both audio and video with interactive problem solving, help, solutions, and quizzes (both on-screen and printable) for a complete, self-contained course. CDs each focus on one or two topics: simplifying, equations, word problems, functions, linear equations, systems of equations, polynomials, factoring, rational expressions and equations, inequalities and absolute value, radicals, and quadratic equations.

Think of each CD as being equivalent to a textbook unit, with a number of chapters within each unit. Each CD has a number of "chapter" sections representing subtopics, with each of those units divided into lessons and quizzes.

Each lesson is accessed by clicking on examples shown to the left of the video screen. Each example brings up a short video presentation of Mr. Maggart teaching the concept on a whiteboard. Another button allows students to view and/or print out a screen summarizing key concepts for the section.

Buttons at the bottom give students seven or eight practice problems on the section topic—1,100 practice problems altogether. For each problem, students have immediate access to visual hints, audio explanation, written explanation, and the correct answer. Practice problems are actually worked on paper rather than on screen. Then students push a button to get the answer and compare it with their own. Additional problems (from a database of 5,000 more problems) are available as a printout; answers for the odd problems are printed upside down on the printout. Complete solutions for odd and even problems are included on an optional twelfth CD. (Tests and solutions are also available at the password protected "instructor's tools" pages at Classmate's Web site.) There are also some "deep thought" problems for those who need a greater challenge.

There is a self-test for each "chapter" and a quiz at the end of each unit, both of which are computer scored. The student's score can then be sent over the Internet to an online gradebook that has been set up by the parent. Parents can then access the gradebook from any computer hooked up to the Internet without having to use the program disk. Students can retake tests, and the gradebook tracks each version of the self-test and each student score. The gradebook feature combined with the printout tests make it easy to check if students are mastering the material when they are working independently.

With 140 interactive lessons and all of the problem solving, this amounts to a tremendous amount of material for instruction and practice. Students can do as much or as little on a topic as needed (or required by parents), and they can choose from some or all of the options for practice problems. The program is very nicely put together and provides one of the most thorough yet easy-to-use options I've seen.

Prealgebra is the second course produced by Classmate. The format and interface is identical to that for *Algebra 1;* however, the teacher for this course is Ms. Gruber. There are fewer units, but more chapters per unit, all contained on nine CD-ROMs. This course is actually quite challenging, reflecting the National Council of Teachers of Mathematics standards. This is especially evident in the last three units on geometry, measurement, and probability and statistics.

Neither of these two courses could be described as entertaining. Material is presented without embellishment or personal comment. Perhaps a need to keep the audio and video within certain limits forced them to cut out anything extraneous. That means that despite the audio and video, these programs lack the personal feel you get from courses such as Steve Demme's *Math-U-See*. On the other hand, students who want "Just the facts, Ma'am" should find the efficiency a plus.

I was able to preview part of *Classmate's Geometry* course that is still in development. *Geometry* is taught by Mrs. Vandersea on about nine CD-ROMs. It uses a traditional approach to geometry, introducing two-column proofs in the first unit. Unfortunately from what I saw, this course seems a bit dry in comparison to some of the other geometry courses available. There is no construction activity by students. Concepts are presented with minimal practical application.

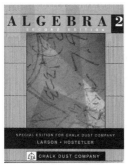

Chalk Dust Math Courses
by Dana Mosely
Chalk Dust Company
11 Sterling Court
Sugar Land, TX 77479
(800) 588-7564
e-mail: sales@chalkdust.com
www.chalkdust.com

Professor Dana Mosely is your video instructor in this outstanding series of math courses for sixth grade through early college levels. High production quality and skillful presentation combine to make these top-notch video courses. Mosely's many years of teaching experience are obvious as he clarifies commonly confusing issues. He keeps the presentation moving at just the right pace, although students can always rewind and review if they don't catch it the first time around.

Courses like these are critical for many families who are deciding whether or not they can handle homeschooling through high school. These courses really do allow students to work independently, which means parents who never went beyond Algebra 1 can still provide their children with a solid math education.

Parents with weak math backgrounds should love these courses since they really do the teaching for you. Even better, purchase of a course entitles students to free technical assistance from Professor Mosely. (Those who purchase complete used courses can pay a $50.00 fee for consultation service per student, per course, per year.)

Courses start with *Basic Math* (sixth grade level) and continue through *Calculus I*. (Chalk Dust also produces *SAT Math Review*, which is not included in this review.) Each course has six to sixteen video tapes; DVDs are also available for all courses. The number of tapes or DVDs per course reflects both the size of textbooks and the complexity of concepts taught.

All courses include a textbook and solution guide. Mosely follows the textbook lessons in order of presentation, with the exception being the geometry course. In that course, Mosely provides different approaches to some topics. In all the courses, he usually expands upon the textbook presentation, sometimes adding his own learning strategies to the lessons. He covers the main concepts, then works out sample problems on a chalkboard with an occasional computer graphic or graphing calculator illustration.

Students should watch a section of the video, then go to the text and work about thirty exercise problems in that particular section in the book. Each section requires about two days to complete. In most of the texts there are far more problems than most students will ever need to complete, so use discretion in assigning exercises. *Chalk Dust* includes a missive with each course explaining how to assign problems.

The textbooks are from Houghton Mifflin, and the lead author on most of them is Ron Larson, one of the most respected and prolific math authors in the United States. However, the *Basic Math* text is authored by Aufmann, Barker, and Lockwood, and these authors are also responsible for the *Prealgebra* text. Some texts are identical to those used in schools, while some have been published as special editions for Chalk Dust. *Algebra 1* and *2* texts are softbound standard with a hardbound option for an extra $20.00.

The textbooks are designed for classroom teachers, so they do not function well on their own for homeschooling students. However, the combination of video presentations and solution guides with the texts results in excellent courses that work well for independent study.

This series of texts is strong on real-life applications and word problems that enhance conceptual understanding. They include calculator use at all levels. In addition to lessons, examples, and practice problems, textbooks also have reviews and tests.

The softbound solution guides for all courses include complete solutions to all problems, with the exception of guides for *Trigonometry* and *College Algebra*. Their guides are student editions that have worked-out solutions to the odd problems from student exercises, although they have all solutions for test questions. Solution guides are a valuable component in these courses. You can purchase components separately, but you really need all three components—text, videos, and solution guide.

Chalk Dust's Web site has short demos of programs available for free viewing, so you can check them out before purchasing. An "evaluation tape" (volume 1 of the series) can be ordered for any program if you agree to return it within thirty days. Full-set orders include a thirty-day money back guarantee, a one-year VHS tape replacement warranty, and a thirty-day DVD warranty. Also available on the Chalk Dust Web site (www.chalkdust.com) is information about creating tests (if you need to retest from time to time), grading tests, and assigning test and course grades.

Basic Math (2003)

6 videos or 2 DVDs, text, and solutions guide—$225.00

The text for this course is Houghton Mifflin's *Basic Math, Second Edition*, by Aufmann, Barker, and Lockwood, but it is a special edition published for Chalk Dust. The course functions well for remediation or reteaching of basic concepts students might not have mastered at earlier levels.

While Chalk Dust lists it as a sixth grade course, it is not a complete course by some standards because topics such as geometry, area, volume, and integers are not included. The Chalk Dust course covers basic concepts and operations, including exponents and order of operations with whole numbers, fractions, and decimals. It also covers ratio and proportion, percents, and graphs. Also, new to this edition are the topics of statistics, probability, U.S. customary units of measurement, and the metric system of measurement.

Many practical applications appear in examples and word problems, and an entire chapter is devoted to business and consumer math skills such as percent calculations in making purchases, computing interest, calculating the cost of buying a home or car, calculating wages, and balancing a checkbook.

Although the course is not typical of sixth grade math due to the omission of several topics mentioned above, those topics are covered in the next Chalk Dust course, *Prealgebra,* so *Basic Math* may be regarded as a foundation in the basics necessary for upper level work.

I would use it with an average student at seventh grade or higher who needs remediation before going on to a grade level course. A four-function calculator might be used along with this course, but it's not absolutely essential. If you are looking ahead, you might want to go ahead and purchase a TI-83 Plus graphing calculator since it can be used with all courses.

Prealgebra (2002)

10 videos or 6 DVDs, text, and solutions guide—$335.00

This prealgebra course is fairly similar in content to *Saxon's Algebra 1/2.* The text is *Prealgebra, Second Edition,* by Aufmann, Barker, and Lockwood, published especially for Chalk Dust Company by Houghton Mifflin Company.

This approximately 650-page, hardcover textbook includes instruction, examples, exercises, tests, and answers to odd-numbered problems in the exercises. It comes with a softcover *Complete Student Solutions Manual* that contains step-by-step solutions to both even- and odd-numbered problems.

The text first reviews basic math skills and concepts, including exponents and radicals, before moving on to topics such as polynomials, first-degree equations, the rectangular coordinate system, measurement, proportion, percent, geometry, statistics, and probability. Even though this level of math covers many algorithms with no immediate applications, this text still includes many word problems and practical applications.

Periodically, lessons include mention of how to use a scientific calculator, with a few questions directing students to perform calculator operations. Calculator use is introduced at this level, and students should use a scientific or graphing calculator with the course.

Courses such as this used to be considered eighth grade level, but the new math standards have advanced the math agenda, so this is now considered seventh grade level in most states.

Algebra 1 (2001)

11 videos or 6 DVDs, text, and solutions guide—$354.00

The text for this course is *Algebra 1* by Larson and Hostetler in a special edition published for Chalk Dust. This is a traditional course targeted toward the average student. Mosely's thorough presentations plus the combination of video instruction with textbook reinforcement should make it easy for most students to master algebra while working independently through the course. In addition, the solution guide will help when both students and parents are stumped.

While this text does not incorporate geometry instruction (as does *Saxon*) it does include algebraic applications in geometry. (Chalk Dust offers a separate *Geometry* course, as do most publishers.) The *Algebra 1* course has lessons and exercises for using a graphing calculator. In addition, the book's appendix adds sections on graphing calculators, geometry, and statistics, but the appendix sections are not included on video.

Algebra 2 (2001)

14 videos or 8 DVDs, textbook, and solutions guide—$429.00

The textbook for this course is *Algebra 2* by Larson and Hostetler in a special second edition published for Chalk Dust Company. Mosely closely follows the lessons as presented in the textbook. Many first-year algebra concepts are reviewed at length, a boon for students who have taken geometry after one year of algebra and need a refresher. The solution guide covers all the problems.

The scope and sequence is a bit different from some other Algebra 2 courses. While it covers functions at length along with radicals, inequalities, conic sections, systems of equations, matrices, and logarithms, it does not even introduce trigonometry. The inclusion of elementary trigonometry techniques is a relatively recent trend in Algebra 2 courses, and Chalk Dust follows the more traditional approach in offering trigonometry as a separate and much more comprehensive course.

Instructions for using a TI-83 graphing calculator are part of the video instruction and also appear in a separate section in the appendix. Additional calculator information appears as "technology tips" in sidebars throughout the book. Occasionally, video lessons actually show the calculator and its screen so that students can use their own calculators and follow along performing operations.

In my opinion, this is the most practical solution for covering Algebra 2 unless parents are great at math and have time to teach it themselves. Even though the cost seems high, keep in mind that everything can be used with other children, then resold when you are finished, or you could share a set of tapes with another family.

College Algebra (2001)

12 videos or 9 DVDs, textbook, and solutions guide—$409.00

The *College Algebra* textbook is by Larson and Hostetler. The text follows the same format as do Larson's other algebra books. As you might have guessed from the course title, *College Algebra* is really a college course rather than a high school course. However, you might use it after *Algebra 2* or, in exceptional cases, instead of *Algebra 2*.

The course reviews much of the material covered in *Algebra 2* but takes it to a deeper level in most instances and at a more rapid pace. For example, in the section on graphing equations, you encounter new types of equations and graphs. In the study of functions, you will encounter more complex functions than you did previously.

It might be possible for outstanding *Algebra 1* students to skip *Algebra 2* and move directly into this text, but for most students it should follow an Algebra 2 course. Some students will be able to skip the first section of the course that reviews fundamental concepts of algebra.

The solution guide for this course is actually a student edition, so complete solutions are shown for only odd problems from student exercises (this is typical of college math textbooks). All test solutions are shown.

Although the course is titled *College Algebra*, it is only a little more challenging than *Algebra 2*. In comparison to *Saxon*'s math series, the content of *College Algebra* is somewhat equivalent to algebra coverage in *Saxon*'s *Advanced Math*. However, *Saxon* also covers geometry and trigonometry, which this course does not. Chalk Dust offers separate *Geometry* and *Trigonometry* courses and also covers trigonometry within its *Precalculus* course. On the other hand, this course covers statistics and probability, which receive little attention in *Saxon*, and it also has more coverage on conic sections. The use of a graphing calculator is highly recommended, but the course can be completed without one.

College-bound students who do not need calculus and trigonometry will have a very solid math background if they continue algebra studies through this course. Students completing the Chalk Dust *College Algebra* course should be able to test out of college algebra at the college of their choice.

College-bound students interested in an engineering or science degree are advised to take the Chalk Dust *Precalculus* course, which covers topics in both the *Trigonometry* and *College Algebra* courses plus other material. An additional benefit of taking *Precalculus* rather than *Trigonometry* and *College Algebra* separately is the cost: $514.00 for *Precalculus* versus $818.00 for the other two courses.

Geometry

11 videos or 7 DVDs, textbook, and solutions guide—$399.00

This course reflects the positive side of what the standards movement in education has been trying to accomplish. The approach used in this course, which aligns with the math standards, combines conceptual learning and computational skills while teaching with both construction activity and traditional proofs.

The text used is Houghton Mifflin's *Geometry: An Integrated Approach* by Larson, Boswell, and Stiff. I believe students should use the text with this course even more than they might with other Chalk Dust courses because videos and text complement each other rather than repeating all the same (or very similar) material.

While the text is fairly good on its own, explanations of some concepts are perfunctory. Professor Mosely expands the lessons wherever necessary. For example, the book's presentation on slope is very brief, so Mosely uses visual aids for a much lengthier, more complete teaching of the topic. On the other hand, construction activity is used throughout the book, and some inductive methods similar to those in *Discovering Geometry* show up in "Special Projects," "Chapter Explorations," and "Lesson Investigations" in the text. The text also features some optional computer and calculator activities. The projects, explorations, investigations, and computer and calculator activities are presented only in the text, not on the video. I highly recommend that students tackle as many of the projects, explorations, and investigations as they are able. A computer drawing program is necessary for the computer activities and a graphing calculator for the calculator activities. However, neither is crucial to the course as a whole.

The course covers typical content, including a brief introduction of trigonometry. Proofs are introduced in the second chapter, then used throughout the text, although the stress on logic is not at the level we encounter in Harold Jacobs' *Geometry* text.

The text is heavily illustrated with lots of practical application: e.g., "Why does a 'baby gate' not have a bi-directionally rigid framework while a bridge using a similar parallelogram structure is rigid?" (p. 282). Some of this carries over to the videos, but the video presentations focus primarily on key concepts and skills. Algebra is applied within geometry lessons, and some "mixed reviews" in the text offer opportunity for problem-solving practice on algebra problems to help students retain skills.

After lesson 13 in the text, there are seven "Excursions in Geometry," which are optional short lessons dealing with topics such as Platonic and Archimedean solids, topology and Mobius strips, and fractal geometry. Most of these are very interesting and not overly challenging, so consider using them if you have time.

Overall, I think this course is great for homeschoolers. It includes some of the elements I like so much from *Discovering Geometry* (application, inductive thinking, construction activity, and interesting presentation), and it can be used by students working independently, while *Discovering Geometry* really needs a teacher.

Trigonometry (2001)

12 videos or 9 DVDs, textbook, and solutions guide—$409.00

The text for this course is *Trigonometry, Fifth Edition*, by Larson and Hostetler. This is a traditional course covering both trigonometry and some analytic geometry. Graphing calculators are referenced throughout the text and demonstrated throughout the video as well. Although these calculators can be somewhat expensive, they can be critical in demonstrating equations and the relationship between the algebraic form (the equation) and the geometric form (the graph). The TI-83 Plus is recommended.

If students are not already familiar with the calculator, they should go through the user-friendly instructions that come with it and learn the calculator techniques on a need-to-know basis as they are encountered during the course. Keep in mind that Chalk Dust provides technical support by phone or e-mail so calculator issues are not a big deal.

The solutions guide is a student edition, so complete solutions are shown for only odd problems from student exercises. All test solutions are shown. (Note: *Precalculus* covers the content of *Trigonometry* and *College Algebra*, so students need not do either of those courses in addition to *Precalculus*.)

Precalculus (2001)

16 videos or 13 DVDs, textbook, and solutions guide—$514.00

There are more tapes or DVDs for this course than for other Chalk Dust courses because this course is really two courses in one, college algebra and trigonometry, with the addition of even more material not contained in either of the other two. There are more than forty hours of video presentation associated with this course.

Professor Mosely follows lessons in the text, expanding explanations and working out sample problems. With this course, students really should stop the video occasionally and try to solve example problems so they can fully grasp the concepts.

This would be a one-semester course at the college level, but high school students should definitely take a full school year or more to complete it. The text used in the 2004 version of this course is *Precalculus with Limits, A Graphing Approach, Third Edition,* by Larson, Hostetler, and Edwards. Both content and presentation in the textbook help make the course more appealing. There are a number of fully-explained examples for each topic in the book. In addition, the text has some full-color illustrations; historical/biographical sidebars; and real life, business, and science applications within the chapter problems.

With the combination of videos, textbook, and the complete solution guide (with solutions to all problems), students really should be able to learn independently. After completing this course, students should be ready for college-level calculus, so they should be able to test out of college algebra and trigonometry or out of precalculus.

A graphing calculator is standard equipment for this course. The TI-83 Plus is recommended. (See the review of *Trigonometry* for comments on the calculator.)

Calculus 1 (2001)

12 videos or 8 DVDs, text and solutions guide—$409.00

The text for this course is *Calculus of a Single Variable, Sixth Edition,* by Larson, Roland, Hostetler, and Edwards. The text actually covers two courses—Calculus 1 and Calculus 2—but the videos and the solutions guide cover only Calculus 1.

This is a true college level course. I suspect that most students tackling such a course will want to earn college credit if possible, so students should check with the college of their choice beforehand to make sure they will have the opportunity to test out of Calculus I once the course is completed. I would not be surprised if the college uses the same text since it is one of the most popular calculus texts in the country.

Chalk Dust for the Elementary Grades

1 CD or online access plus binder—$80.00 per course

I have to add a note about Chalk Dust's new computer-based math courses for the elementary grades, marketed under the trade name *Math Matters*. These courses for grade levels 3, 4, and 5 (thus far) were developed under the direction of Dana Mosely of Chalk Dust. The courses include colorful illustrations and animations as well as voice instruction for a key topic in each lesson.

You can choose to purchase either online access to a course or the CD-ROM that contains the course. Both come with a three-ring binder that includes tests, answers, and other material.

Each course has approximately 180 lessons and covers an entire year's math curriculum. All lessons include cumulative review. Some of the lessons allow the student to type answers in blanks provided, while others call for written work from the student. Written midchapter and chapter tests are provided in the binder.

Unlike other math courses offered by Chalk Dust, students are not expected to work independently. Parents will still have to monitor and control the learning experience due to the grade levels involved.

Math Matters offers a unique assessment and placement test that may be taken whether or not the student signs up for a course. The cost is $15.00, but about half that cost will be deducted from the cost of any *Math Matters* course you purchase. The online tests accessed through the *Math Matters* Web site, adapts as students answer questions, providing easier or more difficult questions as needed so that the end result is a very precise evaluation of a student's ability throughout a spectrum of topics.

Students also have the opportunity to take tests written in the standardized format called *MCAT* (*Math Comprehensive Assessment Tests*). These self-correcting tests appear at the end of each chapter. As with all Chalk Dust courses, *Math Matters* offers technical support online or by phone.

Sample lessons and more course information are available at the Math Matters Web site, www.mathmatters.com or by phone at (888) 693-6284.

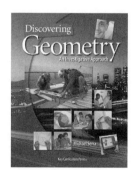

Discovering Geometry: An Inductive Approach (third edition)
Key Curriculum Press
1150 65th Street
Emeryville, CA 94608
(800) 995-MATH
(800) 338-7638
e-mail: info@keypress.com
www.keypress.com

Student book—$53.70, teacher's edition—$79.43, solution manual—$35.95, assessment resources—$37.90

I used this text twice, each time with groups of three students with widely diverse mathematical aptitudes. Amazingly, after completion of the course, all my students actually thought geometry was fun!

That's because *Discovering Geometry* truly uses a different approach to teaching the subject. This is a complete college-preparatory course that is more inviting than any other I have seen.

The first thing students encounter in the book is art—geometric art. The art leads students into their first investigations about lines and shapes. Investigations by students help them discover postulates and theorems by inductive reasoning. Many investigations involve students in activities, especially making and working with constructions using a straightedge and compass.

Word problems are imaginative, although the latest edition (third edition) has dropped many of those we liked best from earlier editions. Real-life applications are more true-to-life than in some other texts. Mathematical thinking is the goal of this text rather than mere memorization of postulates and theorems.

The text moves from the concrete to the abstract—a strategy essential for many students to be able to succeed in geometry. In the teacher's edition, the author explains his philosophy of gradually working through levels of thinking to the point where students are able to deal with proofs.

Paragraph proofs are introduced in chapter 2 as a means of getting students to organize data and make conjectures. Flowchart proofs are taught in chapter 4, and column proofs are saved for the last two chapters (12 and 13) after students have mastered concepts and understand relationships between theorems. Even though formal proofs are not taught at the beginning of the course, students are applying both inductive and deductive reasoning and working with logic and language leading up to use of two-column proofs.

Now, here's the hangup that explains why more homeschoolers are not using this text. It was definitely designed for classroom use. It requires cooperative learning with two or more students working together. It is possible that a parent could function as a second student for some of the activities, but it is more than a bit tricky for a parent to function simultaneously as teacher and student. Lest you view the cooperative learning requirement as a negative, I must tell you that it is one of the features that makes it so enjoyable. This is primarily where students have the many "Aha!" experiences of this course. It will be well worth your while to pull together even a small group class to make this course work.

You need both the student text and the teacher's edition. The hardcover student text is printed in full color. It has "Hints for Selected Exercises" at the back, but no answer keys.

In addition to the aforementioned straightedge and compass, students will need a protractor and a ruler. Numerous other items are used to make this a hands-on course, although most of the time their use is optional. Among these items are drinking straws, interlocking cubes, geometric shapes, geoboards and rubber bands, a meter stick, modeling clay, patty paper (the lightweight paper used to separate burger patties), toothpicks, cubes, and uncooked spaghetti.

The teacher's edition is a larger hardcover edition that includes reproductions of student pages, with some answers overprinted in magenta, plus teaching information, solutions, and other helps in margins and at the bottom of the page. Additional teacher information is in the front matter and at the beginning of each chapter. One valuable part of this information is course outlines that will help you schedule lessons, tailoring the course for "standard," "enriched," or "block" schedules. Answers to all problems are found either in the chapter or at the back of the teacher's edition. A separate solution manual shows the steps leading to the answers. Parents who are not strong in math might want to have this on hand in case they get stuck.

Every exercise set in the student book includes some review questions. Reviews at the end of each chapter consist of about fifty or more problems. Assessment Resources (quizzes and tests) are available separately.

The third edition has upped the number of opportunities to incorporate technology into learning, although it is not required. The author suggests that students have a graphing calculator and/or software such as *Geometer's Sketchpad*. *Geometer's Sketchpad* ($39.95 for a student edition) is a computer program (either Macintosh or Windows version) that can be used in conjunction with *Discovering Geometry* or other geometry courses. I expect that *Geometer's Sketchpad* might help compensate if you absolutely cannot find a second student. Students can create numerous constructions quickly on the computer and compare results, whereas it would be too time consuming to do many of them manually. However, you would not want to use the software as a total substitute for a student learning to create constructions with compass and straightedge.

Elementary Algebra
by Harold Jacobs
W. H. Freeman
Homeschool orders should be directed to VHPS
16365 James Madison Highway
Gordonsville, VA 22942
(888) 330-8477, press 1 for order entry, then 3 for high school orders

(*Note:* All orders placed by homeschool parents must be placed with a credit card. All homeschooling orders that include teacher's materials must be accompanied by a current certificate from your state or other source documenting homeschooling status.)

Student text (#0716710471)—$50.00, instructor's guide (#0716710757)—$25.00, test bank (#0716710773)—$25.00

This is an atypical algebra text. *Elementary Algebra* covers all concepts typical of a first-year algebra course, but it invites students to explore algebra concepts in a friendlier environment than other texts. Cartoons, comic strips (e.g., *Broom Hilda*, B.C., *Wizard of Id*, and *Doonesbury*), interesting and creative applications, puzzles, and even poetry capture the interest of students who struggle with abstract mathematics.

For example, a lesson on mixture problems opens with the story of Archimedes and the King of Syracuse's golden crown that the king suspected was not really solid gold. Jacobs then sets up a volume/weight equation based on the problem.

In addition to stories and practical applications, Jacobs uses the rectangle-building concept throughout the text to demonstrate how concepts work. This is the same rectangle-building idea used by *Math-U-See* and some other manipulative systems. While Jacobs' book shows pictures and doesn't require use of manipulatives, students can still use them if they are helpful. I think most students really benefit from this approach when they are learning to multiply and factor polynomials. (This last feature makes this text a particularly good one to use after *Math-U-See*'s *Prealgebra* level. If you don't already have manipulatives, check out either *Algebra Tiles* or *Algebra Base 10 Kit* from Nasco (www.lcsc.org/nascomath.html, 800-558-9595).

The book is divided into seventeen chapters, with each chapter subdivided into a number of lessons. A summary and review section is at the end of each chapter. Four exercise sets are at the end of each lesson, with problems ranging from simple computation, through word and application problems, to challenging thought problems. Generally, you will choose two of these sets for students to work. By assigning appropriate problems, the text can be used with students of varying capabilities. Answers to questions from one of the sets from each lesson are in the back of the student text so students can see if they are getting the correct answers. The instructor's guide is the source for the rest of the answers. A test bank is also available.

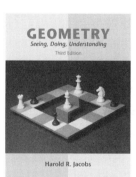

Geometry: Seeing, Doing, Understanding (third edition)
by Harold R. Jacobs
W. H. Freeman
(See ordering information for *Elementary Algebra* by Jacobs above.)
Student text (#0716743612)—$52.50, instructor's guide (#0716756072)—$30.00, test bank: book (#0716756080)—$30.60 or CD (#0716756102)—$66.30

Jacobs has managed to write a user-friendly geometry text that is heavy on logic and proofs. This is one book where you don't want to skip the introduction that introduces students to Euclid and teaches them the basics of construction with a straightedge and compass.

In the newly revised third edition, the first chapter is an introduction to vocabulary, tools, and basic ideas of geometry. But it ends with a lesson titled "We Can't Go On Like This," a lesson that takes students through some intriguing problems to demonstrate the necessity for a logical approach to geometry.

Then in the second chapter, Jacobs begins to teach logic. Many people cite the value of geometry as being the development of logical thinking skills. Jacobs takes this idea seriously, ensuring that students are truly tuned in to logical thinking before tackling other geometry topics. Given the foundation in logic, students then immediately begin work with proofs, which continues throughout the text.

Jacobs uses entertaining illustrations (including cartoons), as well as practical-application explanations and engaging word problems. For example, the lesson on similar figures and ratio begins with a comparison of movie and television screens, including the "letter box" option that changes the ratio.

Topic arrangement is different from what I have seen in most texts. For instance, work with circles follows introductory lessons on trigonometry. The trigonometry is introduced as a natural progression in the study of triangles, so this is not really an outlandish arrangement. Even if the arrangement is unusual, there is a clear continuity to topics, building one upon another.

There are sixteen chapters in the book, with each chapter divided into a number of lessons. Each lesson has three problem sets. All students should try to complete the first two sets, but skip the second set for struggling students. The third set frequently features really intriguing investigations, but these should be used as a challenge for better students who have the time. A summary and review at the end of each chapter includes specific algebra review.

Construction activities (using straightedge and compass) are minimal. Because of this and the emphasis on logic, I recommend this text for abstract thinkers rather than hands-on learners. But I suspect that even some students who struggle with the logic will like this text because the presentation is so appealing.

Problems from SAT tests are interspersed throughout the exercises. They are labeled as such so students preparing for the test can be sure to master these.

Selected answers for about one-fourth to one-third of the problems from each lesson (selected in no numerical sequence) are at the back of the student text. All answers are in the instructor's guide. A separate test bank is available in either book or CD-ROM format (both Windows and Mac versions on one disk).

Horizons Mathematics

Alpha Omega

300 North McKemy

Chandler, AZ 85226-2618

(800) 622-3070

www.aop.com

Sets for each level include teacher handbook and two student workbooks: K—$59.95, grades 1 through 3—$69.95 each; grades 4 through 6—$71.95 each

Those familiar with Alpha Omega's *LIFEPAC* curriculum are often surprised when they check out Alpha Omega's *Horizons Mathematics* because they are so different in both format and methodology. Whereas *LIFEPAC* courses are comprised of ten (in most cases) individual worktexts through which students work independently, *Horizons Mathematics* follows a more traditional format. In *Horizons*

Mathematics, the teacher handbook is the main part of the program, although each level does have two full-color student workbooks.

The teacher handbook outlines every step of each lesson, listing objectives, materials needed, stories, poems, and games. Some preparation time is needed, and lessons must be taught. However, lessons are purposeful; they don't waste time on peripheral topics as do some other math programs, such as *Saxon* for younger levels.

Horizons uses a variety of manipulatives throughout all levels, although far more in the early grades than fifth and sixth grades. Among manipulatives used are dominoes, counters, play money, place-value materials (might be craft sticks or something similar), flannel board and numbers, abacus, beads, and flash cards, along with household items such as bags, a calendar, an egg carton, a ruler, and straws. For the most part, these are either household items, things you can make easily yourself, or easy-to-find and relatively inexpensive items. *Base Ten Blocks*® used at upper levels would be one of the more costly items. Charts at the front of each level's teacher handbook list manipulatives to be used and lessons for which they are to be used. It also indicates which are essential and which are optional.

Each lesson has instruction on a new concept and practice or review of previously learned concepts. This continual practice and review marks this as a "spiral" curriculum.

Each lesson includes a number of activities that require interaction between teacher and student, often with hands-on materials. For example, one lesson in the first grade program includes paper-and-pencil work with a hundreds chart, regrouping demonstration with place-value manipulatives, oral number chart work, time-telling practice using small clocks, written place-value practice, addition practice, writing the words for large numbers, and word problems.

Alpha Omega explains their scope and sequence and course layout in great detail at the beginning of each teacher handbook, making it very easy to see what should happen when. A readiness evaluation is also found there, so you can make sure that each child is ready for this level and also spot weaknesses.

The teacher handbook is very well designed, with each part of the lesson clearly labeled. Novice home educators should especially appreciate the easy-to-follow layout. Activity instructions are numbered and spaced so they are easy to locate and read quickly. All instruction is provided through one-to-one teacher instruction, demonstrations, and hands-on activity, although there is less and less of this as you move into the upper levels.

Students have two separate workbooks (each about one-half inch thick) to cover each level. This is a lot of workbook pages (two to four per lesson depending upon grade level), especially for kindergarten, but they are appealingly designed with full color, large print, and variety in the layout—illustrations, puzzles, and lesson explanations take up some space. Simple instructions are included with each activity in the workbooks.

I suspect that many parents will be tempted to hand their children the workbooks and ignore the teacher handbooks, but there are some important lessons and presentation ideas in the handbooks you should not skip. You should review the lesson plans and determine how much of each presentation is useful for each student.

Supplemental, reproducible worksheets are also included in the teacher's handbook with clear indication of the lessons to which they correlate. Periodic tests are in student workbooks. Answer keys to workbook pages, including tests, are in the teacher's handbook.

Each level goes beyond most other programs by spending more time on development and practice of concepts and skills. The scope and sequence is purposely advanced in keeping with the national mathematics standards.

Alpha Omega's educational philosophy is also evident in this program. They believe repetition and review are essential until a subject has been mastered to the point where it becomes second nature. They view math, in particular, as both a basic functional skill and a communications skill that develops precision in thinking. Within this framework that emphasizes mental discipline, they have done an excellent job of breaking tasks down into manageable increments and also building in learning methods that address the needs of various learning styles.

However, this also means that you might not need to use everything in each lesson with each of your children; they might not need all the multisensory instruction, and they might not need all of the practice and review (in spite of instructions to the contrary in the teacher's handbooks). You will need to exercise some discretion as to what you might skip. Also, keep in mind the advanced speed of the program, and slow down if necessary.

Quarterly tests and a final, plus answer keys for workbooks, worksheets, and tests are all in the teacher's handbook, except for level K. There is also a test after every ten lessons in the student workbooks.

This program was designed very much with home educators in mind, so there are few classroom-only type activities that must be adapted or skipped.

Horizons Mathematics K

The *Horizons Mathematics K* program follows an advanced scope and sequence, closer to some publishers' first-grade programs. Students are doing addition and subtraction (two digits plus or minus one digit) with no regrouping by the end of the year. However, lessons are taught with visual aids and manipulatives to better help young children grasp concepts. Time, money, measurement, ordinal numbers, and introductory fractions are among other concepts covered. For home educators who want an academic math program for kindergarten, this is a practical solution.

Horizons Mathematics 1

The first grade program begins with concepts such as place value and counting by twos and fives—all within the first ten lessons. Addition works up through addition of triple-digit numbers with carrying from the ones column. Subtraction works up through three-digit numbers, but without borrowing. In addition to basic number concepts (e.g., counting, addition, subtraction, place value), this level teaches time, money, the calendar, measurement, fractions, sets, shapes, bar graphs, and estimation.

A solid foundation in number recognition and meaning along with other concepts (such as colors and shapes) is essential before beginning this level. This foundation is laid in *Mathematics K*. Readiness assessment tools in the teacher's handbook will help you evaluate readiness. If children are weak in some areas, extra lessons in the handbook can be used to cover some topics. However, some children in first grade might need to start with *Mathematics K*. Choose levels according to appropriate skill levels rather than equating them to grade levels.

Horizons Mathematics 2

Mathematics 2 expects that children have learned two-digit addition and subtraction with carrying, but it still reteaches the concepts, then moves on to larger numbers. Multiplication facts for 1 to 10 are taught along with place value, number order, sets, correspondence, cardinal and ordinal numbers, shapes, graphs, fractions, measurement, temperature, estimation, ratio, the calendar, time, money, area, perimeter, volume, and decimals (in money).

Horizons Mathematics 3

Mathematics 3 covers the same topics as *Mathematics 2* but at more challenging levels; for example, multiplication teaches up through four-digit multipliers, division works up through two-digit divisors with remainders. Algebraic thinking is introduced with equations like $n + 5 = (7 + 2) + 4$.

Horizons Mathematics 4

The readiness test at the front of the book will help you know whether or not your child is able to work at this level. It asks students to reduce fractions, multiply four-digit numbers by multiples of 10, perform short division, compare values of fractions with unlike denominators, round off numbers, understand ratio, add fractions with common denominators, and solve simple algebraically-expressed addition equations.

Lessons are designed to be presented by the teacher as with lower levels, but students should be able to do the majority of their work independently. Lesson objectives are clearly spelled out in the teacher handbook. Materials or supplies needed are listed, and you might have to plan ahead to procure some of these. One lesson describes a bingo game for the teacher to construct, but most materials are much more standard—counters, flash cards, rulers, *Base Ten Blocks®*, a clock, and play money. While much of the lesson activity takes place within the two student workbooks for this level, there are additional activities such as mental math or manipulative work described in the lesson plans. About every other lesson uses a worksheet, for which reproducible masters are found in the teacher's handbook.

Among concepts covered by the end of the course are long division with two-digit divisors, adding and subtracting fractions with unlike denominators, converting fractions to decimals, adding and subtracting decimals, metric measurement, and multiplying or dividing to find equal ratios. Time, money, geometry, and graphs are also covered.

Horizons Mathematics 5

As in *Mathematics 4*, there is a four-page readiness test at the front of the teacher's handbook to help determine whether students are ready for this level. Among concepts they are expected to know *before* beginning this course are division of two-digit divisors into dollar amounts with decimals; acute angles; diameters and radii of circles; similar and congruent figures; simple perimeter, area, and volume; ratios; addition of fractions with unlike denominators, addition and subtraction of mixed numbers, decimal values, and metric measurements. As with earlier levels, there is a great deal of review, so if your child has not yet covered all of these concepts, he or she might be able to pick them up easily through the review that is built into Level 5.

Among concepts taught by the end of this course are multiplying three-digit by three-digit numbers, values of exponential numbers, finding averages, division by two-digit divisors, types of triangles, least common multiples, multiplying and dividing fractions, all four functions applied to decimal numbers, percent, and probability. Calculators are used, primarily for checking answers. This course continues to stress both computation skills and understanding of concepts.

Horizons Mathematics 6

Students *beginning* this level are expected to know how to work with fractions, decimals, and percent, although not all types of functions (e.g., division with decimal divisors). Some other concepts covered in *Horizons'* earlier levels might not have been taught yet in other programs: congruency/similarity; diameter, chords, and radius of a circle; and different types of averages. However, the continual review and spiral approach used throughout the program mean that these concepts are reviewed and/or retaught at this level. Still, the program moves beyond the level of most others. For example, *Saxon's Math 76* introduces the idea of ratio while *Horizons Mathematics 6* teaches cross multiplication to solve for *n*. Geometry coverage is more complex, with students learning to construct geometric figures using a compass and straightedge. Students continue to work with fractions, decimals, and percent. Consumer math topics such as check writing, banking, budgeting, and calculating interest are covered along with more advanced equations, graphs, measurement, and problem solving.

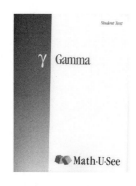

Math-U-See

1378 River Road

Drumore, PA 17518

(888) 854-6284

www.mathusee.com

Teacher packs (include VHS or DVD plus teacher manual): Primer—$25.00, levels Alpha through Zeta—$35.00 each, Prealgebra through Geometry—$50.00 each, Algebra 2—$75.00, Trigonometry—$70.00

Student kits (include student text and test booklet except for Primer, Algebra 2, and Trigonometry levels): Primer level—$15.00, levels Alpha through Geometry—$20.00 each, Algebra 2 (text plus Extra Practice Sheets book)—$27.50, Trigonometry—$15.00

Starter set of manipulatives—$30.00, completer set—$35.00, Fraction Overlays—$30.00, Algebra and Decimal Inserts—$20.00, skip-counting tape or CD with book—$12.00

Steve Demme, creator of *Math U-See*, combines hands-on methodology with incremental instruction and continual review in this manipulative-based program. It excels in its hands-on presentation of math concepts that enables students to understand how math works. It is the only truly multisensory math program I know of that covers all grade levels.

Manipulative blocks, Fraction Overlays, and Algebra and Decimal Inserts are used at different levels to teach concepts, primarily using the "rectangle building" principle. This basic idea, consistently used throughout the program—even through algebra—is one of the best ways to demonstrate math concepts.

Taking a tip from Saxon, Demme incorporates another key feature—a spiral design for the problem pages, continually reviewing and practicing previously learned concepts.

In the newly revised editions there are eight books for elementary grades titled *Primer, Alpha, Beta, Gamma, Delta, Epsilon, Zeta,* and *Prealgebra.* The Greek letter designations were chosen particularly to emphasize the order of learning rather than grade level designation. Students should move on to the next level once they've mastered the content of a book. These first eight books are followed by *Algebra 1, Geometry, Algebra 2,* and *Trigonometry* (in unrevised editions). Placement tests for the different levels are available free at the *Math-U-See* Web site.

For those familiar with the original series, the concepts covered in these books are the same as those in the original books, but the formatting and arrangement have been greatly improved. Improvements have been made in coverage of some topics, review, word problems, and layout of all the components.

First I'll discuss the lower-level books, saving high-school-level courses for later. These eight books have thirty lessons each. They should take about one year each to complete, but students can take more or less time as needed.

For each level except *Primer* there are four basic components: a video (your choice of VHS or DVD), teacher's manual, student worktext, and test booklet. The *Primer* level has no test booklet.

The program also uses plastic blocks, color-coded to correspond to each number. The blocks snap together like Legos because of their raised surfaces. The Starter Set of manipulative blocks is required for all levels. At *Alpha* level, you will probably want to add the Completer Set so you will have plenty of manipulative blocks. You will need the Fraction Overlays at level *Epsilon.* And the Algebra and Decimal Inserts will be needed for levels *Zeta, Prealgebra,* and *Algebra 1.*

All books are comb bound and designed to be written in. Both teacher's manuals and student books are printed on only one side of each page so there is extra room for teacher notes and student work respectively. Student books contain three lesson-practice pages and three review pages for each lesson. Word problems are included in both types of pages.

The test booklets have tests to be used at the end of each lesson plus four unit tests and a final exam. Answers are in the teacher manuals. Neither student worktext pages nor tests are reproducible; you need to purchase books for each student or come up with a creative solution such as using a wipe-off overlay.

Primer will generally be the starting place for most kindergartners. At the early levels, you will also want to use the *Skip-Counting and Addition Songs* cassette tape or CD. Both a Bible version and a science and literature version are included on the tape or CD.

Parents must watch the videos or DVDs to understand the basic concepts that are the foundation of the program. On the videos, Demme works through each level, lesson by lesson, demonstrating and instructing. Although the videos are very basic (two cameras focused on Demme with a whiteboard), Demme's presentation is enthusiastic and engaging. Although he is actually teaching the lessons to a class, we don't see or hear the students except on rare occasions. Demme clearly explains why and what he is doing. He throws in lots of math tricks, the kind that make you scratch your head and ask why they never taught us that in school.

The video presentations are critical components of the courses, although teacher's manuals have briefer lesson presentations of the same material covered on the videos.

I expect that most parents will have their children watch the videos with them, although it is fine if parents choose to watch the videos and then do their own presentations to their children.

After the initial viewing or lesson presentation, parents and children work through lessons together for as many days as it takes for children to master the concepts. Once students have grasped a concept, they practice and do problem pages on their own with occasional assistance. Typically, children should be spending about a week per lesson, but you need to take as long as necessary for your child to learn each lesson.

All books are printed in black-and-white with no illustrations. This is not a particular problem in the first four levels if students are watching the videos, working with the colorful manipulatives, and learning the skip-count songs. In other words, the other multisensory experiences make up for the bland worktext. However, as older students need manipulatives less and less, the "plainness" of the worktexts is a point to consider.

The program covers all basic math concepts, including time and money. It does not try to correlate with the national math standards. Thus, for example, children are not working on graphing and probability in the early levels.

The *Primer* level begins with essential number concepts and continues up through adding to make 10, telling time, and introduction to subtraction. Children use manipulatives more than in upper levels of the program (and far more than in most kindergarten math programs). While I generally don't recommend formal math programs for kindergarteners, I make an exception for this one because its design makes it more developmentally appropriate than most others.

Alpha level focuses most heavily on place value, addition, and subtraction. *Beta* level teaches regrouping for both addition and subtraction. *Gamma* primarily covers multiplication, while *Delta* moves on to division. Fractions are the main topic in *Epsilon,* while *Zeta* tackles decimals and percents. Of course, other topics are included alongside these primary themes, topics such as money, measurement, geometry, time telling, graphs, estimation, prime and composite numbers, Roman numerals, and solving for unknowns. Prealgebra topics are similar to those in other such courses: positive and negative numbers, exponents, roots and radicals, order of operation, geometry, ratio and proportions, and other such topics. One unusual topic for this level is irrational numbers.

I have heard from a number of parents that as their children get older, they use the manipulatives less and less. Sometimes, by *Epsilon* or *Zeta* levels, students will skip the manipulatives altogether, moving through lessons more quickly.

When students complete the *Prealgebra* level, they can move on to *Math-U-See*'s *Algebra 1* or to *Saxon*'s *Algebra 1/2. Math-U-See* is slightly behind most other courses at this level, so students who want to shift to another publisher for Algebra 1 should first take a placement test for the course if one is available. However, if the Algebra 1 course has a decent review section at the beginning, students might be able to make the transition with no problem.

As we move into the high-school-level books, I have some reservations about the layout of the courses. Each course has videos, a teacher's manual, and a student text. Instruction is in the videos and teacher's manual but not in the student book. If a student needs to review a topic or, perhaps, look up a geometry theorem covered in an earlier lesson, they must use the teacher's manual or go back through the video. Even using the teacher's manual might be a challenge because indexes at the back of each volume are sparse. While the books have glossaries and charts of symbols and tables, *Geometry* lacks any list of theorems and postulates. How much of a problem any of this might be depends on how well students retain knowledge.

High-school-level math is challenging to start with, so presentation matters a lot in overcoming student resistance. The fact that student books are strictly black-and-white with no illustrations other than graphs and geometric forms is a negative feature, especially since students are no longer working with manipulatives all the time. While the algebra courses feature many word problems and applications, these are missing from the geometry and trigonometry courses. This lack, coupled with the visual lack of appeal, makes the latter courses significantly less attractive than other alternatives. (I expect some of these deficits will be addressed when new editions of these courses are published.)

In *Algebra 1,* manipulatives (the standard set plus the algebra and decimal inserts) are still used, but not as much as in earlier levels. For example, manipulatives are used to demonstrate basic equations, including the use of unknowns and negative quantities. However, they are not used to teach line slope since the graph itself is very visual and manipulatives would be cumbersome at this point.

Demme presents concepts simply and clearly, avoiding dense-sounding mathematical abstractions common to many algebra textbooks. At this level there are two videos with a total of four hours of instruction.

The format at this level is the same for all lessons: two pages of lesson practice concentrating on the new concept followed by three lesson sheets for additional practice and review of other concepts.

The teacher's manual has complete solutions to student exercises and tests. Tests themselves are in a separate book. These include weekly tests, cumulative unit tests, and a final exam. All are in multiple-choice format similar to standardized tests.

Algebra 1 does not cover as much territory as do most other first-year algebra courses. For example, quadratic equations, complex work with radicals, and motion problems are taught in *Algebra 2*, although they are included in most other first-year courses. Consequently, I would recommend this course for students who are average to slow in math.

Geometry has two videotapes providing four hours of instruction covering thirty lessons. Following the same format as *Algebra 1*, each lesson has two practice sheets and three lesson sheets in the student book. Students rarely use manipulatives, but they do need a protractor, a compass, and a straightedge to draw constructions.

This course is fairly traditional in presentation and coverage, although it is an easier course than most. While it covers the standard topics, it does not go as far in depth as *Discovering Geometry*. For example, Demme deals only with regular polygons when teaching about interior and exterior angles of pentagons, hexagons, etc. There is minimal work with tangents compared to both *Discovering Geometry* and *Jacob's Geometry*.

However, Demme introduces geometric proofs in lesson 24 and uses them through the end of the course. He also introduces trigonometry and transformations in the last three lessons. Algebra is reviewed from time to time within the lessons.

As with *Algebra 1*, I would consider using this course with average to slow students.

Algebra 2 has five and a half hours of instruction on either two videotapes or DVDs covering thirty-one lessons. The student book has four practice pages per lesson, and a book of extra practice sheets adds another two pages for each lesson. Tests and solutions/answer keys are in the teacher's manual.

This course moves on to new material rather quickly (as compared to many other second-year algebra courses), so it brings the total of *Math-U-See*'s algebra coverage up close to that of other publishers. It introduces matrices and determinants in the last lesson but does not get into functions at all. Students should be able to move on to either precalculus or trigonometry courses after completing *Algebra 2*.

Trigonometry has four hours of instruction on two videos. The student text has twenty-six lessons plus two review lessons, with four practice pages per lesson. Students need a protractor, a ruler, and a scientific calculator. (Note that this is the only *Math-U-See* course that uses a calculator.) The teacher's manual has more pages per lesson than other courses, with up to eleven pages for one lesson. Probably because the teacher manual is already bulky, solutions are published in a book with the tests.

This is a straightforward and relatively unexciting course, but the video teaching might make a huge difference for many students since Demme does a great job explaining and illustrating concepts.

Modern Curriculum Press Mathematics series, Levels K and A through F

Modern Curriculum Press/Pearson Learning Group

P.O. Box 2500

Lebanon, IN 46052

(800) 393-3156

www.pearsonlearning.com

Student book—$28.50 each, teacher's edition—$29.50 each, set of both—$45.50

MCP Mathematics is one of the most practical and affordable math resources for the elementary grades. The student book comes in worktext format, so lesson presentation and work pages are combined in one place for the most part.

I sometimes use the MCP Mathematics teacher's manual as an example of what a good teacher's manual should look like. It is very useful, even though children can do much of their work independently. It features reduced student pages with answers overprinted, so it is easy to check your child's work. Around the outside of the reproduced pages are lesson objectives, items you might use for a hands-on presentation for some lessons, mental math activities for practice, and very brief instructions for lesson presentation. The teacher's manual also has error pattern analysis that can help you determine why children make certain errors. I really appreciate this format where everything you might need is visible on a two-page spread. It is easy to pick out what you want to use, so lesson preparation time is minimal.

Instruction within student books includes explanations of concepts, usually with visual diagrams and sometimes with suggestions for using hands-on materials. Base Ten Blocks® are pictured from time to time, so they might be a good choice for math manipulatives to use alongside this series. Word problems combine with the conceptual presentations to help children develop mathematical thinking skills.

Many parents find that their children can work through lessons without parental lesson presentation, so this series works well for independent study situations as well as for more interactive situations.

A weakness of this series is that it deals with only one subject per lesson, reviewing previously learned concepts at infrequent intervals on tests. This does not usually present a problem up through third grade, but by fourth grade you need to either supplement with other means of review or do as one mom suggested—skip occasional problems in each lesson, then come back and use those for review.

This series moves at a slower pace than A Beka, Horizons, and Saxon (e.g., long division is usually taught in fourth grade, but in MCP it is taught in fifth). However, it does a good job on concept development through lesson presentations and word problems that are often quite challenging. Level K for kindergarten is very easy and not really necessary. I would begin with Level A (first grade) and use the series through Level D (fourth grade), perhaps moving children at a faster rate than suggested by the publisher.

This series *does not* reflect the national standards for math, a factor that might be considered both positive and negative. With its narrower focus on the most important math concepts and skills, it does a better job of teaching foundational math skills than do many resources that try to cover "everything." However, the slower progression might put children behind their age-mates in covering even the basics like multiplication and division.

Moving with Math

Math Teachers Press, Inc. (MTP)

4850 Park Glen Road

Minneapolis, MN 55416

(800) 852-2435

Fax: (952) 546-7502

www.movingwithmath.com

This program offers a compromise between the extremes of a totally manipulative-based approach and a workbook approach. You can actually shift back and forth between the different program components depending upon whether or not you want to use manipulatives to cover each topic.

The original *Moving with Math* program, Levels A–D, offers tremendous flexibility for designing the program to fit your child's needs using the diagnostic/prescriptive tools and instructions that come with the program. The scope and sequence is slower than most other programs. It spends more time on concept development, so it cannot cover as many concepts as quickly as other programs.

The original program, which I will describe first, is divided into four levels: A for grades 1 and 2, B for 3 and 4, C for 5 and 6, and D for 7 and 8. There are three essential components at each level: *Math Capsules*, *Moving with Math* (student workbooks), and *Skill Builders*. These are all consumable, so you will need extra sets for additional students. (The publisher does have reproducible versions available, so check them out if you are teaching more than one or two children.)

Much of the instruction comparable to that found in a teacher's manual is in *Skill Builders*. *Skill Builders* also contains activity pages—some using paper-and-pencil and some also using manipulatives. This is a substantial part of the program.

Moving with Math workbooks include basic instruction and practice along with instruction for some manipulative activity. Answers are in the teacher's guides. It is not absolutely necessary to use manipulatives with the workbooks, but it is strongly recommended.

Math Capsules contains pre- and posttests for the entire level; however, there are also pre- and posttests for each chapter or unit in each *Moving with Math* workbook. *Math Capsules* contains a detailed key to the objectives, but you can see the objectives by simply reading the table of contents in each book—they read like a scope and sequence list. While this is useful, the most important part of *Math Capsules* is "Maintenance Tests"—reproducible, short quizzes to be used for continual review of previous concepts. Every question in each maintenance test is matched to an objective so parents always can identify what their child does and does not know. Another feature of the Level A *Math Capsules* component is "Oral Drill," exercises to be used along with the "Maintenance Tests."

To use the program, you identify which objective you wish to work on, then plan a combination of both the workbook and *Skill Builder* sheets and activities that is most appropriate for each child.

This really is not that confusing, but some parents and teachers have had trouble making decisions about what to use. So the publisher has put together teacher's guides that lay out step-by-step lesson plans showing which program components to use when. The teacher's guides are not essential if you can figure this out for yourself. You do not need to follow their lesson plans if you find another arrangement more suitable.

If you use the teacher's guides, you should still be making the underlying decision of whether or not your child actually needs to do each lesson. MTP recommends that most homeschooling parents purchase the teacher's guides to understand how to organize instruction and teach with the manipulatives. I suspect that many home educators will want the guides since they will save much time in lesson planning and help parents understand concepts they are trying to teach.

MTP also provides home educators with free *Instructions with Daily Calendar* for each level that show you how to break down program material into one-year programs, suggest how many days to spend on each objective, and provide record-keeping and planning forms. Trained educational consultants are available at MTP's toll-free number to answer questions.

You might also be interested in MTP's hour-long video, *Moving with Math: An Overview for Home School*, which describes the philosophy and components of the program, the role of manipulatives in bridging the gap from concrete to abstract, and practical suggestions from a homeschool parent. It also shows students from various levels working with manipulatives.

There is a PreK-Kindergarten level available to begin with three- and four-year-olds, but I generally recommend that parents begin with Level A since the PreK program is high in cost for what children actually learn.

Level A for grades 1 and 2

Homeschool set that includes *Skill Builders*, three student workbooks, *Math Capsules*, *Using Models to Learn Addition and Subtraction*, and manipulatives—$150.00, *or* separate grade 1 and grade 2 programs, each with student book, teacher's resource manual, and essential manipulative set—$185.00 each

Level A has three workbooks: *Parts I* (numeration), *II* (addition and subtraction), and *III* (fractions, geometry, and measurement). It reviews basic number activities taught in kindergarten, so it is possible to begin arithmetic instruction with Level A. The Level A package integrates one more component that is especially useful to those with no experience teaching with manipulatives—a book titled *Using Models to Learn Addition and Subtraction Facts*. Manipulatives needed for Level A include *Base Ten Blocks®*, a Number Stair, Geoboard, and Unifix® cubes, all available from MTP.

Those beginning *Moving with Math* at second-grade level might appreciate an option that MTP has developed. They have broken Level A into separate grade 1 and grade 2 programs to make it easier for those with second graders to jump into the program. This does not save you money, but it does eliminate material that your child already knows so you do not have to spend as much time figuring out which elements of the program to use. (Free *Instructions with Daily Calendar* are still available for grades 1 and 2.)

The grade 1 and grade 2 programs teach the same objectives as Level A but separate the material into two grade levels and present it a little differently. These versions are enhanced by children's stories (from the library or bookstore) that are integrated with the math lessons. Students have a single workbook each for grade 1 and grade 2. You will need a student book for each student plus the teacher's resource manual.

The teacher's resource manual for each grade includes detailed lesson plans. They are scripted, telling you what to say as you follow each step-by-step lesson plan. Smaller-sized copies of student pages show correct answers. Within the lesson plans are suggestions for using more than 280 children's books and extensive activities that help children see math in the real world. Combined with additional art activities, this approach might be more appealing to children with literary or artistic "bents."

Also within the teacher's manual are the reproducible *Skill Builders* and *Math Capsules* that come as separate books in Level A. The grades 1 and 2 versions offer more security for parents who are uncertain about their teaching ability and want less decision making and planning.

Level B for grades 3 and 4

Homeschool set—$150.00

There are three primary components: *Skill Builders B*; three *Moving with Math* workbooks—*Part I* (Numeration, Addition, and Subtraction), *Part II* (Multiplication and Division), *Part III* (Fractions, Geometry, and Measurement); and *Math Capsules*. The layout and components for Level B are similar to those of Level A omit "Oral Drills."

Multiplication covers through two-digit multipliers, but division covers only through single-digit divisors. Considering that this level is supposed to cover through fourth grade level, the program's overall rate of progress is slower than that of *A Beka*, BJUP, and Modern Curriculum Press. Part of the reason is that *Moving with Math* is designed for mastery of objectives with long-term retention rather than the constant review found in some of the other programs. (Of course, students can move on to higher levels as quickly as they are able.) For example, two-digit division, which is typically introduced at fourth-grade level in other programs, is introduced at Level C (grades 5 and 6). This might be an important factor for those concerned about standardized tests since those tests are geared toward earlier introduction of some of these concepts. However, Math Teacher's Press proudly points to an outside study that shows very positive test results in schools where *Moving with Math* has been used. (A one-page summary is available from MTP if you are interested.)

This level also includes the book *Using Models to Learn Multiplication and Division Facts*. *Using Models* should be especially helpful to those unfamiliar with the use of manipulatives. Manipulative activities need one-to-one presentation as will many of the worksheet activities, but there are many pages students will be able to do alone. If you already have level A, you can purchase only the additional manipulatives you need rather than the whole set for each new level.

Level C for grades 5 and 6

Homeschool set—$150.00

Components: *Skill Builders C; Moving with Math* workbooks—*Part I* (Numeration and Problem Solving with Whole Numbers), *Part II* (Fractions, Decimals, and Percent), *Part III* (Geometry, Measurement, and Problem Solving); and *Math Capsules*.

Part I stresses problem solving using various strategies. At this level the need for manipulatives is not universal; but for those students who need hands-on work, this program is one of the few that really addresses that need well.

There is a moderate amount of manipulative work in the *Moving with Math* student workbooks, but it may be enough for many students. Those who need more will benefit from the lessons in *Skill Builders*, which often require more manipulative work. The diagnostic tests (for identifying which areas need attention) and maintenance tests (for review) in *Math Capsules* are very important at this level.

At this level, the need for manipulatives for whole number concepts is often greatly reduced; however, students benefit from the Fraction Bar activities for developing fraction concepts, *Base Ten Blocks®* for developing decimal concepts, and the Geoboard activities for increased understanding of geometric concepts.

Level D for grades 7 and 8

Homeschool set—$180.00

This program is one of only two I know of for students who still need extensive manipulative (hands-on) work at this level. The layout is similar to earlier levels, but there are five *Moving with Math* workbooks covering numeration and problem solving with whole numbers; problem solving with fractions and decimals; problem solving with percent; geometry and measurement; and prealgebra.

Calculator activities that emphasize estimation, checking answers, and looking for patterns are integrated throughout the Level D teacher guides, but you can use calculator lessons as you wish if you don't have the teacher guides.

Progress in Mathematics

Sadlier-Oxford, a division of William H. Sadlier, Inc.

9 Pine Street

New York, NY 10005-1002

(800) 221-5175

www.sadlier-oxford.com

Package prices for each grade: K—$110.00, grade 1—$160.00, grade 2—$220.00, grades 3 through 6—$250.00 each

Progress in Mathematics is a classroom-designed math program that reflects the national math standards. I generally don't review many such programs since their publishers are usually not set up to deal with homeschoolers and because the classroom design makes them cumbersome and expensive for homeschoolers. In addition, adherence to the national math standards often skews such programs so that they skimp on basic computation skills in favor of all the other concepts that are in the standards.

I'm making an exception for Sadlier for a few reasons. Some families are looking for a nonsectarian math program that thoroughly implements the new math standards and is more similar to what is used in "regular" schools than are some of the most popular programs among homeschoolers. Sadlier has always published solid academic materials since their primary market has been parochial schools. Thus, basic computation skills receive plenty of attention along with coverage of all the other topics in the standards. (They supply the math program for William Bennett's *K12* program.) In addition, Sadlier is one of the few publishers of such programs interested enough in the homeschool market to create homeschool "packages" of their program.

Primary components for each level are a teacher's edition, a student textbook, and a student workbook, although the workbooks might be optional. (Packages for all levels except kindergarten include these three components plus others described below.) Student textbooks for grades K through 2 are softcover, while third grade and up are hardcover. Workbooks are softcover.

Teacher's editions for the textbook are hefty, spiral-bound volumes that include detailed lesson plans with smaller-sized copies of student pages surrounded by instructional information. Answers are overprinted in red on student pages. They also have reproducible tests and blackline masters for both essential and extended activities. These manuals are loaded with information, even though some of it is targeted at larger classes. There are valuable helps here for teaching to different learning styles, addressing difficulties, and assessing progress. These manuals also indicate when you might use pages from the other program components.

It might be possible for parents to use the kindergarten through second grade student books without the pricey teacher manuals, ordering books individually rather than purchasing the package. You will be missing mental math exercises and some reproducible masters from the teacher's manual as well as the very detailed lesson plans, answer keys, and extra helps. However, many parents should be able to figure out how to use the student books for K-2 without missing essentials.

Student textbooks are beautifully printed in full color. Books for grades K through 2 include punch-out pages of heavy card stock to use as manipulatives. These substitute for coins, a ruler, geometric shapes, and manipulative blocks. Classroom-sized sets of manipulatives are also available, but they are prohibitively expensive for most families. Of course, you can purchase other manipulatives on your own to use with this program if you decide you need more than the punch-out pages.

The student textbooks provide adequate practice problems, including computation and word problems. Each lesson covers a single topic rather than using a spiral approach such as Saxon's. This is true for both the student textbook and student workbook.

The student workbooks mirror the lesson content, often with a brief explanation at the top of the page and problems similar to those done in the textbook. Think of the workbook pages as homework pages (one single-sided page per day) that students complete outside school time. While the workbooks provide additional practice and reinforcement, use your own judgment as to how much each child should complete. Separate teacher's editions for workbooks serve as answer keys.

The supplemental *Spiral Review Practice Books* that come with all but kindergarten level provide continual review of this sort that helps keep students up to speed on previously taught concepts. However, in the first few levels, the *Spiral Review* books tend to stick with the lesson topic rather than reviewing. The *Spiral Review Practice Books* have only half a page of problems per day, so these might be used as warm-up exercises before beginning a new math lesson.

In addition, packages for grades 1 through 6 include a *Skills Update Practice Book* that reviews concepts and skills taught the previous year. However, this is a fairly thin workbook. Using both the *Spiral Review* and *Skills Update* books will help students retain what they have learned. Both *Skills Update* and *Spiral Review* workbooks have separate, relatively small teacher editions that serve as answer keys, also included in each package.

Grades 4 through 6 packages add one more component, an *Intervention Workshop* student workbook and teacher's edition. The substantial teacher's edition targets key concepts with scripted step-by-step lessons to use when children need remediation on particular topics. I suspect that most students will not need this component.

While there is more in these packages than most students will need, the complete program provides everything that you might need to help children of different abilities and learning styles.

Saxon Math 54 through Calculus

Saxon Publishers, Inc.

6277 Sea Harbor Drive

Orlando, FL 32887

(800) 284-7019

e-mail: info@saxonhomeschool.com

www.saxonhomeschool.com

The *Saxon* math program for upper elementary grades through high school has retained high popularity among homeschoolers year after year because of its comprehensive content, reasonable price, and its instructional methodology that allows for and encourages independent study.

Homeschool kits for each level include everything most students need. In 2004, Saxon introduced an updated version of its *Math 54* through *Math 87* homeschool kits, developed to meet the educational needs of fourth- to seventh-grade students. These programs feature new content and components especially designed for homeschoolers. Each of the kits includes a nonconsumable, softbound student edition textbook, a solutions manual, and a consumable test and worksheets workbook. Homeschool kits for *Algebra 1/2* and above include hardcover student textbooks, tests, and answer keys. Solutions manuals are purchased separately at these upper levels.

There are no teacher editions for the *Saxon* program since each lesson in the student text provides the explanation of the concept to be learned. Each lesson includes an introduction and explanation of the new concept, examples and practice problems, then a set of problems that not only reinforces the new lesson content but also reviews previously learned concepts. Parents might help students work through the beginning of the lesson, but most students will be able to work through lessons independently. Parents need to check daily assignments and tests, ensuring that students are understanding what they are learning. The program requires virtually no preparation time.

While most parents appreciate not having to directly teach this program, the newest editions of *Math 54* through *Math 87* have added a valuable feature that does require some interaction. The "warm-up" box at the beginning of each lesson should be used orally. In that box typically are math-fact drills, mental math problems, and a thought-provoking problem to solve. This interactive time should also give parents an informal tool for assessing student performance and understanding of concepts.

One significant feature of the *Saxon* series that sets it apart from many other math programs is the incremental method in which concepts are taught. Once a concept is introduced, it is not dropped but is incorporated into the mixed practice that students encounter every day. In later lessons, the concept is developed more fully. Over time and through repeated exposure to a developing concept in a spiral process, students gain understanding and mastery. Unlike traditional chapter books where one content strand is taught and fully explained over a few consecutive lessons, *Saxon* has students work with a concept many times over the course of study. (Note that some students prefer this approach while others would rather have the entire concept fully explained all at once.)

Although this "incremental" methodology is used in *Saxon*'s program for all grade levels, the rest of the methodology for this series for the upper grade levels is very different from that of the program for the primary grades.

At levels *54* and above, *Saxon Math* has a "rules" orientation in its presentation, more like *A Beka's*, rather than a hands-on conceptual orientation like *Math-U-See* and *Moving with Math*. *Saxon*'s own primary grades program is more conceptually oriented than these upper levels. In a very simplified nutshell, that means that younger *Saxon* students use manipulatives to see what actually happens when they multiply, while older students memorize the rules and facts for multiplication.

Even though the program is not strong on teaching concepts, thinking skills get a good workout. This means that the program works best for students who do not need manipulatives and who tend to figure out mathematical concepts without a great deal of explanation. It is also good for those who like "brain teasers" like those troublesome time/rate/distance problems.

The latest editions of *Saxon Math 54* through *87* correlate well with the new math standards, having incorporated more on topics like statistics and probability, additional word problems to develop mathematical thinking skills, and twelve topical investigations in every book. However, *Saxon* does not teach the use of calculators until *Algebra 2*—a move I applaud even though calculator instruction is called for by the standards.

Another helpful addition to these revised editions is reference numbers in the mixed problems sets. If a student misses a problem, the reference number next to the problem provides the number(s) of the lesson(s) where the concept was taught. Reference numbers are also included on the assessments. The new editions have also added a second color to the black-and-white presentation, but the *Saxon* books still lack visual pizzazz.

In the past, *Math 87* was optional within the sequence. Originally, students often skipped *87*, completed *Algebra 1/2* in seventh grade and *Algebra 1* in eighth grade. However, some students were not ready for this rapid progression into advanced mathematical thinking. The introduction of *Math 87* provided an option for students who need the extra time and practice. Saxon encourages students to take both *Math 87* and *Algebra 1/2*, but since the new edition of *Math 87* has substantially more content, including prealgebra instruction, Saxon now recommends that a student who has completed it successfully skip *Algebra 1/2* and move directly to *Algebra 1* in the eighth grade.

From *Algebra 1/2* and up, each textbook has answers to odd-numbered problems at the back. Answer keys have answers to all problems in each textbook plus tests and test answer keys. Most parents will want to also purchase the optional solutions manuals in case neither they nor their students can figure out how to solve a problem.

Saxon has placement tests (free downloads from their Web site) to help you determine which book is the correct starting place for each student. Placement tests can be accessed at www.saxonhomeschool .com/pg/index.jsp. The Web site also has additional helpful information on their program, including a FAQ (Frequently Asked Questions) section.

Math 54, third edition

Homeschool kit—$64.50

This textbook should be appropriate for most fourth graders and those fifth graders who lag slightly behind grade level. Among topics covered in *Math 54* are addition (review), subtraction, multiplication (up to multiplying a three-digit number by a two-digit number), division (up through dividing by two-digit numbers), time, measurement, money, area, perimeter, fractions, mixed numbers, arithmetic algorithms, geometry and measurement, negative numbers, powers and roots, two-step word problems, decimals, averaging, estimation, patterns and sequences, statistics and probability, and Roman numerals. Saxon also sells Basic Fact Cards ($5.50), an optional set of flash cards for working on addition, subtraction, multiplication, and division, which might be useful at this level.

Math 65, third edition

Homeschool kit—$69.50

This text is appropriate for the average fifth grader. Students who need extra time at this level might spend more time in this text, perhaps skipping the *Algebra 1/2* book later on.

It continues developing arithmetic skills through multiplication and division of fractions and decimals while reviewing and expanding concepts of place value, addition and subtraction, geometry, measurement, and probability. Powers and roots, prime and composite numbers, ratios, and order of operations are also taught. Extra math drills for each lesson are at the back of the book. A few students might have difficulty with this text because it requires them to work in more abstract ways than for which they might be ready.

Math 76, fourth edition

Homeschool kit—$74.50

Math 76 is for average sixth graders or slower seventh graders. This text is especially good at providing a cumulative review and expansion upon topics covered through earlier grade levels. Among topics covered at this level are fractions, mixed numbers, decimals, percents, ratios, rounding, estimating, exponents, working with signed numbers, square roots, beginning algebraic expressions, surface area, volume, angles, circles, prime factorization, ratios and proportions, and statistics and probability. Especially notable are word problems that cause children to think of math concepts in a number of different ways to ensure understanding. These features make this a great choice for many students at this level.

Math 87, third edition

Homeschool kit—$79.50

Math 87 reviews material introduced in the prior texts, especially *Math 76*, and provides prealgebra instruction. The new edition covers word problems, scientific notation, statistics and probability, ratios and proportions, simplifying and balancing equations, factoring algebraic expressions, slope-intercept form, graphing linear inequalities, arcs and sectors and the Pythagorean theorem.

Algebra 1/2, third edition

Homeschool kit—$63.50, solutions manual—$31.50

This prealgebra text can be used after completing *Math 87*. Plenty of review, a spiral learning process, thought-provoking word problems, and clear instruction that works for independent study make this one of the top choices among other options available for this level. As is typical of the upper level *Saxon* books, the level of difficulty rises sharply toward the end of the text. If your student starts to have more difficulty toward the end of the book, consider doing only half a lesson each day.

Among topics covered are fraction, decimal, and mixed number operations; scientific notation; exponents; radicals; algebraic expressions and solving equations with one variable; working with signed numbers; order of operations; ratios; geometry fundamentals; and graphing. Saxon has resisted the inclusion of calculator instruction even though most other texts for this level include it. While students can use calculators to solve problems when it is appropriate, they are not instructed to do so.

Algebra 1 and Algebra 2

Homeschool kits—$64.50 each, solutions manuals for either text—$31.50 each

Saxon's Algebra 1 is probably the most widely used algebra text among home educators. *Algebra 1* coverage is comparable to that in other first-year algebra texts, although *Saxon* has chosen not to include calculator instruction or use. The spiraling method of presentation and constant review help students work fairly independently, a major advantage for parents who lack time and expertise.

Saxon seems to work fine for students who grasp math fairly easily, but not so well for those who struggle with the abstract thinking required. Overall, the book is fairly easy for students to work through on their own. Interestingly, I have yet to find a text that does a better job with distance/rate/time problems than does this one, even though I know that students still struggle with them in *Saxon*.

If students have used *Math 76* and *Math 87*, they might be ready for this book in eighth grade. Although many eighth graders will have no problem with this book, there are many who will not be developmentally mature enough to begin algebra for another year or two. If you feel that your child is not ready for *Algebra 1* at eighth grade level, either academically or developmentally, alternatives might be to use *Saxon's Algebra 1/2*, a consumer math program such as *A Beka's Business Mathematics* or *Barron's Essential Math*, or a specialized topic study such as one or more of the *Key to . . .* series (Key Curriculum Press) before continuing with algebra. Or you might have your child begin *Algebra 1* in eighth grade, but move at a slower pace, taking a year and a half or two to complete it.

It is important to consider the design of the entire *Saxon* lineup of high school math courses before starting *Algebra 1*. *Saxon* takes an approach that, while common to other countries, is uncommon in the United States. They have integrated algebra, geometry, and trigonometry into three textbooks, titled

Algebra 1, Algebra 2, and *Advanced Mathematics.* Most high schools teach one course in algebra, then geometry, then return to algebra.

While *Saxon* does an excellent job with algebra, the geometry is weak. Originally, very little geometry was found in the first two books. *Advanced Mathematics* provided the bulk of the coverage, which was insufficient. More geometry was then added to *Algebra 1* and *2*, but it is scattered and presented very briefly in both books. By the time students have completed both books, they will have studied about one semester's worth of geometry. They complete their geometry requirement with the *Advanced Mathematics* book. Explanation of geometry topics is fairly brief, and does not begin to compare with the quality of presentation in such texts as *Discovering Geometry.*

A student planning to take only one year each of algebra and geometry (not recommended for college bound students!) could use *Saxon's Algebra 1,* possibly skipping over geometry instruction and problems, then switch to another publisher for geometry.

Students who complete both *Algebra 1* and *Algebra 2,* but who do not intend to continue through *Advanced Mathematics,* need to use another resource to complete geometry requirements. They too might skip geometry activities within *Saxon's* first two books.

However, if a student is going to go through *Advanced Mathematics,* tackling a separate geometry course is likely to be redundant and overwhelming.

Algebra 2 covers standard second-year algebra topics, although its inclusion of a significant amount of trigonometry is not a standard feature of all second-year courses. Students will need a scientific calculator for this course. You might want to invest in a graphing calculator while you are at it so it will be useful for future math courses.

Saxon's program is generally strong on skill development but weak on conceptual explanation and application. The inclusion of the "investigations" in the revised middle-school-level books reflects *Saxon's* awareness of this problem. They will likely include such investigations in the next editions of upper level books. For now, other publishers' texts do better on the "How do we use this?" question.

Advanced Mathematics, second edition

Homeschool kit—$67.50, solutions manual—$31.50

This highly recommended text is one of the easiest for most homeschoolers to work with to cover advanced algebra, geometry, and trigonometry. Originally designed to be a one-year course, Saxon now recommends that students take at least a year and a half to complete the course unless they are very bright.

It includes the equivalent of the second half of geometry, plus advanced algebra, precalculus, and trigonometry. In the revised second edition, much of the geometry was moved to the front of the book rather than being spread out. This should make it easier for students who need to get through the geometry in preparation for PSAT tests in their junior year. In addition, geometric proofs are taught early on, then used throughout the first half of the book.

Students will need a graphing calculator to use with this text, although the calculator is not used as much as in other texts for this level. Parents might decide to allow students to use a calculator more than is required.

Among other topics covered are logarithms, conic sections, functions, matrices, and statistics. This text moves even more into the theoretical math realm than do earlier *Saxon* texts.

By the time students complete *Saxon's Advanced Mathematics*, they should be on par with students who have completed a precalculus course. This course is particularly good for preparing students to do well on college entrance exams.

Saxon also has a text titled *Calculus with Trigonometry and Analytic Geometry*. Since few students seem to be tackling calculus on their own, I will simply mention that the text is available. The review of that text is posted at www.CathyDuffyReviews.com.

For extra help:

D.I.V.E. Into Math (Genesis Science, Inc.) offers instruction for each *Saxon* text, from *Math 54* up through *Calculus*, on CDs that play on your computer (discs for either Windows or Mac systems available). D.I.V.E. stands for Digital Interactive Video Education, a technique that uses a computer "whiteboard" (which is blue on your computer screen) so that it looks and sounds like a class lecture. However, there is the added advantage that students can rewind, pause, and fast forward whenever they need to. On each CD, Dr. David Shormann explains the topic of each lesson and works through practice problems on the whiteboard. Students see only the computer whiteboard on their screen while listening to the audio explanation. Although there's nothing glitzy about it, this type of instruction might be just the thing for students who need more multisensory input to be able to work through the *Saxon* lessons. Genesis Science sells CDs for $50.00 per course and also offers packages of the *Saxon* homeschool kits plus the CD, discounting the CD price by 10 percent. These packages also include solutions manuals when they are available. While Genesis Science has CDs for all current *Saxon* textbooks, they also have CDs for some earlier editions. Check their Web site for full information and to order. *Note:* Dr. Shormann teaches from a Christian worldview, including a Christian philosophy of mathematics, Christian testimony, and Bible verses on each CD.

D.I.V.E. is not affiliated with Saxon Publishers. (Contact Genesis Science at www.diveintomath.com or call 936-372-9216.)

Singapore Math/Primary Mathematics

SingaporeMath.com, Inc.

404 Beavercreek Road, #225

Oregon City, OR 97045

(503) 557-8100

e-mail: customerservice@singaporemath.com

www.singaporemath.com

Everyone has heard how well Asian students do in math compared to U.S. students, but few people understand why this is so. You will have a better idea of why Asian students excel if you check out this math program. Also called *Singapore Math, Primary Mathematics* is published (in English) by Times Publishing Group and approved by the Curriculum Planning and Development Division of the Ministry of Education in Singapore.

One of the strongest features of this program is that it teaches children to really think mathematically rather than just having them memorize algorithms (the mechanics of problem solving).

There is a huge difference in the scope and sequence between this and all other programs I have reviewed. *Primary Mathematics* is far more advanced. The program uses a three-step process, taking children from concrete, to pictorial, then to abstract approaches to learning. The scope and sequence does not align with state or national standards, but I see that as a positive feature. For example, it leaves coordinate graphs, statistics, and probability for upper levels rather than teaching these concepts in elementary grades. Instead it focuses on laying a solid foundation in basic mathematical concepts and processes.

Because the books were originally written for students in Singapore, the third editions use the metric system and bills and coins from Singapore (which are actually similar in denominations to ours for the most part). The few other cultural differences such as names of fruits and people's names are relatively insignificant. Note also that some of the spellings and vocabulary are British (e.g., *metre* instead of *meter*, *colour* instead of *color*, *petrol* rather than *gasoline*, and, probably most important, the word *brackets* instead of *parentheses*). A few other typographical conventions are unfamiliar: decimals are placed at the mid-height of numbers rather than at the base, and commas are omitted from large numbers.

However, *Primary Mathematics* has proven so popular in the United States, the publishers have come out with U.S. editions that include extra chapters for U.S. measurement (retaining metric system instruction) and replacement of British spellings and Asian typographical preferences with those more familiar to Americans. All levels of the textbooks and workbooks are available in U.S. editions. Teacher's guides and home instructor's guides are being produced for each level of the U.S. edition.

Both teacher's guides and home instructor's guides include answers to all problems, and the home instructor's guides also have complete solutions to many problems.

There are also answer key booklets available for Levels 1–3 and for Levels 4–6 ($6.80 each), with only the answers if you do not want to purchase guides. You will not need teacher's guides if you purchase the home instructor's guides.

The program requires <u>one-to-one teaching throughout</u> most lessons for the younger grades. This is always true for activities directed from guides (if you choose to use them), and almost always true for coursework lessons.

Many of the concrete activities are presented in the teacher's guides, but I suspect that most home-schoolers will rely on the pictorial lessons and oral activity for most lesson presentations. You might want to purchase at least one teacher's guide or home instructor's guide so you understand what they offer. Check their Web site for more information.

Placement tests are available at their Web site as well as at www.sonlight.com/singapore-placement-tests.html.

Each level has two textbooks (A and B) that are the heart of each lesson. There is a student work-book for each textbook (two workbooks per textbook for the third edition up through Level 4). This is not as overwhelming as it sounds since these books range in size from only 90 to 170 pages each. In addition, textbooks and workbooks are about 7 inches by 10 inches, with uncrowded, large, black-and-white print. The amount of written work required of children is very reasonable.

The textbooks present pictorial lessons to introduce new concepts. Parents do these orally with children. Textbook lessons provide little assistance for the teacher in how to talk about each lesson. I think that parents who have a strong foundation in mathematical thinking and confidence in their teaching ability will be able to use these books without much difficulty, but those who want teaching guidance and those unfamiliar with the concrete and pictorial teaching methods might find it difficult to figure out how to teach the lessons. If you are in the latter category, you will certainly want to get the home instructor's guides.

Correlated workbook exercises are indicated at the end of each textbook presentation. The textbooks (full color for Levels 1 and 2) are not consumable and are not intended to be written in, although they are inexpensive enough that you might choose to have your children sometimes write in them. Children should be able to work through workbook exercises independently once they can read directions without difficulty.

Primary Mathematics 1A and 1B

1A and 1B sets—$15.60 each, teacher's guides—$20.00 each.

The Level 1 course begins with an assumption that children already have a basic sense and recognition of numbers. It begins with counting to 10, but by the fourth lesson, students are learning addition. Subtraction is introduced on page 38 of the 88-page 1A textbook. Single-digit multiplication is introduced about halfway through 1B, with division introduced immediately after. (Students are not expected to memorize multiplication facts yet.)

The text stresses conceptual understanding over math-fact drill at this level. (Drill suggestions are given in the guides, but you might want to provide opportunity for more practice with math facts using other resources.) Practical applications are used in lesson presentation and word problems. In addition to the four arithmetic operations, Level 1 teaches ordinal numbers, shapes, measurement, weight, time telling, money, and graphs.

Primary Mathematics 2A and 2B

2A and 2B sets—$15.60 each, home instructor's guides—$14.95 each

Level 2 covers addition and subtraction with renaming, multiplication and division (focusing on the math facts for numbers 2 through 5), measurement, money, introduction of fractions, time telling, graphs, and very introductory geometric shapes and area.

Primary Mathematics 3A and 3B

3A and 3B sets—$15.60 each, home instructor's guides—$14.95 each

This level covers further work on addition, subtraction, multiplication, and division (focusing on math facts for numbers 6 through 9), long division, fractions (equivalent fractions plus adding and subtracting), measurement, graphs, time, and geometry. It also teaches two-step word problems and mental calculation. It will be challenging for most students to begin this program at Level 3 if they have been using a different math program. However, the pictorial lessons do help students pick up concepts they might have not been taught yet. Make sure that if you are just starting this program, you watch for this problem, and provide the necessary teaching before expecting your child to do the lessons.

Primary Mathematics 4A and 4B

4A and 4B sets—$15.60 each, home instructor's guides—$14.95 each

By this level, the advanced scope and sequence of the entire program has created a significant gap between what *Primary Mathematics* covers and the content of most other programs. At fourth level, students learn all four functions with both fractions and decimals. Geometry coverage is also very advanced as students compute the degrees in angles and complex area and perimeter questions. Students also work with advanced whole-number concepts (e.g., factors, multiples, rounding off), money, other geometric concepts, graphs, and averages.

In contrast to most other programs, *Primary Mathematics* introduces two-digit multipliers at this level, but doesn't really work on two-digit multipliers and divisors until the fifth level. While students complete quite a few computation problems, the number of word problems seems to gradually increase at this level. Students who want to begin work in this program will not be able to go from most third grade programs directly into this level but will need to first work through at least the third level of *Primary Mathematics*. There is still quite a bit of pictorial lesson presentation, but not as much as in earlier levels.

Primary Mathematics 5A and 5B

5A and 5B sets—$14.60 each, home instructor's guides—$14.95 each

The scope and sequence continues to be quite advanced beyond other programs. At the fifth level, students do advanced work with decimals plus multiplication and division with two-digit multipliers and divisors. They learn to work with percentages and continue with advanced work on fractions, geometry, and graphs. Rate and speed word problems, as well as other types of word problems, are given a great deal of attention. At the end of the course, students are working on beginning algebra concepts.

Some of the geometry taught at this level is rarely introduced before high school level. For example, a workbook problem asks students to find the ratio of the area of one triangle to another, with only dimensions for the triangles given. The rate and distance problems are not quite as complex as the time/rate/distance problems of high school texts, but they get close.

There are many time-consuming word problems and fewer drill-type problems at this level, which accounts for the reduced number of workbook pages.

Students who want to begin work in this program will not be able to go from most fourth grade programs into this level but will need to first work through at least the fourth level, and maybe also the third. Pictorial lesson presentations continue to decrease.

Primary Mathematics 6A and 6B

6A and 6B sets—$14.60 each, home instructor's guides—$14.95 each

Because of this series' advanced scope and sequence, at the sixth level much of the work is more typical of other publishers' high-school-level texts. Students work with fractions, but a typical problem requires students to perform three different operations on four different fractions within a single problem, much like an advanced Algebra 1 type problem, although without variables.

Common geometry problems are set up in proof-style format, although you need not require students to present their solutions in that format.

Among other concepts covered at this level are graphs, algebraic expressions, geometry (e.g., volume of solids and radius, diameter, and circumference of circles), advanced fractions, ratio, percentage, tessellations, and lots of word problems including time/rate/distance problems. It might be challenging for parents with weak math backgrounds to use this level without some assistance.

Students who want to begin work in this program will not be able to go from most fifth grade programs into this level, but they will need to first work through at least the fourth and fifth levels of *Primary Mathematics*.

Videotext Algebra: A Complete Course

VideoText *Interactive*

P.O. Box 19761

Indianapolis, IN 46219

(800) 254-3272

e-mail: customercare@videotext.com

www.videotext.com

$99.95 per module, three modules—$269.00, six modules—$519.00

This unusual course actually combines prealgebra through Algebra 2 concepts (including serious work with functions) in a single course. If you are considering starting this at the prealgebra level, you should know that most prealgebra courses now include geometry, measurement, and other topics that are beyond the scope of this course. This course focuses on number concepts that are foundational for algebra: fractions, decimals, operations, prime numbers, signed numbers, etc. It continues from there to teach algebraic concepts in a different sequence from what is common to most other programs. Equations and inequalities are taught together, concepts are developed in order of degrees (e.g., first degree equations, then second degree equations), and it strives to follow a logical continuity from lesson to lesson as much as possible.

The course is divided into six modules, which should take one to three months each to complete. Consider the entire program equivalent to two years of high school algebra and a supplement to a prealgebra course, even though it should take less than 2½ years to complete.

Five- to ten-minute lessons are presented on the videos—about thirty lessons per module, with about ten lessons per tape. These should be paused frequently for students to consider their own answers to questions posed by the video teacher. Parents should watch the video and discuss concepts with students, but I suspect most parents will prefer that their teens work independently.

A booklet of course notes covering all key concepts and examples comes with each module, so students need not take their own notes as they watch videos. Each module has a nonconsumable student worktext that presents concepts again, using additional examples, then providing practice exercises. A solution manual provides step-by-step solutions for every problem in the worktext. A progress test booklet contains quizzes, tests, and cumulative reviews. Two versions of each test allow for retesting when necessary. Finally, instructor's guides included in each module offer step-by-step solutions to all quizzes, tests, and reviews plus cross references for test problems to the appropriate lessons.

A number of different teachers present the lessons, but because all the lessons were written by a single author, they all use a consistent style that works very well. Presentations are methodical and clear. Videos use animated graphics to illustrate lessons. Emphasis is upon conceptual understanding rather than the memorization of processes.

This is solid algebra instruction that should work well for independent learners. The multimedia presentation is likely to be especially helpful for students who struggle with math. If students need assistance, a toll-free help line is available for them to ask questions. If it does not pose problems for SAT or ACT testing, I recommend completing all six modules before tackling a geometry course.

9

Language Arts

*L*anguage arts is a broad term that encompasses all areas of English communication. Thus, reading and phonics, composition, handwriting, spelling, vocabulary, and speech are all part of language arts. However, in the world of curriculum, we often separate these subjects into separate areas, generally so they each get enough attention.

I've already covered reading and phonics in chapter 7. In this chapter I'll begin with composition and grammar resources since sometimes they are combined within "language" courses. Reviews of my top picks are in alphabetical order, but you will notice that some resources are just for grammar, some just for composition, and some for both.

Spelling and vocabulary resources are separated into their own section later on in this same chapter. I lump them together because many spelling courses actually serve more as vocabulary courses as students move to upper grade levels. Also, if you have a child who is born with the "perfect-spelling gene" or a child who masters phonic/spelling rules in the early grades, it makes more sense to work on vocabulary than to waste time in a spelling program.

Reference work is an important part of language arts education, so you should certainly be using a dictionary and thesaurus (at the appropriate levels). I'll let you choose your own basic reference works, although I could not resist adding my own recommendation for the *Write Source* handbooks at the end of this chapter.

Composition and Grammar

***A Beka Book Language* series**

A Beka Book

P.O. Box 19100

Pensacola, FL 32523-9100

(877) 223-5226

www.abeka.com

I include *A Beka's Language* series in my Top Picks with some hesitation. I know that many homeschoolers have strong negative feelings about these books. However, I think they are very useful when used with discretion. That means parents pick and choose how much of which activities to use within each book. It also means that you should not do every book in the series or you might give your children good cause to hate grammar forevermore.

On the plus side, *A Beka Language* does a really thorough job with grammar instruction. I've yet to find anything I like better, especially at upper grade levels.

Over the years, as *A Beka* has published new editions of these worktexts, they have beefed up instruction in composition skills. However, composition instruction remains pedestrian in comparison to other available options, so you might want to use other resources for developing composition skills.

Grammar and broader language instruction is *A Beka's* forte, and their approach will be especially appealing to parents who want their children to know all the ins and outs of grammar, including sentence diagramming.

As good as the grammar coverage is, it does repeat much of the same material from year to year. So you might use *A Beka* for alternating years. For example, use *A Beka* one year, then the next year focus on composition with one of the other great resources available while using *Daily Grams, You Are the Editor,* or another such tool to review grammar skills.

While *A Beka* has books for first and second grade, I begin my review with the third grade book. The first and second grade books are closely integrated with the rest of the language arts curriculum for teaching phonics, reading, spelling, and handwriting as well as grammar and composition. It is possible to use only the *Language* books (especially *Language 2*) apart from the rest of the curriculum, but there are better resources to use that easily stand alone.

A Beka is well known for strong Christian and patriotic content in their books. They incorporate these topics throughout their exercises. For example, in *Language 3*, a lesson about capitalizing first words of sentences has five practice sentences that, taken together, read as a paragraph about the American flag. In a lesson on quotation marks, one child asks his friend, "Have you accepted Jesus as your Savior?" A punctuation exercise uses the sentence "D. L. Moody was a great preacher." Bible stories are frequently used in this same manner.

All books except those for grades 11 and 12 are in worktext format; instruction and exercises are in a single, consumable student book. This makes it easy for students to complete most of their work independently.

A teacher edition for each book has answers overprinted on student pages. Books for grades 1 through 6 are printed in full color with appealing illustrations. Upper level books are very businesslike in appearance, printed in two colors with no illustrations.

Separate student test books and answer keys are available for every level. A *Beka* also has *Curriculum* books for each course with detailed lesson plans and extra teaching ideas. Homeschool editions of these books for each level coordinate spelling, handwriting, reading, and language lessons from A *Beka* books for those subjects—not just language. These *Curriculum* books are not essential, and I suspect most homeschoolers will be able to function well without them.

The book titles in the series are a little confusing. *Language 1, 2,* and *3* are for grades 1, 2, and 3 respectively. Then *Language A, B,* and *C* are for grades 4, 5, and 6. *Grammar and Composition I* through *IV* are for grades 7 through 10.

For grades 11 and 12, A *Beka* provides a single *Handbook of Grammar and Composition* and companion workbooks for each year. Instruction is in the handbook, while practice activity is done in the workbooks and separate writing assignments.

Language 3

Student Worktext—$12.15, Teacher's Edition—$23.00, Curriculum—$25.00, Test Book—$4.50, Test Key—$9.15

Language 3 reviews beginning grammar skills like punctuation, capitalization, suffixes, and proper word usage that would typically be introduced in resources for earlier grades. It also introduces parts of speech (nouns, verbs, adjectives), simple diagramming, and beginning composition skills.

It is possible to work only from the student worktext, but you should probably also purchase the teacher's edition. The teacher's edition has student pages overprinted with correct answers, explains how the program is to be used, and provides the first ten daily lesson plans from the *Language Arts 3 Curriculum*. This gives you the opportunity to see how useful the *Curriculum* book might be to you before purchasing it.

The *Curriculum* book adds suggestions for developing composition skills not found in the worktext, so if you are relying on this course for composition as well as grammar coverage, you might want to purchase the *Curriculum* book. However, instruction and assignments are in the student worktext, and blank templates for creative writing and journal pages are at the end of that book, so there is some composition coverage without the *Curriculum* book.

A "Handbook of Rules and Definitions" toward the end of the student book is handy for reference. Periodic review quiz pages are in the worktext, but a separate student test booklet and answer key are available.

God's Gift of Language **A**

Student Worktext—$12.55, Teacher's Edition—$23.00, Test Book—$4.50, Test Key—$9.15, Curriculum—$35.00

A *Beka*'s improved composition coverage is readily apparent in this worktext. The first third of the book focuses on the writing process, although it includes mechanics such as punctuation, abbreviations, capitalization, and possessives in this section. The second section teaches all eight parts of speech along with traditional diagramming. The third section concentrates on word usage and dictionary skills. Review exercises or quizzes (depending upon how you choose to use them) are at the end of each section. One quibble: When they teach letter writing and addressing envelopes, they spell out state names in addresses, which is unacceptable to the post office.

A set of *Language Charts* ($8.95) is also available. These are small posters with the steps of the writing process, state-of-being verbs, and other helps that you might post in your "classroom" area. The same charts are used for grades 4 through 6.

God's Gift of Language **B**

Student Worktext—$12.55, Teacher's Edition—$23.00, Test Book—$4.50, Test Key—$9.15, Curriculum—$35.00

Both writing and grammar skills receive comprehensive coverage in this edition. Writing instruction covers topic sentences, paragraphs, and transitions. Outlining, taking notes, and preparing bibliographies are also taught in the context of report writing. Students complete a library research report, including use of note cards and creation of a bibliography.

Capitalization, punctuation, word usage, dictionary skills, and parts of speech are reviewed extensively, with more complex concepts added to those taught last year. The text also introduces complements and use of a thesaurus.

God's Gift of Language **C**

Student Worktext—$12.55, Teacher's Edition—$23.00, Test Book—$4.50, Test Key—$9.15, Curriculum—$35.00

Language C covers most of the same material we find in *Language* B but at more challenging levels. Grammar, composition, and mechanics are thoroughly reviewed. If your child has studied grammar in a "hit or miss" fashion up to this point, this is a good book for reviewing and making sure that everything has been covered. However, it will probably be overwhelming for a child who has studied little to no grammar. The "C" designation allows you to use it for an older child if need be.

The writing process is taught with explanations and examples. However, instruction moves quickly from composing a paragraph to writing a research paper using note cards and including a bibliography. As with grammar instruction, there is some review, but it is likely to be too challenging for the student who has not already done a significant amount of writing. "The Student Writer's Handbook" is a helpful reference tool at the end of the text, with an assortment of tools such as proofreading marks, a checklist for book reports, the Dewey Decimal System, and sample letter formats.

Grammar and Composition, Books I - IV

Student Books—$13.15 each, Teacher's Keys—$17.50 each, Quiz/Test Books—$5.50, Answer Keys—$9.15 each, Curriculum Books—$22.00 each

Suggested for grades 7 through 10, these worktexts offer thorough review of grammar with fairly comprehensive coverage of writing skills. A significant handbook (more than seventy-five pages in *Book IV*) is at the back of each book for handy reference.

Instruction is presented in a rules/explanation format in boxes at the beginning of each lesson. In the composition lessons, the explanation sometimes extends to a few pages. This is followed by practice and application exercises.

Students who have been studying grammar every year will find these repetitious, but those who have neglected grammar for a few years will find them comprehensive enough to catch up on missed concepts since they review parts of speech, punctuation, capitalization, types of sentences, diagramming, library skills, and other concepts students need to know.

Composition skills begin with paragraph structure, outlines, improving style, writing summaries, book reports, and research papers in the first two books. They continue through writing projects—such as critical book reviews, character sketches, and research papers—in the fourth book. The fourth level adds an unusual but helpful section on diction.

Research-paper lessons include footnoting from the first book on. However, explanation and examples are very limited in some of the books, and footnoting information is outdated in texts that have not been recently updated. For example, students are instructed to precount lines of footnotes as if they were using a typewriter, and there is no mention of Internet research or creation of Internet citations. This problem has been addressed in *Grammar and Composition IV*, third edition, published in 2002, and will be fixed as each new edition is released. Meanwhile, you will need to use other resources, such as *A Beka's Handbook of Grammar and Composition* or a *Write Source* handbook for creation of a research paper.

If you purchase only the student text and teacher's edition, you might have difficulty figuring out how to use the writing instruction and assignments. If this is the case, you might want the *Curriculum* book covering that grade level, even if you are not using literature or spelling/vocabulary books from A Beka. At ninth grade level, A Beka has a *Parent Guide/Student Daily Lessons* book ($17.00) rather than a curriculum book, but it serves the same purpose. Separate test and test key booklets are available.

Handbook of Grammar and Composition plus Workbooks V and VI

Handbook—$13.50, workbooks—$6.30 each, answer keys—$10.00 each, test/quiz booklet—$5.50 each, answer key to tests/quizzes—$9.15 each

Workbook V is for eleventh grade and *Workbook VI* is for twelfth, while the *Handbook* is the primary instructional resource used for both. The handbook presents numbered rules with examples in a more comprehensive fashion than many other handbooks since most (other than *Write Source* handbooks) do not include examples. This is an excellent handbook with thorough coverage of both grammar and composition, including research papers. The fourth edition (2003) has up-to-date information on footnotes and citations. Grammar coverage, which includes sentence diagramming, is more extensive than *Write Source* books, although *A Beka*'s format lacks the visual appeal of *Write Source*. The companion workbooks direct students to study particular sections in the handbook, then apply what they have learned in exercises or writing activities.

You will want the answer keys to the student workbooks, but the test books and their answer keys are optional.

Building Christian English series

Rod and Staff Publishers

P.O. Box 3

14193 Highway 172

Crockett, KY 41413-0003

(606) 522-4348

This series is excellent for those who prefer a formal academic approach and don't need any "fluff." Comprehensive coverage, clear explanations, examples, and plenty of practice provide a solid, if unexciting, foundation in the language arts. A great deal of scriptural content as well as frequent references to farm life also serve to differentiate this program's content from most others. Some of the examples and writing assignments reflect Mennonite life so strongly that non-Mennonite children might have trouble relating to them. Despite these possible drawbacks, instruction in grammar and other language arts is better than in most other programs.

Books are all hardbound, printed in black-and-white with minimal illustrations. Children do not write in the textbooks, so they can be reused. The teacher's manual includes teaching instructions plus answers to student exercises. Lessons require teacher involvement and allow for some independent work, increasing the latter as children move to higher grade levels.

Like other classroom-designed texts, these books include extra busywork for classroom purposes, so it is not necessary for children to do all exercises. Both oral and written exercises are included within each lesson. The amount of writing might be too much for some students, especially at the younger levels. If this is the case, more exercises can be done orally or skipped altogether.

Original composition work is included, but there is a minimal amount in comparison to other written exercises until students reach ninth and tenth grades. Students should complete textbook exercises in a separate notebook. Answers, oral reviews, and written quizzes are in the teacher's manuals. For grades 3 through 8 there is a set of extra worksheets ($2.95 each level). Grades 2 through 8 have test booklets ($1.95 each). Tests are combined with editing worksheets for assessment for grades 9 and 10. Worksheet sets are for additional work rather than the primary source of student exercises, except for levels 9 and 10 where they are essential.

Building Christian English 2, Preparing to Build

Student book—$12.90, teacher's manual—$15.25

In keeping with its subtitle, this book lays groundwork by providing substantial work in both composition and grammar. Coverage is very broad and comprehensive for a second grade text. Composition work includes basic sentence structure up through paragraph development and writing poetry. Grammar includes parts of speech (nouns, verbs, pronouns, and adjectives) and usage. Other chapters work on alphabetical order, dictionary use, synonyms, antonyms, and homonyms. Diagramming is not introduced until the third grade.

Building Christian English 3, Beginning Wisely

Student book—$12.00, teacher's manual—$15.25

This level introduces nouns, pronouns, verbs, adjectives, and adverbs as well as noun usage as subject or direct object. Diagramming is taught along with each part of speech. Dictionary work, capitalization, punctuation, and oral communication are also taught. At this level, the teacher's manual states that the worksheets, oral reviews, and written quizzes are not required for the course.

Building Christian English 4, Building with Diligence

Student book—$14.90, teacher's manual—$20.20

The grade 4 text includes all basic parts of speech except interjections, along with diagramming. Original composition writing is included, but it teaches within limited patterns reflecting *Rod and Staff's* educational philosophy. Emphasis is on organization and clear writing rather than upon creativity. There are many student exercises in the textbook, so it is unnecessary to purchase the extra worksheets with even more exercises.

Building Christian English 5, Following the Plan

Student book—$15.30, teacher's manual—$21.90

This comprehensive text covers the eight basic parts of speech, writing skills, speaking, and listening.

Building Christian English 6, Progressing with Courage

Student book—$17.35, teacher's manual—$23.95

This text reviews and expands upon previous levels. There is heavy emphasis upon grammar. It might be too detailed for some students, but *Rod and Staff's* comprehensive grammar coverage in elementary grades allows students to concentrate on other language skills in high school. Composition, listening, reading, and speaking skills are also taught.

Building Christian English 7, Building Securely

Student book—$17.45, teacher's manual—$23.95

Rod and Staff covers grammatical concepts by eighth grade that other publishers spread out through high school, so this text is more difficult than others for seventh grade. It is too detailed for the needs of some students and has extra busywork that should be used only as needed. Using the exercises selectively helps overcome any problems this presents.

Building Christian English 8, Preparing for Usefulness

Student book—$18.05, teacher's manual—$23.95

This book reflects the shift from grammar to application at this level. Remaining elements of grammar are covered, but, more importantly, students work with many forms of written communication.

English 9 and 10, Communicating Effectively, Books 1 and 2

Student books—$14.95 each, teacher's manual—$18.95 each, tests and editing sheets—$2.55 each

By high school, students have thoroughly studied grammar, so the emphasis shifts toward composition and speech. For the most part grammar and mechanics are reviewed, although a few more complex grammatical concepts are taught. Chapters alternate between grammar and composition/speech. Even then, grammar chapters all have subsections on "Improving Your Writing Style," "Improving Your Editing Skills," or "Improving Your Speaking Style," so students are continually working to improve writing and speaking skills.

These two books were also written so that either can be used first. They have much in common, but the first book also covers outlining, arguments, writing book reports, character sketches, letter writing, and poetry while the second covers parliamentary procedure, descriptive essays, expository essays, bibliographies and footnotes, and story writing.

I appreciate the fact that *Rod and Staff* is one of the rare publishers who recognize that grammar skills can be mastered in fewer than twelve years.

Create-A-Story

Create! Press

P.O. Box 2785

Carlsbad, CA 92018-2785

(760) 730-9550

www.createpress.com

Create-A-Story game—$44.95, workbooks—$21.95 each, *Writing Adventures Game Pack*—$24.95

The folks who came up with this board game deserve high praise for incorporating some of the best story-writing strategies into a game format.

The game actually has two parts: the first, moving around the game board and collecting cards that will become components of your story; and the second, putting the pieces together into an actual story, writing, and scoring the story according to how many of your game cards were incorporated into it.

Part of the difficulty for young writers is figuring out what to write about. It is difficult for them to come up with characters, plot, theme, setting, conflict, climax, and resolution, all while using elements of style, such as description and dialogue. This game makes the process much easier by providing a number of these elements for the writer.

There are decks of cards that have topic sentences, settings, characters, plot elements, resolutions (as in how the story turns out), lessons (the moral of the story is . . .), descriptions (e.g., hairy, cold and rainy, majestic), and dialogue (words like "laughed," "questioned," and "roared" that are to be used after direct quotes). Some blank cards are included so you can add story elements of your own.

Every player selects a topic sentence card before play begins, then as they move around the board, they land on other story elements and draw a card each time from the dialogue deck if the space says "Dialogue," from the description deck if the space says "Description," etc. There are some "Free Choice" spaces so players can select a story element they are lacking.

When they reach the end of the game board path, they are ready to put their story together. They need not use all story element cards they've drawn, but they get points for those they do use. They will generally have some cards that just won't fit with the others, but they should still have plenty with which to work.

Each player takes an Outline Sheet from the pad provided with the game and begins to write down story elements he or she plans to use. Players decide which characters will be good guys or bad guys. They choose which plot to use, then write down the key plot elements—what is the conflict, then four steps for what happens first, second, etc. All of this has to lead up to the resolution shown on one of the cards they have drawn.

After they've written down these story elements, they actually write their story. The length of the story should depend upon the age and ability of the child. With a younger child, I might require them to sort through all their cards and limit their selections to fewer than I would allow an older child, just to keep the story brief. Generally, I would expect stories to be anywhere from one to two pages long, but it certainly is possible for students to write much longer stories if time permits.

Once stories are complete, you use the score pad that assigns point values for the various story elements that were used in the story. As the teacher, you can also set your own standards for spelling and grammar, perhaps giving extra points in those areas. Note that references to transition words on the score sheet and in the instructions are a bit confusing since no list of transition words is actually included in the game. The publisher tells me they are posting transition words on their Web site to cover this oversight, but a list is also included at the back of the second workbook (see below).

The game requires adult assistance unless you have older students who have become familiar with the game and who are able to select and fashion story elements together without assistance. There are pawns for up to six individuals or groups of players; children can write stories as teams in a cooperative effort. However, the game will actually work with only one child if you think of it as a tool for writing a story rather than a competition. Ultimately, the stories are the goal more than winning the game, even though children might not catch on to that right away. The story elements in the game will frequently require silliness and creativity to fit them together into a cohesive story, so children are likely to have lots of fun figuring out which ones to use and how to put them together.

Create! Press publishes other products that you might find useful for composition and grammar. Their two workbooks, *Writing Adventures, Books 1* and *2*, teach basic grammar, punctuation, and composition skills in a format that seems most suitable for older students needing remedial work. Beginning with identification of subjects and verbs, the first book presents simplified, condensed coverage that should help a student gain a foundational grasp of grammar. All activities include writing as well as what I would consider optional drawing activities. Composition lessons move quickly from sentence building, through paragraphs, to very short stories (as students might write in the *Create-A-Story* game). The second book adds more challenging grammar lessons and shifts into essay writing. A number of reproducible visual organizers for essay writing are included.

The *Writing Adventures Game Pack* reinforces lesson material in the two workbooks. A double-sided game board comes with sets of cards (that you need to cut out) and playing pieces. You can play numerous variations depending upon which side of the board and which cards you choose to use: identifying parts of speech, punctuation corrections, subject/verb agreement, editing sentences with errors, identifying phrases, constructing sentences from sentence parts collected as they move around the board, constructing compound sentences, and identifying similes. Although designed as a companion for the workbooks, these games work fine on their own.

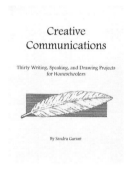

Creative
Communications

Thirty Writing, Speaking, and Drawing Projects
for Homeschoolers

By Sandra Garant

Creative Communications
by Sandra Garant
Catholic Heritage Curricula
P.O. Box 125
Twain Harte, CA 95383
(800) 490-7713
www.chcweb.com
$12.95

This is one of the most interesting and practical books I've come across in a long time. The goal is to teach our children to become better communicators. Much of the emphasis is upon written forms of communication, but it includes oral, artistic, and dramatic forms of communication.

The beauty of this book is that Sandra Garant finds ways to easily incorporate communication activities into everyday life so that children learn the value and importance of developing these skills. I love the way she brings creativity to some of the simplest tasks, such as making signs and lists. But this isn't just a creative-writing resource. Garant stresses the importance of purposefulness in encouraging children to write. Consequently, she has her children communicate in writing many times when most of us would settle for oral communication: writing scripts for the answering machine, making a sign to remind family members when it is safe to let the dog out into the backyard, and writing out directions to your home to post near the phone for children to communicate to telephone inquirers. These are actually very practical ideas!

Communication in this book includes learning how to take phone messages, how to call and ask for information, creating cards with written or drawn messages, creating video presentations, and albums.

There are writing ideas for all ages—beginning writers through adults. Examples of ideas for older children are writing their own tests, creating instruction aids, doing community presentations, and writing action letters. Many of Garant's ideas are brilliant for motivating older nonwriters (see pp. 8–9). She also gives suggestions for informally incorporating grammar into writing activities.

While Sandra writes from her Catholic perspective, including some examples that relate to their religious activities, this book would be great for all families. It functions primarily as a resource book for parents, although toward the end many of the chapters are written directly to students. (There's some inconsistency in this.)

I can't imagine any family that can't use at least some of these ideas to make writing more purposeful and fun.

Easy Grammar series
by Wanda Phillips
Easy Grammar Systems™
P.O. Box 25970
Scottsdale, AZ 85255
(480) 502-9454
(800) 641-6015
www.easygrammar.com

Easy Grammar teacher's editions: *Grades 3 & 4* and *Grades 4 & 5*—$24.95 each, *Grades 5 & 6*—$26.95, *Easy Grammar Plus*—$28.95, student workbooks—$13.95 each for all levels

Daily Grams teacher's editions—$20.50 each, student workbooks—$12.95 each

There are essentially two strands in the *Easy Grammar* series: teaching books and review books. I will use the term *Easy Grammar* to refer to the teaching books and *Daily Grams* to refer to the review books. But to make things interesting, the first of the *Daily Grams* books is actually a teaching and review book! You might choose to use either teaching or review books or both (except at the second and third grade level where they are combined into one).

Let's start with the teaching series. The *Easy Grammar* books are very similar to one another, using the same approach and repeating much of the same material from book to book, albeit at slightly higher levels of difficulty. For example, the first book teaches a list of twenty-eight prepositions while the two highest level books teach a list of fifty-three prepositions.

Each very large (the smallest volume is almost five hundred pages!) *Easy Grammar* book follows a pattern of brief, straightforward grammar instruction followed by examples, then exercises. Most of the time, younger level books combine instruction and activity so that both together take up just one page per lesson. Upper levels sometimes take a page or two for instruction followed by one page of exercises.

You will need a teacher's edition that includes everything in the student book plus answer keys. Student pages in the teacher's edition are reproducible, but that's a lot of photocopying. Instead of photocopying, you can purchase student workbooks that contain instruction and activity pages.

The layout makes *Easy Grammar* self-instructional for the most part. In the teacher's edition, answers are overprinted on student pages right next to the corresponding reproducible page, which makes these answer keys very easy to use.

This program is unique in presenting prepositions before other parts of speech. By teaching students to identify prepositions and prepositional phrases before other parts of the sentence, it eliminates such problems as confusing the object of a preposition with the subject.

Parts of the sentence are designated by underlining, circling, and making notations rather than by diagramming. In addition, it covers phrases, clauses, punctuation, capitalization, types of sentences, sentences/fragments/run-ons, and letter writing.

Author Wanda Phillips strongly recommends that we teach grammatical concepts in order since lessons include cumulative review of previously covered topics. The exceptions would be punctuation, capitalization, and letter writing, which can be taught whenever we choose.

Grammar topics are taught one at a time without significant integration of topics. You will find more grammatical detail taught in programs from *Rod and Staff* and *A Beka* than in *Easy Grammar*, but the essentials for the elementary grades are here. In addition, *Easy Grammar* includes reviews, tests, cumulative reviews, and cumulative tests, all of which help students retain previously taught information.

The format is repetitious and might be enhanced by using it with *Grammar Songs* (Audio Memory), *Editor in Chief* workbooks (Critical Thinking Books & Software), or other resources to add variety.

Easy Grammar is especially good for students who struggle with grammar. In contrast to *A Beka's Language* series, sentences are fairly short, which makes identification exercises easier. Once students figure out what is being done in the exercise, they continue the pattern. Also, there are fewer exercises per lesson than we find in A Beka. However, in my opinion, college-bound students need more challenging grammar instruction after completing *Easy Grammar Plus*. Using one of the A Beka high school grammar courses will take students to a higher skill level.

There are four books in the *Easy Grammar* series: *Grades 3 & 4*, *Grades 4 & 5*, *Grades 5 & 6*, and *Easy Grammar Plus* (for grades 7 and above). These books are not really that specific to grade levels, so, for example, you might use the book *Grades 5 & 6* with a fourth grader and a sixth grader. Also, you do not need to use all of these books since there is so much repetition. You might use one volume, then follow up with *Daily Grams* for a few years before switching back to a teaching volume.

Now, we need to jump back to the combined volume for second and third grade. It is titled *Daily Guided Teaching & Review for 2nd & 3rd Grades*. This is a single volume that contains student pages with an answer key at the back of the book. Thus, you can either have students write in the book or reproduce pages for two or more of your children.

Daily Guided Teaching can be used as the primary teaching tool for the primary grades, although it can also be used as a supplement. Lessons need to be taught rather than used independently, although by third grade students might be doing a good part of the work on their own. Each daily lesson consists of four to five types of exercises that include capitalization, punctuation, alphabetizing, dictionary work, parts of speech, prefixes/roots/suffixes, synonyms, homonyms, antonyms, rhymes, and sentence combining. Rules or explanations and examples are provided within the lessons for each topic that is likely to be new or in need of review. The book has 180 lessons that might be used in one year or spread over two years.

All principal parts of speech through interjections and conjunctions are introduced (only a very brief introduction for each of the more difficult parts of speech). My biggest hesitation with this book is whether or not it is necessary to go that far into parts of speech in the primary grades. You'll have to decide for yourself. Other than that, the coverage of other language skills is great for second and third graders.

Daily Grams are a marvelous tool for reviewing and practicing grammar skills without boring students with an entire grammar course year after year. These books assume students have already been instructed in the grammar concepts, so *Daily Grams* simply provide reinforcement and practice without instruction. Each grade-level book becomes progressively more difficult, reflecting what is assumed to have been taught in corresponding *Easy Grammar* books.

I love the easy-to-use, page-a-day format. It should take only about ten minutes per day. Each page has exercises in capitalization, punctuation, general review, and sentence combining. Answers are at the back of the book. You can make photocopies of the work pages or purchase student workbooks.

There are six *Daily Grams* volumes for grades 3, 4, 5, 6, 7 and junior high/high school.

While you might use these alongside an *Easy Grammar* volume, I would recommend using them between *Easy Grammar* volumes. Focus heavily on grammar instruction for a year, then focus more heavily on composition skills the next year, using *Daily Grams* to help keep grammar skills up to snuff. *Daily Grams* might also be used in the same way with other grammar courses since most repeat the same material year after year and *Daily Grams* reflects a scope and sequence similar to most programs.

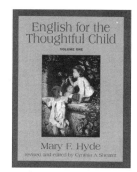

English for the Thoughtful Child, Volumes One and Two
Greenleaf Press
3761 Highway 109 North, Unit D
Lebanon, TN 37087
(800) 311-1508 (for orders only)
(615) 449-1617
e-mail: orders@greenleafpress.com
www.greenleafpress.com
$18.95 each

Cyndy Shearer's search for language arts materials based upon Charlotte Mason's ideas led her first to a book written in 1903 by Mary Hyde. Cyndy updated and revised the book, making it available to home educators. Greenleaf Press later added a second similar volume, also revised and edited by Cyndy.

Volume One assumes that a child has developed basic writing (or printing) skills and is ready to compose sentences. Thus, it is most appropriate for about second grade level. *Volume Two* should work for third grade level. However, neither book has an age or grade designation.

Instead of the repetitious workbook pages found in many English language textbooks, there is a mixture of oral composition (or narration), memorization, written composition, and language exercises. Interesting old pictures—likely retained from the original books—are used as prompts for discussion, narration, and writing in some of the lessons.

Charlotte Mason's philosophy is obvious in the methodology I have described; it's also clear as you read through each book and see the emphasis on thinking skills. Charlotte Mason believed that young children should develop powers of observation and analysis. Some lessons tie in with nature, science, geography—enough so that you will probably need to use the recommended reference book or Web sites from time to time for your child to be able to answer the questions, especially with the second volume. There is plenty of room and encouragement to adapt either volume to suit your own needs. For example, you might find that you end up sidetracking into some of the nature lessons further than originally intended, but that's the beauty of this type of learning.

Volume One covers basic grammar skills necessary for beginning writing—complete sentences, types of sentences, capitalization, and punctuation. Children are actually writing compositions by the end of the book. Literary excerpts used throughout the book are from fables, mythology, and poetry.

Volume Two reviews sentences and moves on to paragraph writing. It also teaches nouns and their usage—common, proper, plural, and possessive; contractions; use of quotation marks; synonyms; homonyms; and letter writing. This does not reflect the typical list of state standards that would at least include more coverage on different parts of speech. The goal of this book is much more on developing a child's familiarity and facility with language, both written and spoken, than with his or her knowledge of language category terms such as "adverb" and "conjunction." Although there are some fill-in-the-blank type exercises, children are also learning to write conversational dialogue and the proper use of words in different situations. In some ways (e.g., thinking, memorizing, writing) it is more challenging, and in other ways (coverage of parts of speech) less challenging than other resources for this level.

English for the Thoughtful Child will work best for those who truly want to implement Charlotte Mason's ideas and are not worried about what everyone else might be covering at the same time. It is a different, yet very effective, approach to language arts.

Classical educators might be divided over this book. While it requires memorization and recitation, it is much more open-ended than some classicists prefer. However, those who value development of thinking skills at early levels might see it as a perfect classical education component.

There are no answer keys—answers should be obvious to parents. Brief teacher information is at the front of each book.

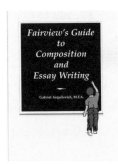

Fairview's Guide to Composition and Essay Writing
by Gabriel Arquilevich
Fairview Publishing
P.O. Box 746
Oak View, CA 93022
(805) 640-1924
e-mail: garquilevich@sbcglobal.net
$20.00

Fairview's Guide to Composition and Essay Writing is a natural follow-up to use after *Writing for 100 Days* by the same author. Although lessons cover basic essay structure, they go far beyond the minimal boring essay. Students create a reading journal in which they analyze many types of professional essays. Think of this as you would an artist who learns to paint by studying and analyzing great artists. Students begin to grasp the creative possibilities available to them as they identify effective techniques in these essays.

While Arquilevich covers some of the same territory as do others teaching essay-writing skills, he often uses unusual approaches. For example, in a lesson on paragraphs, he instructs students to "Find an on-line essay. . . . After duplicating the essay, have someone eliminate all paragraphs so that it reads as a block. Now, locate the best places for paragraph breaks and compare your choices to the writer's" (p. 15).

You might have noticed that the parent/teacher will likely be the one reformatting the online essay into a solid block. Other lessons require either two or more students or else a parent/tutor who will interact with the student on assignments. For example, there is a two-part assignment that requires a writing partner. It says, "First, each person writes one page (any subject) using a lot of qualifiers, intensifiers, informal transitions, and slang. When you're done, exchange papers and rewrite each other's pieces, eliminating the excess. You be the wordsmith and decide what's appropriate" (p. 29).

Fairview's Guide is ideal for small group classes, but it can work with an individual student if a parent or tutor is willing to participate. While some research (i.e., locating professional essays on the Internet or in magazines) is required, the lessons are very well explained and easy to follow. Students who meet periodically as a group should be able to work through lessons independently for the most part, bringing their work to exchange or share at class times.

The first half of the book works on preparatory skills such as those mentioned above, plus tone of voice, audience, word choice, use of quotations, and sentence structures. The second half shifts into actual essay writing, tackling four types of essays: argumentative, comparison and contrast, personal, and mock. For the mock essay, students either imitate an established writer's style or pretend to be someone else and create a style reflecting that personality. Each type is thoroughly developed, including a full-length sample essay of each type.

An answer key at the back of the book has suggested answers for the applicable exercises. While there are a number of such short exercises, students primarily learn by doing lots of their own writing.

Fairview's Guide might be completed in a year, but it is more important to work through each of the skills, taking as long as necessary. It might be used with advanced junior high students, but it is best for high school level.

First Language Lessons

by Jessie Wise
Peace Hill Press
18101 The Glebe Lane
Charles City, VA 23030
(877) 322-3445
e-mail: info@peacehillpress.net
www.peacehillpress.com

Paperback—$18.95, spiral-bound—$20.95, hardcover—$24.95

Jessie Wise, coauthor of *The Well-Trained Mind (TWTM)*, has written a language text that supports classical education as described in *TWTM*. *First Language Lessons* actually combines Charlotte Mason's ideas with classical education elements.

This book mimics many elements found in *English for the Thoughtful Child (EFTTC)*, a book originally written in 1903 and republished in 1990 for use by Charlotte Mason advocates.

EFTTC uses interesting old pictures as prompts for discussion, narration, and writing. Scripted grammar lessons and exercises intermix with the pictures, poems, fables, and other short writings.

First Language Lessons implements all of these ideas from *EFTTC* but with a much stronger emphasis on recitation, repetition, and memorization. This represents the "Dorothy Sayers" line of thought in classical education that young children in the first (or grammar) stage of learning should be learning in this way.

There is much more content in this book than in *EFTTC*. It has one hundred lessons each for grades 1 and 2. Grammar rules, usage, beginning writing skills, and proper oral usage are all covered using four techniques: memory work, copying and dictation, narration, and grammar lessons. Lessons follow a developmental sequence. For example, students do a minimal amount of copying for the first half of first grade, such as copying their own name or a short list of pronouns. They continue with increasingly difficult copywork until second grade when they begin taking dictation.

Let's look at each of the techniques. Children memorize poems, rules, definitions, and short lists. Poetry memorization helps children develop a familiarity with the rhythm and style of good language. Memorization of rules, definitions, and lists helps children acquire the "grammar" of English language.

Copying develops writing skills, familiarity with spelling, and usage. As Jessie Wise says, "Copying allows the student to store in his mind (and muscle memory) the look and feel of properly written language" (p. 15). After students have developed sufficient fluency in handwriting, spelling, and mechanics (lesson 122), they can begin taking dictation. Dictation exercises are never longer than a sentence for this level.

Narration practice prepares children for their own original writing. The parent reads a short fable or story to her child, or the child examines a drawing in the book. Then the child relates key elements of the story or picture. Parents can use the scripted questions to help their children recall or elicit elements of the story or drawing. Drawings are typically used more as a springboard for grammar. For example, one drawing is used to discuss prepositions and the placement of objects in the drawing.

The largest amount of attention seems dedicated to grammar lessons. These are scripted dialogues that call for repetition of rules and oral responses. Sometimes children are prompted to come up with their own examples for categories such as proper and common nouns.

Repetition is used much more than in other programs. For example, the third lesson on pronouns (lesson 48) begins with the student reciting the definition of a pronoun three times. Then the lesson continues with the child continually repeating lists or sentences through the end of the lesson. I imagine you could take the lesson idea and use your own style of presentation if this sounds as boring to you as it does to me. (While the repetition seems excessive to me, I don't think it's as overdone as it is in *Shurley Grammar*.)

Grammar coverage focuses heavily upon parts of speech, covering all eight by the end of the book. *First Language Lessons* covers other elements of grammar, but it doesn't seem as comprehensive as programs such as *A Beka*'s. For example, I could not find anything on plurals, prefixes, or suffixes. However, when children are copying and taking dictation, they learn much of this automatically, so this is not really an issue.

Children are not required to do much writing, but there are occasional enrichment activities for those able to do more than is required. Some of these include hands-on activities that I think would really appeal to all children. For example, one enrichment activity has a child use his body, furniture, toys, and a box to "act out" prepositions.

The book is nonconsumable. Children should have a separate binder where they keep all their work.

I know that some parents greatly appreciate the detailed lesson presentation, the script that tells them what to say, when to have children repeat things, etc. Other parents will find this approach much too structured and controlled. The elements that make it so structured (i.e., memorization of parts of speech, excessive repetition) almost overwhelm the elements reflecting Charlotte Mason's ideas. More narration activity and free-flowing discussion would better reflect Mason's philosophy.

The book is available in paperback, spiral, and hardcover editions.

Format Writing
by Frode Jensen
Wordsmiths
1355 Ferry Road
Grants Pass, OR 97526
(541) 476-3080
e-mail: frodej@jsgrammar.com
www.jsgrammar.com
$22.00

In this outstanding book, Frode Jensen passes on the wisdom and skill he has gained from years of experience teaching writing. His focus is expository writing. I appreciate his strategy of beginning with paragraph writing rather than assuming that students have mastered this skill by junior high—which is rarely the case.

The content covers four major areas of writing that need to be learned consecutively: paragraph writing, essay writing, the principle of condensation, and major papers. Jensen also includes lessons on business writing, including how to write a resumé, which could probably be used anytime after the paragraph lessons. These are the major writing skills that should be developed in junior and senior high school, Jensen's targeted levels for this book.

Students tackle paragraph writing by working with a seven-sentence format that begins with a topic sentence and ends with a conclusion. They write seven different types of paragraphs: example, classification, definition, process, analogy, cause-and-effect, and comparison. The number of each type of paragraph that students produce will depend upon the time available to the teacher.

Sufficient practice at this stage prepares students for the next section—the five-paragraph essay. Students follow the format described in the book, writing seven different types of essays just as they do with paragraphs. In this and other sections, Jensen includes examples.

The section on the principle of condensation teaches students to sort through research information to identify the essentials. They can then transfer the crucial points into their own papers without wasting both their own time and their readers'. Students practice precise writing (condensing and summarizing) with samples within *Format Writing* as well as others the teacher assigns. This is an important skill, largely neglected or treated very briefly in most high school courses.

The final section deals with major papers—reports or research papers of at least 1,000 to 1,200 words. Jensen teaches the traditional note-card organizational method, supplemented with detailed instructions for title pages, citation methods (including CD-ROM or Internet citations), abbreviations, bibliographies, and appendices. Instructions for the various assignments are all quite detailed, and there is an index at the back of the book—both are valuable features for student and teacher.

Jensen includes reproducible check-off forms at the end of the book for evaluating writing assignments. These are extremely useful since Jensen includes a point system and detailed instructions for evaluation that will teach parents with little writing background how to evaluate their teens' work. Sample schedules and scheduling tips also help the inexperienced teacher judge how many assignments to use and how long each should take.

Some exercises are included in lessons as a means of helping students work through some aspects of writing critical to success with the particular format targeted in that lesson. An answer key for the few exercises with predictable answers is included.

Format Writing has Christian content, primarily in some examples and exercises. For instance, students are instructed to write thesis statements for ten different ideas, one of which has to do with explaining the meaning of "faith," and another, comparing two Christian hymns. In the section on book reports, he urges students to write about whether or not the central idea of the book "squares with Scripture."

This book should be suitable for junior high through college level, so you can use it across a wide span of age/skill levels. Also, while Jensen employs a formula approach to writing, it is not as strictly structured as are some other formatted approaches. Jensen's approach should be very helpful for parents who need the structure for themselves as much as for their students. Students can do most of their work independently. However, discussion of some of the lessons would be helpful, and parents need to evaluate student work, so parents should at least read through the lessons.

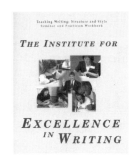

Structure and Style in Writing Seminar

Institute for Excellence in Writing

P.O. Box 6065

Atascadero, CA 93423

(800) 856-5815

e-mail: info@writing-edu.com

www.writing-edu.com

Teaching Writing seminar—$159.00, seminar workbook alone—$22.00, Student Writing Intensive courses—$99.00 for the set, Student Workshops—$60.00 for set of three, Continuation Course—$240.00

A few homeschoolers were so impressed with Andrew Pudewa's *Structure and Style* writing seminar that they went out of their way to make sure I reviewed it. My impression is that their enthusiasm was well founded.

Two things seem to be stumbling blocks for homeschooling parents when it comes to teaching composition skills: the difficulty of finding the right resources and lack of confidence in their own abilities to teach and evaluate. Andrew Pudewa presents writing seminars for parents and students that overcome the confidence barrier better than anything else I've yet to see. And his Institute for Excellence in Writing resources give parents easy-to-use tools that work for a wide range of students.

Since attending Andrew's seminars is not practical for many parents and teachers, he offers those same seminars in the *Teaching Writing: Structure and Style* course on DVDs. Revised and expanded in 2000, the video course consists of six disks (eleven hours of viewing), a seminar workbook, and three *Student Workshop* disks.

The course teaches both structure and style such that students acquire a repertoire of techniques. Parents/teachers learn how to teach both creative and expository writing. In addition, selected grammar skills are taught and applied periodically throughout the course, so students better understand the relationship between grammar and good writing. Students continue to develop and apply the techniques through actual writing activities taught throughout the course.

Parents may watch the entire course all at once or spread it out over weeks or months. Students might watch with them, but this really is focused on teacher training.

Pudewa does not try to cover all types of creative and expository writing but focuses on basic structures and approaches. However, this foundational development should be excellent preparation for students to build upon as they explore other forms of writing.

For example, one of the strategies Pudewa uses is to have students begin by making notes from a model composition. Students come up with key words to convey main ideas. Then they work from their notes to reconstruct the piece, not attempting to copy it, but using their own words, expanding with their own ideas and expressions. This strategy works very well since it provides a secure starting place so students are not worrying excessively about what to say. Instead, they concentrate on structure and style. The basic strategy is then used for various types of writing assignments.

The course as presented to students consists of nine units: Note Making and Outlines, Summarizing from Notes, Summarizing from Narrative Stories, Summarizing References and Library Reports (two units), Writing from Pictures, Creative Writing, Essay Writing, and Critiques. Once past the first few lessons, you can use the lessons in whatever order seems best for your students. The syllabus includes reproducible models that are an essential part of each lesson.

What I like most about this course is that Pudewa walks you through each strategy in detail. His teaching experience is evident as he identifies and deals with problems that tend to crop up for both teacher and student. The lessons move along slowly enough for you to think and work through the process with his "live" audience. This means you are more likely to end up with a solid grasp of the course content.

As mentioned above, the seminar set includes three *Student Workshop* presentations. *Student Workshops* are recordings of hour-long classes conducted with different age groups: elementary (grades 2–4), intermediate (grades 5–7), and high school (grades 8–12). These serve as demonstration classes. You might have students work alongside the "video" class to introduce them to some of the methods of this course.

Even more help is available through *Student Writing Intensive (SWI)* DVDs. These are four disks of actual classes, running about 7½ hours total. Students in the classroom settings reflect the same age-group breakdowns as in the *Student Workshops*. Video classes focus on selected lessons from the syllabus. A binder and a set of reproducible papers (models, checklists, reference sheets, worksheets) come with the set of disks. As with the *Student Workshop* videos, students may work through these along with the "on-tape" classes.

Once you have worked through the basic seminar and *SWI*, the *Student Writing Intensive Continuation Course* picks up where *SWI* ends. It features ten lessons on nine DVDs plus a CD-ROM with all the printable material for you to reproduce as needed. Each lesson is actually a full class, approximately an hour and a half long. Each lesson has an assignment that will take four to five days to complete.

Older high school students (as well as college students) might benefit from the *IEW Advanced Communication Series*. The series consists of three videotapes of classes; tapes are available individually or as a set. Each tape comes with a comprehensive booklet containing the models, exercises, and samples presented in each class. The three titles are *Persuasive Writing and Speaking, Advanced Note Taking: A Dynamic Key Word Approach,* and *Power Tips for Planning and Writing a College Level Paper*.

IEW also offers other related resources in their catalog or through their Web site. Among them are some actual lesson books that will help you implement what is taught in the original seminar. There is a series of four lesson-plan books written by Matt Whitling based upon fairy tales, Aesop's fables, Greek heroes, and Greek myths. These add a classical education element to the *IEW* program. Another book, *Bible-Based Writing Lessons in Structure and Style*, has lessons that you can begin using from the very beginning of the program, while the other books need to wait until a little later. The *IEW* materials are all nonsectarian, with the exception of the *Bible-Based* lessons.

If you want to do a group class, you need to check out the group package options at *IEW*'s Web site.

Learning Language Arts through Literature (LLATL)

Common Sense Press

Publisher sells only through distributors. Contact them for resellers in your area.

(352) 475-5757

e-mail: info@commonsensepress.com

www.commonsensepress.com

Teacher books—$25.00 each, student books—$20.00 each, Red Book package—$85.00

This comprehensive language arts curriculum is based upon Dr. Ruth Beechick's ideas about how to best teach young children—ideas that have much in common with Charlotte Mason's. The program actually begins with the *Blue Book,* a beginning phonics program that I do not include in this review. However, I've chosen *LLATL* as a Top Pick for its comprehensive coverage of language art skills as reflected in the *Red Book* and above.

One of the key features of *LLATL* is literature—in the form of both short excerpts and complete novels—used as a springboard into other areas of language arts. The literature motivates greater interest in both the lessons and the books themselves. In addition, student activity books have lots of variety, and this helps stimulate and maintain students' interest.

Focus shifts from emphasis on developing reading skills in the early grades to more work with composition and literature at upper levels. A Skills Index at the back of each teacher's book shows which skills are covered on which pages.

Following recommendations by Dr. Beechick, once children are able to write independently, they copy short passages from prose and poetry and also take them by dictation. Parts of the ensuing lessons refer back to the literary passage (e.g., identify personal pronouns in the passage). Grammar, spelling, handwriting, vocabulary, and other skills all receive extensive attention.

Student activity books for each level are essential since they contain numerous workbook-type assignments, periodic reviews and assessments, and some pages that need to be cut out for activities. You will also need to buy or borrow novels that are used for most of the levels.

Each book should take about one school year to complete if you use them daily. Although books are suggested for particular grade levels, once past the first year or two, you should be able to use the same level with children over a two to three year grade level span.

The program was designed for home educators and provides plenty of detailed instruction on lesson presentation. However, in the books that include studies of novels, it is not clearly specified when you are actually to be reading the novels. It makes the most sense to me to read the novel and do the book study lessons that focus narrowly on the book first, then tackle the broader lessons that include grammar.

(This is also the order in which lessons are presented.) Minimal lesson preparation is required, but lessons do need to be presented by the parent/teacher. Answers are in the teacher's book.

This is a great program for new homeschoolers who want to use something other than traditional textbooks but are stymied as to how to do it.

The *LLATL* books are written by Christians and reflect Christian attitudes, but religious perspectives are not dealt with in most lessons. A few excerpts from the Bible are used for reading.

I have one negative observation: dictation passages sometimes have unusual or unorthodox punctuation that a student would be unlikely to predict just from hearing the passage. Some such instances are neither pointed out in advance nor explained afterward.

The Red Book package—second grade level

The program for this level comes in a boxed set containing the teacher manual, student activity book, and readers, although you can also purchase books individually. Although six illustrated readers come with the program, you will need to borrow or purchase ten additional children's books.

While lessons are multisensory and interactive, students will occasionally work on assignments in the student activity book on their own. Phonics is reviewed at this level, but instruction also covers beginning composition skills, handwriting (printing), grammar, reading comprehension, spelling, critical thinking, and beginning research and study skills. If a child has already mastered phonics, you might skip those parts of the lessons and focus on new material instead. Periodic assessments help parents/teachers determine how well students are progressing.

Printing instruction is a bit strange. Students are asked to write full sentences from the very first lesson in the book. But at lesson five, they seem to be moving backward since the lesson requires students to trace and print letters and two-letter words. In addition, the style of letter presented for tracing and emulation is more like calligraphy than ball-and-stick or slant-print, but it is presented without explanation. I find this confusing and suggest using another tool for teaching handwriting, either manuscript or cursive.

One other minor complaint: bingo charts and flip books that are to be cut out and put together should have cutting lines clearly marked as well as some explanation of how flip books are to be put together.

The *Red Book* provides a great alternative to traditional workbooks and programs that isolate subjects and skills. In spite of the above observations, it should be fairly easy for even beginning homeschoolers to use.

Yellow Book—third grade level

The broad range of language arts skills covered at this level include grammar, composition, cursive handwriting, spelling, listening, oral presentation, dictionary skills, and critical thinking.

Four "Literature Link" units interspersed throughout the book offer two options: read the recommended book and work with questions and activities that refer to the book, or read the lengthy alternate passage included within the text and use the appropriate questions. The four recommended books for these units are *The White Stallion, Madeline, Meet George Washington,* and *The Courage of Sarah Noble.*

Extra enrichment activities found in the student activity book (e.g., word puzzles, projects, critical thinking and grammar activities, analogies) can be used for challenge or enrichment.

Orange Book—fourth grade level

Four books are used as literature sources for lesson material at this level: *The Boxcar Children, Wilbur and Orville Wright, Benjamin Franklin,* and *The Sign of the Beaver.* A book study of each is followed by additional lessons that integrate literature, vocabulary, grammar, spelling, and composition skills.

Periodically, students copy short literary excerpts or write them from dictation, depending on their abilities. Units on research, journal writing, poetry, newspaper writing, and story writing/book making are interspersed between the book studies.

Purple Book—fifth grade level

The four books studied this year are *Farmer Boy, Trumpet of the Swan, Meet Addy,* and *Caddie Woodlawn.* Students focus particularly on oral presentations, poetry, tall tales, folk tales, and speech making. As is appropriate for this level, the student activity book requires more writing and fewer cut-and-paste activities. Enrichment activities found only in the student book stretch into research, analogies, and logic.

Tan Book—sixth grade level

The four books studied this year are *Carry On, Mr. Bowditch; The Bronze Bow; Big Red;* and *The Horse and His Boy.* There are special units on research and writing the research essay. Lessons are increasingly challenging as students work through activities for reading, grammar, composition, vocabulary, spelling, library skills, and thinking/logic.

Green Book—seventh grade level

The *Green Book* covers grammar (including diagramming), poetry, book study, creative writing (including a short story), topic studies, speech making, and research papers. Literary passages from books such as *Black Beauty, The Borrowers,* and *Eight Cousins* are the foundation for study in many lessons. Other books and a play will be required for book studies that last a few weeks or more. These are *Star of Light, Adam and His Kin,* and Shakespeare's *Much Ado about Nothing.*

Composition and grammar skills receive the most attention in the *Green Book* although all concepts typically taught in seventh-grade language arts are covered. Writing skill lessons are well developed. Reading skills (comprehension, recognition and use of literary devices, structures, etc.) are taught explicitly, while vocabulary work is integrated throughout the lessons. Spelling receives some attention, with an emphasis on rules and generalizations. Study and research skills are both incorporated into lessons.

The content in this book is more obviously Christian than in other books in this series, with the inclusion of some psalms and the book *Adam and His Kin,* a retelling of the first part of the book of Genesis.

The integration of literature with other language arts activities as well as the interactive nature of the program makes this approach more interesting than most traditional courses for junior high.

The Gray Book—eighth grade level

This book definitely shifts students to a more challenging level of work, especially in the areas of writing and critical thinking. Similar in format to other books in the series, this course includes dictation, grammar, spelling, vocabulary, and brief composition activities plus four book studies and four significant writing assignments.

In many of the lessons, students are given passages from well-known literature by dictation. (If this is too challenging, have them copy passages first, then take them by dictation.) In addition, students work on spelling from a list of the most commonly misspelled words coupled with their own list of troublesome words they encounter. Grammar activities and exercises in each lesson often tie in with the dictated passage. Frequent writing assignments develop composition skills, but a special unit on writing teaches students to write four lengthier papers: a narrative, a persuasive essay, a comparison/contrast essay, and a research paper. Four book units are interspersed between other lessons. The four novels students will read are *Across Five Aprils, A Lantern in Her Hand, Eric Liddell,* and *God's Smuggler.*

The student activity book includes an appendix with basic spelling, capitalization, and comma rules; commonly misspelled words list; and space for creating their personal spelling list.

A Christian viewpoint is evident throughout the book, both in the choice of literature and treatment within lessons.

(Also see the *LLATL American* and *British Literature* courses for high school level, reviewed in chapter 7.)

Winston Grammar

Precious Memories Educational Resources

18403 N.E. 111th Avenue

Battle Ground, WA 98604

(360) 687-0282

e-mail: winstongrammar@attbi.com

www.winstongrammar.com

$40.00 per level, extra student packet—$15.00, supplemental workbook and answer key—$17.50

One of the toughest parts of most English language courses is the part that deals with structure and syntax—the sort of thing that diagramming teaches. However, for one reason or another many students just don't get diagramming. Instead of traditional diagramming, you might prefer to use *Winston Grammar.*

Winston Grammar has both *Basic* and *Advanced* sets. All students should begin with the *Basic* set. The *Advanced* set does some review, but it assumes familiarity with the components and methodology introduced in the first set.

Winston Grammar uses key questions and clues for word identification. Rather than constructing diagrams, students begin by laying out color-coded cards in a horizontal fashion that correlates with the sentence under study. Then they use symbols and arrows to "mark up" sentences on their worksheets, showing parts of speech. There are larger colored cards that lead students through strategies for figuring out word functions within sentences. It begins by identifying only articles and nouns, but progresses up through prepositional phrases and predicate nominatives. Overall, it is a much more multisensory approach than most others.

The *Basic Winston Grammar* set teaches parts of speech, noun functions, prepositional phrases, and modifiers. It might be used with students about fourth grade level and above. It includes a teacher manual, student workbook, and the cards in a heavy-duty vinyl case. Four quizzes, a pretest, and a posttest are included in the student book. Extra student packets (student workbook and a set of cards) can be purchased since each student needs his or her own set.

In addition to the above, there is also a supplemental workbook for extra practice. This workbook corresponds exactly with the original in content and difficulty, offering "more of the same" for those students who need it. It comes with an answer key, but workbooks without answer keys can be purchased for additional students ($11.00 each).

Once students have mastered the basic course, they should continue with *Advanced Winston Grammar*, but it should probably wait until students are at least junior high level. The components are similar, but there is an additional quiz in the student book.

This level moves on to more complex noun functions, reflexive pronouns, possessives, gerunds, infinitives, participles, and various kinds of clauses. Some of these sentences get very tricky! I think many of the lessons are fun for a parent and student to work through together, sort of like trying to solve a puzzle.

Precious Memories also publishes *Winston Word Works: A Usage Program* ($26.50). This is a complementary program that focuses on the most common usage errors, such as subject-verb agreement, use of personal pronouns, use of who/whom, correct forms of indirect object pronouns, and comparative and superlative forms of adjectives. This course builds upon the basic *Winston Grammar* procedures for identifying sentence elements. It will be most useful after completing both *Basic* and *Advanced* programs.

Online help is available on the FAQ page at the publisher's Web site, and e-mail questions are welcome.

Wordsmith **series**

by Janie B. Cheaney

Common Sense Press

Publisher sells only through distributors. Contact them for distributor information.

(352) 475-5757

e-mail: info@commonsensepress.com

www.commonsensepress.com

Wordsmith is a series of three books for developing writing skills. These are not age-graded, but they address skills at three different levels. My favorite book in the series is the original *Wordsmith: A Creative Writing Course for Young People*, which targets students around junior high or beginning high school level. My review begins with that book, then discusses the other two volumes in relation to it.

Wordsmith: A Creative Writing Course for Young People (revised edition)

Student book—$16.00, teacher's guide—$7.00

Many students at upper elementary and junior high level have learned the basics in grammar and need some help transferring grammatical knowledge into their writing.

Wordsmith assumes the student knows basic grammar. It moves on from there to work with grammar through written applications. For example, one assignment has them come up with vivid action verbs to replace weak verbs accompanied by adverbs. The goal is to sharpen writing skills by carefully choosing words for the best effect.

After working on grammar, they tackle sentence construction, again with the goal of writing more interesting yet concise sentences. Once grammar and sentence structure are under control, they can apply those skills to compositions.

Although *Wordsmith* does not teach all the different forms of writing, such as reports, research papers, etc., it covers techniques that can be applied in most any writing situation. Lessons work on skills such as describing people, narrowing the topic, and writing dialogue. At the end, students write their own short story. Helps on proofreading and editing are included along with review quizzes.

The student book may be written in or used as a reusable text by doing the brief activities in a notebook. Lesson organization is clear and well designed. Most students should need a year or more to work through all of the lessons. Some teaching, primarily in the form of discussion and evaluation, is required, although students will do much of the work on their own. The author's humorous touches scattered throughout the book add special appeal.

Parents who lack confidence in their ability to teach students how to write will appreciate the inexpensive teacher's guide. It includes answers, lesson plans, teaching suggestions, and ideas for expanding lessons. Parents with strong writing skills will probably be able to manage without it.

Other books attempt to meet the same goals, but the presentation here is better than most everything else at this level.

Wordsmith Apprentice, $16.00

Wordsmith Apprentice is a "prequel" to *Wordsmith: A Creative Writing Course for Young People*. Janie Cheaney translates the same enthusiasm, humor, and energy that so impressed me in the older-level book into this course for younger students.

Using a newspaper-writing approach, she creates interesting writing activities that develop both grammar and composition skills. For example, in the first section teaching about sentences, students learn the four types of sentences, then write four sentences to describe a news photo—mixing declarative, interrogatory, and exclamatory sentences. Stretching beyond the limitations of the newspaper format, students also write invitations, letters, and thank-you notes. "Comic-strips" introduce each new section.

Topics covered are nouns, verbs, sentences, modifiers, prepositions, paragraphs, synopsis writing (often neglected in other courses!), dialogue, opinion writing, and more. These are covered within the context of newspaper tasks such as writing classified ads, travel articles, book reviews, articles, and headlines, as well as editing. Examples and some forms are included, not to stifle or limit students, but to help stimulate their imaginations and give them organizing tools.

Cheaney writes from a Christian perspective, although it comes through subtly. For example, students learn to recognize good synopses by deciding which one of three synopses most accurately conveys the story of David and Goliath. Then an assignment follows to write three synopses, one of which is for the story of the good Samaritan.

This study is designed for students in grades 4 through 6, and it can be used by students working independently (with parents reading and responding to exercises and assignments) or by a mixed age and ability group.

Students who have already been introduced to grammar basics will find this a great way to apply what they have learned. Those without prior grammar instruction will need supplemental study defining and identifying grammatical concepts. All students will need a thesaurus, and they should also have a newspaper to consult for examples. It need not be current, so you can carefully screen a newspaper for objectionable content.

Wordsmith Craftsman, $16.00

Designed for high school students, *Wordsmith Craftsman* can be used after completion of *Wordsmith: A Creative Writing Course for Young People* or any other courses that have built up a basic foundation in grammar, mechanics, and composition. High school students who have done a great deal of grammar but little composition should probably complete *A Creative Writing Course* before jumping into *Wordsmith Craftsman*.

This book is divided into three parts that can be used over a span of anywhere from one to four years depending upon the student. Part One draws students into the writing process with practical, everyday writing tasks, such as note taking, outlining, summarizing, personal letters, business letters, and even business reports (although the last topic is addressed very briefly). Part Two gets more technical with exercises on paragraph writing (narrative, descriptive, persuasive, and expository), word usage, and style. Part Three concentrates on essay writing but builds on paragraph writing skills to create five types of essays: descriptive, narrative, expository, critical, and persuasive.

Cheaney does an excellent job of pointing out different organizational strategies you might use to construct different types of essays. Plentiful examples help students visualize their goals. Cheaney's emphasis on style encourages students to move beyond mechanical correctness to excellence in communication skills.

The book is written for a student to work through independently, receiving feedback and encouragement from a parent/teacher as needed. Students should work through the lessons at a pace slow enough to allow time for them to practice and master the various skills. A ninth or tenth grader should not expect to complete the book in one year, although an eleventh or twelfth grader might do so.

WriteShop: An Incremental Writing Program
by Kim Kautzer and Debra Oldar
WriteShop
5753 Klusman Avenue
Alta Loma, CA 91737
(909) 989-5576
e-mail: info@writeshop.com
www.writeshop.com

Basic set (teacher's manual and *WriteShop I*)—$87.95, *WriteShop I* student workbook—$39.95, *WriteShop II* student workbook—$39.95, teacher's manual—$49.95, *Handbook for Teaching in a Group Setting*—$14.95

WriteShop is another great resource for parents who lack confidence in their own ability to teach their students to write. It takes the guesswork out of the process. *WriteShop* provides detailed daily lesson plans and instructions for teachers, plus student workbooks with worksheets and forms that walk you all the way through activities, evaluation, and grading. Examples, checklists, and evaluation forms show students the objectives and show teachers what to look for in completed work.

Not only do these features make the program easy to use but the authors have structured lessons to build from the ground up, covering sentence and paragraph structure and style before tackling lengthier assignments. The subtitle, "An Incremental Writing Program," refers to the way the program incorporates and builds upon skills taught in previous lessons. Because of this, you should not skip lessons or change the order.

WriteShop is a great starting place for those who have done minimal writing instruction with their children. *WriteShop I* targets students in grades 7 through 10, though it might actually be used with students as young as fifth grade. *WriteShop II* is written for students in grades 8 through 12. The program works well for parents working with one or more of their own children, but it will also work in a group class situation. Co-op teachers will find the *Handbook for Teaching in a Group Setting* a helpful supplement to the teacher's manual.

WriteShop needs to be taught. It is not designed for independent study even though students do much of the writing on their own.

Lessons—each of which might take about two weeks to complete—include "skill builder" exercises that focus on a particular skill, usually related to grammar or vocabulary. The "skill builder" activity feeds directly into the primary lesson. For example, the second lesson is "Describing a Pet." The "skill builder" teaches students to use a thesaurus to come up with more interesting words to replace overused adjectives and weak verbs. This skill is then incorporated into the pet description. Many of the grammar-oriented skill builders help students finally see the use of some of their grammar lessons.

Two weeks per lesson sounds like a lot of time, but the authors have incorporated more than the skill-builder focus into each lesson. For example, the pet description also works with mind maps, topic sentences, metaphors and similes, and concluding sentences. In addition, students are working through the editing and rewriting process on the original assignment. They should also be completing the copying and dictation assignments that build skills of observation and attention while working on various sentence constructions and broader vocabulary.

I think the authors have actually resolved a critical problem some of us have encountered with copying/dictation by *requiring* copying first, followed by dictation of the same piece. This way, students have already encountered unusual punctuation or sentence breaks that otherwise might be unpredictable when encountered only through dictation.

The program is presented in a single teacher's volume and two student volumes, *I* and *II*. The teacher's manual offers more than lesson plans. It also has instructions on how to edit, how to make comments, descriptions of typical student errors, and probable solutions. Student sample writings are accompanied by sample edited versions and check-off lists with teacher comments so you can get a feel for how you might write your own responses to student work. Other helps in the manual are answer keys; reproducible check-off lists, reference sheets, and forms; supplemental activity ideas; story starters; essay topics; and suggestions for writing across the curriculum.

The first student volume focuses primarily on description and narration, although it includes lessons on writing short reports, concise (five-sentence) biographies, and news articles. Skills covered are typical of those covered up through junior high.

The second volume gets into high school level, with advanced narrative and descriptive writing plus heavy emphasis on essay writing.

None of the writing assignments are lengthy. High schoolers will still need to practice writing lengthier papers and research reports than what is required by *WriteShop*. (Keep in mind, the program is not intended to cover all types of writing assignments. For example, there are no lessons on poetry or writing business letters.)

If you start the program with younger students, move through it more slowly, taking at least three years rather than two. Older students might be able to complete both volumes in a single year if they are very diligent and have already developed basic writing skills.

The program is written by Christians; you will find occasional biblical references, primarily in the teacher's manual. However, the author's Christian perspective also appears indirectly in lessons, such as writing a description of a person where the authors caution the student to remember to be gracious and focus on a person's positive features.

Overall, this is one of the best resources I've seen for group classes and for parents who need lots of help to teach writing.

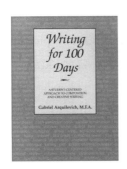

Writing for 100 Days: A Student-Centered Approach to Composition and Creative Writing
by Gabriel Arquilevich
Fairview Publishing
P.O. Box 746
Oak View, CA 93022
(805) 640-1924
e-mail: garquilevich@sbcglobal.net
$20.00

Individual lessons for one hundred days address four areas: composition, fiction, poetry, and writing in action. Assuming the student has a foundation in basic grammar and composition, this book goes on to tackle elements that produce excellent writing. It should work best for high-school-level students, but many of the lessons could also be used with junior high students. I would begin using some of the lessons for seventh and eighth graders, then go back through many of those same lessons again a year or two later as I use the entire book with older students.

Composition lessons work on both style and grammar by focusing on skills such as word economy, word choice, use of dialect and slang, transitions, sentence variety, use of parentheses and dashes, tone, and organization. The strategy is often humorous; sometimes students are instructed to produce a negative example, then a positive example.

In each lesson, instruction is followed by an exercise. Answers to the exercises are provided at the back of the book when appropriate. You need not use all the lessons in order; you can select those that best meet the needs of your student(s).

The fiction section walks students through the actual writing of a story. Poetry addresses selected forms such as haiku, limericks, sonnets, and free verse. "Writing in action" lessons tackle a variety of real-life applications such as business letters, writing news reports, conducting an interview, writing a television commercial, technical writing, and travel writing. For fun, a few "word games" are added.

A list of additional assignments is provided at the end of the book, but I think students will find some of the lesson activities worthwhile enough to tackle more than once. This means that even though the book is only 103 pages in length, it is packed with so many ideas that it can be used well beyond 100 days. Also, you are free to expand, skip, or repeat lessons as you choose.

Ideally, these lessons should be done in a group. Even two students will do! However, most lessons can be used by a single student working independently as long as there is a parent/tutor to interact and evaluate the work. Interaction between two or more students in many of the lessons ranges from helpful to essential, so *do* try to have at least two students work through the lessons if possible.

This book offers a well-balanced combination of skills instruction, motivation, and practice. I often compare it with Janie Cheaney's *Wordsmith: A Creative Writing Course for Young People* because it has a similar playful but effective approach to writing for this age level.

Writing with a Point
by Jeanne B. Stephens and Ann Harper
Educators Publishing Service
P.O. Box 9031
Cambridge, MA 02139-9031
(800) 435-7728
www.epsbooks.com
$12.95

This was my favorite resource for developing essay-writing skills when my sons were at this stage. I might have also considered using *Fairview's Guide to Composition and Essay Writing* or Janie Cheaney's *Wordsmith Craftsman* if either had been available at that time. Nevertheless, both my students and I really enjoyed using this book in small group classes.

It covers gathering and organizing ideas as do other books, but it stresses the importance of communicating in such a way that people want to read it. It teaches writers how to grab the reader with the first sentence, then use description and other tools to maintain interest throughout the piece.

This is a self-contained workbook with instruction supported by examples, then followed by a variety of writing exercises. That means that students can work independently through the lessons. However, they will need feedback and occasional interaction with a parent/teacher. Also, some of the exercises could be done aloud to cut down on the amount of writing.

This book best lends itself to a small group class where students might toss ideas back and forth. Even inexperienced parent/teachers should find it easy to use. Lessons build upon one another, so you should use this book from cover to cover.

Spelling and Vocabulary

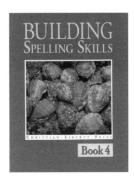

Building Spelling Skills

Christian Liberty Press

502 West Euclid Avenue

Arlington Heights, IL 60004

(847) 259-4444

e-mail: custserv@homeschools.org

www.christianlibertypress.com

Student books—$8.00 each, answer keys—$3.00 each

It doesn't get any more affordable for solid spelling coverage than this series. However, you can't describe these books as "fun" or "colorful." Instead, I would use words like "comprehensive," "thorough," and "businesslike."

They begin in the early grades with a strong basis in phonics, shifting toward word origins and language principles in upper grades. The level of difficulty is higher than most other series and even more so at upper levels. Also, there is Christian content throughout.

Each book is a self-contained, consumable student worktext. Students should be able to work independently through these books for the most part, especially past the early grades. Inexpensive answer keys are available for all but the first book. There are no separate teacher guides. These last features coupled with cost effectiveness make these very appealing for busy families with limited budgets.

Book 1

This first-grade worktext serves as much for phonics reinforcement as it does for spelling. All but the last two lessons are each designed around a phonics rule. (The last two lessons work on syllables.) The first five lessons cover the short vowels, working only on words with the designated short vowel sound. Almost all of the phonograms are covered in *Book 1*. A variety of exercises induce the child to practice writing words over and over. The number of words per lesson seems a little large in comparison to other programs, and the difficulty level also is advanced. Examples of the more difficult words are *voyage, poison, grudge, because, awkward,* and *laundry.* Space for children to take their weekly tests is provided at the back of the book. Teaching instructions are at the front. Some content and inserted verses and quotations identify the curriculum as Christian. No answer key is available or needed.

Book 2

This book accelerates the emphasis on phonics rules with some intense phonics vocabulary. Weekly word lists are introduced with definitions of the phonetic concept, such as consonant digraphs and voiced/voiceless consonants, or rules of syllabication. Some of the lessons deal with root words, prefixes, and suffixes. There are plenty of practice opportunities, but as in *Book 1*, the word lists are more advanced than in other second grade programs. Examples of the more difficult words: *adage, foreign, cyclone, musician, disappear, although, exodus,* and *accomplish.*

Book 3

This book seems to build on *Book 2,* assuming that much of the phonetic vocabulary is familiar. (Phonics background information does appear at the back of the book for reference.) Like *Book 2,* it is very rule-oriented, reviewing previously covered phonetic rules, then moving on to still more. The difficulty level still seems advanced—with words such as *audience, dynamite,* and *luncheon*—but not quite as much so as the first two books.

Book 4

This book continues in the same vein but moves on to accents, more complicated prefix and suffix work, contractions, and possessives, plus calendar and measurement words.

Book 5

Book 5 is subtitled *The World of Words.* The first nine units deal with geography-related words. Remaining units feature individual topics such as birds, sports, anatomy, and economics. Exercises are very eclectic rather than following similar formats each time. One might have students practice with antonyms or suffixes, while others concentrate on the unit topic with vocabulary and practical usage. An example of the latter type of lesson is one on titles for civil officers. Throughout most of this lesson, students learn job descriptions for mayor, notary, auditor, magistrate, constable, assessor, etc. *Book 5* strikes me as one that can be used whenever this type of study seems appropriate for a student rather than at a particular grade level.

Book 6

Book 6 reviews the basic spelling rules students most likely encountered in the early elementary years. This is a good time to review because most students have forgotten that there are patterns to help them figure out the spelling of unfamiliar words, even if they use that knowledge without realizing it. Review does not take students back to one-syllable words but introduces challenging words. Suffixes and prefixes (including Latin and Greek prefixes) are also addressed in depth. Spelling rule coverage is not as thorough as that found in *The Writing Road to Reading* or other resources dedicated specifically to spelling rules. However, this book should be very useful for the student who either never learned the rules or does not use them as a tool when needed. Many junior high students would do well to go through these lessons.

Book 7

Book 7 is obviously more difficult than *Book 6* with its smaller, more abundant print. Suffixes and prefixes are the organizing themes for all lessons, but vocabulary development is the overall emphasis. Students become familiar with many new and challenging words. Since spelling is practiced rather than taught in this book, students lacking spelling skills (rule familiarity) should use *Book 6* first. *Book 7* can also be used with students at older grade levels. Typical of words in the lessons are *infringement, ingenious, befriend, psychic, infirmary, apologize,* and *noticeable.* Examples of some of the more challenging words: *prerequisite, antediluvian, expatriate, ostentatious,* and *recapitulate.*

Book 8

Word origins are the theme of *Book 8,* and this doesn't mean studying only Greek and Latin roots. Instead, lessons explore words from many languages and cultures, including French, Celtic, Arabic, Persian, Hebrew, Spanish, Scandinavian and African languages, Italian, and more. Students need an unabridged dictionary to use alongside the lessons. The lessons are both fascinating and challenging—maybe too challenging for some eighth graders. I would also consider using this book with high school students.

English from the Roots Up: Help for Reading, Writing, Spelling and S.A.T. Scores
by Joegil Lundquist
Literacy Unlimited
P.O. Box 278
Medina, WA 98039-0278
(425) 454-5830
e-mail: joegilkl@aol.com
www.literacyunlimited.com
$29.95 each, word cards—$18.00

Greek and Latin words are the foundation for vocabulary study in the broader sense of word derivations. Children are unlikely to find many of the vocabulary words they learn here in their everyday reading, but they *will* be well prepared for new vocabulary they'll encounter in high school and college. Even more important than the actual vocabulary words they learn is the skill children develop in analyzing new words they encounter and in being able to figure out their meaning.

Each lesson begins with one Greek or Latin word, teaches its meaning, then gives children a list of from three to ten English words derived from the root word. For example, lesson 10 introduces the Greek word *kinesis* meaning "movement." The lesson then teaches five words derived from kinesis: *kinetic, kinesiology, kinescope, cinema,* and *cinematographer.* The word *photos* was introduced in the first lesson, so children are connecting the last word to two Greek words they have learned. Children each need a set of one hundred cards, one for each lesson. Each card has the Greek or Latin word with a border of green for

Greek words and red for Latin words. On the reverse side are the derived words and their meanings. You can purchase sets of premade cards or make them along with your students.

The goal is similar to that of *Vocabulary from Classical Roots* (from Educators Publishing Service), although the vocabulary words here are less commonly used than those in *Vocabulary from Classical Roots*. This program requires teacher presentation and interaction. There is no workbook. Instead, index cards (or purchased sets of cards), a file box, and a good dictionary are the primary learning tools.

The program might be used with students from middle elementary grades through college, but I think junior high through high school is the best time to use it.

Actual teaching information provided is brief but loaded with activity suggestions. The teacher is on his or her own to implement the ideas. Here are some examples of activity ideas. For the root *graph*, a number of related words are presented with accompanying ideas: "Telegraph—Let someone present a research report on Thomas Edison's early days as a telegrapher. Let someone do a report on Morse code and give a demonstration of it." or "Lithograph—Discuss the process of lithography and talk about Currier and Ives. Their lithographs are still used every year as Christmas cards. Make potato or linoleum block prints." These activity ideas could be turned into great unit studies. This resource will be especially suited to the creative teacher who prefers general guidelines rather than detailed lesson plans.

A second volume is also available. It targets a slightly older audience, so it makes a good follow-up to the first volume. It teaches an additional one hundred Greek and Latin root words with new activities and teaching notes.

Sample pages of these books are available on the publisher's Web site. Both volumes can now be purchased together as a set for $49.90.

Spelling Power
by Beverly L. Adams-Gordon
Castlemoyle Books
P.O. Box 520
Pomeroy, WA 99347
(509) 843-5009
www.castlemoyle.com
Book—$49.95, cards—$29.95

Spelling Power can be the only spelling book you use with all of your children through all of their schooling. The basic program is designed for students third grade to adult, but there are also instructions for modifying lessons for children between the ages of five and eight. In order to use this program, the student should be able to write easily and copy words correctly. The "Quick Start Introduction" at the beginning of the book walks you through placement and instructions for using the program.

This very comprehensive spelling program uses a base list of about five thousand frequently used words. A list of the twelve thousand most frequently used and most frequently misspelled words is included as a separate section. These twelve thousand words are coded to show when each should be taught by grade level and in correlation with *Spelling Power*. These words can be used to supplement the basic five thousand already in the program.

The five thousand words are broken down into groups with common elements. Diagnostic tests place students at the proper beginning point in the list. Then each student progresses at his or her own rate, studying only those words with which he or she is having trouble. Frequently used words are reviewed periodically to insure retention. A ten-step study process is used for each word to be learned. This ten-step process should help even poor spellers improve their skills.

Students do all their work in a separate notebook. Castlemoyle sells *Student Record Books* ($5.95 each) that are designed with lines appropriately spaced for different ability levels. However, students can use a spiral notebook or binder instead.

Parental/teacher involvement is essential, although we can note daily activities on the study sheet for older students to do on their own. As children mature and become familiar with the program, they should be able to do much of their work independently. The interaction required between teacher and child in the early grades actually makes this program more ideal for homeschoolers than for the regular classroom. Reproducible study, test, dictionary, and record-keeping forms, plus a whole section of game and activity ideas, are included.

Castlemoyle Books also offers *Spelling Power Activity Task Cards* to facilitate use of games and activities in the program. This is a set of 365 color-coded, four-by-six-inch cards that can be used along with *Spelling Power* or any other phonics-based spelling program. The brightly colored cards are filed in a sturdy box for easy use.

Cards are divided into five categories: drill activities, skill builders, writing prompters, dictionary skills, and homonyms and more. Within each category, cards are further color coded into four categories corresponding to age/skill level groupings covering all grade levels.

Activities designed for auditory, visual, kinesthetic, and tactile learning modalities address learning style needs of all children. Among the activities are games, dot-to-dots, painting, and puzzle making, as well as a variety of writing activities. Most activities can be completed by a student working alone, although a few require a partner.

The *Activity Task Cards* come with a very helpful teacher's manual. The manual tells you how to use the cards, offers suggestions for making your own letter tiles, cross references to *Spelling Power* lessons, and includes answers for the appropriate cards. Cards can be used as supplements to lessons or sometimes in place of lessons. If you are using *Spelling Power*, I highly recommend this set as both a time saver and lesson enhancer. For those using other programs, the *Task Cards* will help supplement lessons through all grade levels.

Spelling Workout, Levels A–G

Modern Curriculum Press/Pearson Learning Group

P.O. Box 2500

Lebanon, IN 46052

(800) 526-9907

www.pearsonlearning.com

Student books—$8.95 each, teacher's edition—$9.50 each

The *Spelling Workout* series, books A through G for grades 1 though 8 respectively, correlates fairly well with MCP's *Plaid Phonics* series. However, *Spelling Workout* may be used on its own. Although books are printed in only two colors, the layout and illustrations make them fairly attractive.

Spelling is taught from a phonics perspective, gradually shifting emphasis to vocabulary and word origins at the upper levels. Lessons for the first six books follow the same format. They begin with a narrative that uses some of that week's spelling words. Then students take a pretest, correcting their own work. The next activity generally focuses on a phonic concept common to the list words. Activities on the third page of the lesson vary; they might be analogies, scrambled words, synonyms, antonyms, definitions, crossword puzzles, dictionary work (in student dictionaries at the back of each book), alphabetizing, or similar activities. The final page of each lesson includes proofreading, a writing activity, and a list of a few bonus words to challenge bright students.

Books F and G are slightly different. They forego the opening narrative and jump right into very brief instruction or review on a topic that might deal with phonics, suffixes, word origins, or anything else relating to how words are spelled. This is followed by vocabulary and dictionary activity, then word analysis and word application activities that might deal with synonyms, parts of speech, analogies, or common word elements.

Every lesson includes a puzzle, most of them crossword puzzles. The final page of each lesson, like those in books A through E, has proofreading, a writing activity, and bonus words.

All levels have reviews every five lessons plus review tests in a standardized (fill-in-the-bubble) test format. Books C and up have a few pages at the back for students to write troublesome words for continued review.

Teacher's editions have answers overprinted on smaller-sized copies of student pages, surrounded by succinct teaching information. Most useful will be the sample sentences to be used for pre- and posttests. Some spelling enrichment suggestions at the back of the teacher's editions might be useful, although most are for classroom groups.

One caution: some children, especially those who are dyslexic, are really confused by misspelled words such as those they encounter in proofreading exercises, or they have trouble unscrambling letters to make words. Their brains absorb the images of the incorrect words, so these children build up a confused memory of what the words should look like. In such cases, skip these activities.

Spelling Workout books require no lesson preparation, and students past the first level or two can work through most of their lessons independently.

Vocabulary from Classical Roots Books A–E

by Norma Fifer and Nancy Flowers

Educators Publishing Service

P.O. Box 9031

Cambridge, MA 02139-9031

(800) 435-7728

www.epsbooks.com

Student books A–C—$9.35 each, D–E—$9.95 each; teacher's guides—$7.10 each

General vocabulary study makes sense for the younger grades, but this type of more specialized study becomes even more useful for older children since they have already built up a foundational vocabulary and can start to make connections with prefixes, suffixes, and roots. The publisher recommends this vocabulary series of *Books A* through *E* for grades 7 through 11, although the letter designations make them easily adaptable to students above and below the recommended levels.

The series draws upon both Greek and Latin roots simultaneously to expand students' English vocabulary. For example, the second lesson in *Book A* begins by introducing the Greek word *tri* and the Latin word *tres*, both meaning "three." It goes on to a study of the words "trilogy," "trisect," and "triumvirate." Greek and Latin words are not always this similar, so lesson 4 introduces the Greek word *pan* and the Latin word *omnis*, both meaning "all," plus the Greek word *holos* and the Latin word *totus*, both meaning "whole."

Students with some exposure to Greek and/or Latin will immediately recognize the derivation of words from those languages. Other students without prior knowledge of those languages will develop some familiarity with Greek and Latin simply by using these workbooks.

Each book is written at an increasingly difficult level. Words with similar roots are grouped thematically for ease of study. A variety of exercises, including work with synonyms, antonyms, analogies, and sentence completion, helps students develop full understanding. Two unusual extras are included: (1) literary, historical, and geographic references help develop cultural literacy, and (2) suggestions for extended writing activities help students to apply new vocabulary. *Books D* and *E* add exercises for testing vocabulary within the context of short articles. One student, who has used earlier levels of this series, pointed out that *Book E* contains creeping elements of political correctness, even though they are subtle and sporadic rather than obvious and pervasive.

While students can work independently through most of the lessons, group or teacher discussion really helps most students.

A teacher's guide and answer key for each level has teaching suggestions, exercise answers, and glossaries of some of the literary and historical references.

Wordly Wise, Books 1–9 (original series)
Educators Publishing Service
P.O. Box 9031
Cambridge, MA 02139-9031
(800) 435-7728
www.epsbooks.com
Student books 1–5—$8.70 each, 6–9—$9.65 each; teacher's key—$6.35 each

I've seen many vocabulary resources over the years, but my favorite for general use remains the original _Wordly Wise_ series, _Books 1-9_. (_Books A_ through _C_ are also available, but I think other academic priorities preclude their use in the early grades.)

In this series, students use one list of words through four or five different types of exercises to become familiar with each word's usage in different contexts as well as their various meanings. Exercises include definitions, recognition of proper usage, word origins, prefixes and suffixes, analogies, and synonym substitution. Crossword puzzles at the end of each unit reinforce learning from earlier lessons. Children must truly understand meanings to complete the activities.

The answer key for each level is relatively inexpensive, and you will certainly want it to save time and energy since the exercises are often quite challenging.

I suspect the popularity of _Wordly Wise_ stems from its effectiveness and reasonable cost as well as the fact that students can work independently most of the time. _Books 1–9_ are intended for grades 4 through 12. However, vocabulary is somewhat advanced, so choose lower level books if your children are average in their vocabulary skills. I suggest starting average to bright students at fourth grade level with _Book 1_.

One drawback of this series occurs in _Books 4–9_. While _Books 1–3_ include glossaries in the back listing all vocabulary words and their definitions, from _Book 4_ on, students must use a separate dictionary.

There is also a newer _Wordly Wise 3000_ series, but it requires more subjective answers, making it more difficult to use. Nevertheless, it too is an excellent vocabulary resource. Eventually, it will replace the original series.

• • •

Although they are not one of my Top 100, you might have noticed my mention of _Write Source_ handbooks in some of the resource reviews. The _Write Source_ actually is a line of products that includes composition and grammar instruction worktexts. But the best thing in the _Write Source_ line is their handbooks. They have a number of editions for different levels—all of them colorful with "cartoonish" illustrations and easy-to-understand language. I recommend using them for third grade level through high school.

Titles and corresponding levels are:

- *Write on Track* (grade 3) $13.75
- *Writers Express* (grade 4) $14.75
- *All Write* (grade 5) $14.75
- *Write Source 2000* (grades 6–8) $14.75
- *Write Ahead* (grades 9–10) $15.75
- *Writers, Inc.* (grades 9–12) $15.75

These are far more than grammar handbooks; they also include guidelines for various forms of writing (including research papers), student models of writing, and reference tools. The *Write Source* goal is to produce better writers, so grammar is presented as a tool for better writing rather than something students learn for its own sake.

Handbooks can be used for instruction, but they actually work best as a reference and review tool. They include grammar and usage rules coded by number.

Here's how I like to use them: When correcting your child's writing, you mark the *Write Source* code number next to an error. Students look up the rule and figure out how they violated it, then make their correction. This forces them to process grammar rules in a way that workbook exercises never do. These handbooks can be used alongside any other grammar/composition resources you might use.

A separate teacher's guide ($21.95 each) is available for each handbook, but they are strictly optional. Although written for classroom use, they do have some useful start-up activities, minilessons, and reviews that you might find helpful.

You might run into occasional content problems, particularly in the examples, since these are written for public school students. (Published by Great Source, www.greatsource.com or www.write source.com, 800-289-4490.)

10

History, Geography, and Cultural Studies

*S*ocial studies is a comprehensive term that includes history, geography, and cultural studies. Some of us cringe at the term *social studies*, equating it with the watered down mush that passes for history education in some current textbooks. But the "social studies" label is not the culprit. The problem lies in emphasis and philosophy. The public school system (in general) has overemphasized cultural studies—and politically correct cultural studies at that—at the expense of history and geography. Social studies has often been used as a tool for social engineering rather than to provide an education in history. Christians have been particularly aware of the secularization of history—the sort of thing that translates our Thanksgiving holiday into a mutual admiration day between the Pilgrims and the Indians without any mention of God. In reacting against the secular bias in textbooks, Christians have sometimes erred in moving to another extreme, rejecting cultural studies and reducing the subject to memorization of history and geography data. Neither approach is correct.

I think a great way to resolve this is to approach social studies as a newspaper reporter. Reporters look for the answers to the questions: Who did what? When did they do it? Where did they do it? and Why did they do it?

So, imitating a reporter, we look at the interrelationships of the three areas: history, geography, and cultural studies. The reporter's first two questions are answered by the names and dates or periods (history). The third question is answered by describing the location (geography). The last question deals with the background of the event and other influences, essentially putting an event in context (cultural studies). Our social studies should be like a good newspaper article, combining all the necessary ingredients.

Choosing Appropriate Resources

A few history/social studies textbooks manage to pull all the above elements together, but then you have to deal with the biases of the authors. It is impossible to write an entirely neutral textbook. Even if the language is not slanted, every textbook will exhibit bias simply in the choices of what is or is not included. Textbooks that cover all of world history while paying little or no attention to the impact of Judaism and Christianity reflect a huge bias that paints a false picture of a world that has developed without any interaction with the living God.

If you are a Christian and want to help your child develop a Christian worldview, then you will probably want to use resources that help rather than hinder that goal. In regard to resources, there are three approaches to social studies. You might use any of these approaches exclusively or mix two or more of them. The three approaches are

1. History textbooks
2. Real books (and I would include Internet research in this category)
3. History through unit studies (which might use texts or real books)

History Textbooks

Most history textbooks are rather boring. They try to cover lots of information, and that usually means they can allot only a few lines or a few paragraphs to each event. Textbook authors don't usually have space to make the interesting connections between events. Other than in the occasional sidebar, they can't tell us the personal history behind extraordinary events such as twenty-one-year-old Nathan Hale's heroic declaration, "I only regret that I have but one life to lose for my country."

Learning history as sets of facts to be memorized and regurgitated for tests might even do more harm than good. Often children learn to despise history if they never get to experience the delight or amazement that comes from reading the "whole stories" of history.

The dumbed down language of some history texts for primary grades is another turnoff. Increasingly, upper elementary level history texts are showing signs of the same malady. Publishers, seeking to make their books more visually appealing, add lots of large color illustrations as they update history textbooks. They steal space for the illustrations from the lines of text, reducing them to short, choppy sentences, for the most part devoid of beauty or human interest. I rarely encourage parents of children in the elementary grades to use history textbooks, especially since we have many better options available to us.

Junior-high-level history books generally are a little better, with more content and fewer pictures. By high school, history textbooks have much more written material than do earlier levels, and there are some worth using.

I know I've made some sweeping generalizations here. There are a few exceptions. I've included reviews of a few history "texts" for elementary grades, but you will note that these exceptions are not the typical written-by-committee, state-approved textbook series.

Geography textbooks might be even worse than history textbooks. I've included only one resource that exclusively targets geography—*The Ultimate Geography and Timeline Guide*. This unusual book is so much better than traditional geography texts that, in my opinion, nothing else comes close.

History through Unit Studies

Most unit studies have a strong historical component. Sometimes history is the primary theme, with other subjects branching off from the study of history. This is a great way to make history interesting.

Unit studies generally recommend real books as the source of historical information. Some unit studies include historical information within their own material, but even then they generally direct you to other resources for further reading.

A few unit studies recommend history texts as the source of information, but they enhance the textbook information with stories and activities.

Some unit studies are structured in chronological order, so if you follow the publisher's sequence of study, you are studying history in its proper order. However, some unit studies are organized around other themes, and their history coverage jumps around—you might be studying ancient Rome one month, then South America the next. In such instances, timelines are essential for children to grasp the actual chronology of events. If they can visually see events on a timeline, it helps them put things in proper context.

Don't forget to check out the reviews of unit studies in chapter 12 to see if you might want to use one of these for coverage of history. One history program reviewed in this chapter, *The Mystery of History*, is designed like a unit study, but I include it here because it is more narrowly focused than most unit studies in that its goal is to cover only history and geography.

Real Books

I'll never forget a television talk show interview with the Colfax family, homeschool pioneers whose sons were probably the first homeschoolers to receive scholarships to Harvard University. One of their sons was talking about his transition from homeschooling to the academic demands of the university. The host was probably trying to get him to acknowledge some deficiencies by asking about his history studies through high school. The young man admitted that he had never read a history textbook before going to Harvard. But, he continued, he had read many real books—biographies, historical fiction, and nonfiction.

He surprised even himself when he discovered that through his reading he actually knew more history than his classmates who had been through ten or more history textbooks each. He attributed his acquired knowledge to his love for the subject that blossomed as he read about history in a way that brought the subject to life.

I have had opportunities to ask groups of veteran homeschoolers what actually worked best for them. The unanimous response is always "real books." Most did not start out with a real-books approach, but after experimenting with it, they gradually shifted from exclusive reliance on textbooks to real books or a combination of both.

Because I believe so much in the value of real books for history, I am including lists of books by historical periods first, followed by reviews of my Top Picks. Real books in the following lists are a mixture of historical fiction, biography, and even some legend.

I've also included some "fact" books, such as David Macaulay's intriguingly illustrated books and a number of colorfully-illustrated information books such as those from Usborne, Peter Bedrick, DK Publishing, Facts on File, and Random House/Knopf. See the boxed review of Usborne's *World History* books on the next page to get a general sense of what these "fact" type books are like.

I suggest using these fact books along with other books that give more complete coverage of at least some topics. Fact books often do a great job on the introductory or supplemental level. But keep in mind that they generally strive for religious neutrality, and religious neutrality often means omission of important religious information and ideas as well as the occasional inclusion of problematic content such as nudity, praise for pagan gods, and distortion of religious positions.

I have *not* read all the books in these lists myself but have compiled the lists from my own experience and the recommendations of others. Therefore I cannot vouch for the content of every book.

Real Books by Time Periods/Topics

Listed here are historical biographies and novels as well as a few informational books that read like stories. You can choose an assortment of such books as the core of your curriculum, adding discussion, writing, and activities to accomplish your educational goals. This is not intended to be a comprehensive list, but it should be enough to get you started exploring history through real books.

I've included some titles that are written for adults but might be read aloud to older children or read independently by mature teens. When I know grade-level information for certain, I've used (y) to indicate books written for children up through about fourth grade level and (o) to indicate books written for at least sixth grade level and older. (If there is no "y" or "o," I'm not certain of the reading level.) I've also used some notations for books that are part of well-known series: (Landmark) = Landmark Books, (CFA) = Childhood of Famous Americans, and (Sower) = Sower series. I've used (FB) by the appropriate titles to indicate a fact book.

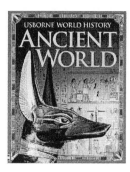 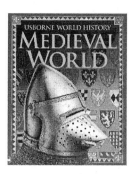

Usborne Internet-Linked Ancient World and *Medieval World*

Educational Development Corporation

P.O. Box 470663

Tulsa, OK 74147-0663

(800) 475-4522

e-mail: edc@edcpub.com

www.edcpub.com

$14.95 each

These two beautifully illustrated history books can be used to cover world history from ancient times up through the Middle Ages for students in grades 4 through 6. History and culture are combined as is appropriate for these grade levels. Although the text is broken up by illustrations, it flows in columns, making it fairly easy to read. Illustrations all have helpful descriptions—children are likely to browse through these books just "reading" illustrations and their descriptions. Timelines running across the bottom of every page are helpful. The selective coverage of history enhanced by the use of the provided Web links should give children a good introduction to world history.

Interestingly, *Ancient World* skips cave men and begins with the first farming communities. It briefly touches on a few examples of ancient towns, then moves on to the Sumerian and Egyptian civilizations. Hittites, Canaanites, Phoenicians, Assyrians, Hebrews, and other ancient civilizations also get brief coverage. Coverage of ancient Greece and Rome is given more space, and China, Japan, Africa, India, and the Americas also get attention.

Medieval World picks up where *Ancient World* leaves off, around A.D. 500. It begins with the Byzantine Empire, skipping over barbarian invasions to discuss the barbarian kingdoms that arose. Arabs and Islam, Vikings, Anglo-Saxon England, Charlemagne, and the Holy Roman Empire typify the range of topics covered next. Castles, towns, trade, and the church all receive attention as significant historical factors. Coverage expands beyond Western civilization to the entire world, including the rise of the Russians, conquest of North Africa, East Africa, Southern India, Southeast Asia, Pacific Islanders, the Americas, and other civilizations up through about A.D. 1400.

I have also added specific dates or time periods by many titles so you can choose books in a chronological sequence if you so desire. In addition, I have sometimes noted the geographical area where a story takes place when I think it might be helpful.

Ancient Egypt

Ancient Egyptians at a Glance by Rupert Matthews (Peter Bedrick Books) (FB)

The Cat of Bubastes G. A. Henty (o)

Pyramid by David Macaulay (FB)

Tales of Ancient Egypt by Roger Lancelyn Green

Golden Goblet and other titles by Eloise Jarvis McGraw

Moses by Leonard Fisher

Motel of the Mysteries by David Macaulay (FB)

The Riddle of the Rosetta Stone by James Cross Givlin

✓ *Pharaohs of Ancient Egypt* by Payne (Landmark)

Into the Mummy's Tomb by Nicholas Reeves

Shadow Hawk by Andre Norton

✓ *The Usborne Time Traveler: Pharaohs and Pyramids* (FB) (y)

Ancient Greece

✓ *The Great Alexander the Great* by Joe Lasker (y)

Classic Myths to Read Aloud: The Great Stories of Greek and Roman Mythology by William F. Russell

Tales of the Greek Heroes by Roger Lancelyn Green (o)

The Illiad translated by Lattimore (o)

The Odyssey translated by Lattimore and another translation by Robert Fitzgerald (o)

Adventures of Ulysses translated by Gottlieb

The Wanderings of Odysseus by Rosemary Sutcliff

Black Ships before Troy by Rosemary Sutcliff

The Children's Homer by Padric Colum (o)

Alexander and His Times by Frederic Theule (o)

✓ *The Trojan Horse* by Emily Little (y)

✓ *D'Aulaires Book of Greek Myths* by Ingri and Edgar Parin D'Aulaire (y)

Archimedes and the Door of Science by Jeanne Bendick

The Librarian Who Measured the Earth (Ptolemy) by Lasky

Discovering the World of the Ancient Greeks by Zofia Archibald (Facts on File) (FB) (o)

The Visual Dictionary of Ancient Civilizations (DK Publishing) (FB)

Bible Times and Ancient Rome

Ancient Romans at a Glance by Dr. Sarah McNeill (Peter Bedrick Books) (FB)

Eyewitness Books: Ancient Rome (Knopf) (FB)

Cultural Atlas for Young People: Ancient Rome by Mike Corbishley (Facts on File) (FB)

Hittite Warrior by Joanne Williamson (1200 B.C., Judea)

Classic Myths to Read Aloud: The Great Stories of Greek and Roman Mythology by William F. Russell

Augustus Caesar's World by Genevieve Foster (63 B.C. to A.D. 14, world) (o)

The Eagle of the Ninth by Rosemary Sutcliff (A.D. 119, Rome)

The Aeneid of Virgil translated by Robert Fitzgerald

Runaway by Patricia St. John (first century, Judea)

Pearl Maiden by H. Rider Haggard (first century, Judea)

Bronze Bow by Elizabeth Speare (32 B.C., Judea)

For the Temple by G. A. Henty (A.D. 70, Judea) (o)

Festival of Lights by Maida Silverman (165 B.C., Judea) (y)

Beric the Briton: A Story of the Roman Invasion by G. A. Henty (A.D. 61, Britain and Rome) (o)

Young Carthaginian by G. A. Henty (220 B.C., North Africa) (o)

Cleopatra by Diane Stanley and Peter Vennema (first century B.C., Egypt)

Saint Valentine retold by Robert Sabuda (third century A.D., Rome)

The Ides of April by Mary Ray (A.D. 60, Rome)

The Lantern Bearers (Britain at the end of the Roman occupation) by Rosemary Sutcliff (A.D. 450, Britain)

Ben Hur, a Tale of the Christ by Lew Wallace (first century A.D., Rome, Judea) (o-read aloud)

The Robe by Lloyd C. Douglas (first century A.D., Rome and Judea) (o-read aloud)

Quo Vadis by Henryk Sienkiewicz (A.D. 60, Rome) (o-read aloud)

The White Stag (Attila the Hun) by Kate Seredy (A.D. 400s, Asia and Europe)

World History from the Fall of Rome through the Middle Ages

Beowulf the Warrior by Ian Serraillier (1100, England)

Dragon Slayer (Beowulf) by Rosemary Sutcliff (1100, England)

Augustine Came to Kent by Barbara Willard (600, England)

Son of Charlemagne by Barbara Willard (780, Europe)

Beorn the Proud by Madeleine Pollard (800s, Ireland and Denmark)

Norse Gods and Giants by the D'Aulaires (Norse mythology)

The Dragon and the Raven or the Days of King Alfred by G. A. Henty (800s, England) (o)

Tristan and Iseult (Ireland and Britain) by Rosemary Sutcliff (legend, England)

The Story of King Arthur and His Knights and other Arthurian Tales by Howard Pyle (legend, England)

Leif the Lucky by the D'Aulaires (1000, exploration of America)

The Usborne Time Traveler: The Viking Age (FB) (y)

The Story of Rolf and the Viking Bow by Allen French (1000, Iceland)

Vikings by Elizabeth Janeway—(Landmark) (1000, exploration)

The King's Shadow by Elizabeth Alden (1000s, England)

The Lances of Lynwood by Charlotte M. Yonge (1000s, Europe)

Wulf the Saxon: A Story of the Norman Conquest by G. A. Henty (1066, England) (o)

The Red Keep by Allen French (1165, Europe)

If All the Swords in England (Thomas Becket) by Barbara Willard (1100s, England)

The Hidden Treasure of Glaston by Eleanore M. Jewett (1171, England)

The Minstrel in the Tower by Gloria Skurzynski (1195, Europe)

The Door in the Wall by Marguerite DeAngeli (1200s, England)

The Lost Baron by Allen French (1200, England)

Winning His Spurs by G. A. Henty (1190, the Crusades) (o)

The Crusades by Child, Kelly, and Whittock (Peter Bedrick Books) (FB)

Magna Charta by James Daugherty (1200s, England)

Cathedral by David Macaulay (1200s, Europe)

Genghis Khan and the Mongol Hordes by Harold Lamb (1200, Central Asia)

The Road to Damietta (St. Francis of Assisi) by Scott O'Dell (1200, Italy)

Adam of the Road by Elizabeth Gray (1294, England)

What Do We Know About the Middle Ages? by Sarah Howarth (Peter Bedrick Books) (FB)

St. George and the Dragon by Margaret Hodges (legend, England)

The Merry Adventures of Robin Hood by Howard Pyle (1200, England)

Men of Iron by Howard Pyle (1300s, England)

In Freedom's Cause (William Wallace and Robert the Bruce and the battle for Scottish independence) by
      G. A. Henty (1300, Scotland) (o)

Ivanhoe by Sir Walter Scott (1300s, Europe)

The Talisman by Sir Walter Scott (1300s, the Crusades)

William Tell retold by Margaret Early (1300s, Switzerland)

Otto of the Silver Hand by Howard Pyle (1400s, Europe)

Sir Gawain and the Green Knight by J. R. R. Tolkien (1400, England)

Joan of Arc by Josephine Poole (1400s, France)

The Trumpeter of Krakow by Eric P. Kelly (1400s, Poland)

The Black Arrow by Robert Louis Stevensonn (1400s, England)

A Knight of the White Cross by G. A. Henty (1480, Europe) (o)

Renaissance to Modern Day (other than U.S. history)

Ink on His Fingers (Gutenberg) by Louise Vernon (1400s, Germany)

The Hawk that Dare Not Hunt by Day (Tyndale) by Scott O'Dell (1494–1536, England)

√*Where Do You Think You're Going, Christopher Columbus?* by Jean Fritz (1492, exploration) (y)

√*Columbus* by the D'Aulaires (1492, exploration) (y)

The World of Columbus and Sons by Genevieve Foster (1400s–1500s, world)

Lysbeth: A Tale of the Dutch by H. Rider Haggard (1500s, Netherlands)

Under Drake's Flag: A Tale of the Spanish Main by G. A. Henty (1500s, England and exploration) (o)

By Right of Conquest or With Cortez in Mexico by G. A. Henty (1500s, Mexico) (o)

The World of Captain John Smith by Genevieve Foster (1580–1631, world)

With Pipe, Paddle and Song by Elizabeth Yates (1750, Canada)

Leonardo da Vinci by Diane Stanley (1400–1500, Europe)

By Pike and Dike by G. A. Henty (1500s, Europe) (o)

St. Bartholomew's Eve: A Tale of the Huguenot Wars by G. A. Henty (1500s, France) (o)

Edmund Campion by Harold Gardiner, S. J. (1500s, England)

Red Hugh: Prince of Donegal by Robert T. Reilly (1500s, Ireland)

Martin Luther, The Great Reformer by J. A. Morrison (1483–1546, Germany)

This Was John Calvin by Thea B. Van Halsema (1509–1564, Europe)

Johannes Kepler by John Hudson Tiner (Sower) (1600s, Germany)

Isaac Newton by John Hudson Tiner (Sower) (1642–1727, England)

A Tale of Two Cities by Charles Dickens (1700s, Europe) (o)

The Scarlet Pimpernel by Baroness Orezy (1700s, France) (o)

Don Quixote by Miguel Cervantes retold by Michael Harrison (fiction, Spain)

U.S. History

✓ *Pocahontas* by the D'Aulaires (y)

Diary of an Early American Boy by Eric Sloan

The Last of the Mohicans by James Fenimore Cooper (o)

Witchcraft of Salem Village by Shirley Jackson (Landmark)

Amos Fortune: Free Man by Elizabeth Yates

Can't You Get Them to Behave, King George? by Jean Fritz

And Then What Happened, Paul Revere? by Jean Fritz

America's Paul Revere by Esther Forbes

Why Don't You Get a Horse, Sam Adams? By Jean Fritz

Sam the Minuteman by Nathaniel Benchley

✓ *Crispus Attucks: Black Leader of Colonial Patriots* by Gray Morrow (CFA) (y)

Ben and Me by Robert Lawson

Mr. Revere and I by Robert Lawson

Ben Franklin of Old Philadelphia by Margaret Cousins (Landmark)

The World of Captain John Smith by Genevieve Foster (o)

George Washington's World by Genevieve Foster (o)

The Cabin Faced West by Jean Fritz

Fourth of July Story by Alice Dagliesh

The Reb and the Redcoats by Constance Savery

Benjamin Franklin by the D'Aulaires

Johnny Tremain by Esther Forbes

By the Great Hornspoon by Sid Fleischman

Pioneers Go West by Steward (Landmark)

Patty Reed's Doll by Rachel Laurgaard

The California Gold Rush by May McNeer

Island of the Blue Dolphins by Scott O'Dell

Streams to the River, River to the Sea (Sacagawea) by Scott O'Dell

Paddle to the Sea by Holling C. Holling

Tree in the Trail by Holling C. Holling

Minn of the Mississippi by Holling C. Holling

Caddie Woodlawn by Carol Ryrie Brink

The Courage of Sarah Noble by Alice Dagliesh

The Matchlock Gun by Walter D. Edmonds

Mother Cabrini by Frances Parkinson Keyes

Carry on, Mr. Bowditch by Jean Lee Latham

The Sign of the Beaver by Elizabeth Speare

Samuel F.B. Morse by John Hudson Tiner (Sower)

✓ *Sitting Bull: Dakota Boy* by Augusta Stevenson (CFA) (y)

Carlota (Mexican War) by Scott O'Dell

✓ *Will Clark: Boy Adventurer* by Katharine Wilkie (CFA) (y)

✓ *Meriwether Lewis: Boy Explorer* by Charlotta Bebenroth (CFA) (y)

Booker T. Washington by Jan Gleiter

A Pocketful of Goobers: A Story of George Washington Carver by Barbara Mitchell

Alamo by George Sullivan

Make Way for Sam Houston by Jean Fritz

Flatboats on the Ohio by Catherine Chambers

Johnny Appleseed by David R. Collins (Sower)

American Girls series

If You Traveled West in a Covered Wagon by Ellen Levine

Daniel Boone and the Wilderness Road by Catherine Chambers

Iron Dragon Never Sleeps by Stephen Krensky

Dragon's Gate (Chinese immigrants and the railroads) by Laurence Yep

Sing Down the Moon (Navaho Indians) by Scott O'Dell

✓ *Clara Barton: Founder of the American Red Cross* by Augusta Stevenson (CFA) (y)

Jed Smith: Trailblazer of the West by Frank Latham

Civil War Period and Slavery

The Life of Stonewall Jackson by Mary L. Williamson

The Life of J.E.B. Stuart by Mary L. Williamson

✓ *Abraham Lincoln* by the D'Aulaires (y)

Abe Lincoln: Log Cabin to the White House by Sterling North (Landmark)

Robert E. Lee, The Christian by William J. Johnson

Robert E. Lee by Lee Roddy (Sower)

Stonewall by Jean Fritz

With Lee in Virginia: A Story of the American Civil War by G. A. Henty (o)

Little Women by Louisa May Alcott (o)

Across Five Aprils by Irene Hunt

Gettysburg by MacKinlay Kantor (o)

Virginia's General: Robert E. Lee and the Civil War by Albert Marrin (o)

The Slave Dancer by Paula Fox (o-read aloud)

Perilous Road by William O. Steele, Jean Fritz

Hang a Thousand Trees with Ribbons: The Story of Phillis Wheatley by Ann Rinaldi

Uncle Tom's Cabin by Harriet Beecher Stowe (o-read aloud)

Rifles for Watie by Harold Keith

The Story of Harriet Tubman: Conductor of the Underground Railroad by Kate McMullan

Tales from the Underground Railroad by Kate Connell

Walking the Road to Freedom: Sojourner Truth by Jeri Ferris

Pink and Say by Patricia Polacco

Charley Skedaddle by Patricia Beatty

Iron Scouts of the Confederacy by McGriffon

The Red Badge of Courage by Stephen Crane (o)

Booker T. Washington by Jan Gleiter

Freedom Train by Dorothy Sterling

Go Free or Die: A Story about Harriet Tubman by Jeri Ferris

Freedom's Sons: The True Story of the Amistad Mutiny by Suzanne Jurmain

Up from Slavery by Booker T. Washington (o)

If You Traveled on the Underground Railroad by Ellen Levine

Incidents in the Life of a Slave Girl by Harriet A. Jacobs

Sojourner Truth; Ain't I a Woman? by Pat and Patricia McKissack

Frederick Douglass Fights for Freedom by Margaret Davidson

Black Frontiers: A History of African-American Heroes in the Old West by Lillian Schlissel

✓ *Mary McLeod Bethune* by Eloise Greenfield (y)

George Washington Carver: In His Own Words by George Washington Carver

The Negro Cowboys by Philip Durham (o)

The Drinking Gourd by F. N. Monjo

Modern U.S. History

American Girls series

Danger at the Breaker (Industrial Revolution) by Catherine A. Welch

✓ *The Story of the Wright Brothers and Their Sister* by Lois Mills (y)

Andrew Carnegie: Steel King and Friend to Libraries by Zachary Kent (o)

Henry Ford: Young Man with Ideas by Hazel Aird and Catherine Ruddiman

Dear America: So Far from Home—The Diary of Mary Driscoll, An Irish Mill Girl, Lowell, MA 1847 by Barry Denenberg

Children of the Dust Bowl: The True Story of the School at Weedpatch Camp by Jerry Stanley

The Bracelet (Japanese internment in WWII) by Joanna Yardley and Yoshiko Uchida

Farewell to Manzanar (Japanese internment in WWII) by Houston and Houston (o-read aloud)

Rosie the Riveter: Women Working on the Home Front in WWII by Penny Colman

Understood Betsy by Dorothy Canfield Fisher

The Yearling by Marjorie Rawlings

Roll of Thunder, Hear My Cry by Mildred D. Taylor (o-read aloud)

To Kill a Mockingbird by Harper Lee (o-read aloud)

Amelia Earhart by Beatrice Gormley

Rocket! How a Toy Launched the Space Age by Richard Maurer

Ronald Reagan by Montrew Dunham

Modern World History

Number the Stars (Danish resistance) by Lois Lowry

The House of Sixty Fathers (China) by Meindert de Jong

The Wheel on the School (Netherlands) by Meindert de Jong

The Winged Watchman (Netherlands) by Hilda Van Stockum

Twenty and Ten (WWII refugee children in France) by Claire Huchet Bishop

The Crystal Snowstorm, Following the Phoenix, Angel and the Dragon, and *The Rose and Crown* (nineteenth-century European politics) by Meriol Trevor

When Jessie Came across the Sea (Jewish immigrant) by Amy Hett (y)

Teresa of Calcutta by D. Jeanene Watson (Sower)

Stalin: Russia's Man of Steel by Albert Marrin (o)

The Yanks Are Coming (WWI) by Albert Marrin (o)

Hitler by Albert Marrin (o)

America and Vietnam: The Elephant and the Tiger by Albert Marrin (o)

Sweet Dried Apples: A Vietnamese Wartime Childhood by Rosemary Breckler

The Land I Lost: Adventures of a Boy in Vietnam by Huynh Quang Nhuong

Help for Figuring Out Which Books to Use When

Many homeschool distributors sell such books as these for various historical periods. Some homeschool catalogs even list books under time period headings so you can easily find those you want to use for history studies. In addition to catalogs, there are other resource books you can buy or borrow that will help you select your own books for historical studies. Three of the best are:

All through the Ages: History through Literature Guide

by Christine Miller

Nothing New Press

1015-M South Taft Hill Road #263

Fort Collins, CO 80521

e-mail: info@nothingnewpress.com

www.nothingnewpress.com

The largest section of the book features listings divided by chronological periods. Selections reflect a strong Western civilization and Reformed Protestant perspective. In addition to chronological divisions, titles within those divisions are further broken down by age groups covering grades 1 through 12. Within age groups there are sometimes further divisions under headings such as overview of the era, specific events, biography, historical fiction, and culture.

Other smaller sections follow a similar format listing books for geography, science, math, the arts, and "Great Books of Western Civilization and the Christian Tradition."

Lessons from History

by Gail Schultz

Hillside Academy

1804 Melody Lane

Burnsville, MN 55337

www.lessonsfromhistory.com

$19.95 each

Gail has written five volumes that are essentially unit study outlines for different periods of history. As a major part of these outlines, she recommends real books for covering not only history but also science, geography, Bible, and the arts. She includes background information, suggested books to read, projects, and discussion questions. These guides will work for students in grades K through 8.

Let the Authors Speak: A Guide to Worthy Books Based on Historical Setting
by Carolyn Hatcher
Old Pinnacle Publishing
1048 Old Pinnacle Rd.
Joelton, TN 37080
(615) 746-3342

Hatcher uses the first half of the book to explain the rationale for using real books for learning and for literature. The second half lists books, first by historical setting (time period, location), then by author. A supplemental section lists myths/legends, fantasy, folk tales, fables, and allegories by time period. Hatcher works from a Judeo-Christian worldview and leans toward a Western civilization background, which is reflected in the lists. However, all books listed are not necessarily Christian.

Internet Resources

I also found three Web sites that list historical literature by time periods. You might want to explore the following:

www.fcps.k12.va.us/FranklinMS/research/hisfic.htm
    Nonsectarian list by date, author, title
http://lexicon.ci.anchorage.ak.us/guides/kids
    Nonsectarian, annotated list by time periods
www.love2learn.net/history/histindx.htm
    Catholic lists with helpful reviews by time period

Reviews of History Resources

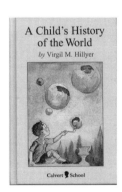

A Child's History of the World
by Virgil M. Hillyer
Calvert School
10713 Gilroy Road, Suite B
Hunt Valley, MD 21031
(888) 487-4652
www.calvertschool.org
Book—$25.00, CD-ROM—$35.00, complete course with textbook—$50.00, course without text—$35.00

Hillyer's elementary-level world history is a classic that will grow in popularity with the beautiful, new, hardbound edition and an electronic edition. For years homeschoolers scrambled to find out-of-print copies of this book, paying premium prices for well-used copies. Finally, recognizing the demand, Calvert

School republished it in an updated edition as well as a CD-ROM version. The update includes the addition of events from the nineteenth century as well as some minor content changes to update archaic expressions and ideas.

The primary appeal is the writing style. Hillyer speaks to children in ways they understand, yet he doesn't talk down to them in the short, choppy sentences typical of most texts written for middle elementary grades. The difference is obvious in the page count—625 pages. Illustrations are minimal: a few maps, line drawings, and, occasionally, words arranged to convey an idea. (Can you imagine any modern publisher offering a textbook this length for fourth graders without color illustrations?)

In spite of these "limitations," Hillyer's book is far better than most of its modern counterparts in my estimation. It offers depth and interest that are lacking in most textbooks. History coverage reaches beyond Europe, the Middle East, and North America by including selective topics on other countries and cultures. Children's imaginations will be engaged by the stories of history told in their proper settings with enough detail to make them come alive.

Hillyer clearly asserts Christian belief, although his biblical references imply a questioning of the truthfulness of Old Testament stories. Also, he sometimes slightly misinterprets the biblical text. For instance, he says, "King Saul had a daughter, and she fell in love with this . . . David the Giant-Killer, and at last they were married." This version overlooks the fact that Saul had promised his daughter in marriage to whomever killed the giant—it wasn't really a matter of falling in love. The beginning of the book also discusses cave men and prehistory in a manner with which some might disagree (e.g., cavemen talked in grunts).

A Child's History of the World really should be read aloud together so such things as I've mentioned can easily be discussed when you encounter them. There are no chapter questions or assignments in the book.

This book and associated lessons are included in Calvert's fourth grade curriculum, but Calvert also sells the book by itself or as part of a new history course. The course adds a lesson manual and a workbook. Lessons include outlines, activity ideas, and discussion questions. The student workbook has two parts. The first part is fill-in-the-blank comprehension questions for each chapter. The second part consists of activity pages: word scrambles, crosswords, projects, recipes, map work, and more.

The CD-ROM multimedia version of this book includes the complete text plus "original art, music, review questions, and computer-scored games."

A Child's Story of America (second edition)
Christian Liberty Press
502 West Euclid Avenue
Arlington Heights, IL 60004
(847) 259-4444
www.christianlibertypress.com
$8.95, test booklet and answer key—$2.00 each

This is one of the most delightful history books I have ever come across. It reads like Hillyer's *A Child's History of the World* (discussed previously). It, too, reads more like a story than like a history text, giving the reader a sense that the author is conversing directly with him or her. Unlike Hillyer's book, however, *A Child's Story of America* includes Christianity in its coverage. The revised second edition markedly expands that coverage with information on the Great Awakening, revivals, and sketches of influential Protestant ministers. This edition now has a strong Protestant flavor that was lacking in the first edition. Information has been updated through the Clinton administration, including his impeachment.

It is important to know that this book had its origins in a much earlier version, written closer to the turn of the last century. The original book reflected attitudes toward Indians that were quite different from today. This second edition reprint has taken pains to update the language and correct inaccurate and incomplete information, but it still reflects some of the original attitude. Keep this context in mind as you read the book.

The second edition features numerous illustrations and maps, printed in two colors. Sidebars add extra biographical sketches or vignettes that enhance topic coverage. Chapter review questions are in the book. A separate test booklet and answer key is available.

Genevieve Foster books

Beautiful Feet Books

139 Main St.

Sandwich, MA 02563

(800) 889-1978

www.bfbooks.com

$15.95 each

Beautiful Feet Books is bringing back some of my favorite world history books for upper elementary grades through high school. This is a series of books by Genevieve Foster that were written around the 1940s. Titles in print thus far are *Augustus Caesar's World*, *The World of Columbus and Sons*, *The World of Captain John Smith*, *George Washington's World*, and *Abraham Lincoln's World*. They reflect a Christian culture although they don't have Christian content.

The beauty of these books is the storytelling approach to history. Foster begins with the day the key person was born and traces "goings-on" around the world throughout his lifetime. Foster makes the connections between people and events all around the globe that are usually lacking in textbooks. Because of this approach, even *George Washington's World* is a world history study. If you read these books in chronological sequence, you cover world history fairly well for the time periods they reflect.

These are great for read aloud time, but only with older students, probably at least fifth grade. Younger children will be overwhelmed with the information and will not have enough background to make the necessary connections. Often the information comes "rapid fire," and even older children will need you to stop from time to time and spend more time discussing or explaining what you have read.

For the adventurous parent, I suggest creating your own unit studies by jumping off on one or more topics within each section of any of Foster's books. While there are no suggested assignments, study ideas, or discussion questions in these books, you could easily come up with some of your own for independent reading and research. Note that the books *do* have indexes that are very helpful when you want to locate information.

Beautiful Feet Books, publisher of the Foster series, also publishes "history through literature" study guides, some of which include study questions for the Foster books. Their *Early American and World History* guide for junior high uses the Foster books on Columbus, John Smith, George Washington, and Abraham Lincoln along with some other books. Their *Ancient History* guide uses *Augustus Caesar's World*.

Greenleaf Press: *Famous Men and Greenleaf Guides*
by Rob and Cyndy Shearer
Greenleaf Press
3761 Highway 109 North, Unit D
Lebanon, TN 37087
(800) 311-1508 (for orders only)
(615) 449-1617
e-mail: orders@greenleafpress.com
www.greenleafpress.com

Greenleaf Guide to Old Testament History
by Rob and Cyndy Shearer
$11.95

The Old Testament is the perfect place to start teaching history since it truly starts at the beginning. Many of us shy away from such a study because of the difficulties we might encounter, but the Shearers have made it much easier with this guide. It covers Genesis, Exodus, Numbers, Deuteronomy, Joshua, and most of Judges.

This guide differs from the other *Greenleaf Guides* in that it is based upon Bible reading and discussion rather than readings from an assortment of books. (Either *The Children's Bible Atlas* or *The Cultural Atlas of the Bible* is recommended as a visual tool, but nothing else is necessary.)

We read through sections of Scripture with our children, then use the guide's questions to lead a discussion. The Shearers suggest using Charlotte Mason's narration technique, where children relate back in their own words what has just been read. The questions generally focus on "who, what, where, when, why, and how" for historical understanding rather than as theology lessons.

Background information is included whenever it is useful. The Shearers also offer practical tips for dealing with the difficult passages, such as Tamar and Judah. You can tell from the suggestions that they have used all of this with their own family of seven children.

This is not like typical Bible study material that uses stories or incidents to teach spiritual truths or doctrine. But even though that is not the primary focus, children will learn foundational spiritual truths. Young children can easily answer most of the questions if they learn to listen carefully, but there are a few questions that will challenge older children to think more deeply. It should take a full school year to complete this book.

Famous Men of Greece, Famous Men of Rome, and Famous Men of the Middle Ages
Edited and updated by Rob and Cyndy Shearer
$16.95 each

Instead of reading dry textbooks, children can learn about ancient history through biographical sketches of influential figures in the *Famous Men* books. Stories often build one upon another in chronological order. The effect is like reading a storybook, although not quite as interesting.

To accompany each *Famous Men* book, we also have *The Greenleaf Guide to Famous Men of Greece*, *The Greenleaf Guide to Famous Men of Rome*, and *The Greenleaf Guide to Famous Men of the Middle Ages* ($8.95 each).

These guides turn the reading into limited unit studies with activities, discussion questions, geography (including map-building projects), and vocabulary for each chapter of each book. Biblical standards are used as the measuring rod when discussing the lives of the famous men. Chronological summaries of people and events are at the end of each book. Project work is optional for the most part, with more emphasis on reading and discussion. Frequently, lessons refer to supplemental resources for further research and readings on Greece, Rome, or the Middle Ages (resources available individually or in Greenleaf "packages").

Of particular note in the *Greenleaf Guide to Famous Men of the Middle Ages* are the "worldview" comparison charts. On one chart we compare creation and end-of-the-world stories from Teutonic mythology and the Bible. Greek myths are compared against the other two belief systems as we consider characteristics of God and the gods, what they value, whom they honor, what they honor, and man's purpose for living. Another chart compares beliefs of Islam with Christianity. Discussion questions in all of the guides cover names, dates, and events, but they go much further than textbooks in dealing with character issues and biblical principles.

Greenleaf also publishes *Famous Men of the Renaissance and Reformation* by Rob Shearer. This book also has a companion guide. These two books are best suited to older students at junior and senior high level. I appreciate the unusual selection of biographies in this *Famous Men* book. We meet such famous men as Petrarch, Leonardo da Vinci, Erasmus, and some of the standard Reformation leaders, including Wycliffe, Luther, Zwingli, and Calvin. But we also encounter characters such as Lorenzo d' Medici, Cesare

Borgia, Niccolo Machiavelli, Albrecht Durer, and representatives of the Anabaptist movement. The result is a richer picture of the period than we typically encounter. The perspective is strongly Protestant.

Greenleaf makes all of this even easier to use with their study packages. *The Ancient Greece Study Package* includes *Famous Men*, *The Greenleaf Guide*, *The Greeks* (an Usborne book), *The Trial and Death of Socrates*, and *Children's Homer*. *The Ancient Rome Study Package* includes *Famous Men*, *The Greenleaf Guide*, *City*, and *The Romans* (an Usborne book). *The Middle Ages Study Package* includes *Famous Men*, *The Greenleaf Guide*, *Castle*, *Cathedral*, and *The Penguin Atlas of Medieval History*.

The Greenleaf materials more than adequately replace textbook material. The *Famous Men* books can be read to children at very young ages, but the actual studies are more suitable for middle to upper elementary grades. Even though the reading level is a little young, junior and senior high students can read the stories. Guide activities can be stretched to meet the needs of most learning levels, although the *Middle Ages* guide seems the easiest to use with older students.

The Greenleaf Guide to Ancient Egypt
by Cyndy Shearer
$7.95

This *Greenleaf Guide* differs from the guides on Rome and Greece in that there is no *Famous Men* book to accompany it. Instead, it uses six other books and the Bible as resources. The books are *Pharaohs of Ancient Egypt*, *Usborne Time-Traveller: Pharaohs & Pyramids*, *Atlas of Ancient Egypt Deserts*, *Pyramid*, *Tut's Mummy . . . Lost and Found*, and *Mummies Made in Egypt*. There are many hands-on activities along with vocabulary and discussion questions. The general tone of this guide is slightly younger than that of guides for Rome and Greece. Since Egypt figures in chronological order before the others, it makes sense to use this book and the *Greenleaf Guide to Old Testament History* as your starting points, then follow with Greece, then Rome and the Middle Ages. Study can be adapted for children as young as second grade level, although it should be perfect for the middle elementary grades.

Guerber History Series
edited by Christine Miller
Nothing New Press
1015-M South Taft Hill Rd. #263
Fort Collins, CO 80521
e-mail: info@nothingnewpress.com
www.nothingnewpress.com

Christine Miller authored *All through the Ages: History through Literature Guide*, which I described briefly earlier in this chapter. Christine recommends using at least one overview-type book for each historical era in addition to titles that might focus on particular people and events. (An overview book functions like a history text in covering the broad range of events in chronological order.)

Because it can be difficult to find appealing overview books written from a Christian perspective, Christine has updated and rewritten a series of books originally written by H. A. Guerber (first published in 1898). These new books vary from minimal rewrites of Guerber's work to incorporation of her material into new books. The six books in this series all begin *The Story of* . . . . The titles continue: . . . *the Greeks*, . . . *the Romans*, . . . *the Middle Ages*, . . . *the Renaissance and Reformation*, . . . *the Thirteen Colonies*, and . . . *the Great Republic* (U.S. history to 1900). It is important to note that all of the material does not derive solely from Guerber's original work. For *The Story of the Middle Ages*, Miller also drew upon some historical works by Charlotte Yonge.

Guerber writes with a lively style that reminds me of Joy Hakim (author of *The Story of U.S.* from Oxford University Press). Christine Miller has retained that same engaging style in her adaptations and additions.

Part of what makes this type of writing more enjoyable is that the author's feelings and opinions show through the narrative. That means we also get some of Guerber's original thoughts and attitudes, and there might be a few of these with which you disagree. However, Christine Miller has added explanations in each book's forward regarding topics most likely to be problematic.

None of these volumes strives to be comprehensive. Instead, they focus on key events and characters. This works fine for an overview in the first four volumes, but I find the topics covered in *The Story of the Great Republic* curious from our twenty-first-century perspective. Because the book was originally written in 1899, events closer to that time period loomed large in the author's consciousness. Thus the Civil War and the Spanish-American War both get more attention proportionately than they do in more recent books. In spite of the original 1899 copyright of this book, it actually continues up through the assassination of President McKinley in 1901. Personally, I would likely use something else instead of this last volume.

The reading level would make these most appropriate for junior high level for independent reading. However, they can be read aloud with children from about fourth grade and up. There are no questions or exercises with any of these volumes, but if you use them as read aloud books, following up with discussion, narration, writing, or other activities of your own, they will work fine with younger students. Older students could be assigned outlining, notetaking, or other written tasks to demonstrate comprehension.

Of particular note is the religious perspective. This series is Christian, and it does a surprisingly good job of fairly presenting both Protestant and Catholic positions. Even in the *Renaissance and Reformation* volume, we read about the good and bad from both sides.

The Mystery of History

by Linda Lacour Hobar

Bright Ideas Press

P.O. Box 333

Cheswold, DE 19936

(877) 492-8081

E-mail: info@brightideaspress.com

www.BrightIdeasPress.com

$44.95 each

Volumes I and *II* of a projected five-volume series hold great promise as history resources for home-schoolers. They are designed so that even inexperienced parents can break free from traditional text-books. They combine read aloud information with age appropriate activities to create a multisensory curriculum for history and geography with a very strong biblical base. They are designed to be used with children in grades K through 8, although the reading level is about sixth grade.

Titles for the five volumes are:

Volume I: Creation to the Resurrection

Volume II: The Early Church and the Middle Ages (A.D. 30–1460)

Volume III: The Renaissance and Growth of Empires (1461–1707)

Volume IV: Revolutions and Rising Nations (1708–1914)

Volume V: The World at War and the Present Day (1915–present day)

Volume I relies heavily on Scripture since the Bible is a source for much of what we know about ancient times. Other than that, the historical information is all presented within this book as it would be in a textbook. No other reference works are required for this study except for research activities older students might pursue. However, other books and videos that expand upon subjects are listed in the appendix, lesson by lesson.

Beginning with creation, the study follows biblical history, incorporating other sources as they fit into the chronological story. Thus, Stonehenge, early Egypt, and the Minoans are taught before Abraham, Jacob, and Joseph. The little we know about world civilizations is represented by inclusion of lessons such as those on Chinese dynasties, India and Hinduism, and early Greek city states up to the point where the historical record broadens and we have more sources for learning about early civilizations. Although Eastern civilizations are given some attention, the focus is much stronger on Western civilizations.

Each volume is structured for a school year, with four quarters divided into two semesters. Lessons are arranged in sets of three with the expectation that you will complete three per week. Each lesson begins with "Around the world" background and introductory information that you will want to read aloud with your children. A pretest follows. Pretests are meant to spark interest, so you want to present these in a light-hearted fashion (á lá a Trivial Pursuit–type game) rather than as a test.

Three lessons follow, each with a similar format: read aloud information is presented from the book, then you choose an activity for each child to complete. An activity is given for each of three levels. For example, the lesson on Noah suggests that young children play a concentration-type card game. Middle grade to older students might use their Bibles to find answers to a list of questions regarding the account of the Flood. Older students might instead tackle the third option, which requires research about the supplies needed on the ark for Noah, his family, and all the animals.

At the end of every third lesson is a reminder for students to create "memory cards." These are three-by-five-inch notecards with key information on each event. A color-coding system helps students group events by time periods. These are used for oral drill, games, or independent review.

Field trip suggestions are sometimes included at the end of the three lessons, but review activities are always included. This includes work on timelines, maps, and a review quiz. Ten reproducible map masters are at the back of the book. Author Linda Hobar recommends that you have both a Bible atlas and a historical atlas for reference for map work.

Linda also shares creative and inexpensive ideas for making timelines, with detailed instructions for using folding sewing boards as the base for portable timelines.

You can see how all of this can break out easily into three days of lessons with their activities; a fourth day for timeline, mapwork, and quiz; and a fifth day for a field trip or focus on other subjects. Other possible scheduling suggestions for different levels are at the front of the book.

I appreciate Linda's explanation of the shift toward increasing student responsibility that should take place over the years. She has a simple diagram that shows high teacher involvement with minimal grading for young children that gradually reverses to low teacher involvement and thorough record keeping and grading at high school level. This approach to education is reflected in the activities suggested for the different levels. Younger children will work more one-to-one with the parent. They have more arts-and-crafts-type activities that are not graded. Older students do more independent research and writing that is graded.

While this is essentially a study of history, it is also a Bible study of sorts with an apologetic flavor in spots. The appendix includes an adaptation of Campus Crusade's booklet used for people to accept Christ. Letters to students at the beginning of the book (different letters for different age groups) direct students to that section of the appendix if they don't already have a relationship with God.

Volume II: The Early Church and the Middle Ages follows the same layout as the first volume, although it is no longer following a biblical chronology. There are fewer lessons, but each lesson has more content information than do lessons in *Volume I*. You will want to have access to an atlas for this volume, and some recommended atlases are listed in the introduction. Lists of additional resources you might use are at the back of the book. Linda's selection and presentation of topics is fascinating. Given the huge time period she covers in *Volume II*, she does a great job of pulling out key people and events so students also get the big picture.

This combination of self-contained history and multisensory activities should really appeal to many homeschooling families.

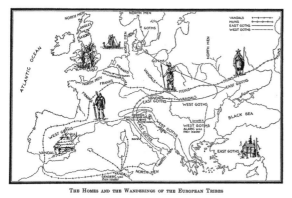

The Homes and the Wanderings of the European Tribes

The Old World's Gifts to the New
by Sister Mary Celeste
Neumann Press
21892 County 11
Long Prairie, MN 56347
(800) 746-2521
e-mail: sales@neumannpress.com
www.neumannpress.com
$26.00

Originally published (and reprinted) in eight printings from 1932 to 1939, this is a delightful Catholic presentation of world history, similar in some ways to Hillyer's *A Child's History of the World*. It is probably best for students in the upper elementary grades. This hardcover book is almost five hundred pages in length, but it has fairly large print, a number of black-and-white illustrations, and a lively writing style that actually make it read rather quickly.

Refreshingly, it begins with Adam and Eve rather than "millions of years ago." It continues up through exploration and settlement of the Americas, including the early colonial period.

As with most history books of the era, this one focuses on the roots of Western civilization with little attention to Africa and Asia. However, it does an exceptional job of connecting people, places, and events in a meaningful way, explaining why things happened as they did, so that it reads like a story rather than a collection of information. I found the illustrations—particularly the photos—quite interesting, but occasionally an illustration had little to no reference within the text—a curious situation.

There are many questions and activities, but they are presented in a somewhat random fashion. Sometimes they are presented as "test yourself," sometimes as recall-type questions, and sometimes as discussion questions. Some activities ask students to retell events in their own words. Among other exercises/activities are drawing or cutting projects and acting out historical scenes. You need at least a small group for the latter. Comprehension questions range from matching to writing a few sentences. These questions/activities appear with no predictability—sometimes in the middle of a unit, sometimes at the end. No teacher guide or answer key is available, but this isn't a significant problem.

I really enjoyed reading this book and found myself reading more than skimming as I frequently do when reviewing such books.

The Story of the World: History for the Classical Child
by Susan Wise Bauer
Peace Hill Press
18101 The Glebe Lane
Charles City, VA 23030
(877) 322-3445
e-mail: info@peacehillpress.com
www.peacehillpress.com

Texts: for Volumes 1–3—paperback $16.95, spiral $18.95, or hardcover $21.95; volume 4 is $1.00 more for each edition. Curriculum guides for volumes 1–3—$29.95 each, volume 4—$32.95. Activity page packets: volume 1—$7.95, volume 2—$9.95; test packets—$12.95 each

The Story of the World by Susan Wise Bauer presents world history through narration and storytelling in this four-volume series. While these books are written to be read aloud to children in grades 1 through 4, they may also be used for independent reading by fifth and sixth graders. The *Story of the World* books are available in your choice of hardcover, lay-flat perfect binding (softcover), or sturdier spiral-bound editions.

Many will recognize Bauer as one of the authors of *The Well-Trained Mind*—an exceptionally good book on providing a classical education. This history series is intended to be used within the context of just such an education, even though it will also work within more traditional approaches.

Volume 1: Ancient Times addresses the time period from the earliest nomads (given a date of about 6000 B.C.) up through the last emperor of ancient Rome—no cave men or Neanderthals included! The book's size of 334 pages means there's actually quite a bit of material in comparison to many world history texts for the early grades. Nevertheless, coverage is not comprehensive because chapters are devoted to lengthy stories about key characters or events rather than tidbits about everything. On the other hand, the book does span civilizations around the world, including India, China, and West Africa, in addition to the usual cast of Western civilizations.

As in *The Well-Trained Mind*, the presentation is not overtly Christian, although it recognizes and includes Christianity. For example, stories of gods and goddesses from other civilizations are retold without value judgments as to their validity. However, the author's own Christianity is still evident in the heavy weighting of biblical stories—lengthy accounts about Abraham, Joseph, Moses, and the beginnings of Christianity, as well as the birth, death, and resurrection of Jesus.

Although there are a few black-and-white illustrations and maps, this is not a colorful history picture book for "browsing" but a basic history resource from which you can build a complete study for the early grades.

To help you do just that, Susan Wise Bauer has also created a companion study guide called a *Curriculum Guide and Activity Book*. This 275-page "book" is a compilation of questions, narration exercises, reading lists (both history and literature), map work, and activities to accompany each section. "Book" is in quotes because you have two options: a softbound book version, or 275 pages with holes pre-punched for insertion into your own three-inch or five-inch three-ring binder. The price is the same for either format.

Reproducible pages in this and other guides are segregated from lesson plans into their own section, which makes copying easier. Parents have permission to photocopy student pages for their family's use. However, Peace Hill Press sells separate packets of only these reproducible pages. Separate packets of tests with answer keys are also available.

You will find some very unusual project ideas in the *Curriculum Guide and Activity Book*: for example, mummifying a chicken and making Greek tattoos with pure henna. Reproducible blackline masters are used for all sorts of things—mapwork, "board" games, paper dolls, making a lighthouse, and more. Another useful feature is "Review Cards"—reproducible pages with four illustrated blocks of information per page. These can be cut and pasted on three-by-five-inch cards and used as flashcards to review key ideas.

I particularly like the review questions that begin each section. These help children focus on the reading from the text. The narration exercises are also very helpful for parents who have trouble figuring out how to implement narration techniques. The guide truly supports the "grammar" stage of classical learning with its focus on information and comprehension.

Cross references are included to *The Kingfisher Illustrated History of the World*, *The Kingfisher History Encyclopedia*, *The Usborne Book of World History*, and *The Usborne Internet-Linked Encyclopedia of World History*. You would do well to purchase at least one of these additional basic resources to supply the colorful illustrations lacking in the core history book as well as more complete historical information. Other recommended books should be available through the library.

Volume 2: The Middle Ages—From the Fall of Rome to the Rise of the Renaissance is very much like the first volume. In her delightful style, Bauer covers a huge amount of territory with selective highlights that actually provide good introductory coverage. She hits touchy territory when it comes to the Reformation, although she tries to balance her presentation better than do most authors. However, I suspect some Catholics might want to skip or "edit" her chapter on Martin Luther.

Volume 2 also has a companion *Curriculum Guide and Activity Book*. This large volume has 236 lesson plan pages *plus* another 176 single-sided student activity pages as compared to the 275 total pages of the guide for *Volume 1*. Like the first volume's activity book, it is available in either bound or loose-leaf format.

Volume 3: Early Modern Times—From Elizabeth the First to the Forty-Niners continues in the same fashion. However, it seems a little "scattered" because it ambitiously tries to cover a huge swathe of worldwide history in fewer than four hundred pages. It seems even more selective and limited in topics covered than previous volumes, although featured topics each get enough attention to present an engaging story. There's much to be said for this approach in contrast to history texts that cover far more information but with little or no depth on any of the topics.

Volume 4: The Modern Age covers from 1850 to the present day. This volume is still in production as I write but should be available by the time you read this book. The curriculum guide and activity books for these last two volumes should also be available by that time.

Both the history "texts" on their own and the study guides are valuable contributions that fill a need for Christian-friendly but classically-oriented history study.

The publisher's Web site has helpful information on choosing and using different versions of the books as well as information about ancillary products.

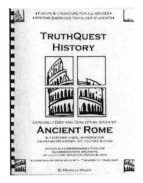

TruthQuest History
by Michelle Miller
TruthQuest History
P.O. Box 2128
Traverse City, MI 49685-2128
e-mail: info@TruthQuestHistory.com *or*
TruthQuestHist@aol.com
www.TruthQuestHistory.com
$22.95 to $33.95 each

I was talking with a group of parents about curriculum choices one evening, and there was a broad consensus in favor of using real books for history among them. However, many parents were insecure about using real books without some sort of guidance. One mom spoke up to recommend *TruthQuest* as the solution. That piqued my interest enough to check it out.

TruthQuest History is a series of ten volumes that serve as guides for a "real books" approach to history. Each guide is divided into many topical sections rather than the typical chapter arrangement. Michelle Miller introduces each of these topics with background information written in a lively, informal, conversational style.

After reading the background information for context, you and your children read from real books to learn more information about the topic. Michelle recommends books, and sometimes chapters or pages within books, for each topic. She recommends a few "spine books"—books that are broad overviews of history, such as Hillyer's *A Child's History of the World*. Then she lists many other books that cover specific topics. You can use spine (or overview) books, topical books, or both; however, using at least some spine books will save you time.

Michelle recommends some out-of-print books that you might still be able to find at a library, but she also includes many that are in print and available if you choose to purchase them.

A unique aspect of *TruthQuest* is a primary focus on the central questions of life: Who is God, and who is man in relation to God? How different people and civilizations answer these questions is reflected in the way they live and the choices they make. So these questions are the underlying focus of background information Michelle Miller writes as she introduces each topic of study.

TruthQuest very much reflects a Francis Schaeffer approach to history. (In his book *How Should We Then Live?* Schaeffer examines religious beliefs and philosophies, showing how historical events, scientific discoveries, artistic endeavors, literary pursuits, etc., were all shaped by beliefs and philosophies.) In addition, Michelle supports a limited government perspective along the lines Richard Maybury presents in his Uncle Eric series (e.g., *Whatever Happened to Justice?*) from Bluestocking Press. Although Michelle writes from her own Protestant perspective, from time to time she discusses conflicting Protestant and Catholic viewpoints on history, acknowledging right and wrong on both sides. I was pleasantly surprised to see this respectful balance, especially in the *Renaissance, Reformation* volume.

As you might have gathered by now, there is a very definite philosophy to these books. However, if you disagree with some of Michelle's philosophy, you can still use these guides by skimming through the introductory material, sharing whichever parts of it you wish with your children, then moving on to the recommended reading and occasional video viewing. Some of the recommended books, particularly some of the spine books, reflect the philosophy described above. For example, *The Light and the Glory for Children* (providential view of history) and *How Should We Then Live?* (described above) are recommended spine books with a strong philosophical orientation. On the other hand, some of Guerber's history books and *Famous Men of Rome* are among others that are more neutral in their presentation. Since recommended spine books reflect a number of different philosophies, your choices of spine books will be particularly important in determining the "tone" of your study.

Enough on the philosophy of *TruthQuest*. Let's get back to how they are structured. Topical sections are further divided into subsections that address important people or events within a time period. For example, the section "The Roaring 20s" has an introduction with a list of general resources. This is followed by subsections with their own resource recommendations on topics such as the Scopes trial; Eric Liddell and the 1924 Olympics; Prohibition, bootleggers, gangsters; women's suffrage; baseball and Babe Ruth; Charles Lindbergh; Bessie Coleman; literary authors; scientists; music; and sports. You won't have time to cover every topic with real books, so it makes sense to either use a spine book for broad coverage along with a few narrower topic books *or* use as many topic books as you can reasonably get through and forgo efforts to cover many topics.

Scattered throughout the books are a number of "ThinkWrite" exercises. These are writing assignments that require students to analyze the historical information they have learned from a worldview perspective. For example, ThinkWrite 5 in *American History for Young Students* says: "Please tell us your thoughts about America winning the Revolutionary War. How did America's Big 2 Beliefs shape the war? Do you think you can see God's hand in it?" (p. 91). ThinkWrite 6 in the Renaissance volume asks:

"What do you think Henry VIII's actions reveal about his *Big 2 Beliefs*? What would it have been like to live under a king who held those beliefs?"

These questions are not intended to solicit only objective information. They require children to make spiritual and practical connections. However, they also tend to support the philosophy of these guides. As long as you are aware of this and agree with Michelle's philosophy, this is not a problem. If you disagree, then you might want to come up with your own ThinkWrite questions.

You will have to watch the level of difficulty in these guides. The three *American History* books are suggested as starting places for children in the primary grades. That does not mean they are only good for the primary grades, since recommended books within these guides are for all levels up through grade 12. My impression is that these and other guides will all work across the entire span of grade levels as long as parents are judicious about how much information they give to each child—don't overwhelm the young ones, and *do* give the older ones plenty to work with. Ultimately, parents need to decide which assignments as well as which books to use with each child.

Titles of the guides are:

- *American History for Young Students, Volumes I, II*, and *III* (suggested as guides to begin with for those with younger children)
- *Ancient Egypt/Ancient Greece*
- *Ancient Rome*
- *Middle Ages*
- *Renaissance, Reformation, and Age of Exploration*
- *Age of Revolution I* (America/Europe, 1600–1800)
- *Age of Revolution II* (America/Europe, 1800–1865)
- *Age of Revolution III* (America/Europe, 1865–2000)

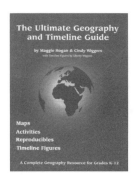

The Ultimate Geography and Timeline Guide
by Maggie Hogan and Cindy Wiggers
Bright Ideas Press
P.O. Box 333
Cheswold, DE 19936
(877) 492-8081
e-mail: geocreations@brightideaspress.com
www.brightideaspress.com

Geography Matters

P.O. Box 92

Nancy, KY 42544

(606) 636-4678

www.geomatters.com

$34.95

Maggie Hogan, author of *Hands-On Geography*, and Cindy Wiggers of Geography Matters, have combined their wisdom and experience to put together this resource book for teaching geography to children in grades K through 12.

It takes a little time to explore the wealth of options found here. The first section, "Planning Your Destination," suggests basic teaching methods, describes notebooks that students might create, and recommends basic supplies. Chapter 2 is a sort of primer course in geography—hopefully a refresher for most of us. It covers basic terminology and concepts, including the five themes of geography identified by the national standards group for geography. Hogan and Wiggers show us how to incorporate the five themes into our studies. Next is a section on maps: different types, how to use them, map games, and more. All this is in just the first of six units!

The second unit focuses on fun, games, and food as tools for teaching and enjoying geography. Unit three teaches us how to teach geography through other subject areas. This is especially important since Hogan and Wiggers are unit study fans and see the inclusion of geography as an important element of such studies. To help us get into unit studies, the authors include two complete unit studies, one on volcanoes and one on the book *Hans Brinker or the Silver Skates*. At the end of this section are tips on teaching geography through the Internet, including a list of great sites.

Unit four presents what most people think of as the nuts and bolts of geography: lesson directions and data on geographical features, climate, vegetation, etc. Lesson ideas are divided into those for middle school and those for high school.

Reproducible maps and activity sheets for games, weather reports, research, and other activities described in this book comprise the next two sections. The final unit is all about creating a timeline and includes hundreds of reproducible figures for your own timeline.

A fun feature of this book is a "Who Am I?" game that uses the reproducible pages of game cards. In addition to all this, the book includes an answer key, a glossary, an index (very useful with a book such as this), and lists of additional resources you might want to use.

In my opinion this approach to geography will be far more interesting than a standard text on the subject. The fact that one book does it all for every grade level makes it even more appealing.

Also check out their new *Hands-On Geography* for grades K through 4 and their new *Trail Guide* books for short daily geography lessons.

11

Science

Let me ask you a few questions about your own experience learning science before we begin with reviews and recommendations. First, did you enjoy science classes when you were in school?

If you are like most people, your answer was no. That was probably because you primarily learned from a textbook. Almost every textbook for the elementary grades takes the same mile-wide, inch-deep approach to science. They cover numerous subjects, but none of them with enough depth to engage a student's interest. At high school level, it switches to another extreme: vocabulary and memorization ad nauseum. High school texts stay focused on one subject but provide the depth through tons of dry factual information. Both approaches are a real turn-off to science.

On the other hand, if you are one of the few who found science enjoyable, what was it about those classes that made the subject enjoyable? I suspect the reason is that your teacher/s did not stick with the textbooks. You learned science by really digging into a topic, perhaps doing experiments or activities that made it fascinating.

Unfortunately, forgoing textbooks is a challenge for those of us who love the security of a textbook that boils a subject down to predictable, manageable, and measurable information. So how do we get past this problem?

Science can be an intimidating subject unless we develop a proper perspective. Science, in terms of education, means the study of God's creation, its purposes, its functioning, and its beauty. We often limit our definition of science education to memorization of plant structure, the names of bones, the periodic table, and other such laborious data without seeing beyond to God's purposes for each aspect of creation. Obviously, we do not have a total understanding of all of God's purposes, but even with our limited understanding we can develop a sense of awe for God's creative genius that has nothing to do with the labels we have come up with for His creation.

It is more useful for children in the early elementary grades to develop an appreciation for God's creation—our bodies, the earth, plants, animals, the weather, and so on—than it is for them to begin memorizing details (although classical educators might argue to the contrary that this is the ideal time to work on memorization). Field trips, experiments, observations, and nature collections will all stimulate interest in children. These should continue to be a major part of your science curriculum for all ages.

In my opinion, attention to vocabulary and acquisition of facts become more important around eight to ten years of age. For those trying to use a classical approach to education, think of this as all being part of the grammar stage. You want children to develop foundational knowledge and skills in science, but you begin by making it interesting so children more easily acquire the knowledge and skills.

I propose the following four goals in teaching science for elementary levels (kindergarten through sixth grades):

1. To turn children on to science so they develop inquiring minds
2. To expose children to many topics in science
3. To teach children the foundations of scientific method—orderly thinking and forming, testing, and evaluating hypotheses
4. To help children acquire *basic* knowledge and vocabulary for science.

I believe the best way to meet these goals is not by using science textbooks. You can turn your children on to science by teaching them to observe, experiment, read, and think about the things that surround us.

Why do they find pill bugs under rocks? Why can they "see" their breath when it's really cold outside? Children are naturally curious about the different areas of science but not usually according to the textbook's scope and sequence. It is far better to respond to an area of interest by an immediate trip to the library or a field trip that gives them information they are personally seeking.

If you limit science to a textbook, you will be missing much. Although textbooks try to introduce a variety of topics each year at elementary levels, they have no way of predicting what will interest each child. Textbook authors cannot know that your family is taking its first trip to the ocean this year, and you want to explore seashells and ocean life in conjunction with that trip. They cannot know that your family just adopted a puppy and your children need to learn all about dogs. They cannot know that your family finally bought a house with a backyard and this will be the year to learn all about gardening.

It is much better if you and your children choose your own topics for science study that relate to your particular interests and activities.

Scientific method is a vital part of science education, but we seldom equate it with the sense of wonder and curiosity that children have. When children look beyond the surface appearances and ask, "Why did that happen?" they are beginning to apply scientific method. Scientific method begins with observations and questions. It continues when you work with your child to form possible answers and ways of testing those possibilities. This is real science, but it is the sort of thing that cannot be easily controlled and explained via a science textbook—you might end up spending too much time on one topic and not get through all the chapters!

However, when you choose your own topics, allowing more time to cover fewer topics, you will be able to follow rabbit trails your child discovers into areas you might not have had on your agenda. This is the sort of learning that inspires great scientists. Think of Thomas Edison tinkering with all of his experiments and inventions, most of which came to nothing in themselves. The time he spent following his own rabbit trails, learning what did not work, ultimately contributed to his amazing successes.

When you use the methods I have described, your children are likely to pick up the vocabulary and basic information painlessly because they are interested.

How Do You Know If You're Doing Enough?

Even if you are willing to abandon the textbook approach, many parents feel insecure at determining what level their children should be working on a science topic. Does making a model of the body systems equally satisfy learning needs of both a seven-year-old and a twelve-year-old? Probably not.

Kathryn Stout's *Science Scope* (Design-A-Study, 302-998-3889, www.designastudy.com) helps you identify appropriate activities for different age groups within each science area. This is an extremely useful resource. Divided into four main areas—general science, life science, earth science, and physical science—it lists specific topics under each heading. Then it suggests methods for use with students at primary, intermediate, junior, and senior high levels. All of this makes it much easier to select appropriate resources for topical science studies.

Another scope and sequence resource, *Teaching Science and Having Fun!* is described on page 248.

What To Do?

Summarizing all of this into a recommendation, for the elementary grades I suggest choosing three or four science topics per year, taking into account the general topics you feel should be covered as well as your children's interests. Then use information books, experiment/activity books (such as those listed throughout this chapter), and field trips to put together an interesting study for each topic.

I can just imagine some parents reading what I've just written and saying, "Oh, great! I've got to go make it all up myself. Forget it!" Those of you who don't delight in creating your own courses can take heart. Others have done it for you. They have chosen one or a few topics, found some real books that make the subject interesting, come up with activities or experiments, and put it all together in one place to make it easy for you to teach science through topical unit studies. If you are using a larger unit study that encompasses many subject areas, you are likely to find this approach to science already incorporated into your unit study.

Following are reviews of science resources. Many of these support the approach to science I have described above. Some are more traditional to fit situations where unit study approaches to science are not practical.

It is impossible to narrow science resources down to "the best" and simultaneously cover all possible science topics. So those you find here are representative of a wide range of useful resources. I hope that just thinking about possibilities will help you figure out what you might want to use with your own children. If you still need inspiration, almost all homeschool distributors' catalogs feature all sorts of fun and fascinating science resources.

Many of the Top Picks in this chapter will work for students beyond the elementary grades. However, I've also created a separate section of reviews of "more traditional" resources for junior and senior high toward the end of this chapter. Because of what needs to be accomplished at those grade levels, most of my Top Picks for older students are more traditional.

"Anything but a Textbook"

If you agree with my philosophy of science education, then you will probably be looking for real books on particular topics rather than textbooks. Many publishers specialize in heavily illustrated, visually appealing topical books. These are the kind of books children will pick up to read on their own. The following are some examples of this type of book:

The Visual Dictionary of the Human Body (DK Publishing, Inc.)

See How They Grow series (great for very young children) (DK Publishing, Inc.)

Let's Explore Science series (information and experiments for ages 4–7) (DK Publishing, Inc.)

Look Closer (nature series for ages 7–10) (DK Publishing, Inc.)

ASPCA *Pet Care Guides for Kids* (ages 7 and up) (DK Publishing, Inc.)

The Way Things Work by David Macaulay (DK Publishing)

Castle, Cathedral, City, Mill, Pyramid, and *Underground* by David Macaulay (these cover both science and history) (Houghton Mifflin)

The Magic School Bus: Inside the Human Body, Inside a Hurricane, On the Ocean Floor, Lost in the Solar System and other titles by Joanna Cole (Scholastic)

Amazing Animal Babies, *Amazing Snakes*, or *Amazing Spiders* (from the *Eyewitness Junior* series for ages 6–10) (Random House)

Butterfly and Moth, *Dinosaur*, *Fish*, *Insect*, *Reptile*, *Car*, *Crystal and Gem*, *Early Humans*, *Flying Machine*, *Invention*, *Plant and Flower*, *Pond and River*, *Rocks and Minerals*, *Seashore*, *Shell*, *Sports*, *Tree*, and *Weather* (from the older level *Eyewitness* series for ages 10 and up) (Random House)

Energy & Power, *Weather & Climate*, and *The World of the Microscope* (from the *Usborne Science and Experiments* series for ages 10–16) (Usborne Books)

Stars & Planets, *Human Body*, *Undersea*, *Electricity*, and *Jets* (from the *Usborne Young Scientist* series for ages 9–13) (Usborne Books)

Introduction to Chemisty, *Introduction to Biology*, and *Introduction to Physics* (ages 12 and up) (Usborne Books)

Blood and Guts by Linda Allison (study of human anatomy and physiology) Little Brown and Co.

Don't forget to include field guides, biographies of famous scientists, and historical fiction about scientific discoveries. Field guides start to seem essential when you concentrate on particular topics. If you study birds, then you become curious about the types that you see in your area. The same thing happens with flowers, trees, rocks, and other such topics. I like the series of guides from Peterson and from Audobon Society best, but look for simpler guides if you start with young children.

As far as biographies and historical fiction, you will find plenty of choices at the library and in home-school distributors' catalogs. The following are a few such titles to get you started:

Archimedes and the Door of Science by Jeanne Bendick (Bethlehem Books)

Albert Einstein, Young Thinker by Marie Hammontree; *Thomas Edison, Young Inventor* by Sue Guthridge; *Wilbur and Orville Wright* by Augusta Stevenson; and other titles (Aladdin Library)

Along Came Galileo by Jeanne Bendick (Beautiful Feet Books)

Benjamin Franklin by Ingri and Edgar Parin D'Aulaire (Beautiful Feet Books)

Galen and the Gateway to Medicine by Jeanne Bendick (Bethlehem Books)

The Mystery of the Periodic Table by Benjamin D. Wiker (Bethlehem Books)

Scientists from Archimedes to Einstein (Usborne Books)

Science: 100 Scientists Who Changed the World by Jon Balchin (reference work with two-page biographies of key scientists—high school level) (Enchanted Lion Books)

Don't limit yourself to books. Science kits, equipment, games, and software can get your children really excited about science. Again, homeschool distributors usually carry these sorts of things. But there are a few companies that specialize in science and have catalogs devoted just to science "stuff." Some of the best are:

- Home Training Tools (800) 860-6272, www.HomeTrainingTools.com
- Nasco (they also have specialized catalogs for art and math) (800) 558-9595, www.nascofa.com
- Nature's Workshop, Plus! (888) 393-5663, www.naturesworkshopplus.com
- Tobin's Lab (800) 522-4776, www.tobinslab.com

Science Experiment Books

Absolutely crucial are hands-on experiences with science. Experiment and activity books often supply the magic ingredient that draws children into science. I particularly like the books that pose questions and stimulate thinking rather than the books that simply outline steps in an experiment. Again, the possible choices are numerous, but I have chosen a couple of Top Picks that I think especially good.

AIMS Program

AIMS Education Foundation

P.O. Box 8120

Fresno, CA 93747-8120

(888) 733-2467

e-mail: aimsed@aimsedu.org

www.aimsedu.org

Most books are $21.95

This series of activity books combines science with math activities in fun projects for experiencing science in action. There are more than eighty books on all sorts of topics. Here are just a few examples.

The Sky's the Limit deals with flying and aerodynamics. *From Head to Toe* studies the human body. *Floaters and Sinkers* makes the concepts of density, volume, and mass come alive. *Down to Earth* has an unlikely combination of activities for geology, meteorology, and oceanography. *Fun with Foods* is one of my absolute favorites. Food items like popcorn and bananas are used in ways most of us would never dream up on our own. For example, one activity has to do with the amount of popped corn obtained from various brands of popcorn. As they proceed, students learn about ratio, volume, value-for-cost, etc.

Reproducible worksheets are included for recording data from the activities. Books cover grade-level groups such as K–3, K–4, and 5–9. These are fantastic for all types of learners, although some will not enjoy recording and analyzing the data as much as others.

You will need to gather some resources and do some prep work for these sessions. The lessons themselves are totally interactive. You can mix children of different ages, assigning tasks according to their abilities. Of course, you should expect older children to do more analysis, data recording, "hypothesizing," and explaining than younger children.

These activities work well across all learning styles: Wiggly Willys love the hands-on part. Sociable Sues love the interaction and discussion. Competent Carls love trying to figure out what's going on. And Perfect Paulas like to record the data and organize the activity.

Choose a book that fits in with science topics you are studying. Then plan an afternoon once every week or so for each AIMS lesson, and I expect it will become one of the highlights of your schooling.

Backyard Scientist

by Jane Hoffman

Backyard Scientist

P.O. Box 16966

Irvine, CA 92623

(949) 551-2392

e-mail: backyrdsci@aol.com

www.backyardscientist.com

$8.95 each

Jane Hoffman has written six *Backyard Scientist* experiment books that are at the top of my list because they are educational, practical, and fun. Rarely do experiment books achieve all three! In addition, delightful illustrations make the books visually appealing.

All of the books deal with chemistry and physics principles except the *Backyard Scientist Series Three* and the last book, which is a specialized study of earthworms.

The first and last books are slightly different from the other four in format. The first book, *The Original Backyard Scientist,* sets up each experiment like a mystery investigation. Students "gather clues" as they work to come up with their own solutions. At the end of each experiment in this book, as well as in the others, Jane Hoffman explains the solution or what students should have learned in the experiment—a real help for parents without a strong science background.

The last book in the series, *Exploring Earthworms with Me,* has all sorts of creative experiments to learn about earthworms as well as basic scientific principles. It poses a number of intriguing questions in the middle of each experiment.

The middle four *Backyard Scientist* books are titled *Series One, Series Two, Series Three,* and *Series Four.* Each experiment in these books starts with a question that will start your child wondering. For example, "Will a bottle filled with water float when placed in a container filled with water?" Students go on to experiment with a full bottle, empty bottle, half full bottle, etc., to learn basic principles of flotation. In another book, students start with the question, "Can rocks absorb and hold oil?" They proceed to a more challenging experiment about properties of different types of rocks and oil.

Experiments vary in level of difficulty, although there are few that I would describe as very complex. *Series Two* and *Series Four* have the most challenging experiments; *Series Two* is targeted at ages nine to fourteen and *Series Four* is designed more for groups or for older students. *Series Four* has some experiments with dry ice and others such as one where students make an electric buzzer (probably the most complex experiment in the series)—adult supervision is definitely required. (You could use some *Series Four* experiments for a themed birthday party!)

Backyard Scientist also publishes a supplement, *Biblical Applications from the Backyard Scientist,* as a companion to the other books. A biblical correlation for each experiment (but not all) in those books adds another dimension to your science studies.

I particularly like the presentation in the Backyard Scientist books because they stimulate thinking rather than simply directing students through steps of an experiment. Most of the supplies are either easy to obtain or already available in your home. And the experiments really work, something that can't be said about many other experiment books.

Science for Every Kid series

by Janice VanCleave

John Wiley and Sons, Inc.

www.wiley.com

$32.50 hardcover, $12.95 paperback each

Janice VanCleave's science experiment books are very popular among home-schoolers. I will describe one book from the series, *Physics for Every Kid: 101 Easy Experiments in Motion, Heat, Light, Machines, and Sound,* to give you an example of how the books are designed.

Experiments range from extremely easy to slightly involved, but none require fancy equipment. The most complicated activities are things like building a wheel-and-axle contraption out of pencils, a spool, and string. The cost for doing experiments and the hassle of finding what you need is minimal.

Experiments are designed for children ages eight to twelve and have been child-tested. Each experiment lists the purpose, materials needed, step-by-step instructions, results (what should happen if all goes well), and an explanation. Everything is very straightforward and easy to understand. One criticism I have is that this book lacks the "wonder quotient" we find in some books, such as *The Backyard Scientist,* that prompt kids with "wondering why" questions before they begin.

A valuable asset of this book is its organization. We can easily select experiments to go along with whatever topics we are studying because they are divided into categories: electricity, magnets, buoyancy, gravity, balance, flight, simple machines, inertia, motion, light, heat, and sound. Also—unlike most experiment books for children—it has an index that helps us connect experiments with particular concepts. Other science titles in the *For Every Kid* series are *Astronomy, Biology, Chemistry, Constellations, Dinosaurs, Earth Science, Food and Nutrition, The Human Body,* and *Oceans.*

Try This On for Science
by Ron and Peg Marson
TOPS Learning Systems
10970 South Mulino Road
Canby, OR 97013
(503) 263-2040
e-mail: topsideas@yahoo.com
www.topscience.org
$10.00

In our early days of homeschooling, I tried a number of science experiment books with mixed results. One of the toughest areas for us was experiments with batteries and/or electrical circuits. We purchased the TOPS book on *Electricity,* and were amazed when every one of the experiments worked! Even better, they required minimal equipment and expense. That book alone sold me on the rest of their books.

TOPS actually has two different series of books: Task Card Books and Activity Page Books. However, apart from slightly different formatting, these books are very similar in the way they work.

Each activity page has clearly numbered and illustrated instructions. The cartoon style illustrations used are very appealing. Information for the teacher lists the objective, some details that will help the experiment work out, answers, extension activities, and a list of materials needed. Extension activities often are substantial enough for another entire lesson! You are free to reproduce the pages for your own families or "classes."

Books are targeted for different age groups, but a large number are for junior and senior high. Most books, especially those for older levels, include math application. Even some of the younger level books include data recording. While other experiment books introduce scientific principles, this approach takes students to a deeper level of learning that really prepares them for challenging science courses.

There are thirty-five different books available that work for homeschooling. Each book addresses a single topic, such as pendulums, metric measure, floating and sinking, oxidation, solutions, heat, pressure, magnetism, light, machines, rocks and minerals, electricity, corn and beans, and planets and stars.

Youngest level books are for grades 3 through 7 or 8 while other books cover grades 5 through 10, 8 through 12, or other such spans. (TOPS has a few other books primarily of interest to classroom teachers.) You can use TOPS experiments as family or group activities, do them one-to-one with your children, or let older students tackle them independently.

TOPS has made it easy for you to sample the entire range of their books with *Try This On for Science.* They have taken one activity lesson each from forty-one of their books and compiled them into this one "sampler." The collection represents the entire level of difficulty and topics so you can preview before purchasing complete topic books. All the activity lessons featured in this book are also available online for free at their Web site, but the convenience of the book is well worth the purchase price. Each lesson page includes a listing of the age range of the source book, number of activities and pages, plus the price.

You can start with the sampler, but I think you'll become a fan, too, no matter which book you choose.

Curriculum

Some science curricula are similar to unit studies, combining a variety of activities and resources for topical science study. *Media Angels* books, *Great Science Adventures*, *A History of Science*, *Living Learning Books*, and *Stratton House Home Science Adventures* are among resources reviewed below that fit this description. They vary in the amount of information they include, often sending you elsewhere for resource material. This type of curriculum best reflects my own ideas about how children should learn science.

For parents who want to use a more traditional approach through the elementary grades, I have also included a few such resources.

***Science for Christian Schools* series**
Bob Jones University Press
Greenville, SC 29614
(800) 845-5731
www.bjup.com

If you really want a traditional-type textbook series for science in the elementary grades, Bob Jones University Press's series is one of the better choices. Recognizing that children have different learning styles, they have incorporated activities to fit different styles.

Textbooks are attractively printed in full color and are hardbound for durability.

Scientific thinking is stressed more than fact memorization in the elementary grades. Scriptural principles are incorporated with science applications in the curriculum.

Activities are at the heart of many lessons rather than being presented as optional—especially at the early grade levels. Most activities are outlined in the teacher's editions. That means these courses need to be taught—you cannot just hand your child the text to use on his or her own.

Home Teacher's Editions are essential as are Notebook Packets of student work/activity pages for each level. These teacher editions are well organized and easy to use. Upper levels also have additional visuals, charts, and game pieces that come as part of the Teacher Packet. Everything you need (including tests and answer keys, but *not* materials needed for experiments) is packaged as a kit for each grade level.

These courses do require lesson preparation and presentation time, but if you take time to follow lesson plans from the manuals, you and your children should find the courses very engaging.

While courses are written for particular grade levels, you can use one level for children over a two- or three-year span of grade levels with a little adaptation to suit their abilities. (It will be most challenging to do this for first and second graders who are still developing reading and writing skills.) Because courses are challenging, when you stretch to cover a range of grade levels, you should probably choose a level below that of your oldest student.

Grade 1 kit, $63.50

The text for first grade covers the following topics on an introductory level: senses, heat, sound, wild and tame animals, and the sun, moon, and stars. The supplementary listening cassette (included in kit) is essential for chapters 1 and 11.

Grade 2 kit, $57.50

Both physical and life sciences are introduced in this text. Topics include bones, plants, shape and movement of the earth, forces, and shorelines.

Grade 3 kit, $57.50

Topics at this level include classification of animals, the solar system, photosynthesis, birds, mass, and weight. Student worksheets include some that have students start to record observations from activities. All of these items are in the Science 3 kit.

Grade 4 kit, $79.50

At this level, students are developing scientific skills of observation, classification, and interpretation. The contrast between creation and evolution is introduced with a study of the origin of the moon. Other topics include insects, light, electricity, area and volume, simple machines, digestion, animal defenses, trees, and erosion.

Grade 5 kit, $79.50

This text builds on the thinking-skills foundation begun in the fourth grade text and continues to develop skills of inferring, predicting, and experimenting. However, it is not dependent upon prior study of the fourth grade book. Topics studied include fossils, airplanes, thermal energy, atomic theory, weather, plant and animal reproduction, oceans, forces that cause wind, and tracks. The theme of the limitations of man's understanding and God's omnipotence underlies the study.

Grade 6 kit, $101.00

This newly revised edition also has a companion student activities manual and its own teacher's edition. These, rather than a notebook packet, are included in the homeschool kit along with tests and answer key. The activities manual has pages for recording and evaluating experiments and activities plus some review pages. Among topics studied at this level are earthquakes, volcanoes, weather, cells, classification, atoms and molecules, electricity, motion and machines, the stars, the solar system, plant and animal reproduction, heredity and genetics, and the nervous and immune systems. Scientific method is taught through experiments and activities.

Christian Kids Explore Biology

by Stephanie L. Redmond

Bright Ideas Press

P.O. Box 333

Cheswold, DE 19936

(877) 492-8081

e-mail: info@brightideaspress.com

www.brightideaspress.com

$29.95

I like the balance of information and activity in this science curriculum for grades 3 through 6 that is presented within a single 295-page book. Developed by a homeschool mom, *Christian Kids Explore Biology* is set up, ideally, for two ninety-minute block sessions a week.

The first session each week is "teaching time." It begins with reading and discussing the information from the text. Students complete a daily reading sheet (reproducible form in the appendix), write words and definitions for their vocabulary list in a notebook, possibly work with flashcards, and do extended reading or research.

The second session is "hands-on time" for experiments or activities. These don't require expensive or exotic materials, but it will take a little work to gather the necessary items (e.g., brown pipe cleaner, magnifying glass, old T-shirts, face paints, alligator stickers). There are also some artistically done coloring pages—at least one per unit. Colored pencils are the perfect medium to use for these. The book has numerous smaller black-line illustrations that children might also color. Students should each maintain a three-ring binder in which they keep all of their science work, including coloring pages. You will need to select activities and adjust the amount of work required according to the ages and abilities of your children.

Other reproducible pages in the appendix include an experiment form, field trip form, plant observation form, maps, Scripture memory cards, recipes, supplemental activities, and pictures for an ABC animal kingdom book that students create.

Lengthy lists of recommended resources at the back of the book suggest books, videos, CDs, games, puzzles, and other possible helps for each unit. You don't have to use other resource books, but the study will be much richer for students if you use some of the colorful picture books available on the different science topics. I believe that students in upper elementary grades need more factual information than is provided within the book alone, so I highly recommend using additional books with older students.

There are eight units with a number of lessons per unit—thirty-five lessons in all—so the curriculum should take one school year to complete. Vocabulary words and lists of materials needed are at the beginning of each unit. Each unit concludes with a review, a "test," and a writing assignment.

A biblical worldview is presented throughout with the idea of God as the master designer a key theme. The first lesson advances a creationist perspective, although it takes no position on the age of the earth. However, recommended resource books tend toward a young-earth position.

Considering God's Creation

Eagle's Wings Educational Materials

P.O. Box 502

Duncan, OK 73534

(580) 252-1555

e-mail: info@EaglesWingsEd.com

www.EaglesWingsEd.com

$29.95, additional student books—$13.95

This multigrade science curriculum is for children in grades 2 through 7. Creation serves as the backdrop for science studies that can be easily adapted for multilevel teaching in the homeschool setting. This one-year program is contained in a teacher's manual and a student book. The publisher says it can also be used as a supplement to other curriculum if desired, but I doubt many use it that way.

The teacher's manual contains the lessons, written in an easy-to-use format. Each lesson first describes advance preparation required. Next are vocabulary words listed with definitions and origins. Following is the "introduction"—actually the main idea of the lesson—which can be read to students directly from the book. The words from an original song/poem about the lesson are included. The actual song is on the accompanying professionally recorded audio CD that comes in an attached envelope in the back of teacher's manual. (Cassettes are also available.)

Because the authors believe in hands-on activities for effective learning, at least one such activity is described in each lesson. Many of the activities utilize student activity pages from the 270-page student book.

While a Christian view of science is presented throughout each lesson, a special section called "Bible Reading" directs students to Scripture for verses related to the subject under study. The creationist viewpoint, including belief in a young earth, is a dominant theme. A fun extra, called "Evolution Stumpers," provides tidbits of scientific information with which to challenge the theory of evolution.

A review section includes questions to pose to your children about each lesson. Since the curriculum is designed for a wide age span, the final section, "Digging Deeper," offers suggestions for additional study, activities, investigations, reading, reports, etc., which can be used as is appropriate with each student.

The student workbook consists of work/activity pages. You are free to make copies for immediate family and classroom use only, although you might prefer to order a separate workbook for each student. These sheets are often the foundation for investigations or experiments, or they are used for cut-and-paste activities, all of which are essential parts of the curriculum.

Students compile their own notebooks as they work through these activities and lessons. A few extra items will be needed for activities—crayons, scissors, and glue for most lessons, plus items like flashlights, shoe boxes, rocks, and library/resource books on particular topics.

Topics covered include creation, the universe, the earth, rocks and minerals, weather, plant kingdom, ecology, insects, spiders, fish, reptiles, birds, mammals, amphibians, animal structures, food chains, animal reproduction, instinct, man, and scientists. None of these topics is covered thoroughly, since that would be impossible within a one-year curriculum. If you examine the list of topics, you can see that life science receives the most attention, with earth science filling the remainder.

We definitely need to make decisions about what to require from each child, since some material will be too challenging for young students and some not challenging enough for older students. It also requires significant preparation and presentation time. However, this curriculum is one of the best for homeschool families that want a Christian science curriculum for teaching a broad span of grade levels together.

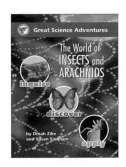

Great Science Adventures
by Dinah Zike and Susan Simpson
Common Sense Press
P.O. Box 1365
Melrose, FL 32666
(352) 475-5757
www.greatscienceadventures.com
$22.00 each

This arts-and-crafts approach to science is totally different from anything else I have seen. One of the authors, Dinah Zike, is well known for her *Big Book of Books and Activities* and other books where she shows how to cut and fold paper into all sorts of creative forms to be used by students as tools for learning and presenting information. In *Great Science Adventures* these are called 3D Graphic Organizers, and they are used throughout the series.

More than half of each book consists of pages to be cut and put together in one fashion or another. About half of these activity pages are for creating little booklets that correspond with each of the twenty-four lessons. These booklets have preprinted pictures and text to convey the factual information on each topic, so we need not use outside information resources unless they are assigned as research for older students.

But lessons are much more than the creation of booklets. Two- to three-page lesson plans give you key concepts, vocabulary words, and a number of activity ideas from which to choose. Each lesson might take from one to three days to complete. You should be able to complete two of the *Great Science Adventures* books per year if you do science two or three days per week.

The authors say the curriculum is appropriate for grades K through 8, but I suspect younger students will find most of the work too difficult. Older students need to be assigned challenging activities from "Experiments, Investigations, and Research" at the end of each lesson plan.

Each lesson begins with reading the corresponding booklet. Some text in small type should be read only by or with older students, but all of the large-type text should be read with everyone. Then you assign appropriate vocabulary words. Instructions for creating a vocabulary book are in the introduction.

Every lesson includes work with some sort of graphic organizer. Other cut-and-paste pages in the book are used to make these. Children might be cutting, pasting, labeling, writing, drawing, or coloring depending upon the topic and their ability level. Children often refer to the booklets for information to write in the organizers.

Detailed lab activities called "Investigative Loops" are in many of the lessons. These require children to use scientific method as they ask questions, make predictions, follow procedures, measure, observe, record data, come up with conclusions, and maybe pursue other questions that arise from the experiment. Common household items are used, but it will take time and planning to gather and prepare materials for the investigations.

Some lessons, instead, have a demonstration or other activity that does not require application of the scientific method.

The last part of each lesson offers a number of optional activities. Some might be done by the group, and some might be done independently by older students. These cover the range of learning styles and age abilities. Some examples from a single lesson: "Use clay to form a mesa, a butte, or both. Compare and contrast the two." "Write a story that takes place in the American Southwest on a mesa." "Research Stone Mountain, Georgia. Report on your findings." And "Investigate hydrodynamics." Sometimes books or Internet sites are listed for reference.

After the lesson plans are two pages on assessment that might be easy to overlook. However, these pages offer some very practical ideas parents will probably want to use, so make a point to read them.

The Great Science Adventures series is divided into three groups: life science, physical science, and earth science. You should probably rotate through these three areas as you choose titles so that children get exposure to a broad range of science. There are sixteen books in the series covering topics such as plants; insects and arachnids; the human body; vertebrates; ecosystems; health and safety; tools and technology; energy, forces, and motion; light and sound; magnets and electricity; atoms, molecules and matter; space; atmosphere and weather; landforms and surface features; oceans and fresh water; and rocks and minerals. Most of these should be available by the year 2005.

You are given permission to reproduce pages for your "classroom," so purchasing one book per topic will be sufficient for your family.

A History of Science

by Rebecca Berg

Beautiful Feet Books

139 Main Street

Sandwich, MA 02563

(800) 889-1978

www.bfbooks.com

Guide—$12.95, complete package—$146.95

This is a guide for a literature-based introduction to science for children in the elementary grades. The guide takes you through a number of real books for a one-year study.

The complete package includes *The New Way Things Work, The Picture History of Great Inventors, Explorabook, Along Came Galileo, Archimedes and the Door of Science, The Story of Thomas Edison, Albert Einstein, Marie Curie's Search for Radium, Benjamin Franklin's Adventures with Electricity, Pasteur's Fight Against Microbes,* a *Scientist's Card Deck, A Science Experiment Pamphlet,* a *History of Science Timeline,* and the guide. A package without the first book (which is optional in the study) is available for $114.95. These are almost all items that I would recommend to you even if you weren't doing this particular study!

There are also lists of additional recommended materials, although these are not essential. Among them are five *Your Story Hour* audiocassettes, *Augustus Caesar's World, George Washington's World,* and some additional biographies.

Lessons start with *The Picture History of Great Inventors,* a new publication from Beautiful Feet Books. This is a colorful picture book along the lines of many of the Usborne books. It's strictly introductory in content. I suspect you will need to provide extra explanation for some of the pictures with younger children. This book serves as a "spine book" throughout the study—start here, then branch off into more depth on different topics. The selected biographies in the package make this very much a "story approach" to the history of science.

Explorabook, A Science Experiment Pamphlet, and seven activities at the back of the Beautiful Feet guide combine to provide substantial hands-on activity.

In addition to activities and reading, students record information in a science notebook they create, color pictures provided in the timeline kit and place them appropriately, do additional research in an encyclopedia, copy related Scripture verses into their notebooks, create and label sketches, and do reports and presentations. Of course, you will need to choose activities appropriate for the ages and abilities of your children.

This is a wonderful introduction to science. It teaches some basic principles, but even better for children in the elementary grades, it connects science to people and real life in fascinating ways. I believe this approach provides an excellent foundation for a classical education in science.

Living Learning Books

112 Heather Ridge Drive

Pelham, AL 35124

(205) 620-3365

e-mail: info@livinglearningbooks.com

www.livinglearningbooks.com

This new science curriculum is different at each of the three levels I reviewed, so be careful when you hear others talking about it to identify which level they are describing.

Each level should take about one school year to complete. All levels have two primary components: a teacher's guide and a student pack. The teacher's guide is the heart of the program at each level. It has detailed lesson plans, activity/project descriptions, suggested reading, narration instructions, Internet links, checklists, and reproducible masters.

The student pack is a nonreproducible set of pages (approximately sixty to seventy-five pages each) that correlate with each level. These are essential, so you will need a separate pack for each student working through the curriculum. Both the teacher guide and student pack come as three-hole-punched packets that you need to insert into binders. Students will need a two-inch binder that will hold these student pack pages, narrations, experiment observations, and other papers created through the course.

The first two levels use real books extensively, while the third level relies upon activities and experiments and incorporates information into the lessons within the book. All levels have writing assignments appropriate to the different levels.

For the first two levels, the publisher sells a pack of key books—all from Usborne—that can be used with the courses. These are not required, but you will have to obtain these or other books covering the same topics. You will also want to borrow or buy some of the other fiction and nonfiction books and videos listed as recommended reading/viewing under the various topics.

Level 1: Life Science was written for grades K through 2. Information about adapting it to work for grades 3 to 6 is available on the publisher's Web site. Three main areas are covered: animals, the human body, and plants. Animal units are introductory lessons on ants, butterflies, eagles, elephants, frogs, pandas, penguins, primates, seals, snails, snakes, and whales. Human body units explore senses and some of the body systems. In plant units, children learn about leaves and roots, growing things, flowers, trees, and carnivorous plants.

Parents/teachers need to plan ahead to collect books and resources for activities, but nothing is very complicated at this level. Lesson plans follow a standard outline for each topic. You begin the lesson with reading about the topic. Students who are able to read independently, and all students maintain a reading log (reproducible form is included). Most student pack pages for this level are coloring pages. Many of them appear to be high-quality original artwork, although a few seem to be enlarged computer images with "pixellated" lines.

Optional enrichment activities tend toward arts and crafts and cooking more than experiments in the animal units, but experiments take center stage in the human body and plant units. Don't skip the Internet links. There are some great links to video clips, slide shows, pictures, games, and much more.

Charlotte Mason fans will appreciate the incorporation of narration into the lessons. Children do narrations about books or projects that can be taken by dictation, written by the children themselves, or some combination of the above depending upon the child's ability.

Vocabulary gets some attention, but you are really on your own to select words and to decide how to teach vocabulary.

Level 2: Earth Science and Astronomy targets grades 2 through 6. In many ways it is similar to *Level 1*. The basic format is the same, but it clearly addresses the needs of older learners. It has additional detail that I find very helpful: in the lesson plans it includes review questions, specific pages to be read from a recommended book, and suggested projects to correlate with each lesson. Projects are more complex than in *Level 1*.

Topics addressed under astronomy are rockets, solar system, stars and constellations, space shuttles, space stations, astronauts, and telescopes. Earth science covers day/night/seasons, the earth's crust, rocks and fossils, soil, disaster preparedness, volcanoes, earthquakes, the water cycle, storms, rivers and caves, and seas and oceans. *Level 2* also has an appendix of Scripture readings that relate to the various topics—use these or not as you choose.

The student pack still has some coloring pages, but it also has word search puzzles and pages for students to create their own planet books. The pack includes a reproduction of an American Red Cross *Disaster Preparedness* book that has both instruction and coloring pages.

Level 3: Chemistry substitutes experiments and activities for reading because of the nature of the topic. Very few elementary level books, fiction or nonfiction, are written on this topic, so children learn mostly by doing, although some reading material is included in the student pack pages. This level is recommended for grades 3 through 6.

Lessons follow a new format: read the short introductory passage, conduct an experiment, record results of the experiment, review the reading passage, copy key words and definitions into their binders, and complete unit review pages.

Children start to learn scientific method at this level, although the focus is primarily upon observation and comprehension rather than analysis.

Parents will need to plan ahead to gather supplies for the experiments. Although they don't require expensive or complicated equipment, it will still take time to round up everything you need.

I especially like the reformatted teacher guide pages at this level. A left-hand column shows correlated student pages, reference pages in two Usborne and Kingfisher books that might be used, and project supplies. Clearly the author is continually working to improve the product as each new level is developed.

Media Angels Science

15720 South Pebble Lane

Fort Myers, FL 33912-2341

e-mail: mediangels@aol.com

www.mediaangels.com

Media Angels is a team of two authors, teacher Felice Gerwitz and geologist Jill Whitlock, both of whom are also homeschooling moms. Media Angels publishes science unit studies as well as a guide to creating your own such studies. The guide *Teaching Science and Having Fun!* is optional, but I will begin with it in case you prefer to do it all yourself.

Teaching Science and Having Fun!

by Felice Gerwitz

$12.95

Felice Gerwitz provides detailed science scope and sequence for grades K through 12 while also explaining how to create either topical studies or comprehensive unit studies based upon science topics. She stresses the importance of knowing and applying scientific method at all grade levels, emphasizing the vital role that experiments play in learning scientific method. Because of this, Felice offers extensive suggestions for creating lab activities for high school level science where they are required, including lots of budget-conscious substitutes. She adds extensive resource lists with commentary so that you can find other resources to flesh out your courses.

Teaching Science and Having Fun! addresses the big picture—Why teach science? How do you teach children of differing ages? What topics do you need to cover?—rather than attempting to offer complete course outlines. She also addresses problem areas such as what kind of microscope to buy. This is an inspiring, practical, and helpful resource for teaching science to children of all ages.

The educational philosophy of this book is reflected in all the Media Angels science books.

Creation Science: A Study Guide to Creation!

by Felice Gerwitz and Jill Whitlock

$18.95

This is one of a series of unit study guides from Media Angels. The other three volumes are *Creation Anatomy, Creation Astronomy,* and *Creation Geology* ($18.95 each).

This series very much reflects what I think science education should look like with its combination of real books, experiments, and other interesting activities that truly engage children in the study of science.

Each study should take about six to eight weeks to complete. The guides are set up for multigrade teaching, with activities divided into levels for K–3, 4–8, and 9–12.

These are actually unit studies that stretch beyond science, although they do not provide complete coverage of any of the other subjects. Activities for each level are divided under the headings of Science Activities and Experiments, Geography/History, Reading Ideas List, Vocabulary/Spelling List, Vocabulary/Spelling/Grammar Ideas, Language Arts Ideas, Math Reinforcements, and Art/Music Ideas. Science receives the most attention, with a good deal of background information for the teacher included in a "Teaching Outline" section in each book. (Read through this section in each book before you begin to teach the unit.)

Lots of extras are included in each guide: bibliography of videos, books, and computer resources; materials list; field trip guide; science experiment instruction pages; and reproducible activity pages.

Activity instructions are fairly well spelled out—they are much more than lists or outlines of suggestions. The suggested reading list includes titles that are referenced within some of the activities. Suggested books are a mixture of nonsectarian and Christian titles.

You will need to plan ahead to determine which activities to do and what resources you will need. All studies are presented from the young-earth perspective and rely on a literal interpretation of the Bible. Otherwise, the religious perspective is generically Christian rather than Protestant or Catholic.

I think you will want to use the *Experiment and Activity Packs* that complement the books ($12.95 each). While there are separate packs for each of the *Creation Astronomy* and *Creation Anatomy* books, there is a single pack to be used along with *Creation Science* and *Creation Geology.* Packs feature reproducible pages of activities and experiments with step-by-step instructions, questions, games, puzzles, a glossary, and more. Experiments are most appropriate for the elementary grades up through junior high since they do not require any of the mathematical analysis necessary for high school courses.

from **Discovering Birds**

Stratton House Home Science Adventures
17837 First Avenue South #186
Seattle, WA 98148
(800) 694-7225
e-mail: hello@homeschoolscience.com
www.homeschoolscience.com

If you want to do activity-based science, but you don't have time or inclination to find experiments and gather materials, Stratton House kits are a great option. Designed by a homeschooling family, they can be used with children in grades 1 through 8. Materials for two children are included, but extra materials are available from the publisher.

While Stratton House sells kits on individual topics, their three-topic combo kits are the best deal. Two of these combo kits are available. One is *Astronomy, Birds, and Magnetism* ($66.50) and the other is *Microscopic Explorations, Insects, and Light* ($69.50).

These kits offer much more than science kits like those you find in children's stores. They include actual lessons in a parent guide—forty lessons in the first kit and forty-three in the second. It should take about a year to complete each kit.

Kits include the parent guide, reproducible worksheets for children, and the materials needed for the activities. For example, the first kit includes items such as binoculars, birdseed, bird identification book, star charts, and magnets. Lessons are laid out with clear, illustrated instructions, so they are easy for even the inexperienced parent. The parent guide has additional ideas and topics for discussion to make the most of your children's curiosity.

Sample lessons are available on their Web site so you can check it out before buying.

More-traditional Courses for Junior and Senior High

Apologia Science series
by Dr. Jay L. Wile
Apologia Educational Ministries
1106 Meridian Plaza, Suite 220
Anderson, IN 46016
(888) 524-4724
(765) 608-3290
e-mail: mailbag@highschoolscience.com
www.apologia.com

Dr. Jay Wile is the primary author of most of Apologia's *Exploring Creation* science curricula for junior and senior high. These Apologia courses are among the few options for college-prep lab science courses that do not require a parent to teach the courses. Another factor that makes them popular is their very reasonable cost.

Apologia offers courses for general science, physical science, biology, chemistry, and physics. Among them are both standard courses and supplemental ones that provide the equivalent of AP courses. I appreciate the options that accommodate a range of student goals, from the nonscience oriented student who just wants the basics, through the ambitious college-bound student who wants AP level courses. Some courses also offer choices of lab experience options to offer more activity for ambitious students or more limited options that might fit a family's limited financial resources.

Most courses are available in traditional textbook format or in new CD-ROM versions. Textbook courses come as two-volume sets ($75.00 to $85.00 per course). The first book is the hardbound primary text; all texts have color illustrations. The second book is a softbound solution and test manual with complete answers and explanations for questions from the student book and the tests. Step-by-step instructions for lab experiments appear in chapters alongside the concepts they illustrate.

CD-ROM versions ($65.00 per course) contain all of the textbook and solutions manual content plus multimedia video clips, animations, pronunciation guides, and other helps. They also have nifty indexing so you can simply click on an index entry to go to that topic in the correct module on the CD.

Those who choose the textbook version of one of the second edition courses (*Physics* and *Chemistry* thus far) can purchase a companion CD-ROM that has only the extras not already contained in the textbook ($15.00 per CD per course). Icons in the textbook alert students to available video clips they might want to view.

A Christian worldview permeates these courses. Dr. Wile brings in not just creationist views but also other scientific issues and ideas in relation to Christianity (e.g., geocentric versus heliocentric viewpoints).

Courses were written for independent study. Dr. Wile's conversational style of writing makes these texts much easier reading than most others. He speaks directly to students, assuming they will be working through the courses on their own—a realistic expectation in most families. Brief information for parents/teachers is at the beginning of the solution and test books. Free support is available via e-mail, voicemail, fax, and snail mail.

Students who need more oversight or outside prodding might want to enroll in one of the Internet courses based on these texts. Apologia has information about such courses in their catalog and on their Web site.

In student textbooks, the text typestyle is large compared to other science texts, but this makes it easier to read and less intimidating. (That also means there has to be slightly less content than in an equivalently sized book with smaller type.) Books are divided into modules rather than chapters. Within each module are "on your own" questions and problems. Students are to answer these as they proceed through each section, and answers can be self-checked within the textbook. At the end of each module is a "study guide" that has questions and problems for which answers are in the solutions and test book. A test and answer key for each module is also found in that book. Students also need to keep a separate lab notebook to record observations and conclusions from their experiments.

All textbooks have glossaries and indexes plus other helps, such as the periodic table and lists of elements and their symbols. At the beginning of the book are lists of lab materials needed. Dr. Wile specifies lab materials that, for the most part, can be found at grocery and hardware stores. However, the biology and chemistry labs need some more sophisticated equipment, such as a scale, microscope, and test tubes. Using nontraditional lab equipment means students will not be familiar with the more complex scientific equipment, but this should be a very small liability given the practical advantages of these types of labs. Lab equipment and resources for high school level courses are available in various sets either from Apologia or from Nature's Workshop Plus!

Exploring Creation with General Science and *Exploring Creation with Physical Science* are junior high courses targeted at grades 7 and 8.

Exploring Creation with Biology, Exploring Creation with Chemistry, and *Exploring Creation with Physics* meet requirements for high school lab courses. However, Apologia also offers advanced courses in biology, chemistry, and physics that, combined with the foundational course, cover the content of an Advanced Placement (AP) course.

The advanced courses are titled *Advanced Chemistry in Creation, Advanced Physics in Creation,* and *The Human Body: Fearfully and Wonderfully Made* ($75.00 to $85.00 per course). These are similar in format to the foundational texts, but the first two courses are illustrated only in black-and-white. CD-ROM versions of the advanced courses are scheduled with *The Human Body* due first and others to follow over a two-year period.

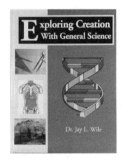

Exploring Creation with General Science

This is a broad general science course for junior high students that includes a significant amount of lab work. The course is set up in sixteen modules that should take about two weeks each to complete.

Topics covered include the history of science, scientific method, how to perform experiments, simple machines, archaeology, rocks, minerals, fossils, geology, paleontology, evolution and interrelated theories (uniformitarianism and catastrophism), living organisms, classifications, the human body, and organisms and energy.

Exploring Creation with Physical Science

This large, 450+ page text is the foundation for the most user-friendly, yet academically challenging, physical science course for homeschoolers of which I am aware. It qualifies as a lab course, with extensive experiments and recording activity. In fact, Dr. Wile begins the first lesson with an experiment. He carefully details how to perform the experiment and the expected results. He describes possible corrections if it's not working as it should. Then he uses the results as a platform to provide a basic explanation of molecules, atoms, and chemical reactions.

The book is divided into sixteen modules, each of which should take about two weeks to complete. Topics covered include "the basics," air, atmosphere, water, the hydrosphere, earth and the lithosphere, weather, motion, gravity, electromagnetic force, electrical circuits, magnetism, atomic structure, radioactivity, waves and sound, light, and astrophysics.

While the content is appropriate and challenging, it is not as difficult as some physical science texts. For example, in discussing chemical bonds, it addresses overall positive and negative charges without going into valences as do some physical science courses.

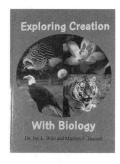

Exploring Creation with Biology

This text is coauthored by Marilyn F. Durnell. It is very similar in format and presentation to the physical science course. While it is traditional in its approach for the most part, it does not include study of the human body. Instead, human anatomy and physiology are covered in a separate course, *The Human Body*, which Apologia considers an advanced biology course. Students preparing for AP exams or wanting to list an AP course on their transcript need to complete both courses.

Clear explanations teach concepts in a friendly fashion without oversimplification. Questions provoke thought and not simply recall.

With this text, lab activity becomes more demanding, although you have a choice about how much of it your student needs to complete. There are three levels of lab activity: household labs require minimal equipment and should be completed by all students; optional microscope labs require a microscope and slide set (kit available for $285.00); dissection labs are also optional, but the dissection kit is only $40.00. Instructions for all labs are found in the text.

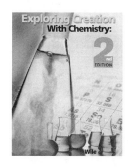

Exploring Creation with Chemistry

This text covers essentially the same content as most high school chemistry courses. Algebra 1 is a prerequisite. While Dr. Wile assumes that the student has this math background, he does do some math review. Solutions to test questions include the math work, so students weak in math can figure out what they might have missed. This sort of help is very rare in chemistry courses. The text presents concepts and guides students through practice exercises before leaving them to work on problems.

Dr. Wile has done a great job constructing lab activities with low-cost equipment while providing enough experience for a solid college-prep course. The labs are exacting in detail, achieving a great deal of precision with minimal equipment. *Nature's Workshop Plus!* sells a basic equipment set for this course ($55.00). All the chemicals you need are items available at the grocery or hardware store. However, the second edition of the text for this course added optional extra lab work for which you need a "secondary lab set," available from MicroChem Kits, that includes more specialized chemicals.

One negative point: chemicals are frequently introduced by formula but not by common names. This seems odd in a text that is generally good at making practical connections for students. However, Dr. Wile explains the reason for this: "When you introduce every chemical with its name, the student is quickly overwhelmed by the names and thus ceases to remember them. Therefore, I only introduce the names of practical chemicals that the student will encounter in everyday life. As a result, the student remembers the important names and does not get overwhelmed with chemical names he or she will never encounter."

Apologia's *Advanced Chemistry* course combined with this foundational course is equivalent to an AP or university level chemistry course.

Exploring Creation with Physics

This course will be quite challenging for students who attempt to work independently unless parents are knowledgeable and can help from time to time. However, it is still a good course for the student who does not intend to take much science in college. Coverage is adequate but not as complete as in some other high school physics texts. For example, there is no treatment of the properties of matter, heat transfer, atomic and nuclear physics, relativity, or quantum physics. (Such topics are covered in some, but not all, high-school-level physics courses.) These shortcomings not withstanding, Dr. Wile's casual and illustrative prose goes a long way toward helping both teacher and student grasp inherently difficult subjects.

Science oriented students should consider adding Apologia's *Advanced Physics* course. Together the two courses are equivalent to an AP or college level physics course.

Lab activities are fairly simple for a high school physics lab course. Lab experiments seem to be designed to illustrate principles more than to provide opportunities for serious scientific work. Nevertheless, this course will satisfy most college entry requirements for a physics course with lab.

This is a math-based course; prerequisites are algebra and beginning trigonometry. However, the math is not overly complex, and example problems are worked out in clear and thorough detail. A primer on the subjects of conversion of units, scientific notation, and measurement precision and accuracy is available for free by mail or on the Internet in case students need to review these topics.

The second edition of this text, released in 2004, includes additional experiments and practice problems plus icons corresponding to multi-media content on the companion CD.

The Human Body: Fearfully and Wonderfully Made

by Dr. Jay L. Wile and Marilyn M. Shannon, M.A.

I'm including a brief review of this "advanced biology" course since I suspect many parents will want to cover human anatomy and physiology as part of their teen's biology instruction. However, be forewarned that this is a challenging course with some content (especially the large amount of vocabulary to be learned) more likely to be encountered in a college level course rather than a high school course. That's why it is suitable for AP test preparation!

Along with the student text and Solutions and Tests book (which comes with the student text for $85.00), students will need a microscope, a set of prepared slides, a dissection and specimens kit (tools, cow's eye, cow's heart, and fetal pig), and *The Anatomy Coloring* book by Kapit and Elson. All of these resources are available through Nature's Workshop Plus! If students opt not to do all the lab work, they should still purchase *The Anatomy Coloring Book* since it has far more detailed illustrations than does the text. As with other Apologia courses, students need to keep a separate lab notebook.

Although this is a very challenging course, it is designed such that students can complete all work independently. The publisher recommends it for twelfth grade but says it can also be used from tenth grade on if students have the prerequisites.

The Rainbow
by Durell C. Dobbins, Ph.D.
Beginnings Publishing House, Inc.
328 Shady Lane
Alvaton, KY 42122
(800) 831-3570
e-mail: dcdobbins@aol.com
www.beginningspublishing.com

Complete year 1—$254.00, year 2—$143.00, text and *Teacher's Helper*—$96.00, text only—$80.00, lab workbook—$18.00

Serious science is coupled with a lighthearted approach and lots of hands-on activity for this two-year course targeted at junior high level. Written specifically for Christian homeschoolers, it has a beautiful full-color textbook (softcover) and huge lab set with all sorts of interesting items. The course is also unusual because the text is intended to be used for two years. In the first year students study physics and chemistry, and in the second year they study biology and applied science.

The Teacher's Helper is a teacher guide for both the text and the labs, covering both years. The first year's lab set includes both durable equipment and consumable supplies plus a lab workbook. For the second year, you need additional equipment and supplies and a new lab workbook, all of which is sold as a "year 2" set.

I really enjoy Dr. Dobbins personal, friendly writing style, and I think most junior high students will too. Here's a short excerpt to give you the flavor:

So you've given up on dissolving oil and vinegar together without killing people, but you are still convinced you are a smart chemist. So what do you do? Like every other good chemist in the world, you pick up the bottle of salad dressing and shake it really hard, then fret to remove the cap and pour the dressing before it separates again. But unlike the untrained nonchemists, you know the word for what you just did. You created a *suspension*.[1]

Dr. Dobbins explains concepts simply, frequently relating concepts to familiar experiences such as the above. Each small section has "exercises"—questions that can be used for discussion or written assignments.

The Teacher's Helper outlines a schedule for three days per week for thirty-two weeks per year. It also has the purpose of each lesson, section review quizzes, answers, and troubleshooting ideas in case a lab experiment doesn't turn out as it should. A separate *Lab Workbook* for the student gives detailed (and often humorous) instructions for the weekly experiment.

The complete kit includes a neatly packaged set of lab materials with everything needed to carry out the experiments, including such items as safety glasses, a marble roller assembly, a baseball, resistors, magnets, light bulbs, glass tubing, syringe, PVC tubing, dye, and much more. You could conceivably collect your own materials from the list provided on the publisher's Web site, but it's such an odd assortment that you would be better off purchasing the kit from Beginnings.

If you have more than one student you will need to add an extra lab workbook. Each lab workbook comes with a pair of safety glasses, an essential item for each student. Other than that, students should be able to work cooperatively on the experiments with what comes in the kit. Those using this program with a larger group need to order multiple kits.

The curriculum is obviously Christian with its numerous references to God. Dr. Dobbins's treatment of the theory of evolution is interesting. He says, "In this text we will attempt to teach the general theory of evolution because a good education in the sciences requires it. We present it as a theory . . . which we ourselves do not accept" (p. 136). However, it does not seem to me that evolution is taught in this text so much as it is undermined. Dr. Dobbins does not take a position on the age of the earth.

Another sensitive subject might be human reproduction, but it is tastefully and conservatively explained.

Overall, I think this course prepares students with a solid foundation for more in-depth high-school-level science courses. Beginnings also has a high school course, *The Spectrum Chemistry*. I didn't have time for a complete review of this course, but the format and tone are the same as *The Rainbow*. The content appears to be solid college prep (the author claims "honors course" level) with plenty of lab work. There's a separate lab book and set of equipment. Like Apologia's course, it is written directly to the student so he or she can work independently.

12

Unit Studies and All-in-One Programs

Textbooks were created for classroom management purposes—not because authors prefer to write them. Too often textbooks are written by committees, warped by state and federal goals, censored by publishers' agendas (with which we might or might not agree), written with no sense of style, and boring beyond belief. Of course, there are some exceptions, but not many. And even good textbooks reflect a compartmentalized approach to learning. Math stays in one book, while language remains in another. Spelling is in yet another compartment, and literature has to stay separate from both spelling and language.

Making Learning Come Alive

Real life is not compartmentalized. Unit studies try to make learning more like real life by bringing a number of subjects together around a central theme for study. Unit study themes are infinite. Some follow historical themes, some use character traits, some use novels, some use science topics, and some use Scripture.

Unit studies can be narrow topical studies, such as a single unit on the theme of horses. In such a study, children might study breeds of horses, the history of their development, how horses have been used through history, horse anatomy and physiology, and famous horse stories. This sort of study might cover science along with some history and language arts.

Other unit studies are more comprehensive. Most of these larger unit studies are at least year-long programs that cover history and science completely, while offering varying degrees of coverage of language arts and math. Most have arts and crafts mixed in, and many have strong religion components.

Many parents, but especially Perfect Paulas, like the idea of unit studies but find it overwhelming once they get into it. In many unit studies, parents must choose which books to use, find those books at the library or figure out substitutes, choose among a number of activities, organize all of this, and then keep records of everything. The insecurity and worry about making "wrong" choices paralyzes them, and they quickly return to safe and predictable textbooks. Fortunately, some unit studies have taken this into account and provide much more direction and fewer choices—features that make it possible for worriers to still take advantage of unit studies.

Addressing Learning Style Needs

Unit studies can be a marvelous way of meeting all the different learning style needs of children while providing an education vastly more interesting than what comes out of standard textbooks.

While unit studies vary in the types of activities they include, there are almost always some hands-on and multisensory activities to engage Wiggly Willys. Sociable Sues usually thrive on the interaction that is so much a part of most unit studies. Although Perfect Paulas might be uncomfortable with unit studies that change the lesson structure all the time, they generally do well with ones that follow a somewhat predictable format and spend plenty of time developing academic knowledge and skills (as opposed to continual craft and cooking projects). Competent Carls usually love the independent reading and research required by many unit studies.

By selecting unit studies with the elements that best fit your children, then selecting the appropriate activities for each child, you can bring everyone together studying the same topics.

Unit studies also work to overcome learning style weaknesses. After children have already been introduced to a topic or skill via a method that is best for them, choose other activities from the unit study that have them apply that knowledge or skill in ways that are not as comfortable. For example, Sociable Sue learns about a history topic as you gather everyone together to read and discuss a biography related to the historical event. Sociable Sue learns the background and some interesting details of what happened in a way she enjoys. After that, you can assign her to do further independent reading on the same topic, requiring her to come to you to do a narration about what she has read. She would have a difficult time if she were to begin with the independent reading, but sandwiching it between two interactive activities makes it more palatable.

These Are Not Your Only Choices!

I have selected some of the best unit studies on the market as examples of different types available. There are many more excellent ones I would have included if this book were about the top 200 or 300 products! Names and short annotations for more unit studies follow the reviews.

Five in a Row
by Jane Claire Lambert
Five in a Row Publishing
P.O. Box 707
Grandview, MO 64030-0707
(816) 246-9252
e-mail: lamberts@fiveinarow.com
www.fiveinarow.com
$19.95–$24.95 each

Five in a Row volumes have been written for preschool through eighth grade levels, although they are best known for use in the early grades since that was the target of the original volumes. Consequently, this is a less intense approach to unit study than *KONOS*, *Weaver*, *Tapestry of Grace*, and others that were designed to cover all grade levels.

Let's first look at the basic *Five in a Row* volumes written for children ages four through eight. All four volumes available in this series follow the same format. For each volume, author Jane Claire Lambert has selected a number of outstanding books for children, then built a "mini" unit study around each one. Volume 1 has nineteen units, volume 2 has twenty-one units, and volumes 3 and 4 each have fifteen.

Each study should take one week, with more or less time spent each day depending upon which lesson elements you choose to use. While there are no biblical references in the primary volumes, *Five in a Row* repeatedly teaches positive character qualities such as forgiveness, compassion, and honesty that tie easily to Scripture. Likewise, the selected stories are not overtly Christian, but reflect godly principles. For those who want more explicit Christian "connections," a separate *Five in a Row Bible Supplement* ($17.95) contains more than two hundred Bible lessons relating to the fifty-five studies in volumes 1 through 3.

Examples of selected books are *The Story about Ping*, *Who Owns the Sun?*, *Mike Mulligan and His Steam Shovel*, *Clown of God*, *Katy and the Big Snow*, *Wee Gillis*, *Make Way for Ducklings*, *All Those Secrets of the World*, *Harold and the Purple Crayon*, and *Gramma's Walk*. You will need to purchase or borrow the required storybooks for each volume. However, Five in A Row Publishing also sells packages of these books if you prefer to buy them all at once.

Each story is to be read aloud every day for one week (five days). You select activities for social studies (the term loosely used to cover character qualities and relationships in addition to geography, history, and cultures), language arts, math, science, and art to build lessons from the story. There are numerous hands-on activities and projects, although much of each detailed lesson plan is presented as "talk about this" type activities. An example of the activities is "story disks" in each volume, one per unit. These are to be cut out and laminated (by mom), then used by students to locate where stories take place on a world map. These disks are also available as a ready-to-use set, printed in color and laminated for $15 for the set of fifty-five.

You can choose to select only one subject area per day or select a variety of activities from among the subject areas. Activities range from those appropriate for nonwriters and nonreaders to those for children who have mastered these skills. Thus, you can use the lessons to meet the academic needs of younger and older learners up through about third grade level.

This is not intended to be a complete curriculum for math and language arts. It does not teach phonics, writing, or math in any sequential progression. In fact, you are encouraged to use stories in whatever order you please. (A calendar linking stories to calendar events suggests a possible progression you might follow.)

For younger children, the material might be more than adequate to meet their learning needs. For six- and seven-year-olds, the social studies, science, and art are likely to be much better than they might get from textbooks, so you might want to add only basic phonics and math, and possibly other language skill development for the oldest children.

An index lists what is covered under each subject area, sometimes broken down further under subheadings. This helps you if you have specific goals of your own. A reproducible planning sheet helps you with weekly lesson plans. Instructions for activities are quite detailed. Lambert includes valuable tips on questions to ask your children to guide discussions. *Five in a Row* is very user-friendly, especially for the inexperienced homeschooler.

Other *Five in a Row* volumes are available for older and younger children. Those with preschoolers might want to use *Before Five in a Row*. This volume was developed for children ages two to four. Plenty of activities center around twenty-three books written for young children. The format is somewhat similar to that of the volumes described above.

Those with older children (approximately grades 3 through 8) should check out *Beyond Five in a Row*, volumes 1–3. These three volumes were authored by Becky Jane Lambert, daughter of the original series author, Jane Lambert.

These are excellent one-semester courses. Four books for each volume are the foundation for each unit study. For example, volume 1 includes *The Boxcar Children, Thomas A. Edison—Young Inventor*,

Homer Price, and *Betsy Ross—Designer of Our Flag*. Subject areas covered include literature, some language arts, history, composition, science, and fine arts.

Lessons are set up so that you read a chapter from the book, then work through your choice of the suggested activities. These vary greatly from day to day.

Quite a bit of historical and scientific information is included within the book, but you need to use outside resources for additional research. Many such resources are suggested in the lessons. Lessons often include "Internet Connection" activities for students to do research at a particular site or sites on a topic related to the study.

About half of the lessons include an essay question; you will need to tailor requirements on these to suit the age of each student. Occasional "Career Paths" sections help students consider career possibilities and offer suggestions for further research and/or experience in the field. Timelines are recommended as a means of helping students understand chronological relationships between people and events. Numerous hands-on activities are included: art projects, cooking, science experiments, learning sign language, etc.

A list of all topics covered (a form of scope and sequence) is located at the back of each book; this will help you for both planning and tracking your accomplishments.

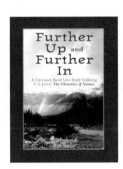

Further Up and Further In

by Diane Pendergraft

Cadron Creek Christian Curriculum

4329 Pinos Altos Road

Silver City, NM 88061

(505) 534-1496

e-mail: marigold@cadroncreek.com

www.CadronCreek.com

$50.00

Subtitled *A Literature Based Unit Study Utilizing C. S. Lewis's The Chronicles of Narnia*, this recent entry into the unit studies field provides detailed lesson plans for teaching children in grades 4 through 8, although it might be adapted to suit younger and older students.

While the publisher considers it adequate coverage for all subjects except math, grammar, and spelling, I think coverage of history is a little light. It is very strong in Bible and in character education even though the latter is not a specified subject area.

You will need the seven-volume *Chronicles of Narnia* (1995 printing of the Scholastic edition is referenced in this study), access to the Internet or an encyclopedia, a dictionary, a Bible, a Bible concordance, and a thesaurus. Additional recommended resources that are used so frequently that you ought to own them are *Genesis: Finding Our Roots* by Ruth Beechick, *Surprised by Joy* by C. S. Lewis, *Poems* by

C. S. Lewis, and *Tales from Shakespeare* by Charles and Mary Lamb. Other books and videos are recommended for each of the units along with a grammar and composition handbook such as one of the *Write Source* books for all units.

Some shorter readings, such as poems and portions of *Hamlet,* are actually reprinted in the back of the book along with some recipes and games. Another useful help is found on pages 261–64; this is a "Subjects Covered" list that organizes topics covered under subject area headings for quick reference.

Art activities, cooking projects, game ideas, and field trips are included in this unit study, but, overall, it is more book-based than activity-based like *KONOS* and some of the other unit studies. For example, most science assignments are reading rather than experiments. When the topic of light is introduced, students are told to use an encyclopedia or book to study light. They are given a few questions to explore and some vocabulary words to define.

The study is arranged with one unit per book in the *Chronicles* series. Each unit should take about one month, so that leaves time for extending units if you wish.

A planning guide at the beginning of each unit lists materials and resources you will need, topics for which you will need research information (from encyclopedias, books, or the Internet), suggestions for field trips, and Bible memorization. Then the study of each book is broken down into four sections so that you are reading four chapters per week. Lessons are given for each chapter. Subjects, other than vocabulary words for every lesson, do not seem to be covered in any consistent pattern but depend upon content of each chapter. Thus, in one week there are assignments for history, English, and art one day; Bible, English, science, cooking, and critical thinking the second day; art, English, critical thinking, and history the third day; and critical thinking and cooking the fourth.

Some activities need to be done together, but many can be done by students working independently.

Students use a three-ring binder and divide it into sections to create notebooks for vocabulary, plant studies, and animal studies, plus notebooks for each of the *Chronicles* books. This could be done with ten separate spiral notebooks, but the binder keeps it all in one place.

Further Up and Further In is likely to appeal to families who love to read together, enjoy variety, and who have children who like to do independent reading and research.

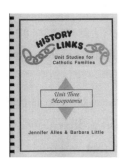

History Links

by Jennifer Alles, Barbara Little, and Kim Staggenborg

Wooly Lamb Publishing

P.O. Box 411

Dickinson, ND 58602

(701) 260-2777

e-mail: woolylamb@worldaccessnet.com

$15.00–$20.00 per volume

History Links is a Catholic approach to unit studies that can be used to teach preschoolers through high school level. Thus far there are nine volumes available, with others in development. Completed volumes are in chronological sequence, although you need not use them in that order. Most volumes should take from two to four months to complete, so you would complete approximately three volumes per school year. The first unit, *General Studies*, should take only one to two months. Apparently some families using *The Well-Trained Mind* approach are completing four or five units per year, albeit with more superficial coverage of each time period.

History Links is designed such that you can go back through the entire series at least once more, using the more challenging activities suggested for upper grade levels. The units available thus far are *General Studies, Creation, Mesopotamia, Ancient Egypt, Ancient Israel, Ancient Greece, Ancient Rome: The Republic, Ancient Rome: Pax Romana,* and *Ancient Rome: The Roman Empire. Early Medieval* (at least two units long) is in the works.

This is truly a family-designed curriculum. Activities are presented for four levels: "P" for preschoolers, "1" for kindergarten and early elementary grades, "2" for intermediate through middle school levels, and "3" for advanced junior high through high school. In addition, ideas for keeping toddlers occupied are included at the bottom of many pages. For those enjoying new babies, there are suggestions for following the "baby track" that pares down the more time-consuming or messy activities. While *History Links* works well as a family curriculum, it might also be used in co-op settings for once or twice a month gatherings.

You will need reference resources: an encyclopedia, a Bible, a dictionary, a globe or world map, and the *Catechism of the Catholic Church*. Much of the resource information might also be found on the Web. Some other books (e.g., *Usborne Book of World History, Usborne Book of the Ancient World, English from the Roots Up, National Geographic* magazines, *The Antiquities of the Jews* by Josephus) are recommended but are not essential. The authors purposely tried to keep costs low by having just a few essential resources, then recommending materials that you can usually get from the library or online.

The units also incorporate ideas from *Teaching Writing: Structure and Style* (Institute for Excellence in Writing)—another of my top picks, but the authors encourage you to purchase the seminar itself.

History Links provides complete coverage of history, religion, critical thinking, research, music, art, and crafts. While it also includes science, language arts, and some math, activities in these areas should be considered supplemental. The authors suggest using other science unit studies between some of the *History Links* units to maintain the unit study approach while ensuring adequate science coverage. (Consider science units from Media Angels for this purpose.) I expect that *History Links* should take about one to two hours per day, depending upon which activities you choose.

Everyone needs to start with *Unit One: General Studies*. The first half of this book explains the methodology used through all the units. The second half presents brief introductory studies on the four key areas covered within all the units: history, geography, archaeology, and theology.

The same format is used in these introductory studies and throughout all the other units. Each unit begins with prayers and hymns to learn, vocabulary lists, punctuation and capitalization items to be learned, a "Library List" of recommended resources (books, videos, recordings, periodicals, Web sites, encyclicals, church documents, etc.). The bulk of each unit or book is presented under subtopics with brief introductory, background, or explanatory information followed by activities coded by subject area and level of difficulty. Extensive appendices in most volumes include many of the source documents you might need. The more recently published units also include resource guides that help you select age-appropriate materials for your children.

Activities address all types of learning styles, but those for the upper two levels direct students toward independent research, reading, and writing much more than traditional curriculum and even more so than some other unit studies. For example, here are two activities from *Ancient Rome: The Roman Empire*:

- "Research Arianism. What belief did Arians promote? What role did Constantine play in this conflict? Who was the staunchest opponent of Arianism? What Church council was held to settle this dispute?" (p. 37).

- "Do you think it is true to say the ancient philosophers lacked 'faith, humility, and chastity? (Although we have already studied the works of Cicero, advanced students might want to do a research project and locate Cicero's and Ambrose's De Officiis to compare them.)" (p. 42).

While these type activities might seem very challenging, I believe they provide the best type education. In addition to developing academic skills, they help students think through and develop a thoroughly Catholic worldview. They draw on classical education ideas in the use of primary sources, comparison of ideas, and focus on important questions in addition to coverage of information.

Lest you think all the activities a bit overwhelming, here are two examples of activities for younger students:

- "Divide an orange, cantaloupe, or other fruit. Draw a line around it, and then cut it on the line. Then discuss the concepts of hemisphere and symmetry. Did Diocletian actually divide his empire in 'half'? Did he divide the Empire along a line of symmetry?" (p. 31).

- "Constantinople is now called Istanbul. Why? (The Ottoman Turks renamed it.) Locate Istanbul, Turkey, on a map. Why was this such a desirable location for a city?" (p. 36).

Note: Children will have already learned something about Constantinople before tackling this activity.

Like other unit studies, *History Links* requires parental preparation and presentation time. You will probably need to work quite closely with young children, while older students will need occasional assistance. Once students have developed their own research skills, they can work more independently than they might at first. However, you will not have simple answer keys to consult to "check" their work.

Of course hands-on activities like art projects and cooking will demand more of your time, but you can choose how many such activities to undertake. With younger students, you can research and read material together, then choose whether to have students do written work or discussion. Such choices should depend upon their abilities and your time.

One of the unique benefits of *History Links* is that because it is presented in small units, it's a great way to try out unit study without making an expensive commitment.

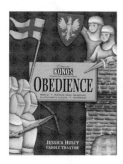
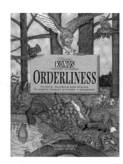

KONOS Character Curriculum
P.O. Box 250
Anna, TX 75409
(972) 924-2712
e-mail: info@konos.com
www.konos.com
Volumes 1, 2, and 3—$95.00 per volume, timelines—$59.95 per volume, curriculum/timeline combo—$144.95, index—$20.00, *KONOS In-A-Box*—$175.00 each, *KONOS In-A-Bag*—$90.00 each, *History of the World: Year One* or *Year Two*—$150.00 each

KONOS features character traits as unit themes in their unit studies for children in grades K through 8. There are also two high-school-level volumes that I will discuss later in this review.

Subjects included in *KONOS* are history (primarily American history), Bible, social studies, science, art, music, drama, practical living, health, critical thinking skills, and character training, as well as some language and math. The authors suggest we use other math and language programs as needed. If you use all three volumes of *KONOS*, you will cover material typically covered in history and science programs in elementary grades with the exception of world history, which *KONOS* reserves for higher levels.

Because the authors believe children learn best by "doing," this program is strong on activity—an ideal program for Wiggly Willys. The real strength of *KONOS* is in the number of activities from which you can choose. There are *many* more ideas than you can possibly use. Some people are overwhelmed at the choices, but the many alternatives allow you to choose how much time you spend, the amount of hands-on activity, field trips, books, etc. that fit your situation.

Lesson plans list materials and preparation needed, then recommend activities for younger, middle, and older children. The lesson plans are a tremendous help to those who are overwhelmed by too many choices and also to those who want just a little help in quickly sorting through all the ideas. *KONOS* lesson plans provide structure, yet they leave much room for individualizing. Moms who prefer a set structure and routine might have trouble using *KONOS*, while those who prefer variety will likely enjoy it.

While Volume 1 should probably be the first volume used with children in grades K to 3, any volume, including the third, could be used at any level. Each volume of *KONOS* can be used for two years. *KONOS* provides detailed background information for some activities, but not all. Library books and other sources will be needed to round out the lessons. Detailed lists of resources and activities are under each heading. It is necessary to plan ahead to get books and other resources that you will need. For those who have difficulty getting books from a library, *KONOS* has arranged with Lifetime Books, Alabaster Books, and other companies to carry books that specifically correlate to *KONOS* units. With so many titles to choose from, you can be guaranteed the availability of appropriate resources.

Because *KONOS* covers history in a nonsequential fashion, you should use timelines to tie historical events together coherently. You can make your own, but *KONOS* sells beautifully laminated timelines that coordinate with each volume of the curriculum, plus a *Bible Timeline.*

The *KONOS Index* ($20.00) is a separate book that shows which topics are covered where in each volume of *KONOS*. This is most valuable to those who have accumulated two or more *KONOS* volumes or who want to use *KONOS* activities to jazz up their traditional curriculum. If you want to locate information on a particular topic, the *Index* will help you find it quickly.

Those who like the methodology of *KONOS* but feel overwhelmed with what it requires from the parent/teacher should love *KONOS In-A-Box.* There are two of these nine- to eighteen-week unit studies derived from the original *KONOS* volumes. The titles of the two volumes are *Obedience* and *Orderliness.* The *Obedience* unit contains the teacher's manual/curriculum (also sold separately), craft materials (e.g., copper foil, wire, brads, whistle, tapestry set, fake jewels), eight resource books, and timeline characters—all packaged in a sturdy cardboard case with carrying handle.

They are laid out with detailed, daily lessons, and they come with just about everything you need. No more frantic trips to the library and the craft supply store. *KONOS In-A-Box* covers the same subjects as the original *KONOS* but is more comprehensive than the original, particularly in the area of language arts and literature where students are taught how to write and to analyze literature. Again, math and phonics are not covered.

There are still some choices to be made. The studies can meet the needs of students in grades K through 8, but you must choose which activities to require of older and younger students. For example, when it says "Write five simple sentences on index cards about what you learned yesterday about light," you might ask your third grader to write only three sentences, then spend time with your kindergartner on basic reading skills while older students write their sentences.

While some preparation time will still be necessary, it will be a fraction of that required for the original *KONOS.* If you've always wanted to try unit studies, but felt that it might be too overwhelming, this is a terrific way to try it out. Many families find that after using *KONOS In-A-Box,* they can easily handle the regular *KONOS* volumes.

Similar in concept to *KONOS In-A-Box* is *KONOS In-A-Bag.* There are two units available in this newest format that *KONOS* calls its "New Culture Curriculum Series." The two "bags," *Russia: The Land of Endurance* and *Africa: The Land of Stewardship,* couple country or continent themes with a character trait identified with each one. A detailed two-hundred-page curriculum manual can be purchased on its own, although it is included in the bag that also has all the items needed for the study. For example, the

Africa tote bag includes the manual, a beautifully illustrated Dorling Kindersley book, a map, and five craft kits with supplies for three children.

The culture series differs from the box series in that the curriculum does not include the in-depth writing lessons or literary analysis.

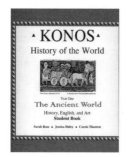

KONOS *History of the World*

Those with older students who would like to continue this style of teaching through high school should check out *KONOS History of the World*, written for high school students. *KONOS* for high school is quite different from the younger-level volumes in that it is written directly to the student rather than the parent. It includes a student book, a teacher's guide, and a timeline/map kit. Each volume covers Bible, history, English, and art for a full school year, but students can easily gain credits in drama, and geography as well.

As with other *KONOS* volumes, students are not expected to do all activities but should work with parents to select those necessary to provide sufficient work in each subject area and to cover the main topics adequately.

The beginning section of *Year One* teaches students how to study and how to use this curriculum. (*Year Two* repeats the same information in case students are starting there.) Each lesson follows the same basic format. It begins with the "Lesson Focus," listing the main ideas to be learned. Bible study is next, with passages to read, study, and memorize. The map/timeline packet includes full-color, self-sticking figures that students cut out and place on the timeline as they study each civilization—interpreting the details of the figures themselves serves as a review or study prompt. For example, you might want to ask your children why Diogenes is pictured inside a barrel?

Students construct a large map with the pages included in the packet. Vocabulary words for each lesson are to be written on three-by-five-inch cards, then studied and reviewed.

A number of other resources are used for study, a few of which are used so frequently that students should own them. In addition to some basic study tools and reference works, students should own either *Streams of Civilization* (Christian Liberty Press) or *A Picturesque Tale of Progress*, which is out of print but worth trying to obtain through a book search service. The other recommended books are worth owning but not essential. Some videos are also recommended.

Activities for each weekly lesson are listed. Some are marked with symbols indicating that they are writing, art, or map activities. A mortarboard indicates advanced activities college-bound students should tackle. Record-keeping boxes next to each activity allow students to record which assignments were done and the time actually spent doing them. This allows students to keep track of hours for credits.

Students also maintain a notebook in a three-ring binder that includes a journal, book lists, weekly schedules, essay questions, English reports, and tests. Evaluation questions at the end of each section help both student and parents assess progress. There are very few questions that require exact or predictable answers, but those answers are found in the teacher's guide. Students are also told how to create a portfolio of their work that can be used to validate their high school studies for high school graduation or college entry.

The entire curriculum is oriented toward developing a biblical (Protestant) worldview with a deep understanding of the impact of philosophy and religion throughout history. Worldview ideas reflect a conservative political viewpoint. Students do a great deal of reading, and there are numerous opportunities to write stories, essays, and papers. Rigorous academics are balanced by *KONOS*'s characteristic hands-on activities, such as setting up Passover for your family, creating a pharaoh costume for Egyptian night, or sculpting a Greek amphora out of clay.

In *Year One,* ancient history coverage is comprehensive from the time of Abraham's departure from Ur up to pre-Rome (the Celts and Etruscans), and history is the organizing theme throughout the year. English activities stress literature, vocabulary, and writing, with detailed lessons on various forms of writing incorporated into the different sections. Art is an ideal combination of art history, appreciation, and expression. Bible coverage is extensive, particularly in the historical study of the Hebrews. Study for these subjects will be time consuming, so the authors recommend that students tackle only a few additional subjects, such as math and science. *Year Two* adds an introductory Latin course equivalent to about a half unit of credit. Although the format of the curriculum is not traditional, the level of learning is quite challenging. This is definitely a high school curriculum, and it might even be too challenging for some ninth graders. Parents should assist students as they make decisions about resources and assignments. Each student must have his or her own book since students do record keeping on lesson pages.

While students can do much of the study on their own, discussion is a vital part of the program. Parents should read the primary books that students are reading, then plan two to four hours per week for some great discussions.

Eventually, there will be volumes covering all of world history, but thus far we have the first two. *Year One: The Ancient World* covers Mesopotamia, the Egyptians, the Indus Valley, the Hebrews and their neighbors, the Greeks, and the foundations of Rome. *Year Two: The Medieval World* covers Rome, the Byzantines, Moslems, Vikings, Charlemagne, the early Church, Medieval times, and China to the present day.

It, too, is quite challenging, especially as it requires students to analyze philosophies and ideas in light of both history and current events. For example, students are asked to complete activities such as comparing the merits of multinational armies such as the one that existed in Rome prior to its fall to the present-day United Nations armies. Early church history, church fathers, and development of doctrine also receive far more attention in this volume than in other programs. The reading list for *Year Two* includes Shakespeare's *Julius Caesar,* Augustine's *City of God,* Dante's *Inferno,* Chaucer's *Canterbury Tales, Black Arrow, Beowulf, Quo Vadis?,* and *The Good Earth.*

Parent Helps

Tapes and workshops on implementing unit study methods are available from KONOS. Their tapes (both audio and video) are loaded with practical information and examples based on the experiences of the homeschooling authors.

I recommend the book *KONOS Compass: An Orientation to Using KONOS* ($25.00) to anyone using *KONOS*. It gives an overview of all three volumes along with a comparison to typical state requirements so you can see if you are covering the necessary material. *KONOS Compass* also provides teaching information and sample lesson plans.

Another alternative is *KONOS: Creating the Balance* ($150.00), a seven-hour video set covering critical topics, such as the father's role, multilevel teaching, planning and scheduling, dealing with toddlers, discipline, and how to choose library books. In addition, it features two hours of Jessica Hulcy teaching her children hands-on.

Tapestry of Grace
by Marcia Somerville
Lampstand Press
P.O. Box 5798
Rockville, MD 20855
(800) 705-7487
www.TapestryOfGrace.com
$130.00 per year-plan, also available as five individual units/packages per year-plan for $30.00 per unit

Tapestry of Grace (TOG) is a unit study curriculum that covers most of the major subject areas for students in grades K through 12. Some features that make it especially appealing are Christian worldview studies incorporated throughout the curriculum, a chronological approach to history as the basic organizing theme, and a classical education approach based on the grammar, dialectic, and rhetoric stages of learning.

Subject areas covered include history; English (writing and literature); fine arts; some science; geography; church history, including missions (more extensively covered than I recall seeing in most other curricula); Bible; and history of fine arts and sciences (reflecting a classical approach). You will need to use other resources for phonics, English grammar, math, foreign languages, and high school lab sciences.

While the *TOG* volumes include actual *World Book Encyclopedia* information on many topics as background information for you as the teacher, for the most part students will read information from recommended books that you purchase or borrow for them. Some books you will use frequently and should purchase (e.g., a basic history textbook and a *Write Source* grammar handbook from Great Source). Some will be used over a long enough period of time that they also should be purchased (e.g., *Tales from Shakespeare* by the Lambs). Others will be used for only a week or two and might be borrowed. While some titles are strongly recommended, in most cases there are a number of choices listed, which helps families who need flexibility due to limited resources. If you don't have a big budget, living close to a library will be a real asset if you use *TOG*.

The lengthy resource lists in each level (referred to as "Year-Plans") of *TOG* list all recommended books by category, with informative annotations for most that will help you decide which will be most useful for your children.

Like many other unit studies, while *TOG* uses many books, it also includes multisensory learning options to address different learning styles and interests. These range from reading, writing, and simple art projects through costumed reenactments.

TOG covers the same general topics for all students simultaneously, but instruction and activities are divided into four levels of learning reflecting the classical Trivium (with the Grammar stage divided into two sections). The divisions are: Lower Grammar (K–3), Upper Grammar (3–5 with a purposeful overlap here to address the reality that young students the same ages are rarely progressing at the same rate), Dialectic (6–9), and Rhetoric (10+). If you are unfamiliar with these terms, you should read up on classical education in books such as *Designing Your Own Classical Curriculum* or *The Well-Trained Mind* or search for one of the many Internet sites on the subject.

The author describes numerous options for starting at different times and for families with children of different ages. Permission is given for reproduction of pages for your immediate family. Co-ops can reproduce pages if every family has purchased that Year-Plan of *TOG*. Classroom licenses are available for larger organizations.

There are four Year-Plans to *TOG*, and the idea is that you will progress through each Year-Plan at one level of difficulty (lower grammar, upper grammar, etc.), then go through each again four years later, shifting children up to the next level. You can see that the youngest children might go through each Year-Plan three times. A possible alternative is to take two years to cover a Year-Plan of *TOG* if you are starting with younger children. (The flexibility of this program is one of its major assets!)

Year One: The History of Redemption covers creation through the fall of Rome. *Year Two* includes Medieval World through the signing of the U.S. Constitution. *Year Three: The 1800s* addresses both American and European history. *Year Four: The Twentieth Century* covers world history, although U.S. history is a major component.

Each Year-Plan of *TOG* actually consists of four units plus a base component of materials that span the entire Year-Plan—materials such as introductory notes, the writing component, and resource list. This structure allows you to start in *TOG* at lower cost by purchasing a base plus one unit to begin for only $60.00. It also allows you to select areas of history to cover. For example, if you have already studied ancient civilizations up to but not including Ancient Rome using another curriculum, you can begin with only the units you need rather than the entire Year-Plan.

While the first impression is a bit overwhelming, once you've gotten familiar with the layout, it should be fairly easy to use. It's logically organized for each week. Using tabbed separator pages for each week—available for $12.50/set from Lampstand Press—will make it easier to locate things. The parent/teacher should familiarize himself or herself with the background material and discussion threads for each week. Overview charts actually work as general lesson plans. I think I would be likely to copy a set of these for each child to have in his or her assignment binder. The overview charts are followed by student pages for each level that should be photocopied for each student. These pages include questions, activity instructions, charts to be completed, etc. Watch for a CD-ROM that will soon be available with overview charts in PDF format. This will allow you to print as many copies as you need from your computer.

In the base component are about 150 pages divided into Writing Scope & Sequence and Writing Assignment pages. Parents/teachers draw from the first part to determine what writing instruction and activities are appropriate for each student. Much instructional material is actually included here, although you will need additional resources such as *Easy Grammar* or *Write Source* books. The second section pages include writing assignment charts for each of twelve levels (think grades 1–12) for each of the four "years" of *TOG* plus worksheets and evaluation forms. All of this makes the task much easier for the parent/teacher who is unsure about how to teach writing skills.

Like most extensive unit study programs, *TOG* requires a significant amount of parent/teacher preparation and presentation. Parents/teachers should dedicate a large block of time over the summer to plan and prepare for each school year. Keep in mind that most parents and teachers will be getting a great deal of education of their own as they work through *TOG!*

Overall, I think *TOG*'s use of classical education methods combined with the chronological approach helps overcome one of the weaknesses of some unit studies—that children read good books and participate in fun activities but sometimes fail to make connections between topics studied and their chronological relationships. In addition, the worldview threads provide themes for discussions (ideally, directed by parents using Socratic methods) and activities that help children make important connections and understand the significance of what they are learning. *TOG* comes from a Reformed Protestant viewpoint, but it respectfully tries to include Orthodox and Catholic views as it explores church history. Consequently, *TOG* should be easier for those of the latter religious persuasions to adapt than many other unit studies might be.

Each Year-Plan purchased (or separate units thereof) includes three-whole-punched pages plus cover and spine for a binder, but the binder and tabs are not included.

The thirty-six Weekly Topics covered by each Year-Plan and the resources used are listed (and sometimes shown) on the *TOG* Web site along with other information about the curriculum. The site also hosts a bulletin board (called the Forum) where *TOG* users can get support from experienced users as well as from the author herself. In addition, the site links to complementary Web sites for various topics covered in *TOG*.

A World of Adventure: A Unit Study Based on World History

by Dorian Holt

Learning Adventures

1146 Kensington Court

Seymour, IN 47274

(812) 523-0999

e-mail: Dorian@Learning-Adventures.org

www.Learning-Adventures.org

AWOA—$75.00, AWOA game—$34.00, AWOA student pages—$20.00; ANWOA—$90.00, ANWOA student pages—$26.00

Two volumes are available thus far in a planned five-volume unit study program. Each volume is a full-year program (180 school days) covering Bible, history/social studies, science, language arts, and fine arts for students in grades 4 through 8. Math, P.E., cursive writing, and/or keyboarding will need to be covered separately. Science, social studies, and language arts occupy the bulk of study time.

The unique feature of this series is that read-aloud and background material is built into each volume so parents need to spend less time finding information books and selecting which information to present to their children. While you still need to use some additional books, studies do not depend upon those books to the extent all the others do.

Each volume comes as packets of prepunched pages. Binders are not included. You will want to purchase at least two to three large binders to hold each volume.

Daily lesson plans provide for a mixture of read-aloud/together time and independent work, including discussion and a significant amount of writing. Lesson plans provide complete literature, grammar, vocabulary, and spelling lessons, although parents will need to copy some of the material (e.g., sentences to be marked for grammar, spelling lists) onto a whiteboard or some other media to present it to students if you do not purchase the student page packets. Please note that the spelling and vocabulary lists might be a bit challenging for some fourth graders, so use your judgment as to what to require from your own children.

Science lessons explain various topics in language that can be read directly from this book. Then you direct students to do independent reading on topics. Once in a while in the first volume there are science activities or experiments, but there are lots more in volume two.

Fine art lessons, likewise, provide material to be read aloud, sometimes followed by activities or reading. The second volume recommends resource books that you should use for visual examples of art, sculpture, and architecture. In the first volume, coverage of fine arts relates more to history than actual art activity, although the author recommends Barry Stebbings's art courses (see review of *Feed My Sheep* in chapter 14) to round out art experience. The second volume suggests many more art activities. In music, hymns are the primary focus in the first volume, while the second volume branches out further into classical, patriotic, and colonial music.

Aside from the extra books, there are many other required items—everything needed for each day's lesson is listed at the beginning of each subsection. These items are not that difficult or expensive to obtain (e.g., eggshells, CD or tape of Handel's *Messiah*, cooking ingredients). However, planning ahead is essential. You can plan unit by unit, but I think accumulating many items as you prepare during the summer, then leaving only library books and perishable items to worry about as you approach each section will save you grief.

Most unit studies are weak on accountability—how do you know students are really learning anything? To solve this problem, *A World of Adventure* has included questions for students similar to those you typically find in textbooks. These are found within each volume along with answers, but the questions are also available in separate student page packets in an easy-to-use worksheet format. As with the main volumes, pages are pre-punched for insertion in binders. There are 176 pages for the first volume and 395 for the second. These student pages seem essential to me, since questions in the main volume are really set up more as an answer key.

Learning Adventures has come up with a great review and reinforcement tool. Each volume will have a companion game. The game set for the first volume is called *Worlds of Adventure*. The game set has six laminated game boards, each covering a major area (e.g., Ancient Egypt) studied in that volume. There are six corresponding comb-bound question booklets with a total of 3,300 multiple-choice questions. Questions are in order according to the units, so you can use any game board selecting only questions from units covered thus far. You can even combine game boards and questions from all the different units to have a marathon game. This type of review can be more effective and certainly more fun than quizzes or tests.

The perspective throughout the study, particularly evident in history and science lessons, is Christian (Protestant) and also supports a young-earth viewpoint.

The first volume, titled *A World of Adventure (AWOA)*, is a 790-page book covering ancient Egypt through the Age of Exploration, dividing content into six subsections that also include study of ancient Greece, ancient Rome, the Middle Ages, and the Renaissance and Reformation.

Required resources are a Bible, a hymnal, a dictionary, *The Golden Goblet*, *Aesop's Fables*, *Classic Myths to Read Aloud*, *The Bronze Bow*, *Adam of the Road*, *The Door in the Wall*, *The Swiss Family Robinson*, and two biographies from a suggested list. Many additional books are recommended within each section, but extensive lists offer many choices. You can borrow these from the library or purchase them. Those available through homeschool catalog companies are listed separately. In addition, you will need student notebooks and/or folders for each subject, note cards and file boxes for the cards, a world map or atlas, a globe, and potting soil and herb seeds to grow chives, dill, parsley, mint, basil, oregano, and thyme.

The herbs highlight an unusual feature of this unit study. Students grow the herbs, which then come under study in the Middle Ages section. They also use them in a variety of recipes reflective of different geographical and chronological eras.

The second volume, *A New World of Adventure* (ANWOA), covers the years 1600–1800. At 1,613 pages, it is about twice as big as the first volume! It contains even more background and commentary as well more guidance for teaching writing and for covering science and fine arts. Other expanded areas are review and the practice exercises and activities—there are even more choices for children of different ages and abilities.

I would judge *A World of Adventure* a valuable entry into the unit study market, especially for parents who appreciate having much of the work done for them, but there is one major omission—an index. An index would allow parents to easily locate topics for review or reference or perhaps even to present them out of order.

The other three books in the *Learning Adventures* series will cover the following periods: Book 3, *Westward and Onward*—1800–1860; Book 4, *A Nation Torn and Mended*—1860–1900; and Book 5, *Adventures in a Modern World*—the twentieth century. American history will be the primary focus, although "other countries, personalities, and events will also be covered as they apply to events in America." This unique approach actually covers world history, but in connection to U.S. history. For example, study of the Gold Rush includes study of the Chinese people who came to America, which then leads to a side study of China itself. This is an unusual way to tackle world history, so it will be interesting to see how it plays out in future volumes.

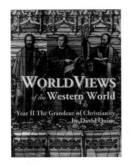

World Views of the Western World
by David Quine
Cornerstone Curriculum Project
2006 Flat Creek
Richardson, TX 75080
(972) 235-5149
www.cornerstonecurriculum.com

Starting Points—$45.00; *Starting Points* package—$125.00; Syllabus for each of years I–III—$125.00 per volume for first student, $75.00 for each additional student in the same family, packages for years I-III range from $520.00–$675.00

This is a four-volume worldview unit-study curriculum that draws heavily upon the works and ideas of Dr. Francis Schaeffer. Each volume is published in an easy-to-handle, lay-flat-binding book. Each of these books serves as a course research-teaching syllabus for students. It is designed so that students can work independently, although this would not preclude group discussion and interaction. In fact, the courses best lend themselves to a combination of independent and group work.

Following through the weekly lesson plans, students read from the research-teaching syllabus and answer questions and write essays directly in it. They are also directed to view videos, listen to audio-cassettes, and read extensively from other sources. For each volume, you will need to purchase or borrow a number of other resources, most of which you will probably consider to be valuable additions to your library rather than resources to be used only for school. The list of resources seems daunting for a student to get through for all but *Starting Points*, but students will only use excerpts from a number of them.

This curriculum particularly suits the dialectic (logic) and rhetoric stages of classical education. Although it uses a mixture of Great Books and good books, it draws out of these books the important life questions. While Socratic dialogue is missing, Quine poses questions to students that direct them through the type of thinking that occurs in a Socratic discussion. In addition, students are challenged to logically defend their positions and conclusions in writing. Parents could also create a Socratic discussion them-selves using the syllabus, although they would have to be familiar with the material to do so. Even though students cover a huge amount of information, focus throughout is upon ideas and critical thinking rather than on memorization of information.

Starting Points: World View Primer can be used by junior high or high school students. This is an intro-ductory course that most students should complete before tackling the other three volumes. However, it was developed after the original volumes, and it is possible for high school students to skip it and begin with volume I.

Starting Points lays a foundation for developing a biblical Christian worldview consistent with Schaeffer's Reformed Protestant perspective. Alongside this central theme is a subordinate theme advanc-ing the concept of limited government.

The first part of the syllabus directs students through chapters of James Sire's *How to Read Slowly*, Paul Little's *Know What You Believe*, and David Quine's *Answers for Difficult Days*. This is a rather directive study that guides students into acceptance and support of the biblical worldview. It requires neither per-sonal research nor a study of primary documents to evaluate all available options. Although it deals with contrary beliefs, it does so in a cursory fashion most of the time. This first section might be the most prob-lematic for those with different interpretations of what constitutes a biblical Christian worldview.

The second section deals with literature and movies as they present worldviews that are either con-sistent with or contrary to a biblical Christian worldview. Students learn what to look for and how to ana-lyze what they read or view as they work through *The Chronicles of Narnia* (three books), *Frankenstein*, *Dr. Jekyll and Mr. Hyde*, *It's a Wonderful Life*, and *The Wizard of Oz*.

The third part of the syllabus guides students through C. S. Lewis's *Mere Christianity* and Christian Overman's *Assumptions* as they move into cultural applications of worldview, both positive and negative.

This section of *Starting Points* as well as the next both bring in philosophical background that helps students understand motivating ideas that shaped our country.

The final section uses Gary Amos's *Never Before in History* as the foundation for a study of the founding of the United States, drawing upon information and ideas raised earlier in the study.

High school students can derive one credit each in Bible, literature, and United States history with this course. They will be required to do a significant amount of writing, including lengthy essays. As with the other volumes, assistance is provided within the syllabus for developing each essay.

The next three volumes follow a chronological timeline. Volume I, *The Emergence of Christianity*, begins with an introduction to the course and covers the basics of defining worldviews. Thus, students could skip *Starting Points* and begin with this volume. From there it moves on to a comparison/contrast of a biblical Christian worldview and Greco-Roman worldviews roughly covering the time period 1200 B.C.–A.D. 1200. (Primary attention is given to Ancient Rome and Greece and the Middle Ages.) In-depth studies of the book of Job, *The Iliad*, and *City of God* are representative of David Quine's strategy of using significant pieces of literature as "springboards" for integrated study in each area. The second half of volume I shifts to the Middle Ages, examining changes in philosophical and theological ideas and their consequences through this era and beyond. Among other resources used with this volume are *The Aeneid* by Virgil, *Affliction* by Edith Schaeffer, *How Should We Then Live?* by Francis Schaeffer, *The Republic* by Plato, *The Universe Next Door* by James Sire, the *How Should We Then Live?* video series, Cornerstone's *Adventures in Art* and *Classical Composers and the Christian World View*, audiotapes by Francis Schaeffer, and audiotapes from the *Knowledge Products* series on figures such as Aristotle and Plato.

The second volume, *The Grandeur of Christianity*, covers 1200 to the 1800s, addressing the Renaissance, the Reformation, the Revolutionary Age, political theory, early American history, and the rise of modern science. A primary focus is comparison and contrasting of the Renaissance view of life with that of the Reformation. Volume II uses such resources as Calvin's *Institutes of the Christian Religion*, *Reformation Overview* videos, Sire's *The Universe Next Door*, Machiavelli's *The Prince*, *Knowledge Products'* audiotape about John Locke and his *Two Treatises*, *The Shorter Catechism*, Luther's *95 Theses*, Bastiat's *The Law*, *The Communist Manifesto*, *Hamlet*, *A Tale of Two Cities*, and *Animal Farm* along with extensive, in-depth study of *The Divine Comedy*. Development of Reformation theology is a major theme.

The third volume, *The Loss of Truth*, continues from the 1800s (the Age of Reason and the Age of Fragmentation) to the present, covering both world and American history with a "Western civilization" emphasis. Volume III compares and contrasts the theistic ideas of the Bible with the naturalistic ideas of the twentieth century. Examples of resources used with volume III are dramatized audiocassettes on famous philosophers such as Hegel, Nietzsche, Marx, and Sartre; Hazlitt's *Economics in One Lesson* (audiotape); Johnson's *Darwin on Trial*; *The Plague* by Camus; *The New Evidence that Demands a Verdict*; *Walden Two* by Skinner; C. S. Lewis's *That Hideous Strength*; three of the *Star Wars* movies as well as the movies *Gettysburg* and *Gone with the Wind*; Schaeffer's *How Should We Then Live?* book and video series; and the

Of Pandas and People science text. Quine's continual use of comparison and contrast effectively helps students to understand both the underlying beliefs and the cultural outworking of different worldviews.

Rather than aiming for comprehensive coverage of history, these volumes instead focus upon key ideas that dominated each period. Following the lead of Francis Schaeffer in *How Should We Then Live?* (both the book and the video series), study centers primarily around the areas of philosophy/religion, literature, music, and the fine arts. It also ventures beyond Schaeffer into economics, law and government, and science. Extensive writing is required throughout all volumes, and basic paragraph and essay writing skills are taught for the lengthier assignments.

A chart at the beginning of volume I shows how many credits might be given for each subject area for the high school transcript; the entire three volumes are equivalent to 16 Carnegie units, so this is a major part of a student's high school course work. It includes enough units for requirements in English, history, government, and fine arts, with the equivalent of 2 units of philosophy/theology, 1 unit of science history, and surplus units in government, political theory, and economics (the latter of which look great on a transcript). You will need to add math, lab science, and foreign language classes—plus health, physical education, driver's ed, and other such extras—to complete high school requirements.

While students can work through these volumes independently, there are no built-in mechanisms for accountability—no tests or quizzes. However, there are numerous essay questions and writing assignments. Parents should be looking over this work and discussing the course content with students. However, most parents are not familiar with the course content, which makes this rather difficult.

Ideally, parents should also participate in the study, at least reading through the material, watching videos, and listening to the tapes. If this is not possible, having a student narrate lesson content to the parent, summarizing what they have learned, might be adequate although less than ideal. Consider having a few students who are working through the study (simultaneously but independently) meet with a knowledgeable adult periodically to discuss course content.

If none of these ideas are practical, all is not lost. We might leave accountability at the student's doorstep: they get out of it what they put into it. When you consider how little students retain of what they "learn" under the most stringent accountability systems, there is something to be said for allowing them to absorb as much as they can without outside coercion. After all, this is most often how adults function when they want to learn something. The key here is student motivation. I have found in teaching worldviews that once most students grasp the idea of worldviews and how important it is, learning follows naturally. They easily understand that this is learning that matters!

Note that each volume is a consumable course and is intended for use by only one student. No photocopying or resale is allowed. Thus, you need to purchase a separate book for each student, although additional books are purchased at discounted prices. Packages include the tapes, videos, and books needed for each level. However, you can also purchase selected items from any of the packages if you already have access to some of them.

Some Other Unit Studies to Consider

The ABC's of Christian Culture by Julia Fogassy (Our Father's House, 206-725-0461, www.ourfathers house.biz)—chronological Catholic unit study. Great content but requires quite a bit from the parent/ teacher.

Ancient History: Adam to Messiah by Robin Sampson (Heart of Wisdom Publishing, 800-266-5564, http://heartofwisdom.com)—biblically-based chronological study.

Amanda Bennett's Unit Studies series by Amanda Bennett (AABennett Books, 423-554-3381, www.unitstudy.com)—innovative, inexpensive, topical unit studies on interactive CD-ROMs. Titles available: *Patriotic Holidays, Pioneers, Gardens, Baseball, Thanksgiving, Sailing Ships, Lighthouses, American Government, Easter, American Hero Stories,* plus *A Unit Study Journal* and *Unit Studies 101* on how to create your own unit studies.

Blessed Is the Man and *Far above Rubies* (All-Around Education, 334-273-7888, www.far andblessed.com)—two different volumes respectively focus on raising young men to be godly fathers and heads-of-the-household and young women to be godly wives and mothers; junior high-high school level.

Christian Cottage Unit Studies (Fountain of Truth Publishing Division, 303-688-6626, www.christiancottage.com)—combines traditional texts and real books for chronological unit studies.

Diana Waring's Unit Studies (Diana Waring-History Alive!, 605-642-7583, www.dianawaring.com) —combines Diana's tapes and supplemental books for units that primarily cover religion (Protestant) and social studies with some work in other subjects.

Learn and Do Unit Studies by Kym Wright (Alwright! Publishing, P.O. Box 81124-W, Conyers, GA 30013, www.alwrightpub.com)—inexpensive unit studies on topics such as color, arachnids, botany, photography, turtles, and the library.

Lessons from History by Gail Schultz (Hillside Academy, 1804 Melody Lane, Dept. W, Burnsville, MN 55337, www.LessonsFromHistory.com)—inexpensive chronological unit studies that serve more as frameworks and outlines than comprehensive programs. See comments in chapter 10.

Life in America series by Ellen Gardner (Life in America, 877-543-3263, www.lifeinamerica.com)— chronological unit studies centered around U.S. history.

My Father's World from A to Z by Marie Hazell (My Father's World, 573-426-4600, www.mfwbooks.com)—comprehensive unit study programs for kindergarten and first grade that even include reading instruction.

Night Owl Creations Unit Studies (Night Owl Creations, Inc., 352-242-9842, www.geocities.com/ nightowlcreationsinc)—topical unit studies that primarily serve as supplements.

Patchwork Primers (Patchwork Primers, 850-951-0399, www.patchworkprimers.com)–chronological unit studies for those who like to do some of their own research.

Polished Cornerstones and *Plants Grown Up* (Doorposts, 888-433-4749, www.doorposts.net)—focuses on practical life training and developing godly character for elementary through high school levels.

Prairie Primer by Margie Gray (Cadron Creek Christian Curriculum, 505-534-1496, www.cadron creek.com)—units are built around the nine books in the *Little House on the Prairie* series.

Interdisciplinary Units (Teacher Created Materials, 800-662-4321, www.teachercreated.com)—these limited, topical unit studies are nonsectarian and should be used as supplements.

TRISMS (Trisms, 918-585-2778, www.trisms.com)—chronological unit studies for junior and senior high.

The Weaver (Alpha Omega, 800-622-3070, www.home-schooling.com)—comprehensive unit study following a scriptural timeline and centered around books of the Bible.

Where the Brook and River Meet (Cadron Creek Christian Curriculum, 505-534-1496, www.cadron creek.com)—literature-based study based on the Victorian era.

Zephyr Unit Studies (Zephyr Press, 800-232-2187, www.zephyrpress.com)—nonsectarian, topical unit studies. These are not as comprehensive as most of the others listed but might make good supplements.

13
Foreign Language

This is an especially tough area to come up with Top Picks since I do not have room to pick a best product for every language, much less differentiate products for younger students and older students in each language. So I've picked two top publishers that produce language resources for many different languages that also address the needs of both older and younger learners.

Then I made an exception and got specific for the Latin language since it is increasingly popular for study among homeschoolers and is not covered by the other two publishers.

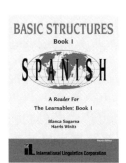

The Learnables—French, German, Spanish, Russian, Chinese, Japanese, Hebrew, Czech, or English

International Linguistics Corporation

12220 Blue Ridge Boulevard, Suite G

Kansas City, MO 64030-1175

(800) 237-1830

www.learnables.com

(for most languages) Level 1 book with tapes or CDs—$49.00–$53.00; Basic Structures 1—$45.00–$65.00; Level 1 and Basic Structures 1 package for Spanish, French or German—$89.00;

Level 2 package for Spanish, French, or German (includes Learnables 2, Basic Structures 2, and Grammar Enhancement 1)—$169.00

Check Web site or brochure for more pricing details

The Learnables approach to foreign language works well for homeschooling families for at least four reasons.

1. Flexibility for different age learners. Using the different components, *Learnables* can be used to instruct children from elementary grades through high school (and even adults!).

2. Does not require the parent to know or teach the language

3. Multisensory format works for many different learning styles

4. Inductive, experiential methodology is a more natural learning method than traditional approaches to foreign language acquisition

The Learnables features an unusual approach that uses picture books (no text with the pictures in the basic book for each level) and cassettes or CDs to build up vocabulary and teach sentence structure from repeated usage. The methodology is to develop understanding and comprehension first, then follow with reading, speaking, and writing skills, in that order. This is similar to the way most of us learned English, although a child learns to speak before reading.

The same picture books are used with each language. All ages should start with Level 1, which includes a book with five audiocassette tapes or four CDs. Tapes or CDs begin with words and short phrases whose meaning is obvious from the pictures. Translation is not given. If the student is in doubt, repetition of a word in another picture will likely clear things up. Sentences become more complex as do the pictures. Pronunciation is very clear. There are similar sets of books with tapes/CDs for four levels in Spanish, French, German, Russian, and Chinese. Fewer levels are available for Hebrew, Czech, and Japanese.

This approach is certainly more enjoyable than typical programs of either the textbook variety or the tapes that have us simply repeat the foreign language phrases after the speaker. The learner must think about what is happening in the pictures to understand the meaning. This methodology also adds visual memory association to the words students hear, enhancing vocabulary retention.

Children in the early elementary grades can work through the picture books and tapes/CDs. However, older students need to learn to read and write the language and to understand its grammatical development, especially if they are seeking credit for high-school-level courses. The *Basic Structures* and *Grammar Enhancement* programs add these elements.

Basic Structures programs are designed as companions for each level. Thus far, the *Basic Structures* program is available for four levels of Spanish, three levels of French and German, and one level of Russian and Hebrew. (International Linguistics is in the process of converting from cassette tapes to CDs, so you will need to check the availability of the different media.) The number of tapes or CDs varies depending upon the language.

Basic Structures 1 for Spanish, French, and German each include a book and three CDs. *Basic Structures* books include pictures with phrases or sentences plus a very few reading/writing activities without pictures. The primary goal with the *Basic Structures* program is learning to read the language rather than learning to write it. Vocabulary in each *Basic Structure* program is very similar to that of the corresponding picture-book program. Children listen to the CDs, read the phrases and sentences, and sometimes do matching, fill-in-the-blank, or similar written exercises. These could be done on separate paper so you can reuse the same book with more than one child. However, additional books are available without CDs if you need them. *Basic Structures* might be used with students from about fourth grade and up. Junior high and high school students definitely should use *Basic Structures* after completing each level of the *Learnables* picture books.

Grammar is not taught directly within either the picture books or *Basic Structures* programs, but students *do* acquire practical grammatical knowledge from actually using the language. At elementary levels this does not present a problem as it does for high school where students are expected to study the grammar of whatever foreign language they are learning. This is where *Grammar Enhancements* come in.

Grammar Enhancement programs are available for Spanish, French, and German. Each *Grammar Enhancement* set includes a book and either five audiocassettes or four CDs ($63.00 each). These are designed to be used after completion of level 1 of a language, both the picture-book program and *Basic Structures*. Thus, you could have young children working through only the picture book, intermediate children adding *Basic Structures,* and teens continuing through *Grammar Enhancement*. Alternatively, you could have students complete both levels 1 and 2 before tackling *Grammar Enhancement*.

The publisher sells a package of *Grammar Enhancement* with level 2 materials, suggesting it be used at the beginning of level 2. However, if you are trying to create something comparable to a typical first-year high school language course, *Grammar Enhancement* is essential. It uses vocabulary from level 1 and adds a great deal more. For example, in the Spanish course, the preterit tense is introduced in *Grammar Enhancement* but not in the other level 1 books. Yet, the preterit tense is typically taught in a first-year course.

Grammatically, *Grammar Enhancement* focuses on prepositions, pronouns, plurals, and verbs. (Future *Grammar Enhancement* books will deal with even more topics, such as "to be" verbs, advanced prepositions, future tense, and the conditional.) The present book contains the words from the tapes/CDs as well as pictures, but no instruction is given in English and no grammar rules are provided. Instead, many examples are given so students learn the sometimes subtle distinctions as they look for patterns and listen to the correct usage. This method might be more effective for some students than traditional instruction about grammar rules.

None of the components require any significant amount of writing, and there is no built-in requirement that students actually speak the language. However, I think parents and teachers can easily work on these two skills depending upon the ages and abilities of students. For example, parents might have students read aloud the *Basic Structure* exercises after students have had time to first listen to them. Older students could be required to write their own captions for pictures in either *Basic Structures* or *Grammar Enhancement* (covering up the written material in the book), then compare what they have written to the book.

The program is set up with four levels for most languages. Each level follows a similar plan, although the other three levels have five to six cassette tapes each. Spanish students also have available to them a fifth level as well as specialized vocabulary books on eating, transportation, walking, and placement. German students can continue with levels 5, 6, 7, and 8, or they might work through any of eight specialized vocabulary study books.

It is impossible to correlate levels of this program directly with traditional language courses, although the combination of *Learnables 1*, *Basic Structures 1*, and *Grammar Enhancement* could be considered a first year course. The publisher claims that the four levels of Spanish are equivalent to four high school years, while four levels of German and French are equivalent to 3.5 high school years. High school students should aim to complete the four levels using all basic components available for each level. The specialized vocabulary books would be optional elements.

Christians might also want to use the supplemental *Bible Stories in Spanish, French,* or *German* (includes a book and CD) after completion of level 2.

The Rosetta Stone (CD-ROM computer programs)
Fairfield Language Technologies
135 West Market Street
Harrisonburg, VA 22801
(800) 788-0822
e-mail: info@RosettaStone.com
www.rosettastone.com
Level 1—$209.00, level 2—$235.00, set of both levels—$349.00 per language

Are you looking for a language program that will help your student understand the spoken words as well as the written ones? Do you want your child to learn a language that you do not know? These CD-ROMs are similar to *The Learnables* audiotapes and CDs in methodology but are more interactive and give students more options.

First you look at four photos or drawings and listen to words by native speakers that are illustrated by the pictures. Listen to the sequence over and over, or choose a particular photo and hear the words as many times as you wish. You also have the option of having the words appear on the screen if you are one of those who need to see a word in order to hear it correctly. After you go through the ten preview screens of the lesson, pick the style of exercise that is most helpful to you. Hear a word and click on the correct picture, or see a picture and choose the correct word. Especially for languages that look very different, such as Arabic or Chinese, it would be helpful to use the exercises that give you a chance to try matching the sound of the word to its printed form.

You can repeat a lesson as often as you like, test yourself, and keep a record of your progress. If you have a microphone with your computer, you can even evaluate your pronunciation.

The photos are multicultural to be appealing to all types of students, and some even include very short video segments to clarify what is happening (such as showing the difference between tying and untying shoes).

Homeschool editions include a Student Management System that allows parents to create individual lesson plans and track progress for an almost unlimited number of students.

The foreign languages that are available in two levels are: German, Dutch, Spanish (either Latin American or Castilian), Portuguese, Arabic, French, Italian, Russian, Japanese, Chinese, and English (both U.S. and U.K.). The first level is also available in Latin, Polish, Welsh, Arabic, Hebrew, Thai, Vietnamese, Korean, Indonesian, Turkish, Hindi, Danish, Swedish, Pashto, and Swahili.

Those who want writing practice can order workbooks for the German, Spanish, French, and English programs. Currently there are study guides for the first level of those languages, with notes on grammar and usage. I would consider these essential for most teens trying to complete a course for high school credit. A quiz book is also available for Spanish.

Programs are recommended for ages 8 and up. The programs run on Windows 95 or higher (requires a Pentium system and microphone for speech recognition) or Mac OS 8.6 or higher systems. Rosetta Stone has a free online demo, or you can request a demo CD at no charge.

Henle Latin courses
by Robert J. Henle, S. J.
Loyola Press
3441 North Ashland Avenue
Chicago, IL 60657
(800) 621-1008
e-mail: customerservice@loyolapress.com
www.loyolapress.com
$16.95 each, answer keys—$1.00 each, teacher's manual—$2.00

This four-year Latin course, originally published in the 1940s, has been reprinted without significant change. The course focuses on mastery of the forms and vocabulary. Classical readings (particularly from Caesar, Cicero, and Virgil) are incorporated throughout the course along with some Christian readings (including a few from Scripture) and some expressly Catholic. (*First Year* has a particularly strong Catholic flavor at the beginning of the book.) The classical approach of this book fits perfectly with other elements of a classical education.

In the *First Year* book, grammar and vocabulary instruction take precedence as students work through numerous practice exercises. Some are labeled "essential" for students who master the material quickly and need not do all the exercises. The entire book may be covered, but if students complete up through lesson 26, it is sufficient for Latin I.

The *Second Year* book reviews the material, including explanation of material taught past lesson 26 in the first book for those students who might not have covered it. In the *Second*, *Third*, and *Fourth Year* books, the first half or more of each is readings to translate. In *Second Year*, notes and definitions are at the bottom of pages (footnote style), while *Third* and *Fourth Years* feature copious notes, background, and explanations on facing pages. Exercises are found in the second half of each of these three books, with accompanying instruction on new concepts. Reference helps and Latin-English and English-Latin vocabulary lists are at the back of each book.

Companion answer keys for each book are inexpensive photocopies. You will definitely want to purchase these. There is also a small, 105-page *Teacher's Manual for Henle Latin Series First and Second Years* by Sister Mary Jeanne, S.N.D., that explains the philosophy of the course and teaching strategies. It was written in 1955 for classroom situations, but there are many helpful ideas that will be useful in homeschooling situations.

There are other good Latin programs available, but none are this reasonably priced for such a solidly academic Latin course.

Loyola Press also publishes *Henle's Latin Grammar* ($9.50), which is extremely useful alongside this series.

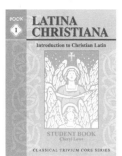

Latina Christiana, 2000 editions

by Cheryl Lowe
Memoria Press
4103 Bishop Lane
Louisville, KY 40218
(877) 862-1097
e-mail: magister@memoriapress.com
www.memoriapress.com
Books I and II: student books—$15.00 each, teacher's manuals—$20.00 each, CDs—$4.95 each

Cheryl Lowe believes that Latin is the ideal foundation for a classical education for children in grades 3 through 8. Ideally, Latin study replaces some English language study (particularly grammar and vocabulary) through these years. It also serves as the focus for study of history and geography to a minor extent. Cheryl explains how to integrate your studies in her teacher's manuals, correlating history questions based on *Famous Men of Rome* (from Greenleaf Press) throughout both volumes.

Parents with no Latin background should find these courses very easy to use. Lesson preparation is minimal unless you choose to develop some of the optional activity ideas Cheryl suggests. These are not independent study workbooks; you really need to use the teacher's manuals for lesson presentations.

She advocates using *Latina Christiana I* and *II* for grades 3 to 5, then using a first-year high school Latin text in grades 6 to 8 to complete the foundation. Students are then prepared for further language study and for reading Latin literature in high school. They should also find study of English and any of the Romance languages much easier.

Latina Christiana uses medieval or "church" Latin pronunciation rather than the "classical." You should find the companion CD very helpful for learning pronunciation. Words and phrases relating to Christianity are included; content should be appropriate for both Protestants and Catholics.

Lessons need to be taught following instructions in the teacher's manuals. The teacher's manuals are very nicely designed both in appearance and functionality. Smaller-sized copies of student pages are surrounded by lesson information. Answers are overprinted so you do not have to go to a separate answer key.

Lessons are learned through repetition, memorization, and drill, but Cheryl presents a number of ideas for making this interesting: vocabulary flash cards, games (e.g., Latin "Pictionary"), songs, and an audio CD.

The student books are less intimidating than most other foreign language workbooks since they were written for young students. Students do oral work with new vocabulary, study words and phrases, learn a well-known Latin proverb or phrase, and complete exercises in their books (or on blank paper if you wish to reuse the books). Students also listen to the CD that comes with each level and complete a tape exercise form that helps them review vocabulary, conjugations, and declensions. Most lessons include memorization of Latin prayers (e.g., the "Pater Noster" or "Our Father") or songs (e.g., "Adeste Fideles").

The courses were developed with small classes of homeschoolers, so Cheryl suggests gathering a small group for class. However, the courses should work well for a single student and parent.

Book I covers first and second declension noun and adjective forms, first and second conjugations and three tenses, subject/verb agreement, personal pronouns, gender, and use of the nominative case. Book II covers the third through fifth declensions, third and fourth conjugations, present and imperfect tenses, use of accusative and ablative cases, third person personal pronouns, and principal parts of selected verbs. Both levels include lists of English words derived from Latin vocabulary words in each lesson.

Helpful appendices include lists of all the vocabulary words and their meanings, charts of declensions and conjugations, and other helpful reference material.

Memoria Press also publishes *Prima Latina* ($32.95 for three items), an easier course that can be used prior to *Latina Christiana*. It covers some of the same vocabulary, but more slowly and in a different format. *Prima Latina* provides a "gentler" introduction to Latin, since *Latina Christiana* is likely to be quite challenging for most students in the elementary grades. While Memoria Press says *Prima Latina* can be used by children in grades 1 through 4, they qualify this by saying that it is "for students who are still becoming familiar with English grammar but are competent readers." I would add that students need to be fairly competent writers since there is quite a bit of writing in the course.

The teacher's manual for *Prima Latina* has general teaching guidelines and reproducible vocabulary drill forms and tests. Other than that, it has only overprinted answers on pages identical to those in the student text rather than expanded lesson plans. The companion CD helps with pronunciation and includes beautiful Latin hymns from another Memoria Press product, *Lingua Angelica*.

Lingua Angelica is a supplemental study of Latin hymns. It consists of a single CD with twenty-four hymns, two levels of student books with teacher manuals, and a songbook ($39.95 for first level, CD, and song book). The same songbook and CD are used with both levels. While you can purchase the CD alone just for the beautiful music by a six-voice Gregorian chant choir, the workbooks do not function as a stand-alone course but must be used alongside a beginning Latin course.

Optional DVDs or VHS tapes with lesson presentations are available for both *Latina Christiana* and *Prima Latina*. The video presentations teach the content of the books, but you still need the course books for student exercises, practice, and review. Parents worried about their ability to teach Latin, as well as those short on time, should really appreciate this option. Check the Web site for price and availability information.

14

Electives, Online Classes, and All-in-One Programs

After sorting through all sorts of curriculum, checking out new items, and making my initial list of Top Picks, I discovered I already had close to one hundred items before even touching electives. I could not bring myself to totally eliminate any electives, since you might get the impression that they don't matter! On top of that, I had already decided that it was critical to include some of the online, all-in-one, and computer courses so you have an idea of the increasingly sophisticated and helpful options available.

So I "demoted" a few of my original Top Picks to join the rest of my reviews available at www.CathyDuffyReviews.com. This gave me just a little space to add a few elective items that are especially good while also keeping my reviews of the unusual programs that don't fit into any other category.

Obviously what I have included here is a miniscule sampling of what's out there. I haven't touched many topics at all. Music, physical education, keyboarding, handwriting, home economics, driver's education, economics, worldview, and many other topics are not represented here, and it's not because these subjects are not important or useful. There is a logic to my narrow selection of health, critical thinking, and art resources. I believe the resources I have chosen represent "electives" that are essential for *all* students. You need not use these particular resources, but I believe that health education, critical thinking, and basic drawing skills are essential for a good education. I could have included handwriting, music, home economics, and a few other subjects in that list, but I omitted them for reasons such as the following:

- Handwriting: There are many excellent handwriting courses available. The style of handwriting you choose is a matter of personal preference as far as I am concerned (and I am aware that there are some advocates of one style or another who believe theirs is the only right way to teach handwriting!).

- Music: Where to begin? It all depends upon what direction you want to go—music appreciation, keyboarding skills, string instruments, voice.

- Home Economics: There is no single Home Economics text or course that I would rate as a better choice than a real books and hands-on approach. However, some unit studies come close.

Thus, the following are reviews of items I think most homeschoolers need to include as electives.

Health

Total Health: Choices for a Winning Lifestyle and *Total Health: Talking About Life's Changes*
by Susan Boe
Purposeful Design Publications, a division of ACSI
P.O. Box 65130
Colorado Springs, CO 80962-5130
(800) 367-0798
www.acsi.org

Choices: $28.95 hardcover or $23.95 softcover, teacher's edition—$35.95, test and quiz book—$15.50, *Parent Connection*—$12.50; *Talking About:* $22.95 softcover or $26.95 hardcover, teacher's edition—$36.95, test and quiz book—$15.50

Up until recently, there was no comprehensive health textbook written specifically for Christian day schools *and* homeschoolers. Now we have two texts, *Talking About Life's Changes* for middle school and *Choices for a Winning Lifestyle* for high school. Both books are definitely written from a Christian perspective. Spiritual principles emphasizing our relationship with God play a major role throughout both books. In addition, both books are similarly divided into four large units on physical, mental, social, and spiritual health.

The Parent Connection is a book for parents only! It correlates with topics covered in both texts, supplying background information, discussion topics, problems to watch for (e.g., depression, eating disorders), and suggestions for dealing with touchy topics such as contraception and masturbation. Note that the topic of contraception is not addressed at all in the student books. *The Parent Connection* touches on different forms of contraception, how they work, and their relative effectiveness, but the issue of the morality of contraception, even within marriage, is not raised.

The *Choices* text is 464 pages. Although there is a teacher's edition, you shouldn't need it. (The teacher's edition features chapter outlines, suggested course plans, vocabulary exercises, worksheets, transparency masters, activity suggestions, and discussion questions.) The test and quiz master book for *Choices* includes fairly brief teaching instructions plus quizzes, tests, and answer keys.

Choices covers all of the topics addressed in other health texts, although the amount of time devoted to many of the topics is very different. For example, human reproduction is covered very briefly without full details or illustrations. Instead of spending pages and pages describing various types of drugs, it discusses drugs and drug abuse in a more general fashion in about eight pages. For many home educators, this approach makes far more sense since we spend more time on positive health and nutrition issues and less time on the negative issues that seem to require so much attention in public schools.

Also, while other texts address physical, mental, and social health, *Choices* adds a section on spiritual health. Social health deals with personal care, first aid, attitudes, responsibility, and relationships, including dating. Although very conservative in approach (encouragement to group date and avoid sexual activity of all kinds), the author treats dating as acceptable.

Treatment of topics such as health, fitness, and nutrition is generally mainstream—no discussion of homeopathy, herbology, alternative medicine, etc. While this course might not be as radical in some of its positions as some home educators are, it does seem to be the most comprehensive, conservative alternative designed with home educators in mind.

The layout makes it very easy to use. Chapter reviews focus on both comprehension and application, providing natural opportunities to expand on topics of special interest.

Talking About is very similar in many ways to *Choices*, although at 336 pages, it is less comprehensive. There is also a greater emphasis on the changes young teens undergo than in *Choices*.

You don't need to use both texts, and I think *Choices* would be the better one to use if using only one. If you want to use *Talking About*, the middle school level, there is a more than seven-hundred page teacher's edition, student book, a test and quiz master book that includes its own answer key plus keys to chapter reviews, and a companion workbook and answer key.

Critical Thinking and Logic

Logic beat out other electives for inclusion in this chapter because I am convinced that a grasp of logic (at a minimum, what is called "informal logic") is essential to a good education. If you can't think straight and then express your ideas logically, if you can't spot the shysters and the propaganda and sort through it all to the truth, then your education is incomplete.

In addition, many logic books on the market are fun to use. My eldest son says that one of the best books we used in all of our homeschooling years was a small paperback titled *How to Lie with Statistics* (W.W. Norton and Company). This little gem has been reprinted numerous times since it was written in the 1950s. It will have you in stitches with some of its examples. It's a terrific way to inoculate your older teens against marketers, politicians, and media manipulation. The reason it's not in my Top Picks list is because it really serves as a supplement to logic studies rather than a primary resource and because it does require "parental editing"—read it yourself first before using it with your older teens since there are sections you will probably want to skip.

Even with the logic/critical thinking resources I selected, I cheated a little by including Critical Thinking Company, a publisher with hundreds of items, most of which are supplementary. They are not the only publisher of critical thinking resources for younger children, but they have by far the broadest and best selection. Their line includes what I would call "prelogic" books for young children, books relating to different subject areas that appeal to children of different learning styles, books for teens that address informal and formal logic, and software programs. These are great for challenging your children to stretch their thinking skills as well as helping them learn to function in other thinking/learning modes.

The Fallacy Detective and *With Good Reason* are great resources for younger and older teens respectively to introduce them to informal logic—a required course for all students if it were up to me.

If you want to explore formal logic, a good place to start is *Traditional Logic: An Introduction to Formal Logic* by Martin Cothran (Memoria Press). For more about teaching logic and available resources, check out reviews at www.CathyDuffyReviews.com or investigate the articles, reviews, and helps at www.christianlogic.com, a site created by Nathaniel and Hans Bluedorn, authors of *The Fallacy Detective*.

The Critical Thinking Company
P.O. Box 1610
Seaside, CA 93955-1610
(800) 458-4849
www.criticalthinking.com

Building Thinking Skills student books: $22.99—$25.99 each, teacher's manuals—$18.99 each

The *Building Thinking Skills* series is probably the most basic, comprehensive resource for thinking skills at all levels. Each reproducible student book is accompanied by a teacher's manual that offers a combination of lesson plans and teaching information (except for the *Hands-On Primary* book, which requires no manual). Lessons use student worksheets and interaction between teacher and student(s). Each lesson should take about ten to twenty minutes to complete and requires just a few minutes of teacher preparation.

The first three books in the series are written for grades pre-K through 6. The first book, *Building Thinking Skills: Hands-On Primary*, is suggested for grades pre-K through 1. The required hands-on materials are attribute blocks, pattern blocks, and interlocking cubes. Manipulative activities are performed with these materials both prior to and while students complete the worksheets. In the 246-page *Primary* book, children deal with similarities and differences, sequences, classifications, and analogies. Visual-figural skills get a workout in these lessons too.

Level 1 (327 pages), suggested for grades 2 through 4, uses interlocking cubes for a few lessons and broadens activities beyond the primarily visual-figural approach of the *Primary* book. Children work on the same skills as in the *Primary* book but add discussion of five types of analogies, following directions, antonyms and synonyms, "deductive reasoning, parts of a whole, map skills and directionality, logical connectives, spelling and vocabulary building, Venn diagrams, pattern folding, rotation, tracking, mental manipulation of two-dimensional objects," and more.

Level 2 (367 pages), suggested for grades 4 through 7, does all of the above, expands to seven different types of analogies, and adds branching diagrams, overlapping classes, and more. The idea of "implications" is also introduced. Activities vary in difficulty, so select those that seem most appropriate for each child.

***Mind Benders*—$9.99 each**

The *Mind Benders* series consists of sets of smaller, thirty-two- to forty-eight-page books. Each book is self-contained, with teaching suggestions and instructions in the front and detailed solutions in the back. Children organize clues (some direct and some indirect) in grids (except in the introductory *Warm Up* level) to derive logical conclusions. For example, in an introductory lesson, students are told, "Edmund, Ida, Joanne, and Tony are two sets of twins. Tony is a month younger than Edmund. Joanne is a month older than Ida." Students must then answer two questions, "Which pair is the younger set of twins?" and "Which pair is the older set of twins?" The *Warm-Up* book is for grades K through 2. For grades 3 through 6, there is a series of books, *A1, A2, A3,* and *A4.* Some older students will be ready to move up to the second series, *B1* through *B4,* suggested for grades 7 through 12. These activities appeal to children because it seems like detective work as students try to match clues with identities.

The Critical Thinking Company also publishes books that help develop thinking skills within various subject areas such as math, language arts, science, and U.S. history. (Reviews of *Developing Critical Thinking through Science, Mathematical Reasoning through Verbal Analysis,* and *Cranium Crackers* can be found at CathyDuffyReviews.com) You can send for The Critical Thinking Company catalog—called *Bright Minds*—or check out their Web site to determine which resources best suit your needs. (Note: this is a nonsectarian publisher, and you might find occasional, minor content problems.)

More Challenging Logic for Teens

Critical Thinking: Problem Solving, Reasoning, Logic & Arguments, Books One and *Two*
by Anita Harnadek
Critical Thinking Co.
(See address on page 291)
Book One student book—$21.99, teacher's manual—$9.99; Book Two student book—$24.99, teacher's manual—$9.99

These two books, *Critical Thinking, Book One* and *Critical Thinking, Book Two*, are especially good for junior and senior high school as an introduction to critical thinking and logic.

They are lots of fun but will also challenge both students and parents. Some of the exercises are silly but effective. You can skip around to some extent, choosing lessons that are most interesting, easier, or more challenging since they range from popular fallacies through formal logic.

Use these books interactively (teacher interacting with one or more students) since they are not designed for independent work. You will need the teacher's manual for each book.

When we used these books, we occasionally had trouble with the author's politically correct point of view in the phrasing of statements and/or questions. We sometimes used those instances to try to identify her worldview (an exercise in critical thinking!), sometimes skipped them, and sometimes changed them. There isn't anything seriously objectionable on the surface, but attitudes and opinions can be subtle influencers.

The Fallacy Detective
by Nathaniel and Hans Bluedorn
Christian Logic
P.O. Box 46
Muscatine, IA 52761-0001
(309) 537-3644
www.christianlogic.com
$22.00

The Bluedorn family, longtime promoters of Christian classical education, encountered the same problem we did with content in most critical thinking and logic resources, so Nathaniel and Hans Bluedorn put their heads together and came up with this excellent introduction to practical logic from their conservative Christian homeschoolers' perspective. Subtitled "Thirty-Six Lessons on How to Recognize Bad Reasoning," it uses humor, historical references, and real life situations to help teens learn to think and express themselves clearly. Comic strips from *Calvin and Hobbes*, *Dilbert*, *Peanuts*, and *Nuna and Toodles* (the Bluedorn brothers' own creation) are a nice touch that have been added to the second edition.

The style is similar in many ways to the *Critical Thinking, Books One and Two* I described above. However, the underlying perspective comes through in different ways. Verses from Proverbs are used to discuss knowledge and wisdom. One exercise statement reads, "I know everybody thinks Einstein's theory of relativity is correct, but I can't accept it. Einstein believed in evolution." Another on the same page relates this conversation: "Mrs. A: 'I'm going through a logic book with my kids. It's called *The Fallacy Detective*. I really like it.' Mrs. B.: 'Aw, the authors of that book are just a bunch of homeschoolers. What do they know about logic.'" (p. 49).

The Fallacy Detective will likely appeal to many families for another reason: it doesn't need to be taught. Students can read and work through it independently. However, it might be enjoyable for both parent and student for the teen to read the lesson on his or her own, summarize the main idea to a parent, then go through the exercises out loud together. Some exercises require simple identification answers, but others might prompt some great discussion. The authors' answers are in the back of the book.

Instructions for a *Fallacy Detective Game* in which players make up their own fallacies are also at the back of the book. This would make great family fun for those with two or more teens.

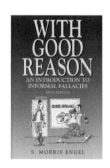

With Good Reason: An Introduction to Informal Fallacies (sixth edition)
by S. Morris Engel
St. Martin's Press, Inc.
175 Fifth Avenue
New York, NY 10010
(order through bookstores)
www.stmartins.com
$36.25

With Good Reason: An Introduction to Informal Fallacies is another good choice along the same lines as *The Fallacy Detective*, but it's better for older teens. It begins with "definitions," but even this potentially boring foundational information is presented with touches of humor that make it both entertaining and interesting. Each brief section is followed by a summary of key points and practice exercises. Answers to a few selected questions are at the end of each section, but parents will need to read along to be able to discuss exercise questions and figure out answers to those for which none are provided—not that difficult a task. (Parents without a background in logic will find that reading this book is time well spent!)

Among topics dealt with in the first section are arguments and nonarguments, missing components, syllogisms, truth, validity, soundness, and deductive and inductive arguments.

The next section deals with language as a medium of communication. It gets into topics such as implied and actual meanings of words, ambiguity, and vagueness. Information here will be valuable to those who want to become more skillful communicators.

The bulk of the book deals with the "fun stuff"—informal fallacies. These fallacies are divided into three general sections: fallacies of ambiguity, presumption, and relevance. Under each section we encounter the more familiar labels, such as begging the question, special pleading, ad hominem attacks, mob appeal, appeals to authority, etc. There are plenty of examples and exercises plus the occasional cartoon for illustration.

An appendix at the end titled "Writing with Clarity and Reason" explains how writing an essay is much like presenting an argument. It offers excellent ideas on structuring and presenting essays.

This book is broader in scope than *The Fallacy Detective*, but it is written for an adult, non-Christian audience. Nevertheless, it should be suitable for mature Christian teens.

Art

Art is a very broad area, but I have focused on a narrow aspect with the following selections. Drawing skill is a form of literacy—being able to communicate with pictures in this case. So with my limited space, I have selected two resources that everyone might use for basic instruction.

Mark Kistler's Draw Squad
by Mark Kistler
Fireside Books/Simon and Schuster
(order through homeschool distributors or bookstores ISBN# 0-671-65694-5)
www.simonsays.com
$17.00

Mark Kistler studied under former Disney artist Bruce McIntyre for twelve years. McIntyre produced his own *Drawing Textbook*, videos, telecourses, and other resources for students to learn to draw, but never quite made the connection with user-friendly children's materials. So Mark Kistler took up the crusade to bring drawing literacy to children via a national public television program and this book.

Drawing, or artistic literacy, is at the heart of *Mark Kistler's Draw Squad*. Author Mark Kistler's basic premise is that everyone can draw. They just need a few basic techniques to know how to get started. As children learn these techniques by working through each lesson, they get immediate and impressive results. Kistler presents the techniques as ten "key words": foreshortening, shading, surface, size, contour lines, overlapping, density, shadows, attitude, and daily use.

The book has thirty lessons with nine components to each lesson. Consequently, a lesson should be spread out over a few days or a week. Since "daily use" is one of Kistler's keys, he recommends some sort of daily drawing activity—and there are plenty of ideas in the book for that!

Lessons include warm-up exercises, instruction in a new skill, exercises with the new skill, examples, evaluation activities, practice and review, and extended activities.

Children actually do much of their drawing right in the book, but you will also want to have extra sketchbooks for all the drawing they will want to do. A pencil is the only other thing you need—no fancy art equipment!

Kistler's book has a jazzy format with cartoon characters popping up occasionally to make things even more interesting. Lessons are well laid out and easy to follow—a fourth or fifth grader can use the book on his or her own. Younger children will need a little help. The format is so appealing that adults will enjoy using it too. If parents don't know how to draw, they should purchase an extra book for themselves and learn right along with their children.

Mark also has some newer drawing books available: *Mark Kistler's Imagination Station* and *Drawing in 3-D with Mark Kistler*.

Feed My Sheep
by Barry Stebbing
How Great Thou ART
P.O. Box 48
McFarlan, NC 28102
(800) 982-3729
e-mail: sales@howgreatthouart.com
www.howgreatthouart.com
$42.95; Bundle Pack—$59.95

This is a combined art text and workbook for teaching drawing, color theory, art appreciation, perspective, portraiture, anatomy, lettering, painting, and more to students ages ten through adult. Older students and adults without art experience should find this a valuable course. It contains more than 250 lessons plus a packet of 17 paint cards. These are 8½-by 11-inch in size and are a heavy 110 lb. stock. For many of the lessons, students need only drawing pencils, a set of colored pencils, a kneaded eraser, a ruler, an extrafine marker, sketchbook, and posterboard. Most of these items come in the Bundle Pack. Later lessons on painting use pure pigment paints and brushes. A drawing board, triangle, and T-square are also helpful in later lessons, but not essential.

Depending upon the age and ability of the student, this can be a three- to four-year curriculum using one lesson per week. One of the primary goals for the course is that students learn to draw realistic images.

However, work with other media and skills, including cartooning, is also taught. You need to select lessons that are appropriate for each student. For example, you might save the painting lessons for older students.

If you want to tackle painting as soon as possible, purchase the Bundle Pack, which includes the book plus a set of pure pigment paints, brushes, Prismacolor pencils, drawing pencils, drawing pen, pencil sharpener, and eraser. Otherwise, start with just the book and purchase paints later so they will be fresh when you want to use them.

Author Barry Stebbing's Christian perspective is evident throughout the course in Bible verses, lesson explanations, art appreciation lessons, and even the choices of examples. The book is written to the student so he or she can work independently. However, younger students will probably need some assistance. Instructions are fairly thorough, so even parents with little art background should be able to help students through all of the lessons.

Art appreciation is incorporated into many of the lessons, and more-focused lessons direct students to the library to locate and copy artists' works or examples from particular periods. Students also research answers to questions posed about art history, styles, artists, etc.

Overall, this is a very comprehensive course. For parents who wish to maintain academic accountability, there are occasional quizzes on art theory and appreciation, with an answer key at the back of the book. This single volume offers a tremendous amount of art instruction at a very low cost. Since students actually work in the book, it is best to purchase one for each student. However, for parents who would rather copy the lessons for multiple children, this is allowed for in-the-home use only.

How Great Thou ART also publishes two less-expensive volumes that cover content similar to some in *Feed My Sheep*. These are called the *Lamb's Book of ART, Books I* and *II*. For younger children, check out *I Can Do All Things: A Beginning Book of Drawing and Painting,* and for older students, the company's flagship book titled *How Great Thou ART.*

Online Classes

Do you want to move your family to Asia for missionary work but wonder how on earth you can manage to continue homeschooling your teen? Did you flunk math all the way through high school and now desperately need someone else to teach your child algebra? Do you have an ambitious, bright student who is begging to go to a "regular" school so she can take AP courses? Does your teen want a course on Greek philosophers with Socratic discussion and you don't have the time, knowledge, or inclination to teach such a course yourself?

All these needs and more can be met with courses available to homeschoolers on the Internet. Homeschoolers are at the cutting edge of online learning because of their openness to new ideas and the unusual needs many families have. For example, Fritz Hinrichs (www.gbt.org) began offering classical courses online back in the 1980s. He has continually developed his courses and delivery methods as new technology and software has developed.

Homeschoolers are not the only ones taking advantage of Internet technology. Even government schools have jumped on board. A challenging dilemma has surfaced as a result. Courses offered by government schools are usually free or of minimal cost to families, while those offered by private organizations can cost hundreds of dollars. But there is a significant nonfinancial cost when a homeschooling family uses courses funded by the government—loss of parental control.

While legal definitions vary from state to state, homeschoolers who enroll in government school courses are no longer considered to be homeschoolers. They are under the authority of the school's teachers rather than that of their parents, even if they are completing their coursework at home under parental supervision. Parents no longer have the final say over course content and requirements unless they pull a child out of the school.

While parents, theoretically, have the ability to oversee what their children are reading and doing, the reality is that in most situations children will work independently, and parents won't know the actual course content. They won't be able to determine in advance if their child's teacher will support or contradict their family beliefs and values. And for those interested in forming a Christian worldview in their children, many government-school approved courses are counterproductive since they adhere to a secular materialistic worldview.

In addition, there are political ramifications of homeschoolers enrolling in government programs that are damaging to the larger homeschool community, but those are beyond the scope of this book. The bottom line is that the "free" courses often come with a hidden price tag.

Content and viewpoint problems can also crop up in online courses offered by private organizations that hold different worldviews than that of your family. However, you are often able to ask questions about teachers and worldviews in these situations. I would urge you to carefully investigate any such program before enrolling your child. There are many good organizations offering online courses that work well with homeschoolers and are up front about their religious beliefs and goals.

In addition to beliefs and goals, there are also choices about structure in online learning. Some programs use the Internet for automated course delivery. Students log on to a course, work through it answering questions as they go, and receive a grade based on their work. Some such courses are mostly text—like reading a textbook—while others are heavily illustrated with computer graphics and animations. Some courses are largely discussion based—this is especially true of classical education courses. Some use bulletin-board posting as a part of course requirements. Some require separate written work, such as essays that are e-mailed to instructors. Some use the Internet sparingly, making assignments in traditional textbooks, relaying assignments and comments back and forth over the Internet, with an occasional student chat room discussion. Anything that might be done is probably being done by some course provider somewhere.

Also, you need to think about your child's learning style when you choose online programs. Because most young children need more active learning and interaction, online education is rarely a good idea for the elementary grades. However, it becomes much more appropriate for junior and senior high students. Even so, an older child's learning style should still influence your choice of such programs. For example, a sociable child will much prefer online discussions to courses where she primarily reads text material online with minimal interaction.

There are two terms you need to know in regard to online courses: *synchronous* and *asynchronous*. *Synchronous* courses mean there are times when students and teacher are online and interacting at the same time—synchronously. *Asynchronous* courses mean courses are either prerecorded or written material that students may access at any time. There are no chats or sessions where students and teachers interact together simultaneously—unless they happen to do instant messaging. Referring back to my last example of the sociable child, she is much more likely to succeed in synchronous courses because of the real-time interaction with others.

Below are some of the online options. The grade levels served by the courses are noted in parentheses. Reviews of just a few of these follow as examples.

- Apex Learning: www.apexlearning.com—nonsectarian; asynchronous (9–12)
- CLASS.com: www.class.com—graphically interesting courses originally developed under University of Nebraska-Lincoln's distance education program; equivalent to public high school courses; asynchronous; nonsectarian (9–12)
- Clonlara's Compuhigh: http://compuhigh.com—asynchronous; project-based learning; non-sectarian (9–12)
- CompassLearning Odyssey: www.childu.com—secular; asynchronous; graphically interesting courses (PreK–6)
- Eagle Christian: www.eaglechristian.org—Christian program using textbooks with some on-line interaction (7–12)
- Escondido Tutorial Service: www.gbt.org—synchronous discussions; classical; Christian (9–12)
- K12 (Bill Bennett's program): www.k12.com—asynchronous; uses a mixture of online activity, real books, and textbooks; nonsectarian. (The big problem with this program is that it tries to enroll home educators in public school programs so they can get the curriculum free.) See review at www.grovepublishing.com/curriculumreviews/elreviews/el_k12.htm. (K–8)
- North Dakota Division of Independent Study: www.thedistancelearning.com/usa/of076.htm—asynchronous; students read from both texts and online lessons; nonsectarian public school program (4–12)
- NorthStar Academy: www.northstar-academy.org—Christian; asynchronous; students access pre-recorded lesson presentations and use traditional textbooks; satisfies U.S., Canadian, or U.K. requirements (7–12)

- Oxford Tutorial Service: www.oxfordtutorials.com—classical; Christian; synchronous discussions (9–12)
- The Potter's School: www.pottersschool.com—Christian; synchronous courses (7–12)
- Schola Classical Tutorials: www.schola-tutorials.com—classical; Christian; synchronous discussions (9–12)
- Scholars' Online Academy (SOLA), Regina Coeli Academy, Agnus Dei Elementary Program: www.islas.org—classical; combination of live conferencing and bulletin-board interaction; synchronous and asynchronous classes. SOLA is Protestant, and Regina Coeli and Agnus Dei are Catholic—all three are branches of the same organization, ISLAS. (4–12)
- Studium Discere Tutorials: www.sdtutorials.com—classical Christian courses; interactive discussion (9–12)

Apex Learning Inc.
315 Fifth Avenue South, Suite 600
Seattle, WA 98104
(800) 453-1454
e-mail: inquiries@apexlearning.com
www.apexlearning.com

Many high school students who want to take Advanced Placement (AP) courses, even within regular schools, have no access to courses in which they are interested. Even the best schools can offer only selected AP courses, if any. So Apex Learning came up with a solution a number of years ago by offering online AP-level high school courses. They have continually expanded the number of courses available, and they have added general education and foreign language courses to their offerings. They have also partnered with other companies to link to a broader range of courses, but these are not Apex's own courses.

Among Apex's own courses at present are fourteen AP courses, eight general studies courses (in math, science, history, government, literature, and computer programming), and six non-AP foreign language courses.

Apex primarily provides services to students within traditional schools. However, they also serve homeschoolers. All courses are nonsectarian, suitable for use within government schools.

I have not examined all their courses, but those I have seen clearly demonstrate that there is no common format used by Apex courses. Nevertheless, those I have viewed all are very engaging, thorough, and professionally presented. Courses are well designed and use audio, video, animations, and other multimedia enhancements that make the content interesting.

Students take courses on a regular school schedule with other students. They work with a teacher from Apex or under another credentialed teacher—you could set up an extension class for homeschoolers with your own teacher using the Apex course for content delivery and your group meetings for discussion, collaborative activities, tests, etc. All courses are designed with multimedia tutorials providing the course content. Students access these tutorials online at a convenient time. Online quizzes and exams are scored and recorded. There are usually additional assignments that students complete and submit to their teachers. Some additional activities and discussions are dependent upon students being enrolled with a group. Nevertheless, students can and frequently do use the courses independent of a group.

Courses sometimes require additional books or resources (e.g., a Norton anthology for a literature course or a graphing calculator for math courses) that you need to purchase separately. Sometimes, optional resources are suggested.

Lab sciences are a bit challenging for homeschoolers. If students do not need actual hands-on lab work, these courses are sufficient with their virtual labs. Those who need hands-on lab are required to complete the labs under a qualified instructor in an actual lab.

Prerequisites and course outlines are available on the Web site for each course. Pretests for AP math and science courses help you determine whether or not your teen is ready for a particular course. Apex also offers separate AP exam review "courses."

Unfortunately, Apex's courses are probably the most expensive online high school level courses available to homeschoolers.

The Potter's School
8279 Raindrop Way
Springfield, VA 22153
(703) 690-3516
e-mail: director@pottersschool.org
www.pottersschool.org
$350.00 per junior high course, $400.00 per senior high course

The Potter's School has grown from small beginnings as it has responded to the needs of home-schoolers. They have been especially aware of the unique needs of families overseas in mission fields.

They have developed individual, online courses—both core and elective—for grades 7-12. While you could probably put together a complete program with their courses, The Potter's School does not offer a diploma. Think of them as a course or curriculum provider rather than a school.

Courses involve videoconferencing once a week for ninety-minute sessions. Potter's School describes these sessions: "The live class sessions employ audio, video, chat, an interactive whiteboard and web presentations to enhance the students' educational experience. The live sessions also provide students valuable interaction opportunities with their peers from all over the world." Potter's offers a number of "sections," or class groups, for each course, each meeting at a different time, so families can select a time that works for them. Teachers are all well-recognized specialists in their areas, and they interact with students enough to actually get to know them.

In addition, there are student discussion forums and online "study halls," individual feedback from teachers, an online yearbook to which students can contribute, a student-published e-zine, and even optional overseas trips in which both students and parents can participate during the summer.

The Potter's School has a Christian (Protestant) statement of faith, and all their courses are taught from a biblical worldview. They actually offer worldview courses.

Among their core courses are high school math courses using the excellent UCSMP math series. (These are some of the very best math textbooks, although I do not generally recommend them to homeschoolers working independently because they really do need presentation by a knowledgeable teacher.)

Potter's has a number of lab science courses using Apologia's excellent textbooks. They also offer courses in history, geography, logic, English, computer programming, Church history, Bible, French, Spanish, Latin, and Greek. Course offerings change from year to year depending upon demand.

A number of their courses are AP level, and all courses are academically rigorous. This is not an "easy way out" for students to get through high school.

Because students "meet" at set times, courses operate on a regular school year schedule. Each section is limited to no more than fifteen students, so early registration is a must if you want a particular time slot or even to be able to get into some courses.

The technology for these courses is sophisticated enough that some families might have trouble getting it to work. Potter's requires families to install and test the software they use before registration to ensure system compatibility. Their conferencing software will not work with Mac systems and might even have problems with some Windows systems (e.g., through proxy servers).

All-in-One Programs

Let's be honest. There are times when you just need someone to put together the whole package for you. Whether or not it meets all your children's learning-style needs or it lines up completely with your philosophy might not matter as much to you as having a program that makes it easy for you to homeschool, particularly if you are just starting out. The package might come from a correspondence school or umbrella school, or it might be a homeschooling program—any of these might be labels for some type of program that gives you everything you need in one nice, neat package.

I'm including reviews here of two very popular programs, each very different in terms of curriculum used and oversight provided (or not). You will find such programs everywhere on the spectrum, from no oversight or teaching services to complete oversight with extensive teacher services. You'll also find programs that offer a wide range of resources from which you can choose, programs that offer you no choices at all apart from their prescribed curriculum, and everything in between. Some programs are Christian; some are nonsectarian. Many follow a fairly traditional approach to education, but some focus on some of the less-standard approaches, such as classical education or even unschooling.

A to Z Home's Cool is a Web site that features Ann Zeise's extensive descriptive listings of programs according to various categories so you can check out more options: www.gomilpitas.com/home schooling/methods/DLPs.htm.

Calvert School
10713 Gilroy Road Suite B
Hunt Valley, MD 21031
(888) 487-4652
e-mail: inquiry@calvertservices.org
www.calvertschool.org

Average course price is under $600.00; average Advisory Teaching Service price is about $280.00—prices are lower for early grades and higher for upper grades.

Calvert offers complete courses for prekindergarten through eighth grade with all materials supplied for each course, including such consumable resources as crayons and pencils. Calvert's strength has always been in their coverage of geography, history, mythology, poetry, and literature, as well as in their teacher's manuals. Art and poetry are included in most grade levels along with basic academic courses, so this is a culturally rich curriculum. Calvert has also created their own math program that adds to the overall academic excellence.

Teacher's manuals provide clear, concise instruction for both the novice and experienced teacher. Even though Calvert makes no such claim, their teacher's manuals effectively teach you how to teach. The quality of individual subject courses within Calvert's program varies from mediocre to excellent. *A Child's History of the World* and other similar books are much better than typical textbooks.

This is not a Christian school, and some of the texts contain evolutionary concepts. However, you are welcome to supplement or substitute lessons reflecting your own beliefs and philosophies for the Calvert lessons. Calvert staff seem to have made good judgments about making assignments from some of these books. For example, in the kindergarten science book there are a few pages about space aliens that have little relation to any science topic. The Calvert manual skips these pages, and so should you.

Prekindergarten and kindergarten programs are a little more challenging than some other programs. Pre-K includes many readiness activities. Reading instruction is introductory and does not use intensive phonics at this level. Kindergarten includes solid phonics instruction through beginning and ending sounds and short vowels. The program includes appropriate work pages and simple readers.

Since subject studies are integrated to some extent, mixing of grade levels is not allowed, with the exception of math. Calvert now offers an option for students to take a placement test and be given a math course at the indicated level. Although these courses are a prepackaged curriculum for each grade level, Calvert allows students to enroll in a program minus the math curriculum or with a "custom math" option. However, Calvert's new math program should please most families.

A second or third child may now enroll in a course already completed by a sibling at a reduced rate since some of the materials can be reused from the previously used course. They get replacements of consumable books, new books when necessary, and a new lesson manual to reflect any changes made.

You may enroll your child and work with him or her independently, or you may elect to include the optional Advisory Teaching Service (ATS) for grades K through 8. With the ATS, tests are sent into Calvert for review and grading by a professional teacher/advisor, who also makes comments and suggestions. At kindergarten level, parents are given progress sheets to use rather than evaluating with tests or grades. Parents submit these sheets along with samples of student work for evaluation by Calvert teachers. Only with the ATS will Calvert issue a certificate of completion for courses.

Calvert also offers enrichment courses: *Beginning French* and *Beginning Spanish* courses for grades 4–8, Levels 1 and 2; *Melody Lane* music course on video for grades K–3 (includes some theory) [$95.00]; *Discovering Art,* an art appreciation course for grades 4–8 [$125.00]; and classic literature courses. Enrichment courses are available to those not enrolled in Calvert.

I'd like to give a little bit more space to one type of enrichment course. Calvert's *Reference Library* courses are available at four different levels of difficulty. I would probably skip the first level for kindergarten and first grades and start with one of the others. I suspect the third and fourth levels ($48.00 each) are the most useful because they target grades 3 to 5 and 6 to 8 respectively—grade levels where reference work is really necessary. These courses each include an appropriate dictionary and thesaurus with a lesson manual. Lessons teach children how to use the books through relatively fun activities. Children do lots of "hunting" for the answers.

Use of enrichment courses for group classes is priced differently than when purchasing for individual use. Call for details.

While you are still restricted on the amount of individualizing you can do with Calvert courses, this is a good choice for new homeschoolers, missionaries, or others who have difficulty rounding up all the necessary materials or creating their own lesson plans. Yes, it is expensive. But Calvert really does make homeschooling very easy for parents while providing an interesting program that works well for most children.

Sonlight Curriculum
8042 South Grant Way
Littleton, CO 80122-2705
(303) 730-6292
e-mail: main@sonlight.com
www.sonlight.com

Sonlight is strictly a curriculum provider—not a school or oversight program. But what sets Sonlight apart from other curriculum providers is that they have designed "grade level" programs with carefully selected resources and instructor's guides that outline lessons for each day using specific pages within the materials provided. In this, they are more similar to Calvert and other such oversight programs. However, there is no option for sending in work for grading, record keeping by Sonlight, or teaching assistance other than what's available on the discussion bulletin boards at their Web site.

Sonlight was begun by a homeschooling family who wanted to provide the best materials at a reasonable cost that would work for families living overseas and working as missionaries. They wanted to base their programs on the educational philosophy of Dr. Ruth Beechick: structured, yet allowing for maximum real-life learning. Influenced by Charlotte Mason's ideas, they also wanted to include real books, but at the same time not create a program that required too much time and work from busy parents. These ideas actually reflected the needs of many homeschooling families, not just those in mission fields. As a result, Sonlight grew to become one of the largest curriculum suppliers in the homeschool market.

But Sonlight is not for everyone. They actually have a page on their Web site and in their catalog titled "31 Reasons *Not* to Buy Sonlight." You should take time to read through this before ordering a program.

Sonlight offers a complete, eclectic, literature-based program integrated around historical themes for kindergarten through high school. They have arranged their program in an unusual fashion. There are thirteen different Core Program Packages, loosely designated for grade levels. However, all of these packages might be used with a range of students over at least three grade levels. This is possible because Core Packages primarily cover history and Bible while also including many read-aloud books plus "readers" (real books rather than reading textbooks). History and Bible instruction are not especially dependent upon skill or maturity levels.

Core Packages focus on one of three broad areas of history: world history, U.S. history, or cultures. Read-aloud books are excellent choices that you would probably love to have in the family library even if you weren't using Sonlight. Bible instruction uses Scripture and other resources, including Christian and missionary biographies. This is essentially a Protestant program, although the level 8 program presents a very even-handed study of church history and doctrinal issues comparing Protestant, Catholic, and Orthodox positions.

Separate language arts, math, and science packages are then combined with your choice of a Core Package to customize the curriculum. Language arts, math, or science packages might be selected for the same grade level or various levels depending upon children's needs. Instructor's guides come with Core, language arts, and science packages. Language arts guides refer to some of the books that come in the corresponding level Core Packages, so if a child needs a particular level of language arts, that might dictate which Core Package you choose. Math and science function independently of the Core Package. Elective packages or resources are also available for critical thinking, foreign language, art, music, geography, Bible study, typing, creation/evolution, church history, driver's education, worldview, and physical education.

Language arts instructor's guides have built in all of the instruction for phonics, grammar, composition, and most other language skills. I am particularly impressed with the weekly writing assignments built into the curriculum, since this area is lacking in so many other programs. Additional books in the packages might be for handwriting or spelling, or they might be a dictionary or thesaurus. Sonlight has created some of their own readers for the early stages of reading, but after that they use real books from other sources.

Science packages include the guide, an assortment of books, and supplies for experiments and activities. The guides for both language arts and science all include lesson plans, calendars, instructions, student activity sheets, answer keys, and much more.

For math, Sonlight offers one or more choices for each level. Answer keys or solution manuals are part of each program, but there are no instructor's guides for math.

All Core guides include week-by-week lesson plans with record-keeping calendars, and thorough instructions. In addition, they have geography and timeline activities, study guides for all history, reader and read-aloud books, answer keys, and much more.

Sonlight emphasizes only those activities that have clear educational purposes; make-work projects and crafts are nonexistent. Though parent-child interaction is required at certain times, little time is required for lesson preparation. What I hear from parents is that the hardest thing is getting time to get through all the read-aloud books.

While Sonlight Curriculum's hallmark is the use of real books—literature, historical fiction, and topical fiction—rather than texts, they still use textbooks and workbooks sometimes. For example, they use *Saxon Math*, *Miquon Math*, *Videotext Algebra*, *Singapore Math*, *Spelling Power*, *Apologia* science texts, and *Italic Handwriting*.

While Sonlight sells complete curriculum packages for each subject in every grade, they also permit you to purchase any individual items out of the complete packages or from their catalog.

On its Core Packages (history, readers, and read-alouds), Sonlight offers an eight-week trial period—use it, and if you don't like it, return your program for a full refund. Customers who purchase a Core Package can take 10 percent off the total cost of their order. Prices for the Core Packages (before discounts) range from about $250.00 to $540.00, while other packages and materials are less. As an example of how this all adds up, if you were to purchase the *Comprehensive 3* curriculum package (Core, math, language, and science, plus art and critical-thinking electives) as a new user, the total cost (with the 10 percent discount) would be $810.30 based on 2003-04 prices. When you just begin with Sonlight, there are some extra costs for resources that are used over a number of years. So costs for subsequent years might be lower.

You save even more if you teach children from the same resources whenever practical, even though they might be at different grade levels for math and language arts. Much of the curriculum is nonconsumable, so you can reuse a large percentage of each level in the future.

Sonlight has proven to be an excellent option for families who want something different from traditional curriculum but lack the experience to put it together on their own. I strongly recommend reading through Sonlight's catalog, either print or online, before determining which program, levels, or resources to use. Both the catalog and Web site are loaded with helpful information, plus the online forums provide an opportunity to ask any questions you might have and get input from Sonlight users around the world.

Computerized Curriculum

I had to create a separate category to cover *Switched-On Schoolhouse*, a computer-based curriculum. This is not the only computer-based curriculum—*Algebra Classmate* (reviewed in chapter 8) is an example of other computer-based programs. But *Switched-On Schoolhouse* is the only one developed for all subjects and grade levels in a consistent format. Thus it doesn't fit under a single subject-area heading.

Switched-On Schoolhouse 2.0
Alpha Omega
300 North McKemy
Chandler, AZ 85226-2618
(800) 622-3070
www.aop.com
$69.95 per subject or $299.95 for complete 5 subject set

Alpha Omega first developed their *LIFEPAC* curriculum, a self-instructional learning system using a number of worktext booklets for each subject. Alpha Omega responded to the proliferation of computers and improvements in technology by using their *LIFEPAC* curriculum as the foundation of their new computer-based curriculum, *Switched-On Schoolhouse*.

Switched-On Schoolhouse is available for grades 3-12 in a completely computerized form that includes full-color graphics, videos and slides, sound, and Internet excursions.

Many parents love *SOS* because it really allows students to work independently. Parents need to set up the initial program, customize lesson plans if necessary, check student progress—which can be viewed in "teacher mode" on the computer—and review writing assignments. Parents can also build supplemental lessons within the *SOS* curriculum.

Computer equipment should be fairly current for the program to run at a decent pace, for smooth viewing of video clips, and for the use of sound. Listed requirements are a CD-ROM multimedia PC system with 500 MHz or higher processor; Windows XP, 2000, ME, or 98 (2nd edition) operating system; 256 MB of memory; and 200 MB hard disk space. Web excursions are not essential to the curriculum, so an Internet connection is not absolutely necessary; however, the Web links add extra interest and additional learning opportunities.

Bible, math, language arts, science, and history/geography courses can be purchased individually or as complete grade level sets. The programs follow the same general format for each subject. A topic is introduced, then students are given pertinent vocabulary words to learn. Activities and/or games help students to quickly master the vocabulary words. Three games—*Spelling Bee*, *Alpha 14*, and *Vocabulocity*—are integrated into all the courses, but not all of them necessarily in every lesson. The latter two games include some sharp graphics, but they are still nowhere near the level of graphic artistry of the enticing games most young people are accustomed to. After they have played the games a few times, students might feel they are wasting time waiting for the program to go through its graphic routine before moving on to the next questions. Students can skip these games if they simply study the vocabulary words and definitions and find the games unnecessary.

Students read through each section of instructional material on the screen, then hit "Show problems" at the bottom of the screen to work through comprehension activities. Questions are presented in crossword puzzles, fill-in-the-blanks, multiple choice, sorting, and matching. Incorrect answers are immediately identified, although students are not allowed to correct them until later on. The program goes back to missed questions to give students another opportunity to get the correct answer.

These section questions in all subjects other than math allow students to scan the "text" material to figure out what the correct answer should be most of the time, but sometimes they must make inferences, read maps, or interpret data to arrive at correct answers. Math programs require students to solve problems. If students miss questions, those that were answered incorrectly are presented again. Sometimes hints are given, such as pointing out that the error was in the spelling or indicating a map to which a student might refer to find the answer. However, such hints seem few and far between.

Once students have answered all questions correctly for a set number of lessons, they take a quiz. It is possible to set the program such that students cannot scan material when taking a quiz, so this is when you will really know whether or not they've learned anything. (The "open book" option allows students to exit and enter the quiz as many times as they wish, presumably allowing them to check the lesson for information they don't know.) Some written responses are required in the exercises and quizzes, and parents/teachers must score these themselves. The program alerts parents/teachers to exercises that need grading while the program is in "teacher mode." Exercises and quizzes are scored by the computer, although parent/teacher override is permitted.

The program is very professional (much improved from the first edition of *Switched-On Schoolhouse*). It allows parents control over which lessons are to be assigned in which order, how lenient or tough to be with spelling of answers, grade format, and access to the Internet. It truly allows students to work independently—a tremendous help for parents with little time to oversee schoolwork. Parents also set up a school calendar that allows the computer to schedule each student's rate of progress. The computer then alerts students if they get behind schedule.

Extra graphic boxes that expand to add additional information are generally very helpful. The programs move at a fairly good pace for the most part so there's not a lot of wasted time, as in software of the "edutainment" sort. While answers are each followed by a verbal affirmation (it would be nice to be able to turn these off and just have something like a green light/red light signal), there are no "cute" graphics wasting time between answers and subsequent questions, except in the games.

The content is nondenominationally Protestant throughout all subjects. Biblical concepts appear throughout all subjects, although less so in math than others.

The Bible program offers solid content, including some Scripture memorization. Map identification is added to the typical questions and answers.

The language program covers reading skills, grammar, composition, spelling, and vocabulary. Periodic writing projects stretch skills beyond the short answers students write within the lessons themselves.

History and geography are combined, with geography and map work intermixed throughout lessons. Essays, reports, and special projects expand learning beyond the computer. Science programs also include a few experiments, essays, observations, and other noncomputer activities.

SOS is a very sophisticated system, so it comes with a 180-page manual. You will need to use the manual to initially set up the system, set up the teacher(s), and set up students and courses since it's not an intuitive process. Once you've got the hang of how to do this, it is easy to add additional courses and students. There is so much customization available to users that most novices will stick with the basics until they get comfortable with the program. But once you've used it for a while, you should experiment with all the fine-tuning features, such as the ability to customize your calendar, create assignment options for students, change grade options, and even edit and create subjects. You should also take time to familiarize yourself and your student with the dictionary and calculator available through the "resource center," available at the click of a button.

SOS makes life easy for parents, but it's not perfect. As I have encountered in many other computerized programs, requested answers seemed highly debatable. Teacher overrides are helpful in dealing with such situations, but that requires more immediate oversight. I am continually surprised at questions curriculum authors come up with that have little value or might even be deemed incorrect by some children. For example, the science curriculum in one lesson focuses at least two questions on defining geraniums as plants that often grow in window boxes. Here in Southern California, geraniums are a common ground cover or bush and only rarely appear in window boxes since they grow too fast for such containers. And is not the focus on window boxes a distraction from more salient features of geraniums?

A problem cropped up in the math program immediately with the presentation of addition and subtraction problems with regrouping. Given three-digit numbers, students will generally work from right to left to solve each problem, yet the cursor begins on the left, and it is a bother to get it to enter numbers in the logical order.

In the language program, students are frequently working from reading selections, answering questions regarding content. Unfortunately, some of the questions are too nitpicky. For example, one question asked students how many trees were in the backyard (13) in a story about family members being friendly to birds and animals. The number of trees was irrelevant unless you really want children to memorize that sort of detail when reading.

The latest release of *SOS* (version 2.0) has a number of improvements over earlier editions; among them are better graphics, interfaces that are easier to work with, more video clips, built-in Web links (previously they had to be set up separately), and the ability to print lessons, problems, assignments, and records.

Numerous *SOS* elective courses—some for elementary grades but most for high school level—can be added to an *SOS* core curriculum or can be used on their own. Among the electives are *Spanish* and *French* courses for elementary grades or for high school, plus consumer math, state history, *The Story of the Constitution, Health,* and *College Planner.*

In summary, I expect that many parents will find *SOS* the tool that makes homeschooling possible for them. Nevertheless, for students this is not a creative approach to learning. It has to be very structured and controlled to be able to work within the computer format.

• • •

Endnotes

Chapter 2

1. Charlotte Mason, *Home Education: Training and Educating Children under Nine* (Wheaton, IL: Tyndale House, 1989), 281.
2. Ibid., 188.
3. Ibid., 141.
4. Ibid., 232.
5. Ibid., 173.
6. Gene Edward Veith Jr. and Andrew Kern, *Classical Education: The Movement Sweeping America* (Washington, D.C.: Capital Research Center, 2001), x.
7. Ibid., 11.
8. Ibid., 11.

Chapter 4

1. Keith Golay, M.D., *Learning Patterns and Temperament Styles* (Newport Beach, CA: Manas-Systems, 1982).

Chapter 5

1. California State Board of Education, "Biology/Life Sciences, Grades Nine through Twelve," accessed September 3, 2004; available at http://www.cde.ca.gov/be/st/ss/scbiology.asp.
2. California State Board of Education, "Grade Two: Mathematics Contest Standards," accessed September 3, 2004; available at http://www.cde.ca.gov/be/st/ss/mthgrade2.asp.

Chapter 11

1. Durell C. Dobbins, Ph.D., *The Rainbow* (Alvaton, KY: Beginnings Publishing House, Inc., 1998), 118.

Index